THE

Philadelphia Citizen's

ALMANAC

Daily Readings on the City of Brotherly Love

THE *Philadelphia Citizen's* ALMANAC

Daily Readings on the City of Brotherly Love

LAURA E. BEARDSLEY

Turner Publishing Company

445 Park Avenue, 9th Floor
New York, NY 10022
Phone: (212) 710-4338 Fax: (212) 710-4339

200 4th Avenue North, Suite 950
Nashville, TN 37219
Phone: (615) 255-2665 Fax: (615) 255-5081

www.turnerpublishing.com

The Philadelphia Citizen's Almanac: Daily Readings on the City of Brotherly Love

Copyright © 2010 Turner Publishing Company

All rights reserved.
This book or any part thereof may not be reproduced or transmitted in any form or by any means, electronic or mechanical, including photocopying, recording, or by any information storage and retrieval system, without permission in writing from the publisher.

Library of Congress Cataloging-in-Publication Data

Beardsley, Laura E.
The Philadelphia citizen's almanac : daily readings on the City of Brotherly Love / Laura Beardsley.
p. cm.
Includes index.
ISBN 978-1-59652-546-7
1. Philadelphia (Pa.)--History--Calendars. I. Title.
F158.36.B43 2010
032.0209748'11--dc22

2010036326

Printed in China

10 11 12 13 14 15 16 17—0 9 8 7 6 5 4 3 2 1

Contents

Acknowledgments ☆ ☆ ☆ ☆ ☆ ☆ ☆ ☆ ☆ ☆ ☆ ☆ ☆ ☆ ☆ ☆ ☆ ☆ vii

Introduction ☆ 1

January ☆ 7

Daily Readings 8

The Battle of the Kegs 39

February ☆ ☆ ☆ ☆ ☆ ☆ ☆ ☆ ☆ ☆ ☆ ☆ ☆ ☆ ☆ ☆ ☆ ☆ ☆ 43

Daily Readings 44

Germantown Petition in Opposition to Slavery 72

March ☆ 75

Daily Readings 76

George Washington to Henry Knox: On His Approaching Retirement 107

April ☆ 109

Daily Readings 110

Lincoln's Assassination: From the Daily Journal of Sydney George Fisher 140

May ☆ 143

Daily Readings 144

The Public Ledger: News of the Philadelphia Centennial Exposition 175

June ☆ 177

Daily Readings 178

Reports of the Kite Experiment of Benjamin Franklin 208

Contents

July ☆ 211

Daily Readings 212

The Declaration of Independence: Letter from John Adams to Abigail 243

August ☆ 245

Daily Readings 246

Concerning the Yellow Fever Epidemic of 1793 277

September ☆ ☆ ☆ ☆ ☆ ☆ ☆ ☆ ☆ ☆ ☆ ☆ ☆ ☆ ☆ ☆ ☆ ☆ 279

Daily Readings 280

Fiftieth Anniversary of the Declaration: A Visit by General Lafayette 310

October ☆ 313

Daily Readings 314

John Jay Smith and the Legacy of Laurel Hill Cemetery 345

November ☆ ☆ ☆ ☆ ☆ ☆ ☆ ☆ ☆ ☆ ☆ ☆ ☆ ☆ ☆ ☆ ☆ ☆ ☆ 347

Daily Readings 348

Casting the Liberty Bell: Letter from Isaac Norris 378

December ☆ ☆ ☆ ☆ ☆ ☆ ☆ ☆ ☆ ☆ ☆ ☆ ☆ ☆ ☆ ☆ ☆ ☆ ☆ 381

Daily Readings 382

The Winter of 1776: A Victory at Trenton 413

Sources ☆ 415

Index ☆ 417

Acknowledgments

The author is grateful to the many friends, neighbors, colleagues, and fellow authors who assisted in the brainstorming and research for this volume. In particular, thanks are due to Marguerite Beardsley and Max E. Moeller for their unrivaled devotion to this project and their uncanny ability to keep the author focused in times of great distraction. The staff and volunteers of Historic Germantown and the Germantown Historical Society, in particular Mark Sellers, Anne Burnett, and Carolyn Faris, were generous with their time, attention, and understanding if some things just didn't get done. Thanks are also extended to the excellent staff of Turner Publishing, especially Michael McCalip and Steven Cox, whose patience and professionalism are truly appreciated.

In quotations of older documents and records, spelling has been adjusted to conform to modern standardization.

For Cora and Owen,
who will always remember "Mommy's book" as an intrusion into their childhood.

Introduction

Introduction

Most of us who live in or love Philadelphia are aware of at least some part of its history. The Liberty Bell, Independence Hall, Benjamin Franklin, and the United States Constitution are Philadelphian to their very core. Known as the Birthplace of the Nation, the City of Brotherly Love, and more recently the "Place That Loves You Back," Philadelphia's greatest attractions are grounded in its social, cultural, and historical past. But for those of us who look more deeply into the city's rich history, other names, places, and events come to light. Philadelphia's past is filled with moments of genius and great despair; of deep inspiration and spur-of-the-moment action; of international acclaim and complete obscurity. It is a history that began more than four centuries ago and continues to delight and inspire those who wish to know more about themselves and the events and people that shaped our city and our nation.

Officially established in 1681 by Englishman and Quaker convert William Penn, Philadelphia and Pennsylvania were founded on the doctrines of the Quaker faith, and as such attracted a diverse colonial population of people seeking land and the tolerance to live as they wished. Philadelphia grew quickly, and by the mid-1700s, the city was home to many leading cultural and economic institutions, among them libraries, theaters, and international merchant houses. It was also home to a growing number of those who were discontented with the British Crown and its control of the American colonies.

In 1774 and 1775, Philadelphia served as host to the First and Second Continental Congresses, colonial assemblies which ultimately led to the creation of the Declaration of Independence and the trials of the Revolutionary War. In 1787 the city was home to the Constitutional Convention, which drafted the United States Constitution, and for the last decade of the eighteenth century was the Capital City of the newly organized United States of America. Philadelphia was the premier city in the country, home to leading national politicians, artists, scientists, and an estimated population of more than 67,000 people. The population reflected the origins of a city bustling with energy, with colonists of English, German, African, Irish, Welsh, and Scottish backgrounds or descent.

By the mid nineteenth century, the venerable City of Brotherly Love was still revered as the birthplace of the nation, but it had lost its place as the leading city in the nation. The racial and religious diversity embraced in the previous century seemed almost to have disappeared overnight in the 1830s and 1840s. Increasingly at the mercy of rioting factions, devastatingly regular cholera epidemics, and a growing disparity between the wealthy and the poor, the future seemed bleak. But Philadelphia was also a place of great industry, beauty, and culture as reflected in the growth of small businesses, the creation of Fairmount Park (still the largest urban park in the world), and the availability of a wide variety of schools, hospitals, and museums.

In 1854, the independent municipalities of nearly thirty townships and boroughs in the county were consolidated into America's newest "great city." Less than a decade later, the Civil

War brought economic opportunity to the city in the form of an increased demand for war materiel, including products such as textiles and ships, both major industries in Philadelphia. This period of growth culminated in the grand celebration of the 100th anniversary of the Declaration of Independence in 1876. Known formally as the International Exhibition of Arts, Manufactures, and Products of the Soil and Mine, the Centennial Exhibition featured exhibits highlighting the preceding one hundred years of American ingenuity and the potential for industrial greatness in the years to come.

In the years immediately following the great centennial exposition, Philadelphia saw the birth of and embraced new technology and became known for big business, big politics, and big profits. Names like Wanamaker, Baldwin, Brill, Cramp, and Widener dominated the city's industrial, political, and social scenes. Philadelphia's population grew in tandem with the growth of industry as thousands of Southern and Eastern European and Asian immigrants arrived by steamship, hoping to fill the newly available manufacturing jobs. As the century came to a close, Philadelphia was crowded with 1.3 million people, making it one of the largest in the nation. Businesses and industries of every kind powered the city's drive toward the future while new amusements drew the masses as well as the elite. No longer defined by its history, Philadelphia saw little change in its role as "workshop of the world," and large industries continued to dominate the region.

The city's many products proved useful to the nation during the First World War and Philadelphia thrived. Shipbuilding, which was on the decline before the war, was the primary industry to benefit from the need to send war supplies overseas. Baldwin Locomotive works began to manufacture artillery shells and railroad gun mounts, in addition to nearly 500 locomotives of various types. The city's leather, textile, and steel industries also saw a dramatic increase in production. Despite the difficulties of war shortages and the disastrous Influenza Epidemic of 1918, the city prospered, even as it began to experience hints of the challenges to come.

Just as New York City, Boston, and Chicago faced similar difficulties following the end of the Great War, Philadelphia found the start of the second quarter of the twentieth century to be marked by economic instability and political change. Reduced demand for Philadelphia goods limited the availability of jobs in the city, until by 1930 the unemployment rate averaged 10 percent and higher. Gangs and organized crime further intensified conflicts between different socioeconomic and ethnic communities.

The Great Depression brought only a few failures to Philadelphia, due in great part to its diversified manufacturing. The Benjamin Franklin Parkway and the Philadelphia Museum of Art were established at a time when private support kept the city's cultural and social environment alive. The city's Republican-dominated government resisted federal encroachment as Roosevelt's New Deal programs gained momentum, and the divide between citizens and local

government expanded, leading to a shift in favor of the Democratics. The city was losing its battle for economic security and a positive future as national trends affected Philadelphia's ability to prosper.

With the threat of World War II looming, Philadelphia set aside many of its local conflicts and prepared once again to serve the nation as the primary supplier of the materials of war. The dramatic growth in the availability of jobs inspired thousands of African-Americans in southern states to migrate north. Rationing, bond drives, parades, and other forms of patriotic expression filled the public lives of most Philadelphians. Once the war had been won, however, tensions re-emerged. The region's economy fell into decline and some of the city's largest companies, including Brill, Baldwin, and Cramp, drastically reduced their production rate or shut down altogether. Inadequate support of the city's older neighborhoods, once havens for the diverse population, drove large numbers of Philadelphians to the new community developments in the northeastern and southern neighborhoods of the city and the suburbs. Neighborhoods closer to downtown were left to the city's poor and unemployed. By the mid-1950s, the aging city was losing its industries and its citizens in what was to be a significant blow to its economic stability.

As the nation faced the upheaval of the 1960s, Philadelphia also entered its most challenging period as riots, ethnic strife, and racial tension overwhelmed the city. Political corruption, crime, and unemployment all took their toll on the already struggling city. Population shifts and the loss of tax dollars led political leaders to seek answers by redeveloping older parts of the city, with some limited success. In response to the federal Interstate Highway Act of 1956, and only after nearly a decade of resistance and contentious public debate, construction on I-95 began in 1965. Running along the Delaware River through much of the city's oldest neighborhoods and river wards, the highway almost completely severed the city's connection to what had once been the basis of its economy. Thousands of families and small businesses were displaced, as the redevelopment of large areas of the old city forever changed the feel of the once-bustling Philadelphia.

Two centuries after the Declaration of Independence was signed, Philadelphia struggled to regain its earlier prominence. The downtown was updated and improved, but at a great cost to the spirit of the city. Large, faceless skyscrapers and massive plazas occupied blocks once ornamented with Victorian odes to the city's industrial strengths. Philadelphia was soon known not for its connection to history but for its impersonal office blocks and failing neighborhoods. The theaters and shops that once had drawn thousands lay abandoned, and the city grew quiet at night. In 1987, the completion of One Liberty Place (which controversially stood higher than the statue of William Penn on City Hall) initiated a new era of development, combining the rejection of old traditions with a shift toward restoration and reuse of classic Philadelphia buildings.

Introduction

Today, nearly every corner of the city is recognized by residents and outsiders alike for the rich and vibrant history it represents. Reclaiming the compelling stories of our region's past is both vocation and avocation for thousands of Philadelphians. The tales found in the pages to follow represent only the smallest fraction of Philadelphia's past. However, it is the hope of the author that readers will be entertained as well as inspired to seek their own answers to the inevitable questions raised by what they can see, remember, or read about the city of Philadelphia. History is everywhere; it is only waiting for us to discover it!

January

January 1

The sounds of year-end revelry in Philadelphia continue into the first day of the New Year with the celebration of the Mummers Parade. Born of the assorted ethnic history of the city, the parade draws from Swedish, English, Irish, German, and African-American traditions, including singing, dancing, costumed mummery, and "calling" on friends. In the eighteenth and nineteenth centuries, roving groups of men dressed in costumes and frequently sporting blackface stopped at neighborhood homes, performing ad hoc skits and songs. Rewards in the form of drink and food were expected, and as the day passed noisemakers and guns were fired in celebration.

In 1808, the masquerades and mummers were targeted as a nuisance and a law was passed banning them. However, within the neighborhoods the revelry continued and by the 1850s the law was repealed with little indication that any arrests were ever made. In 1876, in conjunction with the city's Centennial celebration, the first official parade was organized. The annual event unified the many small clubs and "New Years Associations" and featured increasingly elaborate costumes, comics and clowns, and music. After twenty years of private management, the city assumed sponsorship of the parade in 1901.

Today, the Mummers Parade continues to attract thousands of participants and onlookers each year along the traditional route from South Philadelphia up Broad Street to City Hall. Four distinct divisions of clubs compete: Comics, String Bands, Fancy, and Fancy Brigades. Where once amateur dancers and mismatched costumes held sway, professional designers and thousands of dollars in elaborate costumes and stage sets now rule. A true Philadelphia tradition, the Mummers Parade continues to offer a unique show and a glimpse at the city's remarkable past.

1760: A law prohibiting the production of plays goes into effect. Ten days later a benefit performance of Shakespeare's *Hamlet* is put on by actor-director David Douglas. The law, very unpopular among Philadelphians, is set aside on September 2, 1760.

1785: The Episcopal Academy is founded.

1900: The clock in the tower at City Hall is started for the first time.

1976: The Liberty Bell is moved out of the foyer at Independence Hall to the newly completed Liberty Bell Pavilion, located across the street. Beginning at precisely 12:01 A.M., this is the first official act of the Bicentennial Year celebration.

January 2

Benjamin Franklin is often cited as the father of countless inventions, explorations, and institutions. One of his most prized legacies was founded on this date in 1769 as the "American Philosophical Society Held at Philadelphia for Promoting Useful Knowledge." The society, organized with the specific task of sponsoring and promoting scientific scholarship, was itself formed of a union between two of Franklin's earlier endeavors: The Junto and the American Society for Promoting Useful Knowledge, founded as early as 1727. By the end of the 1700s, the American Philosophical Society would cement its reputation as one of the most revered learned societies in the world.

Franklin's interest in the natural world combined with his belief that the colonies could achieve economic independence by improving their understanding of the science of agriculture, manufacturing, and transportation. These beliefs were shared with some of America's greatest minds. Early members included George Washington, John Adams, Thomas Paine, Benjamin Rush, David Rittenhouse, and James Madison. In 1803–1804, President Thomas Jefferson and other members of the Society would famously support and advise Meriwether Lewis and William Clark as they planned their explorations of the lands westward to the Pacific Ocean. As knowledge of science and the natural world grew, so too did the Society. By the mid nineteenth century, areas of study such as meteorology, paleontology, geology, ethnology, and chemistry formed the core mission of the Society, which continued to elect the finest scientific minds to its membership, among them Marie Curie, Charles Darwin, Thomas Edison, and many others.

Today, the American Philosophical Society continues to promote exploration in the sciences and humanities by supporting scholarship, publications, and public outreach through their research library, lectures, and meetings.

1776: The Continental Congress in Philadelphia establishes the "Tory Act," designed to retaliate and repress Loyalists who continue to support the British king. As a result, more than 60,000 Loyalists and 20,000 slaves flee the original thirteen colonies for Canada.

1787: The first meeting of the College of Physicians, the oldest institution of medical men in the country.

1842: The "Wire Bridge" across the Schuylkill River at Fairmount is opened to traffic. Removed in 1875, it was the first suspension bridge of its kind in the country.

1934: The first state-controlled liquor stores ("State Stores") are opened following the repeal of the 18th Amendment.

January 3

In the battle for the rights of women and against slavery, few people hold the position of Lucretia Mott. Born Lucretia Coffin in Massachusetts on this date in 1793, her lifelong commitment to suffrage for women and African-Americans was heavily influenced by her Quaker upbringing and adopted home. Following a move to Philadelphia to be near her aging parents, she met and married fellow Quaker and teacher James Mott in 1811. Together, they raised five children.

After ten years of marriage and motherhood, Mott became a Quaker minister, speaking out against the evils of slavery and demanding its complete abolition. Fully supported by her husband, Mott traveled the region and earned recognition as a powerful public speaker, gaining friendships among the closely knit community of committed abolitionists, including William Lloyd Garrison. In 1833, James and Lucretia Mott co-founded the Pennsylvania Anti-Slavery Society, the first fully racially integrated abolitionist society.

Conflicts between traditionalist abolitionists and the growing number of outspoken women protesters threatened the abolitionist movement from within. Speaking out publicly was seen as contrary to feminine morals and Mott was heavily criticized for her role in the 1837 Anti-Slavery Convention of American Women. She was also frequently subject to threats of violence and roving mobs looking to stop her activities. In spite of these dangers, Mott continued to advocate for the rights of slaves and freedmen, while also expanding her interests to include the rights of women.

With the organization of the Women's Rights Convention at Seneca Falls, New York, in 1838, Mott and suffragist Elizabeth Cady Stanton first gave voice to a growing feminist movement. Following the Civil War, Mott retained her commitment to women's suffrage, but unlike many of her fellow activists, sought to broaden her efforts to include suffrage and equal rights for all, including blacks. At the time of her death in November 1880, Mott left behind a legacy of activism and compassion still seen today.

1831: The first American building and loan association, the Oxford Provident Building Association of Philadelphia County, is formed at the public house of Thomas Sidebotham in Frankford. Several local businessmen gathered for the specific purpose of forming an association to enable contributors to build or purchase dwelling houses. The association attracted forty charter members, whose contributions matured in ten years. The final payment was made January 11, 1841, with a share value of $500.

1973: Known for their aggressive playing style, the Philadelphia Flyers hockey team is nicknamed the "Broad Street Bullies" by Jack Chevalier and Pete Cafone of the *Philadelphia Bulletin.*

January 4

Liberte! Egalite! Fraternite! With these words the French Revolution (1789–1795) called for changes in the French government, moving from one of feudal hierarchy and monarchy toward that of equality, liberty, and individual rights. In pursuit of those freedoms, however, France would wage war against its own neighbors and bear witness to a period known as "the Terror" during which thousands of aristocrats and those loyal to them lost their lives to the guillotine.

For the newly created United States of America, the upheaval in France would result in the creation of deep divisions within the executive and legislative branches. Claiming to be directly inspired by the American Revolution and the fight against British rule, French revolutionaries hoped to gain support and financial aid from the United States. Guided by former agent to France and then–Secretary of State Thomas Jefferson, the Democratic-Republican Party sought acknowledgment of the French Republic and the establishment of state relations. President George Washington and members of the Federalist Party such as Vice President John Adams had strong reservations about supporting a revolution that resulted in such extreme violence. Further, concerns about maintaining the tenuous business relationship with King George III and Great Britain resulted in a reluctance to show any real support for the French.

In late 1795, a general election among French citizens established a new constitution, creating the first two-house legislature in French history, called the Directoire. Though ultimately guilty of ignoring the constitution and resulting in the 1799 overthrow of the government by Napoleon Bonaparte, the Directoire initially inspired new support for the French Republic among the American people. On this day in 1796 the flag of the French Revolutionary Republic was formally accepted by the United States House of Representatives in Philadelphia, serving as a true "testimonial of the existing sympathies and affections of the two Republics." With the election of Thomas Jefferson to the presidency in 1800, the relationship between the two countries was firmly and permanently established.

1900: James Bond, the leading American ornithologist whose name was adopted by author and avid bird watcher Ian Fleming for his spy character, is born in Philadelphia.

1920: J. Hampton Moore resigns his seat in the United States House of Representatives to become mayor of Philadelphia.

January 5

The storied career of baseball legend Pete Rose would not be complete without the City of Brotherly Love. Born in Cincinnati, Rose began his career with several small, minor league teams before signing with the Cincinnati Reds in 1963 and winning the National Rookie of the Year Award. Known for his intense playing style and high-energy attitude, Rose quickly earned the nickname "Charlie Hustle," said to have been given him by New York Yankees pitcher Whitey Ford. Into the 1970s, Rose regularly contributed to the success of the Reds, helping the team win both the 1975 and 1976 World Series.

Rose continued to play for the Reds until he became a free agent in 1979 and signed with the Philadelphia Phillies. His four-year, $3.2 million contract made him the highest paid player in team sports up to that point. Rose experienced both good and bad seasons, and was frequently benched for poor hitting performance, experiencing the worst season of his career in 1983. Even without Rose's best playing years, during his four years with the Phillies the team earned three division titles, made two World Series appearances, and claimed a World Series victory in 1980. As his relationship with the Phillies soured, Rose refused to accept a reduced role on the team and was granted an unconditional release by the team in 1983.

Rose spent just one year with the Montreal Expos before being traded once again, back to his beloved Cincinnati Reds. He played his last game in August 1986, but continued to manage the Reds until August 1989. In February 1989, Rose was questioned on allegations that he had gambled on baseball, including on Reds games. Rose denied the charges but by late August was banned from major league baseball and sought treatment for a gambling addiction.

In the decade that followed, Rose repeatedly refused to acknowledge the evidence compiled against him and applied for reinstatement in 1997. The application was not seriously considered by then-Commissioner Bud Selig. However, on this date in 2004, fourteen years after the initial accusations were made against him, Rose publicly admitted his guilt in hopes of finally receiving reinstatement and a place in the Baseball Hall of Fame. To this date, he has yet to be welcomed back to baseball.

1777: The 4th Continental Light Dragoons, also known as Moylan's Horse, are raised for service with the Continental Army.

1860: Bishop John Neumann dies. He is later canonized as Saint John Neumann, the first American Bishop to be so.

January 6

On this day in 1785, Haym Solomon, the son of a rabbi born in Poland forty-five years earlier, died in Philadelphia. Arriving as an immigrant to New York City in 1775, the multi-talented Solomon quickly established a successful financial business serving as a broker for merchants specializing in international trading. Inspired by the American fight for independence, Solomon joined the New York Sons of Liberty and was arrested by the British in 1776 for spying. During his forced service to the British as an interpreter, he secretly worked to free American prisoners of war and urged the Hessian mercenaries to desert. Arrested once again in 1778 for his involvement in a plot to burn the Royal fleet in New York Harbor, he was given a death sentence. He managed to escape and fled to Philadelphia, leaving his wife and children to follow shortly thereafter.

Once in the city that represented the center of the revolutionary effort, Solomon quickly sought a formal position with the Second Continental Congress, who chose not to accept his services. Turning once again to a financial business, Solomon opened a bond agency near Second and Market streets. Solomon found he could aid the war effort by brokering a financial deal worth $400,000 to help pay for supplies for Washington's army. It is likely he used much of his own money in creating the fund. By 1780, Solomon was working closely with financier Robert Morris, engaging in dozens of exchanges at an estimated value of more than $650,000 of his own money.

In early January 1785, Solomon was ill, radically in debt, and struggling. Solomon hoped to seek repayment of much of his investment with the government. Unfortunately, he died of tuberculosis before any resolution was made. Indeed, Solomon's children would continue to seek repayment and recognition of their father's service to the country unsuccessfully through the 1860s. At last, a formal acknowledgment of Solomon's contribution to the American Revolution was created with the installation of a statue of Solomon, Morris, and George Washington in Chicago in 1941.

1922: Construction begins on the Delaware River Bridge, now known as the Ben Franklin Bridge.

1996: Snow begins falling in the city's all-time greatest snowstorm, totaling 30.7 inches.

January 7

In the eyes of Robert Morris, a line of credit is a necessity, especially if you are a newborn nation. On this date in 1783, the country's first government-sponsored Bank of North America opened for business in Philadelphia. The bank was the creation of Morris, who was serving as superintendent of public finances in 1781 when he proposed to the Continental Congress that a national bank be established. Morris believed the bank could provide a centralized means of monitoring and increasing public funds and credit, and would greatly aid in funding the American Revolution. A total of 400 shares were sold at $1,000 each, forming the capital necessary to open the bank. With the support of individual state legislatures and Congress, and loans from the Netherlands and France, the Bank of North America established credit for the United States and issued paper currency through the end of the war.

Unlike previous banking institutions in the colonies, the Bank of North America relied on the combined good will of subscribers, debtors, and state and federal governments. States were urged to prevent the establishment of competing banks elsewhere in the country, and to accept the notes of the bank as legal tender in payment of taxes, duties, and debts owed the United States. States were also urged to pass laws protecting the bank, especially against counterfeiting. Granted the power to conduct business in all thirteen states by Congress, in reality the Bank of North America primarily operated in just three: Pennsylvania, New York, and Massachusetts. At its peak, it held nearly $30,000,000 in national debt.

Indeed, as the war drew to a close, the very thing that Morris considered the greatest strength of the bank became its greatest weakness. Growing concerns over how outside foreign interests might control the nation's bank, as well as misunderstandings about the nature of debt and credit, led to the re-chartering of the Bank of North America in 1785. Limited in its powers and less effective as a centralized bank, it nevertheless continued to serve as a successful banking institution through much of the nineteenth century.

1890: William Purvis receives a patent for improvements to the fountain pen.

1982: Owners of the *Philadelphia Bulletin* newspaper announce it is up for sale, suggesting recent financial results do not bode well for the paper, which officially closes on January 29 the same year.

January 8

Inventors always know the value of luck. Walter E. Diemer, born on this date in 1905 and employed as an accountant for the Fleer Chewing Company of Philadelphia, was certainly one of the luckiest. A small family-run business, the Fleer Company first began manufacturing chewing gum in the late 1880s and originated the candy-covered Chiclets brand in the early 1900s. By 1905, Fleer introduced the nation's first known bubble gum, called Blibber-Bubble. Unfortunately, the gum was less than successful. Difficult to chew and easy to break up, Blibber-Bubble was also known for sticking to everything it touched, including faces. While there was clearly a market for bubble-blowing, without substantial improvements in the recipe, the world would remain bubble-less.

One day in 1928, the twenty-three-year-old Diemer was playing around with gum recipes during his spare time when he unexpectedly hit upon an essential improvement. The result of his experiment was stretchier and much less sticky than the average chewing gum and could easily be blown into bubbles. Looking for a way to color the sweet treat, Diemer used the only food coloring handy: red. This is why almost all bubble gum today is pink. Quickly realizing its potential, Diemer took a five-pound measure of the gum to a local retailer. To Diemer's surprise, the chewing gum sold out in just a few hours.

The company, also recognizing the value of Diemer's discovery, named the product Dubble Bubble and began to market it in stores throughout the region. Never patented and therefore open to imitation, Dubble Bubble would nevertheless become one of the most successful bubble gums on the market. By the mid-1970s, Fleer was selling more than five million pieces of Dubble Bubble every day and continues to do so today under the Tootsie manufacturing banner.

For Diemer, who remained an employee of the Fleer Company for most of his life and was eventually made Vice President, the joy of invention was always said to have been trumped by the joy of sharing the results of his lucky accident with the world.

1825: Violet Fahnstock, the first female magistrate in the city, hears her first case. She was sworn in just six days earlier, on January 6.

January 9

Excitement and anticipation were palpable in the yard of Walnut Street Prison. The great French balloonist Jean-Pierre Blanchard was preparing to take to the skies in what would be the first successful balloon ascension in North America. Witnessed by dignitaries and common citizens alike, Blanchard filled his balloon with hydrogen and hoped for the best. Born in France just forty years earlier, Blanchard had earned a reputation as a highly skilled and successful aeronaut when in the 1780s he traveled from France to England demonstrating various designs for hot-air and gas-filled balloons. He became the first to cross the English Channel by air in 1785. Though not alone in his quest for air flight, Blanchard nevertheless made several important advances in balloon safety, including devising the first silk fabric parachutes. Upon his arrival in Philadelphia in December 1792, Blanchard sought funding through subscriptions, hoping to gain enough support for a flight from Philadelphia to New Jersey.

On the morning of January 9, 1793, when the balloon was deemed ready to ascend, Blanchard is said to have walked over to President George Washington, who presented the aeronaut with a passport for easy identification should Blanchard land where no one had heard of the possibility of a flying balloon. Ultimately, Blanchard reached an altitude of more than 5,000 feet, floating eastward and landing across the Delaware River in Deptford Township, New Jersey. Returning to Philadelphia by seven o'clock in the evening, Blanchard visited the president at his executive mansion on High Street at Sixth Street and presented Washington with a small flag he had carried on the balloon.

Blanchard remained in the city for several months and attempted additional flights, some more successful than others. He left Philadelphia in 1794, declaring that technology had not yet achieved the level he required for further developing his ballooning techniques. In 1809, Blanchard suffered a heart attack while in his balloon at a demonstration at The Hague. Falling from the balloon, he sustained life threatening injuries and died a few weeks later on March 7, 1809.

1682: The first meeting of the Society of Friends is held in the new colony, at Shackamaxon.

1776: Thomas Paine's "Common Sense" is published in Philadelphia.

1805: Matthew Pratt, a student of Benjamin West and famed most for his paintings of sign boards in the city, dies in Philadelphia.

On the eve of the Civil War, Philadelphia was a city in conflict. Historically seen as the geographical and political center of the country, the city was nevertheless far from neutral. An aggressive mayoral campaign in 1858 resulted in the surprising defeat of Democrat Richard Vaux by Alexander Henry, who benefited from an unusual coalition of Republicans, Nativists, and Whigs. Most citizens reviled the anti-abolitionist movement in the wake of John Brown's raid in Harper's Ferry, West Virginia, but fervently hoped for the return of the seceding Southern states to the Union. Intimately connected to the South through family, industry, and politics, Philadelphia struggled to find its ideological place among other Northern states. This internal conflict was publicly expressed on this date in 1860 as more than 100 local political leaders voted to urge the state assembly to turn away from "fanatical New England" and align itself with the South.

Despite his election as a Republican, when Mayor Alexander Henry was forced to endorse a national candidate for president in 1860, he chose Constitutional Unionist John Bell over fellow Republican Abraham Lincoln. Local anti-abolitionist politics caused Philadelphia's Republican Party to be less vocal about their anti-slavery platform, choosing instead to focus on the issue of tariff protection. Henry frequently straddled the political fence, managing to diffuse several potential riots and rallies against the rare abolitionist event held in the city. As tensions escalated, many hoped for a peaceful resolution to the split within the Union.

In the days following the January 10 resolution to recognize the city's long relationship with the South, other public statements in opposition to a Northerly agenda appeared. In one prepared on January 16, so-called anti-coercionists raised the possibility that Pennsylvanians might even gather to consider breaking away from the North and choosing their own alliances. Ultimately, as it became clear to all Americans that a peaceful resolution of the South's secession efforts was almost impossible, Philadelphians shifted their collective opinions and awaited the impending conflict with conviction and support for the federal government.

1942: Singer-songwriter Jim Croce is born.

The cold war officially came to Philadelphia on this date in 1976. The Philadelphia Flyers, two-time defending Stanley Cup champions and the National Hockey League's premier team, faced the undefeated Soviet Red Army team (also known as the Central Soviet Sports Army Club-CSKA) in a fourth and final exhibition game of the 1975-1976 playing season. In front of a highly raucous crowd of more than 17,000 Flyers fans, the Soviet team was roundly defeated, 4–1.

Without question, the Soviet team entered the exhibition series as the best team in world hockey. Stacked with the best talent to be found in the U.S.S.R., the CSKA featured players who spent every waking moment practicing and training for team cohesiveness and strength. As the exhibition games progressed, the status of the CSKA remained unchallenged following their defeat of the New York Rangers, the Boston Bruins, and the world-class Montreal Canadiens. In Philadelphia, the Flyers continued to show why they earned their own reputation as the "Broad Street Bullies" through aggressive and energetic play. Not to be underestimated, however, the Flyers also included the skill of head coach Fred Shero and three future NHL Hall of Famers: Bobby Clarke, Bill Barber, and Bernie Parent.

The evening before the game, a meet and greet between teams only fed the intense tension and competitiveness. The night of the game, boos and catcalls filled the Spectrum as the Flyers' passionate fans let their allegiance be known. For much of the game, the Flyers trailed the Soviets. In the second period, the Soviet coach questioned a heavy body check that briefly knocked out one of his players, and pulled his team from the ice. The Americans, believing it was merely a strategic tactic, waited while negotiations to resume the game proceeded. After a sixteen-minute delay, play resumed. Ultimately, the Flyers' quick maneuvering and rapid shots led them to victory.

For many, the win signaled a validation of American hockey strategy over the more considered Soviet style. For Philadelphia fans, the Flyers proved once and for all that they were truly the best hockey team in the world.

1778: The *New Jersey Gazette* publishes a letter from Francis Hopkinson which includes a fictitious account of the fear and panic that gripped the British Navy as a result of the American torpedoes (or "infernals," as the British called them) built by David Bushnell and used to disrupt Royal shipping. His humorous, satirical poem "Battle of the Kegs" appeared anonymously shortly thereafter and became a favorite camp ballad in the American army.

January 12

Longevity in politics is certainly a rare thing. In Philadelphia, known for political dynasties and lifelong service, only one man can lay claim to being the longest-serving mayor: Robert Wharton, born on this date in 1757. Beginning with the Charter of 1701, all of Philadelphia's mayors served a term of just one year, and were elected not by the general public but rather by the Common Council. Indeed, prior to 1747, the mayor received no salary, leading several newly elected mayors to choose to pay a fine rather than accept the position. The first general election for mayor would not take place until 1839. Wharton was first elected in 1798 and served, with a few interruptions, until 1824.

An avid outdoorsman and sports enthusiast, Wharton was known for fox hunting and his leadership of the Schuylkill Fishing Company, a men's social club infamous for its high-society membership. Elected to city council in 1792, he eventually made a name for himself as a man of law and gained a reputation for strength and authority when he put down a riot by sailors protesting for higher wages. In his first year in the Office of Mayor, he once again restored order when a riot in Walnut Street Prison erupted.

Wharton lost in his re-election bid in 1800 to John Inskeep but subsequently regained the office in 1806 for just two more terms. Wharton served additional annual terms during the years 1810-11, 1814-19, and 1820-24, alternating with Inskeep and two other men. Wharton's career, a product of Philadelphia's volatile political atmosphere and quirky charter, has yet to be matched in the number of terms or years served. However, we are not likely to see a repeat under the current charter, which sets a term at four years and limits the number of terms possible to two.

2008: The twenty-second annual Philadelphia midwinter bird census counts ninety-two different species of birds in the city.

January 13

As the eighteenth century drew to a close, the city of Philadelphia was the largest, most significant city in the country. The nation's capital since 1790, Philadelphia was home to magnificent government buildings, the finest cultural and religious institutions, and an assortment of citizens that was almost unmatched anywhere. Thomas Birch, an English-born landscape and marine painter newly arrived to Philadelphia, would provide Philadelphians for centuries to come a true glimpse into how the grand city lived and breathed at its historical peak.

Partnered with his artist and engraver father, William Russell Birch, Thomas Birch drew many detailed views of the city. Subjects included the port on the Delaware River, High Street Market, and the State House (now Independence Hall). In 1800, William Birch & Son published *The City of Philadelphia, in the State of Pennsylvania North America.* Intensely detailed and carefully observed, Birch's work reflects both grand views of notable places and intimate reflections of daily life in the bustling city. Carriages, soldiers, parades, and passers-by mingle in and among Philadelphia's landmarks. The volume of hand-colored prints forms the first collection of views of any American city, and sold well enough to be reissued in four editions, the last in 1827.

Thomas Birch left the partnership with his father in the early 1800s and became a prolific painter known primarily for his marine landscapes and paintings of ships. During the War of 1812, he painted a series of naval battles. Later, he traveled to areas outside Philadelphia, including southern New Jersey and towns along the Delaware River. His paintings, though not often sold, were nevertheless frequently exhibited at the Philadelphia Academy of Fine Arts, the American Art-Union, the Maryland Historical Society, and the National Academy of Design, among others. He died on this date in 1851, in debt and generally forgotten.

1868: Charles Dickens writes to his niece of his arrival in Philadelphia, describing it as "very clean and the day as blue and bright as a fine Italian day. But it freezes very hard."

1933: Tom Gola is born. NBA basketball star, coach for LaSalle University, and City Comptroller, Gola is defeated in a run for Mayor in 1983.

1976: Bobby "Boogaloo" Watts defeats "Marvelous" Marvin Hagler in a controversial ten-round boxing match at the Spectrum.

January 14

The long and difficult war was finally and officially over. A chain of events begun in 1776 with the enumeration of the many crimes enacted against the colonies by the King of England ended with the ratification of the Treaty of Paris by the American Congress of Confederation on this date in 1784. The peace was brokered in France by a five-member American delegation: Benjamin Franklin, John Jay, John Adams, Henry Laurens, and Benjamin Franklin's grandson, William Temple Franklin. Signed by the delegates and a representative of King George III in Paris on September 3, 1783, the treaty was the realization of a nearly decade-long effort to achieve independence and freedom for the United States of America.

The Treaty of Paris consisted of ten individual articles, or points of compromise. Among them, the most important included acknowledgment of the thirteen American colonies as free, sovereign, and independent states; the establishment of national boundaries between British North America (primarily Canada) and the United States; and the protection of Loyalists, prisoners of war, and their property. Despite strongly recommending that individual states abide by the treaty, in reality many ignored the agreement and refused to return confiscated Loyalist property, or absolve the debts of Loyalists. On the other side, British soldiers often refused to leave behind personal property acquired during the war, including slaves.

When the first signatures were affixed in Paris in September, the final article required that the United States Congress sign and return the treaty within six months. Temporarily based in Annapolis, Maryland, Congress impatiently awaited the arrival of its delegates, fully aware of the two months needed to cross the Atlantic. By early January 1784, short of the necessary delegates for a quorum, many in Congress concluded that it was necessary to move ahead with a vote anyway. However, at the last minute, Richard Beresford of South Carolina arrived, ensuring a full ratification. Thirteen official printed copies of the treaty were ordered from Philadelphia printer John Dunlap. In the weeks that followed, governors prepared their own proclamations informing citizens of the newly established peace. For the first time, Americans could look to the future fully independent and free of British rule.

1832: Edgar Allan Poe's story "Metzengerstein" is published in the *Philadelphia Saturday Courier.*

1925: The Horace Trumbauer-designed Ben Franklin Hotel opens at Ninth and Chestnut streets.

January 15

The next in line to a famous and infamous family of English actors, Frances (Fanny) Anne Kemble led a life as dramatic as the most extravagant of scripts. Achieving international fame as a stage actress, her tumultuous marriage and very public divorce from Philadelphia's Pierce Butler would result in a scandal of epic proportions. Born in London, Kemble found success onstage at the young age of twenty when she appeared as Juliet in Shakespeare's famous play. In 1832, she accompanied her father in a much-publicized theatrical tour of America, including an extended stop in Philadelphia. Here, she met and fell in love with one of her most ardent admirers. Pierce Butler was the son of a wealthy and established Philadelphia family whose fortunes lay in the plantations of the South. Kemble, a passionate abolitionist, nevertheless agreed to marry Butler and moved with him to Georgia in December 1838. There she found that what she saw only reinforced her commitment to abolitionism.

The couple returned to Philadelphia and for the next several years fought bitterly, and frequently lived apart. Butler continually harassed Kemble until she was forced to return to England in 1845. To her surprise, Kemble learned in 1848 that Butler was suing her for divorce, claiming that she had deserted him without cause. Kemble returned to the United States to defend herself while avid newspaper readers followed regular updates about the unusual divorce proceedings. Finally, in September 1849, the divorce was made official.

Returning to England once again, Kemble continued to perform and write and in 1863 published her highly influential expose of life among slaves, *Journal of a Residence on a Georgian Plantation in 1838–1839.* Butler suffered severe financial losses, and in 1859 most of his slaves were sold in the single largest sale of human beings in the country's history, an event that became known as "the weeping time." Upon her death on this date in 1893, Kemble left a fascinating and dramatic life, one to rival the greatest of dramas.

1965: Wilt Chamberlain returns to Philadelphia when he is traded from the San Francisco Warriors to the Philadelphia 76ers.

January 16

At precisely 12:01 A.M. on a cold January morning in 1920, the sale and consumption of alcoholic beverages became a federal crime. As the Eighteenth Amendment to the Constitution took effect, Philadelphia enjoyed the amusements offered by more than 10,000 saloons and taverns, with a drinking establishment on almost every neighborhood corner. As the unpopular law faced repeal in 1933, however, it was clear that the "Noble Experiment" was a complete failure, as much in Philadelphia as any city in the nation.

As cities and towns went dry, the demand for alcoholic beverages scarcely dipped. Regional recipes for wood alcohol appeared, with "yak-yak bourbon" (made in old whiskey barrels) proving most popular locally. In Philadelphia alone, a 30 percent increase in the number of speakeasies was noted within five years of the start of Prohibition. Statistics for the city suggested a 100 percent increase in the number of arrests for public drunkenness: from 23,740 in 1919 to 58,517 in 1925, an average of 100 arrests per day.

Across the country and in Philadelphia, organized crime moved in to accommodate the demand for illicit drink. The infamous Chicago crime boss Al Capone, convicted of tax evasion and seeking refuge from the intense government effort to end Prohibition-related crime in his city, went so far as to arrange to serve his sentence in Philadelphia's Eastern State Penitentiary, where he lived in relative comfort for several years.

In the national election of 1932, future president Franklin Delano Roosevelt and countless other politicians swore to repeal the Eighteenth Amendment. Pennsylvania's pro-Prohibition governor, Gifford Pinchot, quickly moved to establish laws for Pennsylvania that would retain some limitations on the sale and consumption of liquor. His efforts resulted in the creation of the Pennsylvania Liquor Control Board just five days before the Twenty-first Amendment ended Prohibition on December 5, 1933. Today, the state's Liquor Control Board remains the single largest purchaser of wine and liquor in the United States, selling on average a remarkable $1.7 billion in products annually.

1808: A crowd of discontented, hungry, and jobless sailors march on Philadelphia to appeal to Mayor Robert Wharton for help during a shipping embargo against American ships.

1834: The play "Pocahontas and the Settlers of Virginia" by George Washington Custis, opens at the Walnut Street Theater.

January 17

The life begun on this date in 1706 in the city of Boston would come to be seen as one of the most influential and compelling lives in American history, much of it lived in Philadelphia. By the age of ten and with only two years of formal schooling, Benjamin Franklin was apprenticed first with his father then with his brother James, a printer and publisher. Denied the opportunity to write for his brother's newspaper, Franklin ran away from his brother and his apprenticeship at the age of seventeen. He ran first to New York, but kept going and finally stopped running when he reached Philadelphia.

After acquiring another printing house apprenticeship and training briefly in London, Franklin dreamed of opening his own shop, which he did in 1730. Through hard work and innovation, Franklin's *Pennsylvania Gazette* became a leading newspaper, gaining him both fame and fortune. *Poor Richard's Almanac,* first published in 1733, would cement his reputation as a talented and driven businessman. He retired from printing at the young age of forty-two and devoted himself to politics and the pursuit of science, as expressed in his experiments with electricity and countless inventions, among them bifocals, the glass armonica, and the Franklin Stove. Founder of many of this country's "firsts," Franklin also sought to serve the public by establishing numerous institutions and organizations, including museums, libraries, learned societies, hospitals, and businesses.

In the years leading up to the American Revolution, Franklin was an essential actor in Pennsylvania politics, leading negotiations with the indigenous peoples during the French and Indian War, fighting the Stamp Act in 1765, and defending the rights of the American colonies while living in England. Following the escalation of tensions between England and the colonies, Franklin assumed the role of elder statesman and served on the First and Second Continental Congress, as well as the Constitutional Convention. Upon his death in 1790, the world mourned a man whose legacy is unparalleled, a Founding Father and Philadelphian whose accomplishments will never be matched.

1771: Novelist Charles Brockden Brown is born.

1781: Inventor and chemist Robert Hale is born.

1832: A patent is granted to William J. Young for improvements to the surveying compass.

January 18

When independence was declared by the Second Continental Congress in Philadelphia, July 1776, an act of treason was enacted. Even as the powerful words were approved by fifty-six delegates representing all thirteen colonies, a veil of secrecy protected those men from possible death at the hands of the British should independence not be won by the fledgling nation. In the hours following approval of the Declaration of Independence on July 4, 1776, the text of the document was prepared for limited distribution in the form of a broadside published by Philadelphia printer John Dunlap. Public readings and newspapers in Philadelphia, New York, and Boston over the next few weeks would begin to spread the word about the intentions of a Congress whose names did not appear anywhere in print.

Within six months, deeming it appropriate that the Declaration of Independence be properly and fully distributed, the Continental Congress (meeting in Baltimore) called for the availability of local presses. This time, in addition to the text the broadside would include the names of fifty-five of the fifty-six delegates. Mary Katherine Goddard, the country's first postmistress and publisher, offered her press. Fully aware of the continued risk in disseminating the Declaration, Goddard published an unknown number of copies on this date in 1777. Congress ordered that a copy be sent to each of the states and formally entered into their records. Within a month, Congress returned to Philadelphia.

Goddard continued to serve as postmistress in Baltimore until 1789, when she was removed from the post despite strong protest among Baltimore citizens. She continued to work as a dry goods dealer and stationer until her death on August 12, 1816. To date, a total of nine Goddard broadsides of the Declaration of Independence are known, making them one of the rarest versions of the essential American document.

1973: An earthquake with an epicenter beneath Wilmington, Delaware, cracks plaster and topples glasses in Philadelphia.

1992: Philadelphia hosts the National Hockey League All-Star game.

1999: A tornado touches down in Marconi Plaza in South Philadelphia; eighteen people are injured.

January 19

Coach Andy Reid had a lot of work to do. Hired in 1999 to bring victory to the Philadelphia Eagles, Reid contributed a great deal to that goal with the drafting of quarterback Donovan McNabb that same year. Forty years had passed since their last national championship, while it was two decades since the Eagles claimed their last NFC Championship and made an appearance in a Super Bowl. Reid and McNabb wanted to prove that the team could be national contenders. Within just one season, the team was once again NFC East champions, preparing to battle for the division title.

For the next three years, the McNabb-led Eagles lived up to their reputation as tough fighters who often lost focus at the most crucial moment. Battling both hard competition and a famously disparaging and emotional fan base, the Eagles played well enough to achieve the best regular season records in the 2001, 2002, and 2003 NFC championships. Much to the dismay of their passionate but increasingly critical fans, the team lost each of those games, perhaps most notably on this day in 2003 against the Carolina Panthers, 14–3.

Finally, the Eagles succeeded in breaking their losing streak and went as far as gaining the division title in January 2004. The following year, on February 6, 2005, the Eagles faced returning champions the New England Patriots in Super Bowl XXXIX and were defeated 24–21. In the years that followed, the Eagles continued to fight for victories, achieving a division championship in 2006 and appearing in the NFL playoffs in 2008. Always thrilling and never predictable while still bearing the brunt of fan displeasure, the Eagles embody the fighting spirit of Philadelphia's sporting history.

1819: William Rawle addresses the annual meeting of the Philadelphia Society for Promoting Agriculture. Rawle was founder and president of the Pennsylvania Historical Society and an attorney who prosecuted leaders of the Whiskey Rebellion.

1996: Three inches of rain and thunderstorms with mild weather cause twenty inches of snow to melt in one day, resulting in the worst flooding in two decades and damages estimated at $1 billion.

2009: Philadelphia celebrates the 200th birthday of Edgar Allan Poe by exhibiting the only known manuscript copy of "The Raven" at the Free Library of Philadelphia.

January 20

It all ended with a single shot. Lieutenant Richard Smyth, second husband of housewife and shop owner Ann Baker Carson, shot and killed his wife's first husband in a duel spurred on by anger, alcoholism, and accusations of bigamy. What would become one of the most infamous trials of the century, the murder of sea captain John Carson on this date in 1816, was the culmination of years of an unhappy marriage and the apparent abandonment of a young wife. Smyth would soon face the hangman's noose for his actions, while his wife desperately sought his freedom until her own untimely death.

Married at the young age of 16 to the over-40-year-old Carson, Ann Baker was frequently left to care for her children and herself while her husband disappeared during alcoholic binges and on the occasional working sea voyage. For more than nine years, she ran all aspects of a china shop business, entirely independent and successful. In 1816, she heard a rumor that her husband had died overseas and soon after married a longtime friend and suitor, Lieutenant Richard Smyth. Unfortunately, Captain Carson returned unexpectedly and threatened his wife's economic and marital independence. In the ensuing argument, Carson was killed in Mrs. Carson's parlor with a gun likely purchased by his wife.

While Smyth was charged and convicted of first-degree murder, Mrs. Carson faced lesser charges of second-degree murder. Permitted to remain free from jail, she worked tirelessly to free her second husband, even making an unsuccessful attempt to kidnap Governor Simon Snyder with the help of several unsavory conspirators. Smyth was never released from jail and was hanged in August of the same year. In 1822, Ann Carson published her recollections and defense of her actions, convincingly portraying her life with an abusive first husband. Mrs. Carson continued her association with criminals and was jailed for her participation in a counterfeiting ring. She died in 1824 while imprisoned, from injuries inflicted by fellow prisoners.

1842: Virginia Clemm Poe coughs up blood while singing and playing piano for her husband, Edgar Allan Poe, at their house in Philadelphia. He realizes that she suffers from tuberculosis.

January 21

In the years following the consolidation of twenty-nine townships and districts into the single city of Philadelphia in 1854, a growing demand for public transportation resulted in the development of several horse-powered street railways. Densely populated areas such as Southwark and Kensington clamored for the opportunity to expand their daily lives beyond the commotion of their immediate neighborhood. On this date in 1858, the Philadelphia and Delaware River Railroad Company opened the first-ever streetcar railway to run within the city. A new era of mobility and progress was at hand.

Initially, demand for public railways seemed to center on lines leaving the city. As early as 1855, the North Penn Railroad was planning a steam line to depart from Front Street at Willow Street up into Bucks County, with the possibility of horse-car spurs extending throughout the city. The need for travel within city boundaries led to the consideration of other options. The first line ran down on Sixth Street and back north up Fifth Street, between Cherry Street in Kensington and Morris Street in Southwark.

Featuring a marked improvement in the speed and comfort of travel, the street railway was an immediate success. As word of the success spread, countless other newly formed companies applied to the city council for permission to run their own lines. Within just two years, nearly twenty charters had been granted for street railways, and an estimated 46,000 people were already riding every day. Such high use led to heavy damage on the rails, and the individually chartered companies often did not live up to their obligations to keep up with repairs. Debates over the fare (5 cents) and the often horrific abuse of the horses raised questions about the need for a new advance in transportation. The next phase was soon to come, with the eventual advent of steam engines and later, electricity. But the value of public transportation had been proven, despite its complications. The city would remain a population on the move well into the next century.

1771: The Carpenters' Company first occupies Carpenters' Hall. The Company, an early trade guild, was incorporated on July 26, 1792.

January 22

On this date in 1948, Temple University dedicated the newly completed WRTI-AM radio studios in the basement of Thomas Hall. Built with the support and assistance of newspaper publisher Walter Annenberg and WFIL-FM, the station formed the core learning laboratory for the university's new radio, television, and film curriculum, known as the Radio Technical Institute, the abbreviation for which gave the station its call letters. Originally intended to broadcast exclusively to those on campus and almost entirely run by students, the station featured programming that included popular music, dramas, news, and sports.

In the late 1940s, Temple University Professor of Communications John Roberts recruited local FM station WFIL and the *Philadelphia Inquirer* to contribute $25,000 toward the creation of a state-of-the-art broadcast studio. Initially available on the dial at 640 AM, WRTI quickly gained in popularity among the thousands of Temple University students and faculty. Within five years, the station received a license to broadcast on FM and quickly became the most powerfully transmitted local radio station, on the dial at 90.1 FM, where it remains today.

Twenty years after the first broadcast, WRTI-FM was moved from Thomas Hall, the oldest building on campus, to the new Annenberg Hall. In addition to radically increasing the available technology and space allotted to the station, the dynamic changed with the inclusion of a new professional staff, supported by student volunteers. No longer operating solely as a training laboratory, WRTI joined the National Public Radio system and began to serve a broader audience, 24 hours a day. The programming was also changed, against the protests of some, to an all-jazz format. In 1997, classical music programming was brought in when Philadelphia's only commercial classical station, WFLN, changed formats.

Into the 1980s and 1990s, the station outgrew Annenberg Hall, eventually finding a home in the university's Entertainment and Community Education Center. The addition of performance studios, advanced soundproofing design, and digital sound technology has brought WRTI-FM into the twenty-first century and prepared it for the next decades to come.

1941: Edward R. Bradley, well-known to viewers of TV's *60 Minutes,* is born.

1965: Jeffrey A. Townes (DJ Jazzy Jeff) is born.

January 23

For some, it is only after their death that memory and legacy are truly appreciated. When actor and activist Paul Robeson died on this date in 1976 at his sister's home in West Philadelphia, he had lived in almost complete obscurity for nearly two decades. A true renaissance man, Robeson excelled as an athlete, actor, singer, scholar, writer, and political activist.

After graduation from Rutgers University as a star football player and valedictorian, Robeson attended law school in New York City where he was also introduced to the joys of public speaking and acting. Receiving much acclaim, he was offered notable roles through the 1920s and 1930s, including *Othello,* O'Neill's *The Emperor Jones,* and in a role written for him, Joe in *Show Boat.* In addition to his work on Broadway and on the London stage, Robeson reprised many of his most famous roles on film for Hollywood, cementing his fame on an international level.

While traveling for his acting and singing career, and achieving international fame as a performer on stage and screen, Robeson began to speak frequently and publicly about his progressive beliefs, calling attention to the many ways in which oppressed peoples sought equal rights and freedom and targeting the capitalist system, not the socialist system, as the offender. He was soon seen as a threat for his communist sympathies by the American and British governments, which were faced with the specter of an expansionist Soviet Union under the genocidal dictator Joseph Stalin. As early as the mid-1930s, Robeson was identified as someone meriting investigation and was then subjected to blacklisting and harassment, which continued for nearly two decades.

As his health declined in the late 1950s, Robeson retreated to Philadelphia. Living in seclusion for the remaining years of his life, the importance of his artistic and political legacy became clearer. Public celebrations of his 70th and 75th birthdays hinted at the growing understanding of how much Robeson had, in fact, influenced and inspired the civil rights movement. Today, his abilities as a vocalist and actor remain highly regarded, securing his place of respect and honor in American performance history.

2000: Southwark Towers is imploded at 8:30 A.M. by Controlled Demolition, Inc., and Haines & Kibblehouse; the two towers were 26 stories tall; the third tower is saved for reuse as senior housing.

January 24

Philanthropy is often the method of choice for those hoping to be remembered for their great deeds or generous actions. Rebecca Gratz, daughter of a prominent and powerful Jewish family in Philadelphia, approached philanthropy less as a means to an end and more as the journey itself. Her lifetime commitment to charitable organizations grew from a belief that all Philadelphians deserved a happy and comfortable life. She firmly believed that the needs of the poor and suffering demanded a commitment from those who could, and should help, regardless of position within faith and community.

Many of the organizations sponsored by Gratz addressed needs within the Orthodox Jewish community, of which Gratz was an observant member. However, Gratz was also known for her ability to comfortably bridge whatever distances might exist within faith or experience. For nearly forty years, she served as secretary on the board of directors of the Philadelphia Orphan Society, which had initially been conceived as a nonsectarian organization, albeit with a Christian orientation. Orphans were provided with a Christian education and abided by strict expectations of behavior and daily order. When protests over the placement of orphaned children in Jewish or Unitarian homes came up, Gratz staunchly defended a religious tolerance that sought only to benefit the children.

On this date in 1822, Gratz and the city of Philadelphia suffered a tragic loss. Just six years after its founding, a fire destroyed much of the Orphan Asylum resulting in the deaths of 23 of the 106 children in residence. The tragedy only reinforced Gratz' commitment to the asylum, and she worked tirelessly to reestablish the people's trust in the charity and rebuild both physically and emotionally. Her hard work inspired countless other men and women, some of whom went on to form their own asylums in cities throughout the country. Gratz continued to serve the Asylum and other charities until her death on August 27, 1869, fully believing that the work she accomplished throughout her life brought relief and meaning to the lives of Philadelphia's most disadvantaged citizens, as well as to her own.

1871: Thomas Augustus Jaggar, Jr., founder of the Hawaiian Volcano Observatory, is born in Philadelphia.

1888: Jacob L. Wortman of Philadelphia receives a patent for the typewriter ribbon.

1970: President Richard M. Nixon presents Philadelphia Orchestra conductor Eugene Ormandy with the Presidential Medal of Honor in a ceremony at the Academy of Music.

January 25

After the first decade of the nineteenth century, a void had yet to be filled. With the formation of the Library Company of Philadelphia and the American Philosophical Society in Philadelphia in the 1700s, science and intellectual inquiry were well represented in the city. However, as the century ended, the physical exploration of the natural world and the scientific ordering of what was found was without a home. On this date in 1812, a meeting of men, many of them members of both earlier institutions, organized the Academy of Natural Sciences of Philadelphia into the oldest natural sciences institution in the Western Hemisphere. In language similar to that which guided other scientific organizations, the academy sought "the encouragement and cultivation of the sciences, and the advancement of useful learning."

From its earliest days, the Academy sponsored many expeditions into the unknown natural wilderness. Explorers such as William Bartram, Stephen Long, and Ferdinand Hayden led study trips throughout the western and southern territories. Each exploration returned with countless specimens, preserved and ordered under the auspices of the academy. By 1828, the collections were first displayed to a curious public. Educational and entertaining at the same time, such exhibitions have remained a staple mission for the academy, as is the care and maintenance of a growing scientific collection, currently believed to number more than 17 million specimens.

Advances in the study of natural history throughout the Academy's history include the first-ever public mounting and display of a dinosaur skeleton, that of a hadrosaurus discovered in New Jersey; the creation of dioramas to display specimens in their natural environment; and the study of biodiversity and environmental sciences. Today, the academy remains one of the most important of American scientific institutions and museums, continuing its mission to expand human knowledge of the natural world.

1858: The Philadelphia banks adopt a clearing house system, modeled after methods first created in New York. Philadelphia was the second city to adopt this improved banking model (which was an improvement over the cumbersome system of exchange).

January 26

Philadelphia has always relied on its waterways for economic survival. Bounded east and west by two highly navigable rivers, including a direct connection to the Atlantic Ocean, the city benefited from the expectation of easy access to coastal and transoceanic travel. Thousands of ships came to dock along the Delaware and Schuylkill rivers, making the city the premier port in North America. Advances in technology beginning in the last decade of the eighteenth century included steamships and the construction of a protective breakwater at the mouth of Delaware Bay. All of these advances, however, could never counter the greatest threat to safe, consistent shipping: ice.

For all its success as a port city, Philadelphia was also located in a temperate zone occasionally subject to harsh winters. In 1793, a law was passed by the Pennsylvania Assembly requiring ship owners to pay river pilots after six days if ice prevented the pilots from bringing the vessel into port. On this date in 1832, a total of 126 outgoing vessels were waiting for the ice to break up. In 1856, the ice was so thick that hundreds of people regularly enjoyed ice-skating across the Delaware River to New Jersey.

By 1836, the steam towboat *Pennsylvania* was in use as an ice clearer. Designed primarily to tow ships upriver from the bay, the *Pennsylvania* was pressed into service as the river and canals froze over, but the ship was unable to break the thickest ice. Following the August 1837 launch of a new iceboat out of Byerly's shipyard in Kensington, the city had a dedicated icebreaker capable of clearing the river. The next year, the boat successfully broke up ice ridges as thick as five feet, making the Delaware River passable once again. As the nineteenth and twentieth centuries passed, the port was no longer at risk of closure due to ice, remaining open year-round.

1767: The first issue of *Pennsylvania Chronicle and Universal Advertiser* newspaper is published by William Goddard and continues until February 8, 1774. The newspaper is best known for publishing John Dickinson's "Letters from an American Farmer in Pennsylvania to the Inhabitants of the British Colonies."

1857: The Academy of Music opens for its first season.

January 27

Water is an essential need, providing a source of life. In the Philadelphia of the 1790s, residents faced a wholly different aspect of water. Dirty and contaminated by surface drainage, the city's wells and cisterns were frequently seen as the carrier of death, the bearer of illnesses and unknown causes of epidemics as devastating as yellow fever and as mysterious as dysentery. On this date in 1801, the first fresh water flowed from an innovative pumping station to the city's Center Square Waterworks. It would prove to be one of the most significant civil improvements in the history of the city.

As early as 1747, Benjamin Franklin served on a committee whose sole purpose was to discuss improving the swampy lands in Dock Creek (now Dock Street) known for its polluted and unsafe waters. By 1798, architect and engineer Benjamin Henry Latrobe was given the task of determining the best method for bringing clean water in from the Schuylkill River. Initially, the city considered constructing a canal from Norristown. However, Latrobe recommended building a basin on the Schuylkill at Chestnut Street, and through a series of canals and tunnels traveling by steam pump to a central station. At Center Square, a gravity-driven reservoir would then deliver fresh water throughout the city through wooden pipes.

The classically designed pump house opened to great acclaim, appealing to citizens not only for Latrobe's delightful architectural design, but also as a remarkable technological feat. Within a year of first pumping water, sixty-three houses, four breweries, and a sugar refinery were supplied with water, in addition to thirty-seven hydrants placed throughout the city. The waterworks at Center Square continued to operate just ten more years, until in 1811 it was replaced with a larger reservoir at Fairmount, now the location of the Philadelphia Museum of Art. Latrobe's building remained in use as a water tank until 1829, when it was demolished, ending the earliest era of water improvement for the city.

1750: A rear tower is ordered for the Pennsylvania State House, begun in 1732 and now known as Independence Hall.

1833: William Rush, artist and sculptor, dies.

January 28

Born in Boston in 1809, Edgar Allan Poe's short and tumultuous life was marked by the heights of genius and the depths of despair. Following abandonment by his father and the death of his mother before Poe was two years of age, he was taken in by John Allan in Richmond, Virginia. Never fully adopted but well educated, Poe attended the University of Virginia and West Point. While still in school, he began to publish his poems and essays. After leaving West Point, he edited several literary publications in Richmond, Baltimore, and Philadelphia, never remaining in one place for very long. Poe developed a reputation for bouts with gambling and drinking, resulting in his removal from several editorial positions.

In 1837, Poe and his young wife, fifteen-year-old cousin Virginia Clemm, settled in Philadelphia, where he hoped to achieve fame as a writer, critic, and editor among the many successful journals and magazines published in the city. Between 1837 and 1844, Poe experienced his most prolific period, publishing some of his most famous works, including "The Tell-Tale Heart" and "The Gold Bug." During this time, Poe earned a limited reputation as a cutting critic and talented poet, becoming embroiled in several contentious literary relationships. Among his rivals was Philadelphia poet Rufus Wilmot Griswold.

In 1842, Griswold published an anthology of American poetry. Poe criticized Griswold's favoritism toward friends, but agreed to write a supportive review for a fee. However, on this date in 1843, another review of Griswold's anthology attributed to Poe appeared, strongly challenging Griswold's work. Poe began to verbally attack Griswold at public readings, and the animosity between the two men grew. Upon the death of Poe in Baltimore in 1849, Griswold falsely related Poe's anti-social behavior and "melancholy" in an obituary published under the pseudonym "Ludwig." Griswold went on to claim editorial ownership of Poe's work and continued to describe Poe as drug addicted, drunken, and mentally ill. Griswold's characterizations of Poe may have been intended to raise interest in the author's work, but the depiction of Poe as a tortured man continues to influence his fame today.

1782: The French Minister of Plenipotentiary notifies Congress that a loan of four million livres is available for their use from the French government.

1935: The first test run of an electric train between Philadelphia and Washington, D.C., is conducted.

January 29

On the whole, I'd rather be in Philadelphia." These words have long been attributed to one of Philadelphia's most famous sons: W. C. Fields, born William Claude Dukenfield on this date in 1880 in the Philadelphia suburb of Darby, Pennsylvania. One of America's most recognizable actors and comedians, Fields' comedic style is said to have been inspired by his mother's mumbled, cutting observations as they watched passersby from the front stoop. The son of a street vegetable salesman, Fields may also have learned the vaudevillian power of juggling by entertaining his father's customers with his fresh produce. As early as age fifteen, he found a home on the road as a member of various traveling vaudeville and burlesque companies, eventually touring across the United States and Europe.

Leaving his young wife and son in Philadelphia, Fields moved on to New York City, where he was eventually picked to join the famous Ziegfeld Follies in 1915. Soon, Fields was enjoying fame as a Broadway star, beginning with *Poppy* in 1923. Following several years in silent films, Fields moved west to Hollywood to star in the earliest talking pictures, further developing a series of wise-cracking, drunken, and mischievous characters. Classically paired with Mae West in *My Little Chickadee,* one of his best-known films, their raunchy banter became a hallmark of Fields' comedic career.

In later years, suffering from poor health as a result of a lifetime of drinking, Fields withdrew somewhat from public life and performing. At the time of his death on Christmas Day, 1946, rumors began that he requested the famous line above as his epitaph. Although there is no evidence to prove or deny this rumor (his marker includes only his name and dates), it reflects Fields' long and public relationship with his hometown. Other lines attributed to Fields about Philadelphia include "I'd like to see Paris before I die . . . Philadelphia will do!" from *My Little Chickadee* and the anecdotal "Philadelphia, wonderful town, spent a week there one night!" He is buried at Forest Lawn Memorial Park Cemetery in Glendale, California, far from home but still a part of Philadelphia.

1901: The American League of baseball is organized in Philadelphia with teams from Buffalo, Chicago, Cleveland, Detroit, Indianapolis, Kansas City, Milwaukee, and Minneapolis.

1927: The first transatlantic cable opens between Philadelphia and England.

1982: The *Philadelphia Bulletin* newspaper closes after 135 years.

January 30

There are undoubtedly hundreds of well-known historical figures for whom myth is as much a part of fame as truth. The storied life of Elizabeth Griscom Ross, more famously known as Betsy Ross, is a fascinating blend of fact and fiction and remains one of Philadelphia's most beloved traditions. Born into a New Jersey Quaker family on New Year's Day in 1732, Betsy and her family moved to Philadelphia in 1735. As an upholstery apprentice, Betsy was trained to sew curtains, bedcovers, and other household objects. In 1773, she met and married fellow apprentice John Ross, son of the Assistant Rector of Christ Church. Opening their own shop, they lived and worked together for just two years before John Ross was killed while serving with the local militia in the Revolutionary War. She remarried in 1777, and again in 1783 after the death of her second husband, who was also serving in the war.

Betsy continued to run her business and in 1777 received a large payment for making flags from the Pennsylvania State Navy Board. Up to this point, much that is known about Betsy can be documented. Unfortunately, the story of her making the "first" American flag was not told until almost thirty-five years after her death on this date in 1836. In 1870, her grandson, William Canby, described a meeting between Betsy, George Washington, and other members of Congress. Impressed with her ability to cut a five-point star in one snip, Washington is said to have asked her to create a flag with a predetermined design of thirteen stripes and thirteen stars.

Canby's story, seemingly supported by affidavits from other family members, was publicized at a time when Americans were beginning to anticipate celebrating the Centennial of the nation's birth. Her home, said to be located at 239 Arch Street, was first advertised as the Betsy Ross House and birthplace of the American Flag as early as 1876. Many patriotic stories were embraced, the need for proof deemed less important than the telling of a proud history. Today, the legend of Betsy Ross is unmatched in popularity, remaining one of Philadelphia's cherished attractions.

1798: Representative Matthew Lyon of Vermont spits on fellow Congressman Roger Griswold of Connecticut in the first of several confrontations between the two men on the floor of the House of Representatives.

1855: City Council passes an ordinance to organize the various volunteer fire-fighting agencies into a Fire Department.

January 31

Like those in other large cities, Philadelphia's Chinatown has its own long and storied history. Growing out of the influx of Chinese immigrants seeking wealth and opportunity in the 1870s and 1880s, Chinatown was initially populated mostly by single men. Faced with exclusionary immigration laws, limited work opportunities, and with a desire to re-create the social connections they knew at home, the new arrivals settled in the area around 10th Street and Arch Street, which remains today the heart of Philadelphia's Chinese-American community.

Following the start of World War II, restrictive immigration laws were lifted as attention turned away from China and toward the threat from Germany, Japan, and Italy. Chinese-Americans stood side by side with other Americans in service to the nation. When they returned from overseas, many arrived as newlyweds, quickly establishing their own families. Other young families followed, and Chinatown grew. Churches, businesses, and social and cultural organizations were formed to support the community.

In the 1960s, urban renewal and other government redevelopment projects began to threaten Chinatown, even as residents sought to improve their community. The proposed construction of the Vine Street Expressway served as a motivator for a growing number of community activists who worked to unify their voice and preserve their neighborhood. Unable to fully stop the development, the residents of Chinatown successfully negotiated a modified plan. Community activism remains an important part of life in Chinatown as expansion and change continue to threaten this vital community.

On this date in 1984, the most recognized symbol of Chinatown, the Friendship Gate, located at 10th Street near Arch Street, was dedicated. Located in the heart of Chinatown, the gate was a joint project between Philadelphia and Tianjin, China. Handcrafted by artisans using traditional methods, the colorful gate is the only one of its kind in the United States. Following a complete restoration, the gate was rededicated on November 19, 2008.

1921: Film and music star Mario Lanza is born Alfred Arnold Cocozza in Philadelphia. He is best known for portraying Enrico Caruso in Hollywood's 1951 film *The Great Caruso,* though his popularity in Philadelphia is unparalleled.

On the night of January 6, 1778, a most unusual naval battle took place along the Delaware River just above Philadelphia. Caleb Carman, of Bordentown, New Jersey, conceived of a way to damage, if not destroy, the British fleet floating in the city's port. A series of kegs filled with gunpowder and spring loaded to explode on contact were to be floated downriver. Carefully piloted by Carman himself, the kegs were successfully released but destroyed only one barge because most of the British ships had returned to the wharves to avoid river ice. British soldiers, alerted to the presence of the kegs, were ordered to shoot anything floating on the river. Disappointed at the limited damage inflicted, Carman and his fellow revolutionaries were nevertheless proud of their effort. Later that year, Francis Hopkinson wrote "The Battle of the Kegs" to the tune of "Yankee Doodle," to poke fun at the British. A fellow Bordentown resident and Signer of the Declaration of Independence, Hopkinson is credited with being one of the country's earliest authors and songwriters.

The Battle of the Kegs

Gallants attend and hear a friend
Trill forth harmonious ditty,
Strange things I'll tell which late befell
In Philadelphia city.

'Twas early day, as poets say,
Just when the sun was rising,
A soldier stood on a log of wood,
And saw a thing surprising.

As in amaze he stood to gaze,
The truth can't be denied, sir,
He spied a score of kegs or more
Come floating down the tide, sir.

A sailor too in jerkin blue,
This strange appearance viewing,
First damned his eyes, in great surprise,
Then said, "Some mischief's brewing.

"These kegs, I'm told, the rebels hold,
Packed up like pickled herring;
And they're come down to attack the town,
In this new way of ferrying."

The soldier flew, the sailor too,
And scared almost to death, sir,
Wore out their shoes, to spread the news,
And ran till out of breath, sir.

Now up and down throughout the town,
Most frantic scenes were acted;
And some ran here, and others there,
Like men almost distracted.

Some fire cried, which some denied,
But said the earth had quaked;
And girls and boys, with hideous noise,
Ran through the streets half naked.

Sir William he, snug as a flea,
Lay all this time a snoring,
Nor dreamed of harm as he lay warm,
In bed with Mrs. Loring.

Now in a fright, he starts upright,
Awaked by such a clatter;
He rubs both eyes, and boldly cries,
"For God's sake, what's the matter?"

At his bedside he then espied,
Sir Erskine at command, sir,
Upon one foot he had one boot,
And th' other in his hand, sir.

"Arise, arise," Sir Erskine cries,
"The rebels—more's the pity,
Without a boat are all afloat,
And ranged before the city.

"The motley crew, in vessels new,
With Satan for their guide, sir,
Packed up in bags, or wooden kegs,
Come driving down the tide, sir.

"Therefore prepare for bloody war;
These kegs must all be routed,
Or surely we despised shall be,
And British courage doubted."

The royal band now ready stand
All ranged in dread array, sir,
With stomach' stout to see it out,
And make a bloody day, sir.

The cannons roar from shore to shore.
The small arms make a rattle;
Since wars began I'm sure no man
E'er saw so strange a battle.

The rebel dales, the rebel vales,
With rebel trees surrounded,
The distant woods, the hills and floods,
With rebel echoes sounded.

The fish below swam to and fro,
Attacked from every quarter;
Why sure, thought they, the devil's to pay,
'Mongst folks above the water.

The kegs, 'tis said, though strongly made,
Of rebel staves and hoops, sir,
Could not oppose their powerful foes,
The conquering British troops, sir.

From morn to night these men of might
Displayed amazing courage;
And when the sun was fairly down,
Retired to sup their porridge.

A hundred men with each a pen,
Or more upon my word, sir,
It is most true would be too few,
Their valor to record, sir.

Such feats did they perform that day,
Against these wicked kegs, sir,
That years to come: if they get home,
They'll make their boasts and brags, sir.

February

February 1

The education of educators is an important process, one that requires care and focus. In Philadelphia, no public "Normal School" for training women teachers existed until this date in 1848, when the Girls Normal School (later the Philadelphia High School for Girls) held its first class. Located in the old Model School at Chester Street below Vine Street and attended by 150 young women (a noteworthy number at a time when most schools were much smaller), it was the first secondary public school for women in Pennsylvania. Within fifty years, the high school refined its purpose to prepare young women for college, not limiting them to a single occupation.

The initial success and popularity of the school resulted in the move to a different facility in 1854, and by 1860 more than sixty-five diplomas had been granted since the first year. That same year, a shift in focus led to the school being renamed the Girls' High and Normal School, as the curriculum supported both teacher training and a general academic education. By October 1876 the school was the third-largest in the city, behind only the University of Pennsylvania and Girard College. In 1933, a new school was built at Seventeenth and Spring Garden streets, but within twenty-five years the school was moved once again to its current location in North Philadelphia at Broad and Olney streets.

Through the twentieth century, Girls' High continued to serve an increasingly diverse community of academically talented women from all parts of Philadelphia. Social traditions such as Big Sisters and Little Sisters, Class Days, and graduation at the Academy of Music evolved as a means of complementing their academic preparations and providing young women the emotional and intellectual support to succeed in the professional world. The school has produced dozens of exceptional graduates, among them artists, politicians, authors, scientists, jurists, and educators. Today, Girls' High is one of the highest-rated public schools in the state. More than eleven hundred young women continue the traditions of Girls' High, looking to the school motto *Vincit qui se vincit* (she conquers who conquers herself) for inspiration in forging their own way in a modern world.

1938: Actor Sherman Hemsley, best known for his work on TV's *The Jeffersons,* is born.

2007: Philadelphia University basketball coach Herb Magee achieves the most Division II victories (829) when his team defeats Wilmington College.

February 2

Much like a garden, cities grow organically but at first only in spots. Small seedlings take hold far from each other but quickly develop and grow into large, overgrown, and tightly packed flower beds. In Philadelphia, the small seedlings of the eighteenth century were the varied districts and boroughs that formed outside the boundaries of the city proper but within those of the county. As laid out by surveyor Thomas Holme in 1682, the City of Philadelphia extended from the Schuylkill River to the Delaware River and from Cedar Street (now South Street) to Vine Street, an area of just two square miles. By the mid-1800s, the city was surrounded by more than two dozen other municipal authorities in addition to the county authority itself, each with its own government. The Consolidation Act of 1854, passed on this date, established the modern boundaries and municipal structures of the city-county of Philadelphia, one of only six in the nation.

In 1850, the city had a population of just over 121,000, while the rest of the county numbered in population nearly three times that amount. Newly arriving immigrants chose to live outside the city itself, resulting in a 110 percent population growth in two northern districts, Kensington and Spring Garden. The loss of tax revenue stemming from this population shift was just one reason for action. Boundaries between city and outlying districts were so porous that criminals regularly "escaped" by simply crossing the rivers, or Cedar and Vine streets, leaving the jurisdiction and preventing the city from properly prosecuting them. Government services were impossible to ensure, as complex dealings from municipality to municipality stymied many resolutions.

In addition to creating the border as it is known today, the Act of Consolidation granted executive power to a city mayor, elected every two years. The City Council assumed control of the city budget, while the mayor's office oversaw the police and fire departments, public services, and all executive departments. A large public celebration held on March 11, 1854, marked the beginning of the modern administration of the City and County of Philadelphia, a structure much of which remains today.

1809: The Walnut Street Theater opens.

1949: Eleanor Roosevelt speaks at the Philadelphia Fellowship Commission, a group attempting to bring the community together.

1968: Wilt Chamberlain becomes the only player in history to achieve a double-triple-double, in which he gains at least 20 of any three statistics. In one game, he scores 22 points, 25 rebounds, and 21 assists.

February 3

Elisha Kent Kane, son of a United States District judge and among the most advantaged citizens of Philadelphia, was born on this date in 1820. Sickened by rheumatic fever while studying at the University of Pennsylvania, he was inspired to study medicine. As a physician, he joined the United States Navy primarily as a means of seeing the world, traveling to China, the Philippines, Malaysia, India, and Egypt, among many other exotic places. After returning home several years later weakened and ill, Kent quickly recovered and sought more adventure by engaging in skirmishes during the Mexican-American War. Welcomed home as a hero, Kane continued to serve the Navy but soon grew bored with his regular assignments. Finally, in 1850, he successfully arranged service with the First Grinnell Expedition, a rescue mission to the Arctic Circle in search of an earlier explorer, Sir John Franklin of Great Britain. The graves of three of Franklin's crew were discovered, but Franklin himself was never found. Once again Kane returned to Philadelphia deathly ill, but immediately began looking for his next challenge.

Pursuing a career as a lecturer, Kane built a reputation as an exciting and adventurous explorer. His love affair with spiritualist and self-professed seer Margaret Fox scandalized the country and only added to his mystique. Convinced that he could find Franklin, Kane pushed for a Second Grinnell Expedition, which departed New York in 1853 under Kane's command. The trip was fraught with challenges and successes as Kane engaged in valuable friendships with local Inuit tribes, made careful scientific observations, and resolved a mutiny. After returning home in 1855, excerpts from his Arctic Explorations were run serially in the *Philadelphia Public Ledger* newspaper, making the travelogue one of the most popular books of the 1800s.

Suffering from lingering health concerns, Kane sailed to Cuba in hopes of recovering his health. He died there on February 16, 1857. His funeral began in New Orleans and traveled up the Mississippi and Ohio rivers to Cincinnati where it boarded a train to Philadelphia. Viewed by thousands of people, it is often considered the largest funeral of the century, second perhaps only to that of Abraham Lincoln. Kane, famed for his courage, adventurous spirit, and engaging storytelling, lived a life of adventure and died young as one of the century's most famous celebrities.

1843: Commodore Isaac Hull, commander of the USS *Constitution*, or "Old Ironsides," dies.

1894: *Public Ledger* newspaper publisher and pioneer George W. Childs dies.

February 4

Unanimity in American presidential elections is a rare commodity. It occurred just two times in the history of the United States under the Constitution, and to just one man. Both elections took place on this date, with the first being held in 1789. Following the ratification of the United States Constitution in 1788, General George Washington was persuaded to come out of retirement in order to serve the new nation in a completely new manner. An obvious and clear choice to lead, Washington was viewed as the only man alive worthy of such an honor. Washington ran unopposed and without actively campaigning. The first general election was held from December 15, 1788, to January 10, 1789, with Washington receiving all of the 38,818 votes cast by eligible citizens, a remarkably small 1.3 percent of the overall population of the country.

The initial structure of the Electoral College as defined by the U.S. Constitution allowed individual states to select their own electors, each member given two votes. In the first election, Rhode Island and North Carolina were ineligible because they had not yet ratified the Constitution, while New York failed to appoint its eight electors because of a deadlock in their state legislature. After the popular votes were counted, all sixty-nine members of the Electoral College unanimously elected General George Washington to be President of the United States. Their second votes were then placed among the remaining eleven candidates, among them John Adams, John Hancock, and John Jay. Ultimately, John Adams received the most second votes, a total of thirty-four, and was elected Vice President.

Washington's first term was generally successful, establishing the ability of the newly formed government to thrive. Four years later, Washington would again be unanimously elected on this same date. At the end of his second term, however, the advent of a two-party system challenged the way Americans elected their leaders, and the first of many contested presidential elections was held. Unanimity within presidential elections would not occur again.

1765: The Philadelphia Medical Society is founded.

1925: Russell Hoban, author of the beloved *Frances* series of books, as well as the youth novel *Turtle Diary,* is born.

February 5

Remarkably, the screen at the Academy of Music was filled with the vision of waltzing dancers, moving to the sounds of the orchestra playing in the pit below. What made this moment notable was the introduction of Henry R. Heyl's "Phasmatrope" in what is generally considered the first-ever public motion picture projection in the world. On this date in 1870, at an evening to benefit the Young Men's Society of St. Michael's Evangelical Lutheran Church, Heyl's improved "magic lantern" was demonstrated to an audience of more than 1,500, each gazing in wonder at the scientific miracle. In addition to the waltz, subjects included acrobats, a menagerie of wild animals, and an actor depicting Brother Jonathan (an early version of Uncle Sam) who seemed to speak to the audience directly, welcoming them to the show.

The "Phasmatrope" was not the first effort to project images on screen, but it was the first to attempt the illusion of motion with photographs of living subjects rather than drawings. Limited by photographic technology, Heyl used a wet-plate process on very thin sheets of glass. To get the effect of motion, Heyl arranged a series of photographic transparencies of people in posed motion along the edge of a large disc and projected them on-screen. The disc was then hand-cranked, passing the images through a projected light source. For the waltz, a series of four poses were taken and repeated four times to create a disc with sixteen images.

Heyl later reported that the event raised more than $350 for St. Michael's. Several weeks later the "Phasmatrope" was again demonstrated, this time at the Franklin Institute. Ultimately, however, Heyl recognized the limitations of his invention and never attempted to broaden its use, turning his attention to other inventions and scientific explorations. Within a decade, Heyl again found a way to improve on known science, acquiring a patent for the first true stapler in 1877. Heyl lived to see the invention of the filmstrip form of projecting images and the eventual exploitation of this technology, fully understanding his own small role in bringing life to projected images.

1932: Vladimir Horowitz, virtuoso pianist, plays Tchaikovsky's Piano Concerto No. 1 in B-flat minor, Op. 23 at the Academy of Music, conducted by Fritz Reiner.

February 6

The most celebrated twins in the world were dead. The original "Siamese Twins" Chang and Eng Bunker died on January 17, 1874, in Mt. Airy, North Carolina. Their deaths signaled the end of a remarkable life. Born the sons of a fisherman in Siam (Thailand), the conjoined brothers were "discovered" at a young age by a British merchant and brought to Europe and America to be the feature in a circus sideshow. As adults, they became farmers and settled down with two sisters from North Carolina, fathering a total of twenty-one children. Several times throughout their lives, the brothers considered surgical separation and consulted with dozens of doctors, many of them in Philadelphia. They repeatedly decided against embracing the unknown, choosing instead to remain conjoined.

When Chang died suddenly in his sleep, Eng refused again to be separated from his brother and died several hours later. The question remained, however: what was the true nature of their connection and could they have been separated? It remained to Philadelphia physicians William H. Pancoast and Harrison Allen to bring the bodies of Chang and Eng to Philadelphia for an official autopsy. The physicians arrived in North Carolina the first week of February and encountered controversy within the Bunker family as to whether to demand payment for the bodies or allow the autopsy to be performed at all. Ultimately, the family agreed to have the autopsy completed with no payment.

The train carrying the brothers' bodies and their investigators arrived in Philadelphia at 3:00 A.M. on this date in 1874. The autopsy conducted at the College of Physicians revealed the band that connected the twins at their chests was primarily cartilage. Their livers were also found to be connected but functioned independently. Only in death was it finally determined that their physical separation could easily have been accomplished. To fully document the event, Dr. Pancoast drafted a report and ordered the creation of a plaster cast of the bodies and the preservation of their joined livers, which remain on display today at the Mütter Museum of the College of Physicians. Returned to their family, Chang and Eng were interred in a local cemetery, laying to rest one of the greatest mysteries of the nineteenth century.

1943: Fabian is born in Philadelphia. He was discovered at the tender age of fourteen sitting on his front steps.

2005: In Super Bowl XXXIX, the Eagles lose to the New England Patriots in Jacksonville, 24–21.

The relationship between Native Americans and colonists in Pennsylvania was heavily influenced by the peaceful intentions of the commonwealth's founder and his Quaker faith. Early treaties and agreements between William Penn and the Delaware and Lenni Lenape tribes living throughout the colony reflected a general tolerance of tribal populations and a desire to build a civil friendship. As the years passed, however, tensions arose over land and settlements along the Pennsylvania frontier west of Philadelphia. As the Indian population declined, European colonists arrived by the thousands. Tribes were increasingly forced into smaller areas, while settlers claimed the land around them. Small skirmishes led to a larger concern among frontier communities who believed that the Quaker political leaders living comfortably in the city were not adequately sensitive to the dangers faced in the outlying settlements.

In May of 1763, a rebellion among tribes throughout the region, spearheaded by Ottawa chief Pontiac, fueled fears among some of Pennsylvania's Scotch-Irish citizens in the Paxtang region west of Philadelphia in what is now Dauphin County. Turning aggressor, the so-called Paxton Boys massacred a small, primarily Christian group of Conestoga Indians in December 1763. The survivors were brought by the government to Lancaster for protection, but the mob broke into the workhouse where the Conestoga were hiding and murdered all but two of the refugees. Efforts within the government to stop the hostilities were unsuccessful, and 250 Paxton Boys marched toward Philadelphia where an additional 140 Indians sought refuge.

On this date in 1764, Benjamin Franklin raised a local militia unit and traveled with British troops to Germantown to confront the Paxton Boys. Franklin successfully negotiated with the vigilante group and prevented further violence toward the Indian population. Several leaders of the Paxton Boys were permitted to present their grievances against tribes to the Pennsylvania Assembly and Governor John Penn. The immediate antagonism was diffused, but relations between Pennsylvania's tribal and colonial communities would never regain their earlier good will.

1776: The Philadelphia Society for Assisting Distressed Prisoners is founded.

1864: Arthur Francis Collins, famed vaudeville performer who specialized in recordings of songs in an exaggerated "black" voice, is born.

February 8

In Philadelphia, the sweet sounds of classical music have long enjoyed a vibrant and appreciative audience. A source of some controversy in the earliest years of the commonwealth, Quaker restrictions against musical and stage performances gave way to the rising demand for sophisticated cultural expressions in the Federal City of the 1790s. Within the first quarter of the nineteenth century, dozens of European and American artists found fame in the various theaters and music halls of the city, among them Fanny Kemble, Jenny Lind, and Edwin Forrest. In addition to musical theaters, social organizations and clubs were also formed in response to the public's demand for more.

The Musical Fund Society of Philadelphia was one of the earliest and most successful of these organizations. Founded in 1820 to offer superior musical concerts and to provide support to aging or struggling musicians, the society strove to present the finest in national and international music. Following the first public performance in 1824, the Musical Fund Hall on Locust Street served as the primary venue for musical performances in the city. The hall also hosted important non-musical national events, including the first Republican National Convention in 1856 and readings by authors such as Charles Dickens and Ralph Waldo Emerson. The orchestra, renowned for the quality of its musicians, moved to the Academy of Music in 1868 and merged with the Philadelphia Orchestra in 1900.

As the center of Philadelphia's musical culture, the Society became known for its exclusive local and national premieres. On this date in 1841, Amadeus Mozart's *Die Zauberflote,* or "The Magic Flute," made its American debut to resounding acclaim. Other premieres sponsored by the society included Hayden's *The Seasons,* Donizetti's *La Favorita,* and Bellini's *La Sonnambula.* The Musical Fund Society was ultimately overshadowed by the advent of the Academy of Music in 1857, but has never stopped seeking and presenting the finest artists and their works. Today, the society honors the remarkable musical history of the city by sponsoring performances and supporting music education, a living legacy to be enjoyed by all who appreciate music.

1803: The city's sole public schoolhouse is completely destroyed by fire.

1836: The Philadelphia Gas Works goes into operation.

1922: WGL Radio, Philadelphia's first radio station, broadcasts for the first time.

1936: The NFL holds its first draft at Rittenhouse Square in a successful effort to eliminate bidding wars among teams. The Philadelphia Eagles claim the first overall pick and choose Heisman Trophy winner Jay Berwanger, who wound up never playing for the Eagles or any NFL team.

The man many people call the Father of Rock and Roll was just fifty-five years old when he lost his battle with cancer on this date in 1981. Bill Haley was born in Highland Park, Michigan, but was raised in Boothwyn, Pennsylvania, outside Philadelphia. He began his career as a country-western singer performing at variety shows and amusement parks. In 1951, Haley and his newly coined "Comets" recorded a rhythm and blues song, "Rocket 88," for the Philadelphia-based Holiday Records label. It was the first of several pioneering efforts that would cement Haley's legacy as one of the most influential rock and rollers in history.

In the early 1950s, Haley and his Comets proved increasingly innovative in their evolution from western swing band to rock and roll. The novel use of guitar, drums, bass, and saxophone in the production of their records brought the seeds of a new sound to popular music fans. "Rock the Joint," released in 1952, was quickly followed the next year with "Crazy Man Crazy," a certifiable hit that shot into the Top Twenty and brought fame and limited fortune to Haley and his Comets.

On April 12, 1954, Haley recorded the song that would change the sound and face of music forever. In New York City, the Pythian Temple Studio on 80th Street shook to the beat of Haley's "Rock Around the Clock." Within a year, more than 75,000 copies were sold, but it wasn't until the song appeared on the soundtrack of teen flick *The Blackboard Jungle* that its fame skyrocketed to legendary levels. Hits like "Shake, Rattle and Roll" and "Birth of the Boogie" continued to demonstrate Haley's electrifying style, and the band was featured in a number of Hollywood musicals, most notably *Rock Around the Clock* released in 1956. The advent of Elvis Presley ultimately led Haley to seek his audiences in Europe, where he toured throughout the 1960s and 1970s. Following his death, Haley was recognized for his tremendous contributions to music and was inducted into the Rock and Roll Hall of Fame in 1986.

1814: A meeting is held by the promoters of a new society, where they adopt rules for what they will name the Athenaeum of Philadelphia. It would open shortly thereafter on March 7, 1814, at the southeast corner of Fourth and Chestnut streets.

1934: Philadelphia's lowest temperature, –11° F, is recorded.

February 10

Singleton Mercer was a young man set on righting a wrong. At least that is the justification he gave for the murder of Mahlon Hutchinson Heberton while riding on the ferry to Camden on this date in 1843. Mercer believed Heberton to be guilty of the most foul of crimes: the seduction of Mercer's sixteen-year-old sister. Just twenty years old himself and believing he was without legal recourse, Mercer responded to his sister's perceived ruin by attempting to murder her, unsuccessfully. He then turned his attention to the seducer, stalking Heberton for two full days before fatally shooting him. The details of the murder and the reasons given for it were sensationally exposed in a public trial held in New Jersey beginning in late March.

The public downfall of a presumably virtuous young woman at the hands of a lecherous older man proved too tempting for most Philadelphians. The very nature of the lurid circumstances sparked unprecedented public interest and inspired strong sympathy for the defendant. Mercer entered a plea of insanity, a rarely used defense. After deliberating for less than one hour, the jury acquitted young Mercer, who was greeted by cheering crowds as he left the courthouse.

The murder and trial inspired Philadelphia novelist George Lippard to write and publish *The Monks of Monk Hall* (or *The Quaker City*) in 1844. Credited as the first muckraking novel, Lippard's work was an expose of the hypocrisy of Philadelphia's elite and an indictment of the dark side of capitalism and urbanization. Despite (or perhaps because of) the shocking descriptions of adulterers, rakish drunkards, and underhanded politicians, *The Quaker City* went on to be the best-selling novel in America until *Uncle Tom's Cabin* was published in 1852. Mercer's crime, and Lippard's depiction of it, drew attention to the need for social and legal reform and inspired efforts to establish laws giving women and their families the right to seek justice in a court of law.

1935: The first electric-train passenger service begins on the Pennsylvania Railroad with the GG1 locomotive, built in Altoona by General Electric.

The citizens of Philadelphia needed medical relief. More than fifty years after the founding of the city, medical care remained elusive for most people, with no hospital or similar public and permanent clinic available. In January 1751, Dr. Thomas Bond and Benjamin Franklin petitioned the Pennsylvania Assembly to establish a public hospital for the purpose of caring for the sick and those "distempered in Mind and Deprived of their rational faculties" who wandered the streets of Philadelphia. Franklin and Bond chose as the institutional seal the story of the Good Samaritan, a reflection of the hospital's commitment to the health and well-being of all Philadelphians. On this date in 1753, the Pennsylvania Hospital admitted its first patients to the wards located at 8th and Pine streets. It was the first step in a long history of innovation and compassion.

Initially, caring for the sick poor was the primary mission of the Hospital. A carefully designed building included separate floors devoted to the care of men, women, servants, and those in need of medical isolation. Opened at a time in history before science understood microbiology and the effect of germs, medical professionals worked primarily to provide comfort and care for the sick. A medicinal garden was established on the grounds and served as an early pharmacy. One innovation was the humane and sensitive care of the mentally ill, who were housed in the basement. Instead of locking them away, a common eighteenth-century "treatment" for the insane, the hospital allowed many patients the opportunity to stroll the grounds, fed them well, and considered many of them to be treatable.

In the first decade of the nineteenth century, the Hospital established its first specialty department, a "lying-in" ward for women and their newborn infants. In 1841, the Pennsylvania Hospital for the Insane was opened in West Philadelphia. The twentieth century brought increased knowledge of medicine and medical training, and the hospital earned a reputation for pioneering work in neurology, coronary care, diabetes, and orthopedics. Today, Pennsylvania Hospital remains one of the highest-rated in the nation, continuing to offer innovative and excellent care.

1839: St. Joseph's Church on Willing Street is consecrated. The congregation is the oldest Catholic community in Philadelphia, founded in 1733.

1895: The Free Library of Philadelphia moves from three rooms at City Hall to Concert Hall at 12th and Chestnut streets, where it remains until December 1910.

Site of the first aerial flight in North America in 1793 (see January 9), a new era in mail delivery dawned for Philadelphia and the country on this date in 1918. The Postmaster General of the United States announced that Philadelphia was one of three cities selected for the inauguration of the regularly scheduled Aero Post, or flying mail service. Delivery to and from Washington, D.C., and New York City would pass through the Bustleton Airport in Northeast Philadelphia in an ambitious plan that hoped to provide regularly scheduled deliveries. Unfortunately, the first leg of the historic flight on May 15, 1918, was less than stellar as it never officially reached Philadelphia. Nevertheless, that single effort marked the end of experimentation and the beginning of a nearly sixty-year history of domestic airmail delivery in the United States.

Under the watchful eyes of the Postmaster General, members of Congress, and President Woodrow Wilson, Army Lieutenant George L. Boyle departed Washington, D.C., at 11:47 A.M. on May 15, 1918. Carrying a cargo of 140 pounds of mail, he was expected in Philadelphia before 1:00 P.M. Flying by sight only, within twenty minutes Boyle was disoriented and headed in the opposite direction of Philadelphia, forcing him to land in Waldorf, Maryland. The mail in his care was transferred to a truck and hauled to Philadelphia the next day. Notified of the mishap, the flight departing Philadelphia nevertheless left Bustleton Field on time, and arrived in New York's Polo Field at 2:50 P.M. The two returning flights were also successful, and by 8:00 P.M. mail from New York and Philadelphia was handed to the President in the White House.

Regular-service airmail was proven feasible, and within four months, the total length of flights from Washington to New York City was reduced from three hours to just two hours and twelve minutes. The service was made available to the public, at a rate of 24 cents per ounce. Airmail continued to provide fast, efficient delivery until 1975, when the separate airmail rate was discontinued. Mail is still carried by airplane when deemed practical, but the special delivery service inaugurated in 1918 has gone the way of balloon-delivery and the bi-plane.

1793: President George Washington signs into law the Fugitive Slave Act, which establishes the legal mechanism for slaveholders to recover a runaway slave and makes illegal the act of assisting an escaped slave.

1918: The first ship's keel is laid-in at Hog Island Shipyard. Construction of the yard began on September 20, 1917, in response to the country's need for ships during World War I.

February 13

As World War I raged overseas, Philadelphia served an essential role as "the workshop of the world," producing thousands of necessary goods ranging from ships and vehicles to uniforms and shoes. But keeping busy was not enough. Like most cities, many in Philadelphia believed the threat of war existed not only in Europe but in their own backyards, as well. By this date in 1918, a total of 6,481 "alien enemies" were registered by the federal government in Philadelphia, many of them German. German-American descendants of Pennsylvania's earliest settlers were also looked on with suspicion. Rumors and suspicions of German-led conspiracies led political leaders in the city to take drastic steps, as efforts to monitor or control the German, Quaker, and Socialist communities were initiated. Some citizens went further, actively seeking to destroy the cultural and social connections maintained since the city's first decade.

In the months leading up to the declaration of war in April 1917, many in Philadelphia took a neutral stance, neither supporting nor opposing American involvement in the European conflict. However, when the United States joined the war effort, patriotic fervor grew. Factories worked overtime and everyone experienced serious shortages in food and fuel. Anti-German sentiment inspired many to turn away from anything remotely German, as sauerkraut and German measles were temporarily renamed "Liberty Cabbage" and "Liberty Measles" and vandals destroyed or defaced public statues honoring German heroes. As tension rose to a fever pitch, German-language newspapers were shut down and the school district suspended German language classes.

In response to these acts, many Americans of German descent chose to increase their own efforts to support the war, publicly declaring their national pride at community gatherings and with the products of their labor. Many also abandoned aspects of their European heritage, most notably the use of their language in religious services and community newspapers. As the war came to a close, fears quieted and Philadelphia moved toward normalcy.

1741: Andrew Bradford publishes the first American magazine, *The American Magazine; or A Monthly View of the Political State of the British Colonies.* It lasted for less than three months.

1886: Artist Thomas Eakins resigns from the Pennsylvania Academy of Fine Arts after enduring several years of controversy over his use of male nudes in a coed art class.

1979: Lawyer and activist Cecil B. Moore dies at age 64.

The mysterious experiment known as "Project PX" was finally ready to be unveiled. Years of planning and innovation reached an endpoint on this date in 1946 when ENIAC, or the Electronic Numerical Integrator and Computer, was made public for the first time at the University of Pennsylvania's Moore School of Engineering. ENIAC, commonly identified as the world's first electronic large-scale computer for general purpose, was a thousandfold improvement over electro-mechanical machines. Conceived and engineered by University of Pennsylvania scientists John Mauchly and J. Presper Eckertt, ENIAC was completed at a cost of $500,000. ENIAC was designed to aid in ballistic calculations for the United States Artillery and was capable of more than thirty-five calculations a second. In one moment, the world was brought into the computer age.

ENIAC differed from earlier computers in remarkable ways. The Atanasoff-Berry Computer, designed in 1941, was the first true electronic computer but was only able to conduct linear equations and was manually controlled. The British successfully designed the Colossus computer, a significant improvement whose function was limited to code breaking. ENIAC stood out because of its ability to be reprogrammed and adapted to multiple facilities. A team of six women did most of the programming, with additional work manipulating cables and switches taking up to several weeks. An astonishing 17,468 vacuum tubes and five million hand-soldered joints reflected the sheer size of the new computer, which was eighty feet long and occupied its own room.

The substantial capabilities of ENIAC were identified early on as valuable for more than just artillery calculations. The first programmed calculations were not related to ballistics study but rather to the Los Alamos project on the hydrogen bomb. After functioning in Philadelphia for six months, ENIAC was shut down and moved to the Aberdeen Proving Ground in Maryland. Started again on July 29, 1947, ENIAC would continue to conduct calculations for the U.S. Army until October 2, 1955.

1760: Richard Allen is born in Philadelphia. Allen would become the first black ordained by the Methodist Episcopal Church.

1791: The first Bank of the United States is incorporated.

1874: The Seal and Arms of Philadelphia is approved by Ordinance of Councils.

February 15

Tensions and conflict among members of the United States Congress are a natural part of political debate, often expressed with words in newspapers and on television rather than through physical confrontation. However, that has not always been the case. On this date in 1798, heightened political differences led to an outright brawl between two members of the House of Representatives: Federalist Roger Griswold of Connecticut and Democrat-Republican Matthew Lyon of Vermont. After several months of verbal wrangling over their political differences, Griswold insulted Lyon by questioning his military past. Lyon responded by spitting in the face of his adversary. Griswold's supporters pushed unsuccessfully to have Lyon expelled from Congress. On February 14, Lyon learned he would be permitted to remain.

In the hours following Lyon's successful bid to remain in Congress, Griswold reportedly sought out a sturdy walking stick. The next morning, as Lyon sat in Congress leafing through a number of papers, Griswold boldly entered the chamber and began to strike Lyon in the head and shoulders. Lyon was pushed to the floor but was soon able to grab hold of a pair of fire tongs. A duel broke out, with Griswold continuing to inflict blows to the head and back of his target. Several fellow congressmen separated the men, but after a brief rest and retreat to opposite sides of the room Griswold once again approached Lyon and began to beat him. A second intervention was successful and this time both men faced charges of inappropriate behavior and likely expulsion.

In a vote that carefully followed the newly evolving party lines, both men were permitted to continue their service in Congress. Public interest in the brawl resulted in dozens of political cartoons, satirical poems, and bawdy jokes. Though this was the first violent altercation in the United States Congress, it would not be the last. Essential ideological differences over topics as diverse as slavery, state's rights, and personal integrity also resulted in physical confrontations among politicians, severely injuring some of the combatants.

1882: Actor John Barrymore is born.

Stephen Girard, the wealthiest American of his time and known for single-handedly preserving the American economy during the War of 1812, had very explicit plans for his wealth. On this date in 1830, Girard completed and signed his will disbursing a fortune of more than $7 million. Childless and widowed at his death in 1831, Girard left a small portion of his estate to family in France as well as to his household servants and their children. However, Girard chose to commit the majority of his estate to the city of Philadelphia and to charitable organizations throughout Philadelphia and New Orleans, many of them committed to serving the educational needs of the poor. A remarkable sum of nearly $5 million was bequeathed to the city for the establishment of a school for "poor white orphans." Girard College, the realization of this bequest, opened on New Year's Day in 1848.

Girard's will is often cited as the most disputed in American history. The enormous amount left to charity was soon challenged by Girard's family in France, but a United States Supreme Court decision in 1844 upheld the distribution of funds. Indeed, although the act of giving to charities and the creation of Girard College as an all-white, all-male institution was initially allowed, by the twentieth century charges of discrimination forced changes in how Girard's wishes were enacted. Decades-long court cases challenging Girard's will and its role in Girard College culminated in a 1968 Supreme Court decision requiring the admission of minorities, and in the early 1980s the admission of girls.

Today, Girard College serves a diverse student body of more than 700 children from first through twelfth grades. Public schools, libraries, and many social services offered in Philadelphia today can look to Girard's benevolence as the starting point from which their long-term success began. Beyond the bounds of Philadelphia, the model of Girard's will and the impact it had on the citizens of Philadelphia was used by other philanthropists in establishing endowments to improve the lives of countless Americans.

1804: Young Captain Stephen Decatur is ordered to use the *Intrepid* to board the frigate *Philadelphia,* captured in November 1803 by Barbary pirates in Tripoli, and intentionally set it ablaze.

February 17

Things weren't going so well for the sports arena known as the Spectrum. Philadelphia's first large-scale indoor sports venue, the Spectrum opened in September 1967 to great fanfare as the new home of the Philadelphia Flyers hockey team. Following its construction in less than eighteen months at a cost of nearly $12 million, a variety of events were also featured in the 18,000-seat stadium, including the Philadelphia 76ers basketball team, musical performances, and popular family attractions. On this date in 1968, as 11,000 spectators waited for an Ice Capades show to start, strong winds blew off a 50 x 150–foot section of the roof, injuring three people standing in a parking lot outside. Engineers assured the public that the structure was sound, and in less than two days $35,000 in repairs were made. The Flyers and the 76ers resumed play just four days after the damage was done.

Less than two weeks later, three additional holes appeared during a windstorm. Luckily, the damage occurred while the Spectrum was empty and no injuries resulted. However, concern for public safety moved Mayor James H. J. Tate to close the arena indefinitely. The Flyers were forced to play away games through the month of March, and the 76ers temporarily used the Palestra or Convention Hall. The seemingly cursed building was further battered when the roof caught fire during repairs. Shortly thereafter, Attorney General Arlen Specter announced that the building had not received proper occupancy certification from the city's Department of Licenses and Inspections, and the reopening was delayed several more weeks.

Finally, on April 4, the Spectrum reopened as the Flyers faced the St. Louis Blues in game one of the NHL Stanley Cup quarterfinals. Following its shaky start, the Spectrum has continued to serve Philadelphia sports, hosting dozens of championship games for the National Hockey League, the National Basketball Association, and the National Collegiate Athletics Association. Finally, in 1996 the 76ers and Flyers left the run-down Spectrum and moved to their new home next door, the Wachovia Center. The Spectrum, equally hated and beloved by Philadelphians, was closed for good in October 2009. Slated for demolition shortly afterward, as of August 2010 the stripped and abandoned icon still stands.

1794: Temporarily delayed by the yellow fever epidemic of 1793, the Chestnut Street Theater opens for its first regular season. Known as "Old Drury," the theater featured three galleries, held 1,165 people, and used oil lamps that could be raised or dimmed.

Like so many other essential city services, the public library system in the city (the Free Library of Philadelphia) was established with the combined efforts of a committed advocate and philanthropic businessman. In the 1880s, Dr. William Pepper, Provost of the University of Pennsylvania, sought to create a fully public library open to all. Private libraries were available (indeed the first lending library in the nation was founded here in 1731 by Benjamin Franklin) but most were considered specialized in topic and exclusive in membership. Pepper understood the burgeoning city's need for a free and general interest library system and looked to a family member for support.

In 1890, Pepper's wealthy uncle, George S. Pepper, bequeathed $225,000 to the city for the specific establishment of a completely new organization, a free public library. On this date in 1891, the Charter of the Free Library of Philadelphia was adopted. Several private libraries filed lawsuits in an effort to claim the bequest, but were ultimately denied. Nearly four years passed before the first branch of the Free Library opened in City Hall. In the meantime, in 1892 a separate institution was created called the Philadelphia Public Library. By the end of 1894, the two were merged and at the end of the nineteenth century had reached a remarkable circulation of more than 1,778,000 volumes, the largest in the country.

The library system continued to thrive, receiving a donation of $1.5 million from philanthropist Andrew Carnegie in 1903. In the wake of a movement to establish a grand boulevard from City Hall to Fairmount Park, a new Central Library site was selected along what is now known as Benjamin Franklin Boulevard. Begun in 1917 and completed nine years later, the classically designed central branch building remains a fixture along Philadelphia's most beautiful thoroughfare. Today, a total of fifty-four library branches serve the citizens of Philadelphia. In late 2008, a number of branches were targeted for closure by the city over budgetary concerns. A citywide grassroots protest successfully held off the closures, providing further evidence of the significance of a single commitment made more than a century ago.

1688: In Germantown, the first formal anti-slavery resolution in North America is penned by Francis Daniel Pastorius and three other members of the Philadelphia Monthly Meeting of Quakers.

Phineas Taylor Barnum needed a new attraction. The infamous showman was known throughout America for his flamboyant publicity stunts and the remarkable Barnum's Museum, with branches in New York and Philadelphia. Following a successful three-year tour of Europe with his most famous "find," the dwarf General Tom Thumb, Barnum learned of Swedish-born soprano Jenny Lind and her success as the world's most popular singer. The "Swedish Nightingale" was herself completing an exhausting operatic tour of Europe. Without having heard a single note but aware of Lind's reputation as a charming, virtuous, and charitable woman, Barnum determined to bring Lind to America. Barnum hired an English gentleman to approach Lind and arrange for a concert tour. Four months later, on this date in 1850, Barnum was in his Philadelphia museum when he learned that Lind had agreed to come to America the following September.

In a grand gesture of faith in her popularity and belief in the potential financial success such a tour could generate, Barnum offered Lind an unprecedented $1,000 per concert, booking her for up to 150 concerts. In addition, all other expenses would be paid by Barnum, including the engagement of a conductor and an Italian baritone to sing in duets. Lind, who saw the tour as an excellent opportunity to advance her charitable efforts and begin a music school, required Barnum to pay in advance. After some difficulty, Barnum succeeded in acquiring a total of $187,500.

In the months leading up to Lind's arrival in New York, Barnum heavily promoted her talent and worthy personality. Her final concerts in Liverpool, England, were touted as farewell events, and staged newspaper articles describing the events emphasized European grief at her departure. Barnum's publicity efforts paid off as over 40,000 Americans waited to greet Lind as she arrived in New York on September 1, 1850. Her first Philadelphia concerts at the Musical Fund Hall on October 18 and 19 were sold out and netted a remarkable $19,000. Ultimately, Lind earned $250,000 over the next two years, most of which she gave to charity. Barnum's profits reached $500,000, proving once again that skilled use of publicity would result in certain success.

1850: P. T. Barnum, at his Philadelphia museum, is first notified that Jenny Lind has agreed to a Barnum-sponsored tour of the United States.

1950: Author of *New York Times* best-sellers *Brothers & Sisters* and *Your Blues Ain't like Mine,* Bebe Moore Campbell is born in Philadelphia.

Like many immigrants to America, Louis I. Kahn (born Itze-Leib Schmuilowsky in Estonia on this date in 1901) would reach the height of critical acclaim only after struggling to overcome an early life of poverty and struggle. Arriving in Philadelphia in 1905, Kahn was a shy but naturally talented artist and musician. Supported through the Philadelphia School District, Kahn received an excellent education and soon chose to focus on the study of architecture, for which he received a scholarship from the University of Pennsylvania. Throughout his subsequent career, Kahn would design hundreds of buildings with only a small percentage being constructed. However, his influence would ultimately prove to be far-reaching, as his unique philosophy established him among the most significant architects of the twentieth century.

As a young student, Kahn benefited from Philadelphia's long-established cadre of internationally known architects and their firms. While learning from and working for architects such as French-born Paul Phillipe Cret, the firm of Zantzinger, Borie & Medary, and George Howe, Kahn was inspired to design sleek, modern structures in the International Style. After graduating, Kahn served as Chief of Design for the Sesquicentennial Exposition, held in Philadelphia in 1926. A long period of unemployment followed, broken by the occasional commission and ended when Kahn assumed a teaching position at Yale University in 1947.

While designing an extension to the Yale Art Gallery, Kahn began to further refine his own architectural philosophy, adopting the perspective that modern architecture did not adequately acknowledge classical forms found in ancient cultures. Kahn's designs attempted to incorporate monumental and spiritual elements drawn from ancient Greece and Rome, while re-envisioning them within a modern context. Projects such as the Jonas Salk Institute of Biological Studies in La Jolla, California, and the Capital Complex in Dhaka, Bangladesh, cemented his reputation as a supremely talented and thoughtful architect. Unfortunately, the rarity of his work combined with a complex personal life resulted in Kahn living the last decade of his life in debt and virtually unknown. He died in obscurity and suddenly from a heart attack on the floor of a men's restroom in New York's Penn Station on March 17, 1974.

1805: Birth of Angelina Grimke, a pioneering abolitionist and advocate for women's rights.

February 21

After the Declaration of Independence was adopted, the Second Continental Congress appointed a committee to draft a form of national governance. The Articles of Confederation and Perpetual Union, drafted in June 1776 and ratified in March 1781, legally joined the former colonies into the United States. Under the confederation, only certain powers were specifically allocated to the central government; all other power was reserved to the states or to the people. The confederation could declare war, negotiate diplomatic agreements, and resolve disagreements among the states regarding the Western territories. The Articles also established freedom of movement among the colonies and made provisions for the addition of states, including pre-approval of the admission of Canada. The Articles were stated as perpetual and could only be altered by approval of Congress and ratification by all of the states.

Problems with the Articles of Confederation soon became apparent. Without the power to tax, any funds for the government had to be raised through voluntary donations from the states. George Washington found the inability to raise funds extremely frustrating in the effort to prosecute the Revolutionary War. The diplomatic arena was also negatively affected by the inability of central government negotiators to ensure that payments or other elements of agreements could be implemented. States also objected to the one state, one vote structure of the Articles, which meant that the larger states were solicited for greater financial support without any accompanying increase in their ability to influence events. Finally, Congress could not regulate commerce, permitting states to control their own trade policies.

On February 21, 1787, Congress resolved that a convention be held in Philadelphia to revise the Articles of Confederation to make the Constitution more appropriate for the operation of government and the preservation of the union. When the 55 delegates at the Constitutional Convention met in Philadelphia, they decided not to revise the Articles, but to draft a totally new constitution, one that was tested at a time of civil war and has been amended, but still governs our nation today.

1861: Abraham Lincoln arrives in Philadelphia on his way to Washington, D.C., where he is to be sworn in as President.

1949: Streetcars and subways of the Philadelphia Transportation Company roll again two hours after workers vote to end a ten-day strike that cost the community $10 million a day. More than 14,850 workers in two separate unions demanded pay hikes.

1961: The Shirelles appear on TV's *American Bandstand* and perform "Will You Still Love Me Tomorrow," and "Dedicated to the One I Love."

February 22

I am filled with deep emotion at finding myself standing here in the place where were collected together the wisdom, the patriotism, the devotion to principle, from which spring the institutions under which we live." With these words, President-elect Abraham Lincoln began his speech to hundreds of onlookers gathered in front of Independence Hall. Lincoln had departed his beloved Springfield, Illinois, just ten days earlier, embarking on a journey through many of the nation's East Coast cities and towns on his way to Washington, D.C., for his Inaugural Celebration, held on March 4, 1861. On this date, Lincoln paused in front of what was arguably the single most historic building in the nation, to consider its meaning and to look toward the future of what would certainly be a history-making term as president.

Philadelphia's support for Southern sentiments and an overall suspicion of African-Americans were set aside during Lincoln's visit in the midst of shared pride in Philadelphia as the birthplace of the nation. Lincoln, fully aware of the hope that he would somehow heal the nation, assured listeners that he would not enter into war without its being forced upon the government to do so. This message was of particular interest to Philadelphians who did not want the government to take an aggressive position in managing conflicts between North and South.

Finally, Lincoln acknowledged his own connection to Philadelphia and Independence Hall when he asserted "I have never had a feeling politically that did not spring from the sentiments embodied in the Declaration of Independence . . . [the] promise that in due time the weights should be lifted from the shoulders of all men, and that all should have an equal chance." He went on to say that if the country could not be saved under this principle, that he would rather be assassinated on the spot than continue. Lincoln would go on to preserve the union, but suffered the ultimate betrayal when he was assassinated on April 15, 1865, only six days after the Army of Northern Virginia under General Lee surrendered to General Grant at Appomattox Court House. He would return to Philadelphia once more, to lay in state in Independence Hall on April 22, 1865, a meaningful and appropriate tribute to his relationship with Philadelphia's most treasured place.

1827: Painter and naturalist Charles Willson Peale dies at the age of eighty-five.

1832: The cornerstone of the Merchants' Exchange Building at Second and Dock streets is laid.

February 23

In the field of medicine, the production and administration of medicines to treat the injured and heal the sick is absolutely essential. By tradition these roles were often combined, as "chemists" or apothecaries took on the responsibility of dispensing medications to their patients directly. However, as the 1700s drew to a close, more and more professional physicians appeared, educated at specialized colleges and claiming special knowledge of caring for the sick. On this date in 1821, a group of sixty-eight Philadelphia druggists united at Carpenters' Hall to assert the role of pharmacists within the field of medicine, as well as to define professional standards and provide rigorous training. The College of Apothecary, the nation's first school of pharmacy, continues today as the University of the Sciences of Philadelphia.

Throughout the decades bracketing the end of the eighteenth and beginning of the nineteenth centuries, many urban centers, including Philadelphia, experienced a series of traumatic outbreaks of contagious disease. Yellow fever, dysentery, scarlet fever, and cholera devastated populations, weakened city governments, and proved a challenge to those doctors and pharmacists charged with treating symptoms and finding cures. While physicians often bemoaned the inconsistencies of quality among apothecaries, a professional rivalry was inevitable in the push to affirm the significance of each professional group. The College of Apothecary offered advanced training in biology and chemistry in a science-based curriculum designed to ensure high quality among graduates. The college, renamed the Philadelphia College of Pharmacy and Science, first admitted women in 1876.

The College was ultimately highly influential in the pharmaceutical industry. Famous faculty and graduates include Professor William Procter (the Father of American Pharmacy), Professor Joseph Remington, and Josiah and Eli Lilly, William Warner, Robert McNeil, and John Wyeth, each a known corporate name decades later. The significance of pharmaceutical study and the essential role of pharmacists in modern American medicine was largely defined by the mission of the College of Apothecaries, whose legacy remains in evidence today.

1778: Baron Friedrich Wilhelm Augustus Von Steuben, the Prussian mercenary, arrives at Valley Forge charged with the task of training Washington's troops.

1850: Philadelphia tailoresses publish a letter in the *New York Tribune* appealing for aid and detailing starvation wages as part of a larger movement to draw attention to the plight of women in the newly industrialized city.

1883: The American Anti-Vivisection Society is founded by Caroline Earle White.

1991: One Meridian Plaza, a 38-story high rise located across from City Hall on South Broad Street, is severely damaged by a blaze that killed three firefighters and caused an estimated $100 million in property loss and over $4 billion in civil lawsuit damages. The building was finally demolished in 1999.

A woman's work never ends—or so the saying goes. For Lydia Bailey, official City Printer for Philadelphia from 1830 to 1850, her outstanding career came to an end upon her death on this date in 1869 at the age of ninety. Lasting a remarkable sixty years, Bailey's professional life continued the tradition of working widows, many of whom acquired their business through the death of a husband or father. For Bailey, working within the printing field began with an early loss and a large debt following the death of her husband in 1808. Faced with a young family and few prospects, Bailey assumed responsibility for the family's printing house, established sometime just prior to the Revolutionary War. Through her hard effort and savvy business sense, Bailey successfully ran one of the city's longest-running printing houses.

The city of Philadelphia has long been associated with the printing business. The first American newspapers, magazines, and classified advertisements all began in the city. Benjamin Franklin, perhaps best known for his political life, made a name first as a printer. With his wife, Deborah, at his side, Franklin did well enough to retire at the young age of forty-two. Unlike Franklin, Bailey continued as a printer for many decades. Shortly after assuming ownership of the business, she published two volumes of poetry by famed Poet of the American Revolution Philip Freneau. Charged in 1811 with printing a census directory of Philadelphia, she soon accepted the commission as City Printer. City ordinances, council reports, and special notices formed the core of her publications.

Like other printers, Bailey also trained apprentices, several of whom later became successful printers in their own right. Most notable among them were Robert P. King, Alexander Baird, and John Fagan. In addition to her printing, Bailey left a legacy by providing an endowment fund for the Third Presbyterian Church of Philadelphia. Today, that endowment lives on, and Lydia Bailey lies at rest in the church cemetery, her work finally done.

1950: Photographer Steve McCurry, best known for his striking picture of a blue-eyed Afghani refugee girl that appeared in *National Geographic* in 1984, is born.

February 25

Few would consider the sport of tennis and the city of Philadelphia to be a natural fit. More famous for baseball, football, and hockey, the city enjoys a special place within the hearts of many who embrace these seemingly all-American contests. However, a song born of friendship would forever establish Philadelphia as the professional home to one of tennis' greatest female performers, Billie Jean King. Inspired by his friendship with King and in support of her newly formed professional tennis team, the Philadelphia Freedoms, Elton John and his songwriting partner Bernie Taupin released "Philadelphia Freedom" on this date in 1975. It quickly rose to the number-one spot on the pop charts, making it the second of three top hits for John that year alone.

King, known for her superior court skills and outstanding victories, cemented her pop celebrity after her victory in the heavily hyped Battle-of-the-Sexes tennis match against self-professed anti-feminist Bobby Riggs in 1973. The following year, hoping to build on the attraction of co-ed professional contests, King helped found the World Team Tennis league and established the Freedoms along with fifteen other teams. Utilizing a unique team approach to tennis, the WTT hoped to inspire interest in tennis among the young by promoting matches among the brightest and best within the sport. Since 1974, the team and league have met with mixed success, but continue today under the leadership of King and partner Ilana Kloss.

Elton John's song has gone on to serve as one of the city's greatest anthems. Raised to significance beyond the game of tennis, "Philadelphia Freedom" is now played at almost every sporting event held in the city. Often used in tourism promotions and as the music heard during a spectacular journey through Philadelphia in the IMAX theater experience at the Franklin Institute, the song once given as a gesture of friendship lives on as part of a vibrant soundtrack to the city.

1791: The Bank of the United States is chartered.

1799: An Act of Congress is passed to build docks for the repair of ships in Philadelphia. Taken in combination with a previous act from March 27, 1794 (to provide for a naval armament), it is considered the origin of the Philadelphia Navy Yard.

Many of the earliest settlers who arrived on the banks of the Delaware River following the founding of Philadelphia in 1682 sought freedoms denied to them because of their religion. Guided by the Quaker principles of William Penn, Pennsylvania seemed to offer the possibility of peace and acceptance with the adoption of the Charter of Privileges in 1701. Followers of non-Protestant faiths such as Catholicism and Judaism found Pennsylvania more open to them but still wary of their presence. In Philadelphia, Catholics often exercised their faith from within private homes and without the leadership of priests or bishops. On this date in 1732, that practice changed as the first mass in Philadelphia was led by Joseph Greaton under the auspices of the newly formed St. Joseph's Church, the only Roman Catholic Church built and maintained in the colonies before the American Revolution.

In many American colonies founded by Protestants, who had fled the religious persecution of Catholicism and other higher churches in Europe, Catholics were generally not welcomed, by law or by tradition. Maryland, a colony founded by Catholics in 1634 and Pennsylvania's nearest neighbor to the south, found that shifts in power resulted in the need to establish a Toleration Act in 1649 to protect the increasingly minority Catholic population from Protestants, who were increasing in both number and influence. The 1702 Act to Prevent the Spread of Popery in Maryland forced some Catholics to migrate north to Philadelphia, resulting in a population of just forty in Philadelphia by 1732.

In Philadelphia, as elsewhere, Catholics were occasionally victims of discrimination and violence. In order to maintain a low-key presence, the site of St. Joseph's was hidden inside a courtyard off a small alleyway. The second Catholic Church built in Philadelphia, St. Mary's was constructed with high brick walls and few windows. Indeed, within one hundred years, Philadelphia would be the scene of countless anti-catholic and anti-immigrant riots resulting in dozens of deaths and injuries. Today, Catholicism in Philadelphia is practiced freely and with pride as the Archdiocese of Philadelphia serves nearly 1.5 million of the faithful, a remarkable 38 percent of the city's population.

1852: John Archibald Woodside, famous Philadelphia sign and ornamental painter, dies.

Few among twentieth-century performers or activists are equal to the brilliant talent or poise of opera singer Marian Anderson, born on this date in 1897. Said to have been possessed of one of the finest contralto voices in living memory, Anderson began her singing life in Philadelphia among the streets of South Philadelphia at the Union Baptist Church where she first began to sing at the age of six years. Throughout her childhood, Anderson's dream of pursuing a singing career was frequently affected by racism and discrimination, as well as personal loss. With the support of her family and the African-American community, she persevered and attained some of the highest achievements possible, culminating in a career that reached every corner of the globe.

After enduring the loss of her father and grandfather within a single year, Anderson and her mother were unable to raise the money to pay for voice lessons. Recognizing Anderson's talent, her church and community arranged for several of Philadelphia's finest vocalists to coach her. When she graduated from South Philadelphia High School for Girls in 1921, Anderson was an experienced and moderately successful performer. Following some success in New York, she traveled to Europe where she generated a devoted following. Upon returning to the United States, she continued her concert tour, further expanding her audience with the inclusion of early spirituals in addition to traditional operatic arias.

In 1939, however, she was quickly reminded of the divisions between black and white. When her manager approached the Daughters of the American Revolution to arrange a concert in their Constitutional Hall, he was rejected purely on the basis of Anderson's color. To counter the DAR's action, First Lady Eleanor Roosevelt arranged for a free public performance from the steps of the Lincoln Memorial in Washington, D.C. As a crowd of 75,000 listened, and radio broadcasts reached millions more, Anderson gave one of her most significant performances. Throughout her career, Anderson continued to quietly but firmly challenge racism and injustice. In 1955, she debuted as the first African-American performer in the history of the Metropolitan Opera in New York, and in 1963 sang once again at the Lincoln Memorial alongside Martin Luther King, Jr. Upon her death in 1993, Anderson was remembered for her great talent and committed activism, an inspiration to many who follow in her footsteps.

1844: Nicholas Biddle dies of heart disease.

1856: The first performance is held at the Academy of Music. It is Verde's *Il Trovatore.*

The Philadelphia Phillies, consistently poor performers and ranked seventh in the National League in 1902, were a team in trouble. Following the creation of the rival American League in 1901, the Phillies suffered sagging game attendance and the threat of defecting players. Team owners Alfred Reach and Colonel John Rogers, in an effort to keep several key players, pursued a court case all the way to the State Supreme Court, eventually winning the case but losing the players when they demanded fines be paid in retribution. Unable to continue the season without more cash, Rogers and Reach reluctantly accepted a loan from Pittsburgh Pirates owner Barney Dreyfuss. Unfortunately, the Phillies remained significantly less popular than their crosstown rivals, the Philadelphia Athletics, and by the end of the 1902 season, Rogers and Reach had determined to sell the team.

On this date in 1903, a syndicate led by Philadelphia socialite James Potter purchased the Phillies for just $170,000. In addition to Potter, the new team owners included Barney Dreyfuss, who hoped to safeguard his previous loan to the Phillies. Potter, lacking baseball know-how, wisely selected Dreyfuss to run the day-to-day functions of the team. Dreyfuss drew on his own stable of baseball talent, putting some of his own players on the Phillies line-up. The 1903 season proved worse than the previous year for the Phillies, and in 1904 Potter sold his interest in the team to another syndicate, which continued to support the slowly improving club over the next few years.

In 1909, the club was sold twice more, landing at last under the apparent control of newspaperman Horace Fogel. A scandal ensued as Fogel, a man seemingly without the means to purchase such a team, was accused of hiding the identity of the real owners. Leading the charge was none other than Barney Dreyfuss himself. Fogel was subsequently banned from baseball and removed from power by the true owner of the Phillies, Chicago Cubs owner Charles W. Murphy. The next year, in response to concerns about financial monopolies within the two baseball leagues, a policy was adopted prohibiting a single owner from holding controlling power in more than one team. The Phillies went on to better years, winning the World Series in 1980 and 2008.

1828: William Strickland begins work on the restoration of the tower of Independence Hall, spurred on by the Marquis de LaFayette's speech in 1824.

1940: The first organization meeting of the Philadelphia Alcoholics Anonymous meets at a private home near 22nd and Delancey Street.

1942: The USS *Jacob Jones,* a destroyer, is struck by two torpedoes from a German submarine U-578 off Delaware Bay, causing heavy casualties and destroying the ship.

One of the earliest settlements in Pennsylvania, the area in northwest Philadelphia known as Germantown, was founded in 1683 by Dutch-speaking Quakers from Krefeld, Germany. Among them was Francis Daniel Pastorius, a lawyer and scholar whose leadership of the Germantown community was based in part on his position as agent for the Frankfort Company, which promoted immigration to Pennsylvania. As Quakers, Pastorius and several of his fellow immigrants were troubled by the seeming contradiction of the presence of slaves and the act of enslavement in a place that represented freedom and religious liberty to others. In 1688, Pastorius led a small group of men to draft the first official protest against slavery, which was submitted to the Philadelphia Monthly Meeting for approval. Unwilling to take a stand, the Monthly Meeting took no action. Subsequent submissions to the Quarterly and Yearly meetings were also met with silence. Finally, after ninety-two years, efforts to end slavery in Pennsylvania were successful in 1779 when the state became the first to pass a law ordering the emancipation of all slaves within its borders.

Germantown Petition in Opposition to Slavery

This is to the monthly meeting held at Richard Worrell's:

These are the reasons why we are against the traffic of men-body, as followeth: Is there any that would be done or handled at this manner? viz., to be sold or made a slave for all the time of his life? How fearful and faint-hearted are many at sea, when they see a strange vessel, being afraid it should be a Turk, and they should be taken, and sold for slaves into Turkey. Now, what is this better done, than Turks do? Yea, rather it is worse for them, which say they are Christians; for we hear that the most part of such negers are brought hither against their will and consent, and that many of them are stolen. Now, though they are black, we cannot conceive there is more liberty to have them slaves, as it is to have other white ones. There is a saying, that we should do to all men like as we will be done ourselves; making no difference of what generation, descent, or color they are. And those who steal or rob men, and those who buy or purchase them, are they not all alike? Here is liberty of conscience, which is right and reasonable; here ought to be likewise liberty of the body, except of evil-doers, which is another case. But to bring men hither, or to rob and sell them against their will, we stand against. In Europe there are many oppressed for conscience sake; and here there are those oppressed which are of a black color. And we who know that men must not commit adultery some do commit adultery in others, separating wives from their husbands, and giving them to others: and some sell the children of these poor creatures to other men. Ah! do consider well this thing, you who do it, if you would be done at this manner and if it is done according to Christianity! You surpass Holland and Germany in this thing. This makes an ill report in all those countries of Europe, where they hear of [it], that the Quakers do here handle men as they handle there the cattle. And for that reason some have no mind or inclination to come hither. And who shall maintain this your cause, or plead for it? Truly, we cannot do so, except you shall inform us better hereof, viz.: that Christians have liberty to practice these things.

Pray, what thing in the world can be done worse towards us, than if men should rob or steal us away, and sell us for slaves to strange countries; separating husbands from their wives and children. Being now this is not done in the manner we would be done at; therefore, we contradict, and are against this traffic of men-body. And we who profess that it is not lawful to steal, must, likewise, avoid to purchase such things as are stolen, but rather help to stop this robbing and stealing, if possible. And such men ought to be delivered out of the hands of the robbers, and set free as in Europe. Then is Pennsylvania to have a good report, instead, it hath now a bad one, for this sake, in other countries; especially whereas the Europeans are desirous to know in what manner the Quakers do rule in their province; and most of them do look upon us with an envious eye. But if this is done well, what shall we say is done evil?

If once these slaves (which they say are so wicked and stubborn men) should join themselves to fight for their freedom, and handle their masters and mistresses, as they did handle them before; will these masters and mistresses take the sword at hand and war against these poor slaves, like, as we are able to believe, some will not refuse to do? Or, have these poor negers not as much right to fight for their freedom, as you have to keep them slaves?

Now consider well this thing, if it is good or bad. And in case you find it to be good to handle these blacks in that manner, we desire and require you hereby lovingly, that you may inform us herein, which at this time never was done, viz., that Christians have such a liberty to do so. To the end we shall be satisfied on this point, and satisfy likewise our good friends and acquaintances in our native country, to whom it is a terror, or fearful thing, that men should be handled so in Pennsylvania.

This is from our meeting at Germantown, held the 18th of the 2d month, 1688, to be delivered to the monthly meeting at Richard Worrell's.

Garret Henderich,
Derick op de Graeff,
Francis Daniel Pastorius,
Abram op de Graeff

March

 March 1 

Pennsylvania's reputation as a place of tolerance and liberty is rightly grounded in the religious and political origins of the state beginning with founder William Penn, a Quaker who himself suffered injustice and persecution for his religious beliefs. Unfortunately, justice was not extended to Pennsylvanians of African descent, many of whom lived as enslaved persons. However, as early as 1688 a formal protest against slavery was drafted in Germantown and as the decades passed other local efforts were initiated throughout the state. Nearly a century after the first protest, and under pressure from Quaker and anti-slavery activists, the Pennsylvania Assembly enacted the first significant law intended to free enslaved Africans across the state on this date. Known as the Gradual Abolition Act of 1780, it was the first such effort in America.

In many ways, the Act of 1780 was a direct result of the American Revolution. Decrying the injustice of slavery within the context of a country at war for independence, Revolutionary War leaders (and newly elected political representatives) such as Anthony Benezet and Thomas Paine pushed to end slavery in Pennsylvania. Most significant, the law banned the importation of slaves while also requiring that all slaves born in the state after 1780 be freed at the age of twenty-eight, at which point they were entitled to the same opportunities as newly released apprentices. Further, all slaves were to be registered with the state within six months; if not properly registered by the deadline, they were to be freed immediately. A 1788 amendment closed several loopholes, including prohibiting the transport of pregnant slaves across state boundaries and prohibiting nonresident slaveholders from rotating their slaves to avoid the state-mandated emancipation.

In the decades following the Act of 1780, more and more Pennsylvanians chose not to own slaves or freed those they could. The Pennsylvania Abolition Society, founded in 1775, committed countless financial and political resources to the purchase and subsequent freeing of hundreds of slaves, as well as the defense of abolitionists and those who had fled bondage. In 1750, a total of 6,000 slaves lived in Pennsylvania, but a century later the number had dwindled to a mere 64, proof that religious, political, and financial principles could be combined to bring about the end of a devastating institution.

1790: The United States Congress passes an act establishing the first United States census, intended to document the population and ensure proper representation in the House of Representatives.

March 2

Among the many ways in which the Quaker beliefs of early Pennsylvania residents and political leaders influenced the lives of everyday citizens, few were so contested as the banning of public forms of entertainment such as plays, theatricals, and musicals. Indeed, for nearly eighty years following the founding of Pennsylvania in 1689, such public performances were entirely forbidden. Concerns about the potential immorality of the content of the performances as well as that of the audience led Quaker leaders to enact several levels of legislation that would not be overturned until the mid-1760s. In reflection of the growing number of Scots-Presbyterian immigrants, themselves anti-theater, the ban was lifted for less than ten years, as new legislation passed in 1774 by the First Continental Congress once again criminalized public theaters. Finally, the advent of Philadelphia's rebirth as the nation's capital in 1790 resulted in a shift toward acceptance of public theater, and the final ban was lifted on this date in 1789.

As the Revolution waned and thoughts turned to supporting Philadelphia as the centerpiece of American culture, members of the strengthening Anglican elite succeeded in legislating the acceptance of public theaters and performances. Seeking talent overseas, Philadelphia's fledgling show business community looked to Europe, most notably England, for actors, actresses, and playwrights. Drawing from the added cachet of British performers, theater owners mounted popular plays dating from before the Revolution. In addition to narrative plays and the occasional musical, theaters throughout the city featured a variety of attractions including lectures, demonstrations, dancers, singers, and even circus acts.

Presidents George Washington and John Adams frequently attended performances in the years after the ban was lifted, as did almost every other segment of Philadelphia society. Accommodating to all types of audiences, the theaters nevertheless established specific hierarchies of seating. While the wealthy occupied boxes alongside the stage, the lower levels were deemed appropriate for the average citizen. Rear galleries offered the least expensive and most rowdy theatergoing experiences. Men, women, laborers, lawyers, and free blacks all sought entertainment within the city's many playhouses and music halls. By the early 1800s, Philadelphia had successfully overcome its staid past and could lay claim to some of the most distinguished and popular American theater of the time.

1962: Wilt Chamberlain becomes the first and only player in NBA history to score 100 points in one game when the Philadelphia Warriors defeat the New York Knicks, 169–147. The game, considered a throwaway within season play, was held at Hersheypark Arena in front of just over 4,000 fans.

March 3

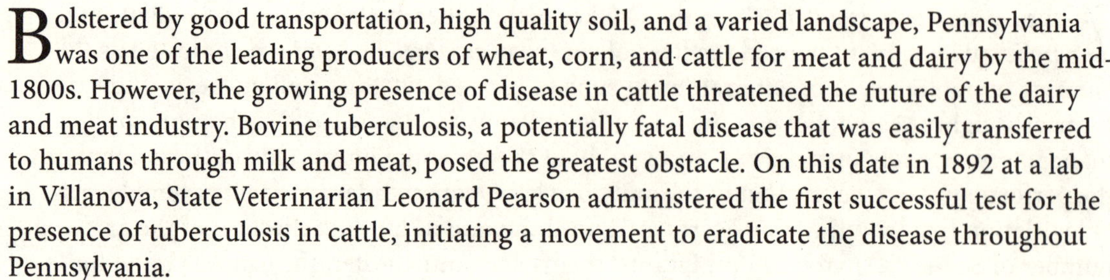

Bolstered by good transportation, high quality soil, and a varied landscape, Pennsylvania was one of the leading producers of wheat, corn, and cattle for meat and dairy by the mid-1800s. However, the growing presence of disease in cattle threatened the future of the dairy and meat industry. Bovine tuberculosis, a potentially fatal disease that was easily transferred to humans through milk and meat, posed the greatest obstacle. On this date in 1892 at a lab in Villanova, State Veterinarian Leonard Pearson administered the first successful test for the presence of tuberculosis in cattle, initiating a movement to eradicate the disease throughout Pennsylvania.

Addressing the twofold problem of public safety and economic stability, Pearson believed that it was possible to use tuberculin as a diagnostic tool on an entire herd. He administered the test to a total of seventy-nine cows; of those, fifty-one reacted. Following post-death examination, Pearson found that all seventy-nine cows were infected. Pearson subsequently led the effort to test as many Pennsylvania herds as possible but met with resistance from farmers, many of whom distrusted the state initiative and its potential impact on their farms and herds. Concerned about conditions that seemed to facilitate the spread of the disease, Pearson mounted a war against the use of traditional Pennsylvania "bank barns," a German and Swiss form of barn that was built into the side of a hill, resulting in damp and dark cattle stalls. Ultimately, however, Pearson succeeded in convincing farmers to follow his lead and have their cattle tested and improve the quality of their barn stalls.

Following his success with testing, Pearson continued to work toward eradicating tuberculosis and by 1896 had produced an effective vaccination. This, combined with increased research into the mechanisms of spreading the disease, eventually resulted in a victory over the fatal disease. By 1936, less than one-half of one percent of Pennsylvania's cattle tested positive for the disease. A parallel drop in the number of human fatalities, especially among children (often the primary consumers of milk), crowned the victory over the pathogen. As a result of Pearson's diligence, one of the state's most significant industries was saved, ensuring economic stability and enhanced public safety along the way.

1790: The Hibernian Society for the Relief of Emigrants is founded.

1871: The United States Congress passes an act to provide for the celebration of the centennial of the Declaration of Independence with an international exposition. Philadelphia was selected as the site.

March 4 

In the months immediately following the swearing in of George Washington as the first American President under the United States Constitution, the practical business of establishing and running a federal government claimed the attention of president and his many political allies and rivals. Alexander Hamilton, advocate of a strong central government, focused his particularly clever mind on the problem of financing and establishing a globally recognized American economy. In 1791, after submitting several banking plans, Hamilton succeeded in establishing the Bank of the United States. Politically contentious yet ultimately successful, Hamilton's semi-public bank played a crucial role in strengthening the position of the young American government. Granted a charter for twenty years, the bank finally succumbed to its opponents on this date in 1811, bringing to an end a significant part of the nation's early success.

As envisioned by Hamilton, the Bank of the United States served several purposes: to provide a repository for government funds, to act as a fiscal agent on behalf of the government, and to regulate currency. Opponents of the plan, led primarily by Secretary of State Thomas Jefferson, argued that the United States Constitution did not grant such powers to the government. Hamilton disagreed, asserting that the power was implied. This was one of many similar arguments that raged within the government in its early years. Once approved, however, the Bank was capitalized at $10 million, of which 20 percent was subscribed by the government. The remaining balance was open to public subscription. Headquartered in Philadelphia, eight additional branches were established in New York, Boston, Baltimore, Washington, Norfolk, Charleston, Savannah, and New Orleans.

In 1809, Secretary of the Treasury Albert Gallatin applied to Congress for renewal of the charter, nearing its expiration in 1811. As had happened during its inception, political debates overcame economic concerns, but this time the renewal was denied by Congress. Jefferson's Democratic-Republican Party, strict interpreters of the United States Constitution, distrusted the Bank and saw it as aristocratic and vulnerable to foreign influence. The legacy of the Bank was ensured, however, in its many successes. By firmly asserting the economic strength of the fledgling government, the Bank of the United States helped move the nation from birth to maturity.

★ ★ ★

1681: The Charter of Pennsylvania is granted by Charles II to William Penn.

1753: The first American arctic expedition leaves from Philadelphia in search of the Northwest Passage. Headed by Captain Charles Swaine on the schooner *Argo*, the failed expedition would return to Philadelphia the same year, in November.

1797: John Adams is sworn in as the nation's second president. Having reached the end of his second term, President George Washington is given a farewell dinner at Rickett's Circus.

 March 5 

On this date in 1810, fierce winds buffeted the shores along the Delaware River. Boats and ferries bobbed in the rough water, while debris whipped through the air. With a mighty crack, the magnificent elm that had stood on the banks of the river for more than 200 years crashed to the ground. Believed to be the site of William Penn's first Great Treaty with the native Lenapes, the elm that had once stood as a unique fixture in the history and landscape of Shackamaxon in Kensington could not withstand the power of the storm. However, its legacy as a physical reminder of the power of peace and the exceptional history of Pennsylvania would be forever remembered through word and image.

Upon his arrival in Philadelphia in 1682, founder William Penn determined to negotiate with the local Lenapes to secure ownership of land essential to his plan to market and settle the commonwealth granted to him by Charles II. Deriving his diplomatic approach from his own Quaker ideals of tolerance and peace, it is believed Penn approached Turtle Clan Chief Tamanend unarmed. Though undocumented, the meeting between Tamanend and Penn is generally accepted as one of the earliest successful interactions between Pennsylvania's indigenous inhabitants and the English. Unlike relations under the remote leadership of the Dutch and Swedes, Penn promised a stable, respectable, and responsive friendship toward the Lenapes. Legend has it that an actual treaty was signed, and continued in place until the mid-1700s. It is believed that the original document, in the hands of the Lenapes, was lost during the French and Indian Wars in 1757.

In 1771, the story of Penn and his Treaty with the Lenapes was further elaborated by painter Benjamin West, who created the iconic *Penn's Treaty with the Indians,* which depicts the singular moment under the spreading branches of the great elm. Over the next two centuries, West's view was copied and reproduced thousands of times, often in order to support the overall legend of Penn as tolerant father and friend to all. Following the felling of the tree in 1810, wood was salvaged and made into a number of commemorative objects, including cups, boxes, and plaques. In 1893, Penn Treaty Park was founded to permanently preserve the place where Pennsylvania's history began.

1756: Four Huguenots from Philadelphia are assigned to disperse refugee Acadians across the colony in order to enforce a new law regulating the Acadian presence in the city.

2004: In a game against the Ottawa team, the Philadelphia Flyers hockey team engages in the most fights recorded in a single game: 21.

March 6

On this date in 1842, a funeral cortege wound its way from Third and Lombard Street past Independence Hall to a small church on Adelphi Street. One of the city's greatest and most honored citizens was laid to rest that day, attended by his family, friends, servants, and employees. Thousands more lined the route to St. Thomas' African Episcopal Church. Unlike others who had enjoyed similar recognition of their lives after death, the subject of their grief was remarkable in both race and status. James Forten, a sail maker who became the wealthiest African-American of his time, was also remembered for his passionate abolitionism and brilliant mind.

Born a free black in Philadelphia in 1766, Forten received several years of Quaker education and apprenticed for a sail maker before volunteering for service as a sailor during the American Revolution. Returning to Philadelphia in the mid-1780s, Forten resumed work for his former boss, Robert Bridges, learning all aspects of the business. Upon his retirement, Bridges offered Forten the opportunity to purchase the business, going so far as to provide a loan from his own pockets. Relying on the labor of a fully integrated workforce of craftsmen, Forten used his inventiveness to create new, more efficient sails and quickly paid off the loan. In the years to come, he built his business into one of the most successful ventures in the city.

In addition to his strong entrepreneurial abilities, Forten was a passionate and effective abolitionist. Throughout his life, he spent nearly half his fortune supporting humanitarian causes. He bought and freed slaves, financed William Lloyd Garrison's abolitionist newspaper *The Liberator,* and co-founded the Free African Society, as well as a school for black children he opened in his home. Initially uncertain of the value of African-Americans leaving America to colonize in Africa, Forten eventually became a strong opponent to the American Colonization Society, refusing requests that he set an example and leave for Africa himself. As attested by the number who mourned his passing, Forten was a true American who believed it was his right to live his life to its best advantage, helping as many people as he could along the way.

1842: Edgar Allan Poe meets Charles Dickens in Philadelphia for the first time. In 1836, Poe reviewed Dickens' *Watkins Tottle* and went so far as to ask Dickens for assistance in getting stories published in England.

March 7

Disputes among inventors are as common as the desire to create new and exciting products. In areas as diverse as technology, food, and entertainment, complex mechanisms are often born of a single idea but frequently realized through the efforts of many. On this date in 1933, Charles Darrow, a young salesman from Philadelphia, began to market the world-famous invention many associate with his name: the ubiquitous board game he called Monopoly. By doing so, he asserted his role as creator of what would become one of the most commercially successful and popular board games in American history. Years later, his relationship to Monopoly remains unquestioned, but is seen more as part of a larger inventive process, involving friends, relatives, and strangers.

As early as 1904, another local Philadelphia inventor created a board game centered on the uneven economic relationship between landlords and tenants. Called the Landlord's Game, Elizabeth Magie's board game was inspired by the economic theories of Philadelphia-born economist Henry George. Dan Layman, a student at Williams College, knew of Magie's game and decided to market it himself under the name of Finance. When friends of Layman moved to Atlantic City in 1930, they added their own twist by using local street names. It was these friends from Atlantic City who later introduced Darrow to the rules and regulations of the game while visiting Philadelphia. Darrow's direct involvement in the invention process lay in the creation of iconic graphic designs, including the large red arrow for "Go" and the faucet, light bulb, and locomotive designs used for the cards and board. Coining the name *Monopoly,* Darrow further cemented his significance by being the first to market the game at Philadelphia's premier department store, Wanamaker's.

Initially rejected by the large game manufacturers Parker Brothers and Milton Bradley, Darrow eventually received a patent in 1935 and negotiated with Parker Brothers to sell them the rights. Within a year, more than 20,000 sets were being manufactured every week. The deal made Darrow a millionaire. In order to ensure their control over the game, Parker Brothers bought the rights to both the Landlord's Game and Finance. Following Darrow's death in 1967, challenges to his place as sole inventor led to several court cases. Today, Parker Brothers continues to portray Darrow as the sole inventor of what for many represents the classic story of inspiration and inventiveness among many that resulted in fame for just one.

1876: Undercover Pinkerton detective agent James McParlan escapes to Philadelphia with enough evidence to hang twenty members of the Molly Maguires.

1914: President Woodrow Wilson visits his oculist in Philadelphia and returns to Washington, D.C., with new glasses.

March 8

Philadelphia has been known as one of the greatest boxing cities since the bare-knuckle days of "Philadelphia" Jack O'Brien. At gyms all over the city and at boxing venues such as the legendary Blue Horizon, often considered to be the best boxing venue in the country, boxers of all weight classes and styles practiced the "sweet science." Home to many champions over the years, the greatest is a man who chose Philadelphia as his home and training base. "Smokin'" Joe Frazier was born in 1944 in Beaufort, South Carolina, the eleventh child in a family of sharecroppers. At the age of fifteen, Frazier moved to Philadelphia, gaining work in a slaughterhouse, where he punched sides of beef to build his boxing strength.

By 1961, he was boxing at a Police Athletic League Gym under the tutelage of trainer Tank Durham. Earning a place on the 1964 Olympic Team, he won the gold in the heavyweight division. Within a year, Joe turned pro, scoring eleven consecutive knock-out victoriesr. Frazier beat Jimmy Ellis on February 16, 1970, to claim the heavyweight world championship. During Frazier's rise to fame, Muhammad Ali was not boxing, having been stripped of his title for refusing induction into the U.S. Army. When Ali was reinstated in 1970, he and Frazier signed a contract for a title fight at Madison Square Garden.

The fight, held on this date in 1971, was heavily hyped as the "fight of the century." Frazier's infamous left hook sent Ali to the canvas, and Frazier won a unanimous decision in fifteen rounds. It was the first defeat of Ali's pro career. Ali and Frazier fought twice more, most memorably in 1975 in the "Thrilla in Manila," in which Ali emerged victorious, a fight that some say was the greatest boxing match in history. Joe permanently retired from boxing in 1976. While the first Ali-Frazier fight was a straightforward victory for Frazier, the feud that began between the boxers over the characterization of Frazier as a "gorilla" by the glib Ali has never been resolved. In 2001, Ali told the *New York Times* that he was sorry, but Joe was quoted as saying, "He didn't apologize to me, he apologized to the paper." For many years Frazier ran a boxing gym in Philadelphia and still lives in the city that adopted him as its champion.

1752: Statesman and Signer of the Declaration of Independence, William Bingham, is born.

March 9

America's first and greatest star of the stage began life in Philadelphia on this date in 1806 as the son of a poor Scottish and German immigrant family. Edwin Forrest, a larger-than-life figure both physically and in international fame, debuted onstage at the tender age of eleven. As a young boy he was inspired to organize a Thespian Club, much against the wishes of his religiously conservative mother. Seeking to learn from the best, Forrest managed to study with the nation's most popular actors, among them Edmund Kean and Junius Brutus Booth, father of Lincoln assassin John Wilkes Booth. As Forrest reached maturity, his reputation was further enhanced by his hard work and commitment to improving his craft, honed by traveling through western Pennsylvania, Ohio, and Kentucky. Following his New York debut in 1826, Forrest embarked on a life as big and dramatic as the dramas he acted onstage.

Contributing to Forrest's appeal was his notable height and muscular physique. At five feet ten inches and possessed of a booming voice and striking good looks, Forrest commanded attention both on and off the stage. Portraying roles such as Spartacus and Jack Cade, his charisma appealed to the masses, while at the same time drawing contempt from the most refined members of his audience, who viewed his manner as vulgar and distasteful. However, Forrest continued to build his repertoire to include Shakespeare and the works of new American playwrights, themselves sponsored by Forrest through an annual competition. At the height of his career, Forrest was performing triumphantly in most leading cities around the world. Much of his public success was eventually tempered by personal failures in the late 1840s.

In 1845, while performing in *Macbeth* in London, Forrest was unexpectedly hissed by the audience. Forrest blamed the incident on rival William Charles Macready. After several years of conflicts, the rivalry culminated in the so-called Astor Place Riot in New York, during which twenty-three people were killed. Forrest's reputation was further challenged by a difficult, and public, divorce from his wife. Accused of infidelity, Forrest countersued for the same reason, only to lose in court. A brief retirement in 1853 allowed Forrest to dabble in politics, but after returning to the stage, illness continued to plague him to the end of his life. Beyond his place as America's first true star of the stage, Forrest left a legacy in the creation of the Forrest Home for Retired Actors, which continues today as part of the Actors Fund home in New Jersey. Forrest, no longer a household name, nevertheless remains a significant figure in America's theatrical past.

1858: The first letterbox sanctioned by the United States Post Office, incorporated into lampposts, is patented by Philadelphia iron products manufacturer Albert Potts.

March 10

On this date in 1880, a small event occurred which reflected the city's unique and sometimes painful role in the history of the captivity of wild animals for display. Columbia, believed to be the first elephant born in captivity in the United States, was born on this date to mother Hebe. Both Asian elephants were featured in Cooper and Bailey's Great London Shows, which wintered in Philadelphia at 23rd Street and Ridge Avenue. Columbia was not the first unusual animal to call Philadelphia home. Indeed, from its earliest years, the city hosted a seemingly unending parade of menageries, exotica, and animal performers, many of whom provided entertainment or enlightenment to Philadelphia's citizens.

As early as the 1720s, camels and elephants were displayed in Boston and New York and it is likely Philadelphia benefited from traveling exhibitions before the Revolutionary War. It is believed that Philadelphia hosted its first elephant visitor by the mid-1790s, at a time when the city was home to the fledgling government and its various employees and supporters. By 1800, painter and naturalist Charles Willson Peale opened his museum on the second floor of the State House (Independence Hall). There, he displayed hundreds of prepared specimens of birds, mammals, fish, and plants. On occasion, he kept live animals in the backyard, among them a grizzly bear and an American bald eagle he considered a family pet. By the 1830s, elephants were frequently seen in exhibitions in Philadelphia. Two elephants drowned while swimming across the Delaware River during an attempt to draw attention to their owner's circus act.

By the late 1870s, the city was home to the first zoological garden in the nation, designed to combine entertainment with the opportunity to learn more about the natural world. The Philadelphia Zoo featured more than 800 animals and welcomed a remarkable 228,000 visitors its first year. In the more recent past, the zoo's remaining two African elephants were moved to a larger facility near Pittsburgh in July 2009. Though some Philadelphians protested the move, many see it as a significant expression of the city's love of elephants and its desire to ensure their future survival.

1753: The new State House bell, today known as the Liberty Bell, cracks after it is first rung.

1826: Henry Lye is awarded a patent for a "leather sewing device," perhaps the first American attempt at a sewing machine.

1974: The Pennsylvania Crime Commission charges that corruption in the Philadelphia Police Department is "ongoing, widespread, systemic and occurring at all levels."

March 11

When the call to arms went out in April of 1861, some Americans rejected President Abraham Lincoln's declared intent to wage war over the secession of the Southern states and the evils of the institution of slavery. Officially members of the Democratic Party and pejoratively called "Copperheads" by those who saw their anti-war rhetoric as poisonous to American unity, these men maintained their stance throughout the war, finding some success in garnering public support. In Philadelphia, the complex social and business relationship between the city and its southern neighbors led to the formation of the Young Men's Democratic Club on this date in 1863. Led by several of the city's most prominent and successful businessmen, the club joined other Copperhead organizations to oppose Lincoln's war, often calling him a tyrant and despot who was bent on destroying the United States and Pennsylvania.

Although never successful in bringing an end to the war, Pennsylvania's Democrats maintained a solid hold on the hearts and minds of many in the state, particularly in the agricultural and mining regions to the north and west of Philadelphia. Heavily populated by Irish and German immigrants, as well as a strong core of Quakers and abolitionists, Pennsylvania was almost evenly divided. Among Quakers, the abolition of slavery and the emancipation of all slaves were seen as essential to the moral and economic future of the country. In opposition, many immigrants feared the product of just such emancipation, envisioning a state overrun by cheap black labor. Additionally, many wealthy businessmen resented the draft and other war-related government edicts.

In reflection of the influence of the Democratic position, state and local elections in 1862 and 1864 resulted in only slight victories for the Republican Party. In 1864, Abraham Lincoln faced considerable opposition for the presidency from his former general, Pennsylvanian George B. McClellan. Officially pro-war, McClellan nevertheless urged a negotiated, rather than military, end to the war. With the official end to the war following General Robert E. Lee's surrender in April 1865, Pennsylvania's Democrats continued to influence politics statewide, eventually losing power to the Republican machine that grew out of the victories of the Civil War.

1795: Philadelphia socialite Charlotte Chambers writes to her mother that "such is the variety of Philadelphia; every day brings some new pursuit, and is passed in the perpetual notation of what is termed pleasure."

1878: The first Morgan silver coin is minted.

1888: A massively destructive blizzard begins, with winds measured at 46 miles per hour.

1907: Noted animator Robert J. Bentley is born. He worked for MGM, Tex Avery, and Hanna-Barbera, among many others.

March 12

The world of retail shopping was changed forever on this date in 1876 when John Wanamaker opened his "Grand Depot" store on Market Street near Juniper Street. Grand in appearance as well as name, the Depot was in fact a renovated Pennsylvania Railroad station, and featured a single large room filled with 129 display counters, arranged in concentric circles. Unlike most retail owners before him, Wanamaker prized innovation and inspiration, looking to new ways to attract (and keep) paying customers. Drawn by Wanamaker's skillful advertising and high-quality products that carried the Wanamaker guarantee, customers came by the thousands, ensuring Wanamaker's success as one of Philadelphia's greatest retailers.

As early as 1861, Wanamaker was conducting business in the city when he founded a men's clothing store called Oak Hall with partner and brother-in-law Nathan Brown. Following Brown's death in 1868, Wanamaker continued to run the business, choosing to expand by purchasing the abandoned railroad station. In addition to men's clothing, Wanamaker offered women's clothing and a variety of dry goods at the new store. By the late 1880s, a total of forty-nine departments served the public. Committed to truth in advertising, Wanamaker ensured that every promise made was kept. Word of mouth contributed to his growing success, as did the first copyrighted advertisements in American history, envisioned by Wanamaker as early as 1874. Retail innovations such as cash refunds, consistent pricing, experienced and well-trained personnel, and services such as an on-site restaurant were also used by Wanamaker to great effect.

Beyond the quality of the merchandise, Wanamaker was concerned with providing a memorable shopping experience. He sponsored the first electrical illumination of a retail store in 1878, creating an awe-inspiring atmosphere. Artwork on the walls, sophisticated window displays, and special exhibitions of scientific equipment and other technological advances set the tone for an informed, refined excellence. Advances made by Wanamaker served him well, allowing him to continue to expand and develop his business into a leader throughout his career. Following his death in 1922, Wanamaker's Department Store retained its gloss for several decades before succumbing to a poor economy and lagging sales in 1978.

1777: Following several months of residence in Baltimore, Maryland, the Continental Congress returns to Philadelphia. Congress initially fled Philadelphia in December 1776 to avoid the British, who were poised to attack the city.

March 13

For thousands of Philadelphia commuters, the quality of one's day is entirely defined by the status of traffic on the infamous interstate highway I-95. Often deemed essential and nearly always reviled, Interstate 95 runs on a north-south route, connecting Philadelphia with New York and Washington, D.C. In between, the roadway plows over, under, and through the city's neighborhoods: from the Great Northeast to South Philadelphia and points beyond. From its earliest inception to its final completion in 1985, Interstate 95 has proven to be the thorn in many a Philadelphian's side; prone to bottleneck traffic jams, speeding cars, and frequent accidents. Love it or not, Philadelphia's busiest roadway has made an impact on the city on every level for almost fifty years.

In response to the growing need for automobile access to America's largest cities, plans for a limited-access highway along the Delaware River similar to those in New York City were debated as early as 1932. The challenge was to maintain access to the Port of Philadelphia while also providing improved high-speed travel. It wasn't until the years after World War II that an expressway linking Trenton and Philadelphia was finally approved. Within a decade, control of the as-yet unrealized expressway was assumed by the Interstate Highway System. Following a pitched battle with neighbors in Society Hill and Queen Village, construction of the alternately elevated and enclosed highway began in the mid-1960s, incorporating the area known as Penn's Landing, a pedestrian-specific access point between the highway and the riverfront. The final section, a four-mile stretch near Philadelphia International Airport, was not completed until 1985, the culmination of the nearly thirty-five-year-old project.

Because the highway winds through some of the most densely populated neighborhoods of the city, Interstate 95 has proven to be one of the most significant methods of transportation in the region, with more than 165,000 vehicles passing through the Center City section each day. The sheer number of travelers often leads to delays, occasionally worsened by events unplanned or unforeseen. On this date in 1996, an immense tire fire was ignited in a Port Richmond tire dump. Severely damaged, I-95 was closed for eight days. In March 2008, a similar shut-down occurred following the discovery of large cracks in a support column. As the highway ages, it seems inevitable that Philadelphia will, at some time in the near future, face more obstacles in its decades-old relationship with the city's most famous, and infamous, roadway.

1844: The City of Camden, New Jersey, is incorporated into the newly formed Camden County, sixteen years after the city is founded.

March 14

The city of Philadelphia lost one of its heroes in the early morning hours on this date in 1919. Thirty-one-year-old police officer James J. Hess was shot to death at DiGildo's Saloon, located on the corner of Clarion and Dickinson streets. As reported in local newspapers, Hess was a recent addition to the police force having previously worked as a city streetcar conductor. At the time of his death, he was unmarried and living at home with his mother. Unfortunately, his death was one of eight police officer murders that year.

The violence enacted on Officer Hess was nothing new. The Philadelphia police department traces its origin back to 1752, when the General Assembly responded to the needs of the citizenry of Philadelphia by establishing the first paid police agency in the British colonies. Benjamin Franklin was the impetus behind this movement, for he recognized that the traditional watchmen who patrolled Philadelphia's streets were increasingly unable to cope with a rising crime rate as the population of Philadelphia soared. By the mid eighteenth century, the upstart city had surpassed both Boston and New York to become the largest city in America, and was second only to London as the most populous English-speaking city in the world.

The continued rapid growth of Philadelphia's industries and resident population in the nineteenth century only worsened the city's struggle against crime and blight. Crowded neighborhoods, poverty, and increasing tensions among diverse ethnic and racial communities put great stress on the modern police department. Hampered at times by corruption in the legal and political system, the Philadelphia Police Department nevertheless remained committed to providing for the safety of all Philadelphians.

The earliest recorded death of a peace officer on duty in Philadelphia occurred in 1828, when Steve Heimer lost his life. The total number of police deaths now stands at just over two hundred and fifty. The challenges of policing Philadelphia have only become more difficult in recent years, as economic and cultural pressures result in greater risk on the streets. To counter this danger, the Philadelphia Police Department now directs a significant part of its work toward building better communities through a multi-layer approach, proudly honoring the past two centuries of service to Philadelphia's citizens.

1800: Charles Hopkins, Edgar Allan Poe's grandfather, makes his debut as a stage comedian in Philadelphia.

1972: The Port of Philadelphia is forced to close when the longshoremen's union begin a strike that does not end until March 30.

March 15

A long, grand line of carts wound its way through the streets of Philadelphia. Unlike almost any other parade in the history of the city, the Procession of the Victualers, held on this date in 1821, included more than one hundred carts loaded with the main attraction: almost 90,000 pounds of butchered and partially butchered cattle, sheep, and pigs. Organized by local butcher (or "victualer") William White, the spectacle was intended to highlight the quality and quantity of meats available in Philadelphia. The parade was so notable that Philadelphia artist John Krimmel documented the event in a watercolor that was later reproduced in at least three printings, all of which were highly successful. As a result, the Procession of the Victualers has remained one of the best remembered of Philadelphia's unique historical events.

In the days leading up to the procession, William White ran newspaper announcements detailing a special exhibition of eighty-seven head of livestock to be displayed at Mr. Graves' stockyard on Sixth Street near Callowhill. Among the displays was a remarkable diversity of animals, ranging from typical livestock such as cattle and hogs to four bears and several deer. After four days, White reported to the newspapers that thousands of people had passed through the stockyard. Part festival and part marketing ploy, White intended to further promote the victualers trade within the city by arranging for the butchering of all displayed animals. Carts would then be loaded with the meat and led through the streets of the city by butchers dressed all in white and mounted on horses. Additional live cattle were draped in floral wreaths and interspersed with the carts. As described by White in additional newspaper coverage of the event, following the procession the meat would be offered up for sale because it was "desirable that it should all be disposed of in one day."

Ultimately, the event was deemed a success by both its organizers as well as the general public. In addition to featuring the quality of individual butchers, the procession also hoped to generate pride in the overall agricultural qualities of the state. The butchers strove to honor the state's excellence in the production of cattle feed, cattle, and the final processed meat, and believed that through the highly public and entertaining mechanism of a spectacle such as the procession they could achieve this goal. Indeed, almost two hundred years later, it would appear they have done so very well.

1707: The city's first Baptist church congregation begins worshiping at the Keithian meetinghouse. The Keithians, who had broken away from the Society of Friends, occupied a frame building on the west side of Second Street, south of Arch.

1804: The floating bridge across the Schuylkill at Market Street is carried away in a flood. Built in 1776, the bridge was removed and stored following the Battle of the Brandywine in 1777 and returned after the British evacuated less than a year later.

1847: Gunner's Run Improvement Company is incorporated, with the purpose of constructing a canal to enlarge trade. Known after April 6, 1850, as the Aramingo Canal, work was begun but never finished, and it was finally paved over in 1896.

March 16

In the world of local politics, few have held a place as significant or controversial as former State Senator Vincent J. Fumo. Known for his sharp mind and skilled political manipulations, Fumo was frequently praised throughout his career for his determination to serve as an advocate for Philadelphia's First District, deep in the heart of South Philadelphia. Unfortunately, following an investigation by federal prosecutors beginning in 2004 and the official indictment handed down on this date in 2009, it was revealed that Fumo had used his tremendous political power for his own benefit in addition to that of his constituents. The indictment, which included more than 130 counts of mail fraud, wire fraud, and conspiracy allegations, was one of the most troubling political events in the city's long history.

Born in Philadelphia in 1943, Fumo applied his abilities to acquiring a top-notch education at Villanova University (B.S., 1964), Temple University School of Law (J.D., 1972), and the Wharton School of the University of Pennsylvania (M.B.A., 1984). Following the conviction of his father for bank fraud in 1976, Fumo assumed leadership of the Fumo-founded First Penn Bank, where he enjoyed tremendous success. Building on a budding political career, Fumo followed in the footsteps of another corruption case when he succeeded First District State Senator Buddy Cianfrani in 1978. He continued to represent the district until the end of 2008.

In Harrisburg, Fumo gained a reputation as one of the smartest and most savvy legislators in the State Capitol. During his twenty years of service, he wielded power in the areas of state appropriations, communications and technology, and several other significant committees. He brought hundreds of thousands of dollars to his district each year through state funding, firmly establishing his popularity among district residents. The 2009 indictment, however, also told of his use of that power for his own personal benefit. In the name of the Citizens Alliance for Better Neighborhoods (a charity run by the Senator), Fumo misused over $2 million in state and charitable funds for repairs on his home and farm, spying on his ex-wife, and funding his re-election efforts. Maintaining his innocence, Fumo nevertheless accepted his sentence of fifty-five months in federal prison, as ruled on July 14, 2009, time substantially less than the eleven to fourteen years called for by the usual guidelines. Fumo began serving his term in prison on August 31, 2009.

1856: The Ferry *New Jersey* runs aground and burns across from Arch Street on the Delaware River.

1879: Pharmacist Robert McNeil opens a drugstore, precursor to the pharmaceutical giant, McNeil Laboratories.

1907: The Sons of St. Patrick present the city with a bronze statue of Commodore Barry, now standing at the center of Independence Square.

March 17

Historically, this date marks the celebration of St. Patrick's Day, a traditional feast day and commemoration of the death of Ireland's patron saint that has been observed for a thousand years. Within Philadelphia's history, March 17 also marks the birth of a significant expression of Irish culture and society in the city. Founded by twenty-four regular members and six honorary members on this date in 1771, the Society of the Friendly Sons of St. Patrick initially offered wealthy Irish citizens and their closest non-Irish acquaintances an opportunity to meet and form fraternal and entrepreneurial bonds. By the end of the 1700s, however, the Society began to address the needs of a new kind of Irish immigrant: the poor and frequently friendless refugees fleeing strife in their homeland.

Several of Philadelphia's brightest and most notable citizens were early members of the Friendly Sons of St. Patrick. These included financier Robert Morris, politician and lawyer John Dickinson, and General George Washington, all non-Irish honorary members. Regular members included General Stephen Moylan, Commodore John Barry, and merchant Thomas Fitzsimmons. During the American Revolutionary War, participation in the Society waned. In the aftermath of war, the role of the Society changed as increasing numbers of poor emigrants from Ireland required support. An extension of the Friendly Sons, the Hibernian Society for the Relief of Emigrants from Ireland successfully helped thousands of new arrivals, especially during the particularly difficult famine years in the first half of the 1800s.

In addition to providing basic services such as food and shelter, the Society supported the Irish-Catholic community when a surge in gangs resulted in several neighborhood riots, most notably in Kensington and Southwark in 1844. Resisting pressure from anti-Catholic groups such as the American Republican Party and the Native American Party, the Friendly Sons stood firm in their belief that Irish-Americans were as patriotic and loyal as any citizen, regardless of religious faith. Today, the combined Society of the Friendly Sons of St. Patrick for the Relief of Emigrants from Ireland continues to support their community by advocating for the recognition of the role of Irish-Americans in history, and by promoting a positive relationship between the United States and Ireland through educational and community programs.

1836: The Girard Life Insurance Annuity and Trust Company is chartered.

1922: WIP, Philadelphia's first commercial radio station and sponsored by Gimbels, goes on the air.

1937: In honor of the 125th anniversary of its founding, the Academy of Natural Sciences begins a four-day International Symposium on Early Man.

1956: The first Mister Softee truck hits the streets and gives out free green ice cream on St. Patrick's Day.

2007: Wildlife authorities report sighting the first bald eagle nest in the city in more than 200 years.

March 18

William Penn stands out in history as a man ahead of his time, who dealt fairly with the native inhabitants he encountered to establish a peaceable kingdom in the new world. Yet while there is much for us to admire in Penn's life, his contemporaries rarely afforded him the same consideration. As the proprietor of a far-flung colony in North America, William Penn spent only four years in Pennsylvania. In effect an absentee landlord, Penn struggled with the government of Pennsylvania to regulate its affairs. But from the founding of the colony in 1681 until 1712, when he suffered a debilitating stroke, Penn spent the vast majority of his time and energy in England embroiled in court intrigue and defending his claim to the colony.

Penn, an open member of a radical religious group known as the Society of Friends, enjoyed a friendly relationship with King James II, a Catholic monarch in Anglican England. In 1688, the Glorious Revolution took place which resulted in James II being deposed. King William of the Netherlands and his wife Mary, the Protestant daughter of James II, ascended to the throne of England. William Penn lost his influential protecter and was placed under house arrest. On this date in 1692, he was stripped of his proprietorship and Pennsylvania was accordingly annexed to New York. During this time, William Penn wrote two important works that were strongly influenced by his forced retirement: *Some Fruits of Solitude, in Reflections and Maxims Relating to the Conduct of Human Life,* which was a personal reflection on life and the wisdom he gained; and *An Essay Toward the Present and Future Peace of Europe,* in which Penn used his free time to objectively assess the state of relations between European nations and envisioned a confederated system of European nations to manage conflict.

William Penn could not be kept down and out for long. On August 9, 1696, Penn regained the proprietorship of Pennsylvania by promising Queen Mary that he would provide for a proper military defense of the colony in spite of his pacifist beliefs. From this time forward, the Penn family would retain possession of Pennsylvania until the American Revolution.

1851: The Assembly buildings on the southwest corner of Tenth and Chestnut streets burn in a massive fire. The buildings were completed in 1834 by a company of gentlemen who hoped to provide suitable quarters for assemblies of any kind.

1857: Arctic explorer Elisha Kent Kane dies in Cuba.

March 19

Spring forward and fall back . . . On this date in 1918, the Standard Time Act passed by Congress inspired the popular mnemonic designed to remind Americans of the shifting of clocks by one hour every spring and fall. Daylight Saving Time, embraced by some and reviled by just as many, was a concept used as far back as Roman days when days were divided into twelve equal hours resulting in longer daylight hours during the summer. Popular belief about the history of the use of a semiannual time shift holds that it was Philadelphia's Benjamin Franklin who first proposed the modern use of daylight saving time, while in fact it was Australian laborer and amateur entomologist George Vernon Hudson who first presented a paper describing the use of a two-hour shift in 1895. Englishman William Willit tirelessly lobbied the British government until his death in 1915, believing firmly in the benefits of extended daylight hours.

The primary goal of most daylight saving plans is to advance clocks in order to allow for more daylight hours in the afternoon. Whether it is for work, leisure, or health, such a shift is often posed as being a benefit. While residing in Paris in 1784, Franklin composed a satirical letter suggesting that Parisians save candles by rising earlier to use morning sunlight. He further suggested that church bells be rung and cannon fired in order to ensure all citizens were properly awakened. Nearly a century later, Hudson hoped to extend his enjoyment of the day (and increase opportunities for seeking insects for his collection) by shifting the clock by two hours. During World War I, Germany and its allies chose to implement a time shift to conserve fuel; as the war neared an end, Britain and America followed suit.

Following the 1918 act, Congress repealed it just one year later under pressure from the agricultural industry, which felt the system negatively affected their productivity and ability to work based on the natural cycles of the sun. The repeal never made it past President Woodrow Wilson, however, who promptly vetoed it. A second attempt to remove federal oversight later succeeded and to this day Daylight Saving Time is regulated on the state level only, resulting in inconsistent use throughout the country.

1792: Death of Peter Jacquett, who was said to have been stolen by Indians as a child. As an adult, he became principal sachem to the Oneidas and served with the Marquis de Lafayette in France. His funeral attracted more than 10,000 mourners.

March 20

American industries, and the lives of workers who made them run, were destined to change forever on this date in 1856. Frederick W. Taylor, often called "the Father of Scientific Management" and a primary advocate for industrial efficiency, was born in the Philadelphia neighborhood of Germantown. Experienced in the day-to-day labor of line manufacturing, Taylor applied his observations and engineering education to the problem of increasing efficiency in the manufacturing process. His management theory became known as *Taylor's Principles* or *Taylorism,* and was broadly adopted throughout American industries. However, his principles were equally despised by many who saw his recommendations as dehumanizing and a misrepresentation of the role of people in manufacturing.

Born into a well-educated Quaker family, Taylor initially chose law as a profession but increasingly poor eyesight redirected his career into that of manufacturing. As a young man he worked on the production lines of several companies, including Enterprise Hydraulic Works and the Midvale Steel Works, where he eventually worked his way up to chief engineer. Later, his employment at Bethlehem Steel led him to a belief that work was worthy of scientific study. He devised four basic principles: replace "rule of thumb" methods with those determined scientifically; scientifically select and train each employee rather than leaving them to train themselves; supervise employees' every detail, leaving nothing to the employee himself to determine; and divide the work equally between manager and laborer, ensuring just as much effort to planning as to implementing the work.

Taylor's push to streamline human labor led to some controversy during his lifetime. As a consultant, he was often brought into a company to pick apart the individual parts of a process, evaluating the specific components that could be made more efficient, be they a machine part or a particular hand movement or action by the worker. His principles frequently met with resistance within laborer ranks, as well as among business owners who distrusted his edicts. Ultimately, however, his theories influenced nearly every aspect of manufacturing. His expectation that productivity is driven by the physical interaction between both laborer and machinery continues to drive manufacturing around the world today.

1825: Thomas Forrest, soldier, dramatist, and member of Congress from 1819 to 1823, dies.

March 21

Peace in "the Family" came to a decisive end on March 21, 1980. Angelo "the Gentle Don" Bruno was found murdered, shot to death in the back of his head while sitting in the front seat of his car. Often considered the last of the old school Philadelphia mob bosses, at the time of his death Bruno was undoubtedly the longest-running mob boss in city history and today may well be considered one of the most successful. Known primarily for his quiet, yet strong personal style, Bruno grounded much of the Family's business in traditional schemes such as bookmaking, loan sharking, and illicit alcohol and gambling businesses. It would be this traditional approach that would ultimately end his leadership.

Bruno was born Angelo Annaloro in Sicily, Italy, in 1910. After immigrating to Philadelphia as a young teenager, Bruno built a close relationship with New York boss Carlo Gambino. With his support, Bruno changed his name (to that of his paternal grandmother) and assumed leadership of Philadelphia's crime family. Choosing to focus his business on nonviolent rackets, Bruno led his crew to financial success. Though he was arrested more than fifteen times in his career, the longest prison term he served was just thirty months, for refusing to testify in a related court case.

As part of his traditional approach, Bruno banned the Philadelphia crime family from dealing in drugs. However, he did permit other Philadelphia gangs to do so, requiring a cut of the profits. This angered some within his family, who resented being denied access to such a lucrative venture. Bruno further angered his family by opening Atlantic City to the New York mob, when in fact the city was traditionally associated with Philadelphia. The resentments culminated in the hit on Bruno arranged by his own consigliore, or close advisor, Anthony "Tony Bananas" Caponigro. Less than a month after Bruno's murder, Caponigro was himself found dead, likely in retaliation for having murdered Bruno without the sanction of the larger Mafia Commission. Within a year, Nicodemo Scarfo assumed the mantle of boss, and led Philadelphia through one of its most violent periods in local mob history.

1835: After years of wrangling, Philadelphia City Council finally passes an ordinance for the construction and management of the Philadelphia Gas Works.

1859: The Zoological Society of Philadelphia is chartered. It remains the oldest zoo in country.

March 22

It went out with a bang—Veterans Stadium, the much loved and much maligned home to the Philadelphia Phillies baseball team and the Philadelphia Eagles football team, was imploded by Demolition Dynamics and the Brandenburg Industrial Services Company at 7:00 A.M. on this date in 2004. Beginning first on the north side and then exploding in a clockwise direction around the building, the demolition lasted only 62 seconds. As early as 1959, the city sought a replacement to the old Shibe Park, home to the Phillies since 1938, and Franklin Field, home to the Eagles. At a remarkable cost of nearly $50 million, Veterans Stadium would become the most expensive sports arena of its time. Delayed a full year due to cost overheads and poor weather, the April 1971 official opening marked the start of a thirty-three-year love-hate relationship between infamously negative Philadelphia sports fans and the odd new arena.

Located in South Philadelphia, near Broad Street and Pattison Avenue, "the Vet" occupied an important place in the developing South Philadelphia Sports Complex, where it joined other sports arenas including JFK Stadium and the Spectrum. The architects called it an "octorad," but the arena is said to have more closely resembled an automobile air filter. Veteran's Stadium seated more than 62,000 fans for football games and just over 56,000 for baseball. One of the largest outdoor venues in town, the Vet was also used for musical performances and related events, including local favorite Bruce Springsteen, Pink Floyd, and the Rolling Stones. The most controversial feature of the stadium was its Astroturf playing field, which served as a frequent fan excuse for losses for both the Eagles and the Phillies from 1971 to 2000.

Prior to playing at the Vet, the Phillies had never won a world championship, but the team went on to win several National League East championships in 1976, 1977, and 1978. Finally, the Phillies beat the Kansas City Royals in the 1980 World Series, a feat not repeated again at the stadium. After repeated (and frequently nationally broadcast) poor behavior among Philadelphia Eagles fans, a special "Eagles Court" was established at the Vet by Municipal Court Judge Seamus McCaffery in 1998. Although the need for such a court has receded, Philadelphia fans reminisce with great nostalgia and affection on the home of their greatest and worst moments in Philadelphia sports.

1822: Horse racing is prohibited on public thoroughfares. The city was undoubtedly host to informal races from its earliest days. In 1854, the name of Sassafras Street was changed to Race Street in recognition of its popularity as a racing road.

March 23

Few citizens of Philadelphia would seem to be in favor of increased traffic, rutted and decaying streets, and the filth associated with thousands of working livestock. Indeed, it was just these concerns which engaged many Philadelphians and a surprising number of competing transportation companies in the aftermath of a single simple civic improvement: the 1831 initiation of a regular stagecoach route along Chestnut Street from 22nd Street to Second Street that ran hourly at a rate of ten cents a ride. The city proper, about two square miles from river to river and Vine Street to South Street, held a population of 175,000. Beyond the city limits, a dozen other municipalities sought the industry and trade that would bring them a thriving economy. The advent of a transportation system within Philadelphia and to points beyond opened the door to issues as varied as the demand for leisure activities and the morality of travel on Sunday.

Following the early success of John Boxall's stagecoach, the number of horse-drawn omnibuses on rails rapidly increased, many running on a subscription basis. Privately run and generally unregulated, early transportation companies cared little for the rapidly deteriorating condition of city streets, or the increasing tensions between residents along the line and the large number of Philadelphians taking advantage of routes to work and a growing number of company-built amusement parks. By the mid-1850s, the demand for street railways led to an explosion of small companies, many of whom received charters within a few months of each other in the spring of 1858. Inventors and engineers raced to improve the technology and gain patents, among them Philadelphian Eleazer Gardner, who received the first patent for a cable car system on this date in 1858. Though never realized, Gardner's patent represented a huge desire to push forward the technology of transportation.

By 1860, the city boasted more than fifteen street railways. The increased traffic and noise led to protests within several communities, but to no avail as public opinion was swayed in favor of the speed and convenience of railway travel. By the mid-1880s, the Philadelphia Traction Company consolidated many of the independent railway companies. This resulted in the formation of an industrial and political monopoly that paved the way for the Union Traction Company to gain control of the Philadelphia street railway system by 1900, contributing to the city's success as a center for industry and growth.

1826: The House of Refuge is chartered.

March 24

The words "William Penn" usually conjure a mental image of a kind looking, plainly dressed, and quietly spoken Quaker man of the seventeenth century. From his tri-corner hat and white wig curls to the simple suit and big-buckled shoes, he holds a place in the hearts of many Pennsylvanians as a symbol of patience, tolerance, and graciousness. Few know of his remarkable powers of persuasion and notable shrewdness, most tellingly seen in his ability to persuade investors to support his young colony. Of those, the Free Society of Traders was ultimately most influential in politics as well as business.

On this date in 1682, the Free Society of Traders was granted a charter by Penn and the Proprietary. The group of wealthy Quakers, based in England but equally represented in Pennsylvania, purchased 20,000 acres of land and was granted manorial rights and exemption from all quitrents in the city. This freedom from taxes and government interference resulted in their ability to quickly sell, and profit from, the high quality properties they held, among them prime locations along the Delaware and Schuylkill rivers. Led by Thomas Lloyd, a delegation from the Traders represented the businessmen in the Provincial Council, indeed dominating the colonial government for a time.

Beginning in 1681 and continuing over several years, William Penn directly solicited the Traders for funds and investment in the colony. Through a series of letters directed to the Traders and other investor groups, Penn detailed the assets available in Pennsylvania. By his accounting, these included "diverse sorts of earth," sweet and clean air, and a native population friendly and open to Europeans. Within just one year, the Free Society of Traders organized and sent more than fifty ships loaded with goods and new settlers to the colony. Seemingly unstoppable in their success, the Traders eventually succumbed to shifts in Proprietary power and the influx of immigrants not associated with their own company. However, they played an essential role in increasing Pennsylvania's European population from approximately 1,000 to more than 20,000 in just twenty years.

1924: Earle Theatre, the most expensive theater built to date in the city, opens with signs proclaiming "World's Biggest Stars."

1986: The Grateful Dead play at the Spectrum.

2010: Two teens are convicted of felony rioting in a Center City "flash mob" incident in which hundreds of teenagers gathered, drawn by text messaging, followed by spontaneous violence.

March 25

The printed word wields a powerful stroke in the history of Philadelphia. From its earliest days, the city has been home to many printing "firsts," among them the first American Bible (in German, 1743) and the longest-running African-American newspaper in the country (1884). On this date in 1836, the city saw the birth of its first penny newspaper, the *Public Ledger.* Unlike other Philadelphia papers before it, the *Public Ledger* was intended for the average citizen. At a standard cost of five cents, most newspapers in the city catered to the wealthy. In addition to cost and frequency, the daily *Public Ledger* also brought innovation to the editorial content of the news and explored advances in the technical production of the paper as well. After experiencing a number of ups and downs and several changes in ownership throughout its life, the *Public Ledger* became one of the most influential newspapers in the nation before it lost out to the competition and ceased publication in 1942.

Founded by a trio of newspapermen, the *Public Ledger* quickly amassed a wide readership, reaching a circulation of 15,000 within five years of the first issue. Inspired in great part by New York's *Herald* newspaper, the *Public Ledger* featured bold headlines. Forging its own advances, the newspaper also began to categorize its advertisements, including items such as deaths, marriages, and "wants" for the first time. Embracing technology, the paper was also among the first to be distributed by Pony Express and to use the electromagnetic telegraph and rotary printing presses. By the mid-1860s, the owners' choice to support the anti-Republican Copperhead policy of seeking a peace settlement with the Confederate States resulted in the loss of much of their readership. Purchased by George William Childs and A. J. Drexel in 1864, the newspaper was redirected toward a Union point of view and soon regained its place in popularity.

Childs and Drexel continued to lead the paper through the last quarter of the nineteenth century, firmly establishing the financial and political success of the *Public Ledger.* Additional innovations included serial fiction (including Dickens), national reporting, and clear editorial positions. Later ownerships by *New York Times* owner Adolph Ochs and *Ladies Home Journal* publisher Cyrus Curtis led to a downward spiral. The paper managed to survive the Great Depression but never fully regained its place as the premier newspaper in Philadelphia.

1850: Cedar Hill Cemetery in Frankford is incorporated.

1871: Presbyterian Hospital is founded.

March 26

Few performers are so directly associated with the Sound of Philadelphia as Teddy Pendergrass, born in Kingstree, South Carolina, on this date in 1950. Though not a native son, Pendergrass grew up in Philadelphia attending but not graduating from Thomas Edison High School. As a young man, he moved from drummer to lead singer in the rhythm and blues band Melvin and the Blue Notes. It was through their collaboration with Kenny Gamble and Leon Huff (simply known as Gamble & Huff) that Pendergrass and a dozen other performers came to be known throughout the country for the signature Philadelphia soul sound, rich with the sounds of strings, deep baseline, and sliding rhythms. Influential beyond the city limits, their sound is identified by many historians as the bridge to disco in the 1970s.

After joining Gamble & Huff's Philadelphia International Records in 1972, Pendergrass and Melvin & the Blue Notes became known for hits such as "I Miss You" and "Wake Up Everybody." Other performers associated with the producers included the O'Jays, Billy Paul, and the Jacksons. Throughout the 1970s, music produced by the label grew in popularity until it eventually eclipsed music giant Motown Records, Gamble & Huff's first and greatest rival. After Pendergrass went solo in 1978, he became the primary representative of the unique Philadelphia sound on the radio.

As the disco rage declined, Philadelphia International Records struggled to hold on to its place at the top of the charts. The future of the label seemed grim following a horrific car accident on March 18, 1982, which left Pendergrass paralyzed from the chest down. The label, and Pendergrass, survived and in the 1990s Gamble & Huff won their first Grammy Award for the remake of the Blue Notes' chart-topping "If You Don't Know Me By Now" by the English band Simply Red. Gamble & Huff continue to produce music today while also focusing their significant talent on charitable and community causes. Pendergrass, who performed briefly in the 1985 Live Aid concert and again in 2007 in honor of his twenty-five years of survival following the accident, formed the Teddy Pendergrass Alliance in support of raising awareness of spinal cord injuries. Pendergrass died on January 13, 2010, following a bout with colon cancer. Born from the talent of these remarkable musicians, the Sound of Philadelphia lives on, heard daily on radio stations and in headphones throughout the world.

1831: Richard Allen dies.

1867: The Fairmount Park Commission is formed by an Act of Assembly of the Commonwealth of Pennsylvania. The Commission was intended to create a public park along the Schuylkill River and to "maintain it forever, as an open public place and park, for the health and enjoyment of the citizens."

1892: Poet Walt Whitman dies in his home on Mickle Street in Camden, New Jersey.

1928: The first galleries are opened to the public at the Philadelphia Museum of Art on the Benjamin Franklin Parkway.

March 27

"Flying your colors" can have great meaning when as a society you feel the need to stand behind a single ideal or symbol. In Philadelphia, it is the city flag which proudly announces our deep connection to our history, as well as our ongoing commitment to unity among citizens. On this date in 1895, the modern version of the city colors was approved by ordinance to include the original arms (now seal) of the city, and to feature the blue and yellow colors indicative of the region's first European settlers, Swedes who arrived as early as 1638. Emblazoned with the motto *Philadelphia Meneto* ("Let Brotherly Love Continue"), the flag represents the richness of the city's three-hundred-year history.

It is unknown at precisely what moment the arms for the city of Philadelphia were originally set. However, it is clear that the intent was to draw attention to the significance of two industries: trading and agriculture. The shield that forms the center of the seal is divided into three horizontal parts. The top section features a plow and the lower a sailing ship, both backed in a light azure blue. A yellow stripe runs between them, completing the homage to the Swedish blue and yellow flag. Above the shield rises an arm holding the balance of justice. On either side stand two female figures: one holds a scroll with an anchor depicted, while the other holds a cornucopia overflowing with the bounty of a harvest. When the original city flag was designed in 1874, this seal was the primary feature and floated in a field of blue. That same year, the motto was adopted, cementing the city's nickname the "City of Brotherly Love."

Although the changes made for the 1895 ordinance were ultimately small, they have remained in place ever since. Henry C. McCook, a hero of the Civil War and designer of the final, adopted version, chose to better highlight the seal by enlarging it and further honoring the city's Swedish history by creating a background of three vertical stripes of yellow and blue, the middle being yellow. Today, the flag flies primarily over City Hall, while versions with or without the seal can be seen elsewhere in the city. A reminder of our long and successful history, the flag stands as a call to community among Philadelphia's manifold citizenry.

1860: Charles Darwin is elected a member of the Academy of Natural Sciences, the first American scientific institution to recognize his achievements.

1975: Susan Saxe, one of only eight women ever to be on the FBI's most-wanted list, is arrested by a Philadelphia policeman who recognizes her from an FBI flyer.

March 28

The nation's worst nuclear nightmare had begun. At 4:00 A.M. on the morning of March 28, 1979, a partial core meltdown of one of two reactors at Three Mile Island Nuclear Generating Station in Dauphin County occurred when a stuck release valve allowed coolant water to drain and the core in Unit T-2 overheated. Caused by a combination of poor engineering and human error, the event has been called the most significant accident in the history of the commercial nuclear generating industry in the United States and serves as a reminder of the potential for disaster in a state where the peacetime nuclear industry was first initiated.

As early as 1957, Pennsylvania was home to a leading innovation in the nuclear power industry. The Shippingport Atomic Power Station, the first peacetime nuclear power plant in the nation, was located near Pittsburgh. Three Mile Island, completed in 1974, served nearly 1.5 million homes when fully running. The morning of the accident, however, a series of mechanical failures occurred that were further complicated by inadequate reporting instruments and poor judgment on the part of under-trained personnel. When the pumps that circulated the coolant water failed, pressure gauges inaccurately reported the state of the interior water pressure and temperature. Steps taken by personnel to correct what was believed to be a build-up of water rather than a loss resulted in the meltdown. Within a few hours, the active event was stopped. However it was not known for several weeks the extent of the damage, which would subsequently result in the shutting down of Unit T-2.

Though the aftermath of the incident is still disputed, no loss of life was recorded as a result of the radiation released that day. Evacuation of the area was voluntary and in the years that followed careful monitoring and regular review of the local environment suggests no long-term repercussions. However, in many ways the nuclear power industry was forever changed. Inspired in part by the Three Mile Island accident and the eerie parallels in the motion picture *The China Syndrome,* released just twelve days before the real incident, greater public demand for oversight and industry transparency has helped to maintain an excellent safety record in the United States, staving off a true nightmare like the Soviet Union's Chernobyl disaster. The remaining Unit T-1 continues to generate power for the region and is expected to do so until the year 2034.

1787: Benjamin Rush writes an open letter "To the citizens of Philadelphia: A Plan for Free Schools" in which he details his desire to establish public schools in the state.

March 29

Like so many other performers before her, Pearl Bailey arrived in Philadelphia as a young woman seeking fame and fortune on one of the countless theatrical stages in the city. Born on this date in 1918, Bailey left her home in Southampton County, Virginia, at the advice of her older brother Bill, who urged her to perform at a local amateur contest. No one could have expected that single contest to be the start of a career that would lead to New York City, Broadway, and national fame.

Known for her lively voice and broad stage presence, Bailey honed her craft in numerous vaudeville and nightclubs in the city through the 1930s. Gaining in popularity, she traveled to various cities and towns on the East Coast. In 1941, she toured the country with the United Service Organization, performing regularly for American troops. Following the war, she moved to New York City and made her Broadway debut in *St. Louis Woman* in 1946. Over the next decade, she performed with several music greats, including Duke Ellington and Cab Calloway. She was also offered several significant film roles, including Frankie in *Carmen Jones* and Maria in the 1959 film version of *Porgy & Bess* starring Dorothy Dandridge and Paul Robeson.

In 1967, she starred in an all-black revival of *Hello Dolly!* on Broadway, for which she was awarded a special Tony Award. Her old friend and performing partner Cab Calloway was also featured in the Broadway show. During the 1970s, a broader audience of Americans was introduced to her through *The Pearl Bailey Show,* which ran for fourteen shows in 1971 and featured musical guests as varied as Louis Armstrong, Robert Goulet, and Moms Mabley. Following her retirement from performing in the mid-1970s, Bailey worked as spokesperson for Duncan Hines baking company and was invited to serve as one of several delegates to the United Nations. She died in Philadelphia, following complications from routine knee surgery on August 17, 1990.

1849: Henry "Box" Brown departs Richmond, Virginia, packed in a shipping crate in a successful bid for freedom along the Underground Railroad. He arrives in Philadelphia twenty-seven hours later.

1853: Pioneering electrical engineer and inventor Elihu Thomson is born in London. As a young teacher at Central High School in Philadelphia, Thomson gives one of the earliest demonstrations of the existence and nature of radio waves.

March 30

Today, the lowly pencil is completely taken for granted. Yet the pencil was a remarkable invention that simplified and revolutionized the process of recording information. The earliest known description and illustration of a lead pencil was recorded in a book on fossils by a Swiss physician and naturalist named Konrad Gesner in 1565. The name is derived from the latin term *peniculus,* which meant "little tail," and was the name of a common brush of similar size. Whilc the lead pencil may not be mightier than the sword, it offered two qualities that other contemporary writing implements could not match in a single instrument: dryness and darkness. No more ink to spill, no more prepared surfaces on which to scratch a metal stylus.

It was a remarkable invention, and the British enjoyed a natural advantage owing to a unique, pure deposit of graphite that was found in Borrowdale, England, sometime in the sixteenth century. Yet pencils were in high demand and over the following centuries inroads would be made in many other countries as inventors found ways to overcome this British supply advantage and improve upon the composition of the pencil. Individual craftsmanship eventually yielded to large-scale manufacturing by the likes of the Johann Faber Company in Germany and the Joseph Dixon Crucible Company (now Dixon Ticonderoga) in America. The quality of pencil lead was strengthened over time to resist breaking; cedar was eventually determined to be the ideal wood for the shaft; and yellow became the standard color of all self-respecting pencils.

And what place does Philadelphia play in this story? It can be argued that a native of Philadelphia named Hyman Lipman perfected the pencil when he placed an eraser on the end, and promptly patented his improvement on March 30, 1858 (U.S. Patent #19,783). Mr. Lipman garnered some success from his small improvement, selling his patent four years later to Joseph Reckendorfer for the remarkable sum of $100,000. Reckendorfer then turned around and sued the Faber-Castell Company for patent infringement following their decision to install erasers on their own manufactured pencils. The case went all the way to the Supreme Court, which invalidated Reckendorfer's claim in 1875. The justices argued that the combination of a pencil and an eraser, two items that previously existed, did not merit an exclusive patent. Regardless, the pencil remains today in use much as it did then, recording the thoughts and history of countless people worldwide every day.

1847: The Pennsylvania Railroad is organized.

1849: Escaped slave Henry "Box" Brown arrives in a wooden box arranged through the Underground Railroad.

1894: A spectacular display of the aurora borealis is witnessed by crowds in the city.

2001: Charles Barkley's number 34 is retired by the Philadelphia 76ers in a half-time ceremony.

March 31

Today, cars and trucks travel quickly over the Ben Franklin and other major bridges spanning the Delaware, but for most of Philadelphia's history, taking a ferry was the way to travel across the river to New Jersey. William Royden obtained the first license for a ferry in 1688; in 1695, the Cooper family operated the ferry under license from Cooper Street for 150 years. Ferry systems at various points along the river on the New Jersey side eventually led to the development of the city of Camden. The Benjamin Cooper house in North Camden is one of the few surviving taverns serving the ferry trade; built in 1734, it is currently used as an office.

The first ferries were open to the elements, but their design evolved to offer rough shelter for passengers. As the cost of a trip increased, the New Jersey legislature attempted to address the issue but ferry interests prevailed; in 1782 the price for a single ticket was nine shillings. Hotels, taverns, and restaurants to serve ferry passengers and the farmers who transported their produce and animals across the river grew up on both banks. Competing ferry companies docked at Market Street and other locations along the Philadelphia riverfront. Sail and oars gave way to steamboats, but danger crossing the river was always a consideration. In 1856, the ferry *New Jersey* burned with the loss of 60 lives.

With the development of train lines of the Philadelphia and Atlantic City railroad in 1877, ferries transported passengers from Bulson Street in Camden to Pier 8 at Chestnut Street. Ferries also transported workers from Camden to industrial sites in the Kensington neighborhood of Philadelphia and in Southwark. In the twentieth century, the construction of the Ben Franklin and other bridges reduced ferry ridership. Finally, on this date in 1952, regular ferry service between Camden and Philadelphia ceased after 264 years of operation, bringing to an end a lifeline between Camden and Philadelphia. Within the last decade, the development of the Camden waterfront and the construction of the New Jersey Adventure Aquarium have renewed interest in a river ferry, and a new service has begun, once again connecting the two cities by way of the ever-flowing Delaware River.

1881: A special City Council committee is called to investigate mismanagement of the Philadelphia Gas Works. Reports include tales of the over-employment of people, chief executive officers selected for political reasons rather than training and experience, and great losses of funds to the city.

1917: Thousands attend a patriotic rally at Independence Mall in support of President Wilson and protecting American rights on land and sea.

1976: A local activist's group announces a formal drive to recall Mayor Rizzo, calling him a "tyrant."

1979: Marvis Frazier, son of Joe, wins the National Golden Gloves heavyweight championship.

A most remarkable event occurred at precisely 12:00 noon on March 4, 1797. For the first time in modern world history, a peaceful transfer of power was enacted as President George Washington stood by to witness the swearing-in of President-elect John Adams on the floor of the House of Representatives in Congress Hall, on the corner of Sixth and Chestnut street. Defined not by monarchal or dictatorial precepts, the moment was a direct expression of the belief that the United States Constitution had created a new form of government, of the people, for the people, and by the people. Elected in a contentious but ultimately clear and open process, John Adams was the first benefactor of one of the greatest strengths built into the new American government. Washington, himself more than ready to step aside and away from the intense politics of the late 1790s, expressed his feelings about this historic moment to friend Henry Knox in this letter of March 2, 1797.

George Washington to Henry Knox, March 2, 1797 (excerpt)

To the wearied traveler who sees a resting place, and is bending his body to lean thereon, I now compare myself; but to be suffered to do this in peace, is I perceive too much, to be endured by some. To misrepresent my motives; to reprobate my politics; and to weaken the confidence which has been reposed in my administration, are objects which cannot be relinquished by those who will be satisfied with nothing short of a change in our political System. The consolation however, which results from conscious rectitude, and the approving voice of my Country, unequivocally expressed by its Representatives, deprives their sting of its poison, and places in the same point of view both the weakness, and malignity of their efforts.

Although the prospect of retirement is most grateful to my soul, and I have not a wish to mix again in the great world, or to partake in its politics, yet, I am not without my regrets at parting with (perhaps never more to meet) the few intimates whom I love, among these, be assured you are one.

The account given by Mr. Bingham and others, of your agreeable Situation and prospects at St. George's, gave me infinite pleasure; and no one wishes more sincerely than I do, that they may increase with your years. The remainder of my life (which in the course of nature cannot be long) will be occupied in rural amusements, and though I shall seclude myself as much as possible from the noisy and bustling crowd, none more than myself, would be regaled by the company of those I esteem, at Mount Vernon: more than 20 Miles from which, after I arrive there, it is not likely I ever shall be.

As early in next week as I can make arrangements for it, I shall commence my journey for Mount Vernon. Tomorrow, at dinner, I shall, as a servant of the public, take my leave of the President Elect, of the foreign characters, heads of Departments, &ca. And the day following, with pleasure, I shall witness the inauguration of my Successor to the Chair of government.

On the subject of Politics I shall say nothing; you will have an opportunity of seeing and conversing with many of the Legislators; from whom, so far as it relates to the proceedings of their own body, they can give you the details. The Gazettes will furnish the rest.

Mrs. Washington unites with me in every good wish for you, Mrs. Knox and family, and with unfeigned truth, I am yours always, and affectionately.

—George Washington

April

April 1

In a game often cited as one of the greatest upsets in NCAA Men's basketball history, on this date the eighth-seeded Villanova Wildcats defeated top-seeded Georgetown, 66–64 to win the 1985 championship, missing only one shot the entire second half of the game. Fans delighted in the victory, but the historical basketball rivalry in Philadelphia is the Big Five, an association of universities in the Philadelphia area: La Salle, the University of Pennsylvania, Saint Joseph's, Temple, and Villanova. The Big Five is not a conference; the member teams represent three separate conferences: the Atlantic 10, the Big East, and the Ivy League. Formed in 1954, the purpose of the alliance was to provide a showcase for Philadelphia basketball and to help pay for the upkeep on the Palestra, the venue on the University of Pennsylvania campus where the games have been played for decades. Round-robin tournaments and double-header games were a means of creating extra interest and excitement.

Built in 1927, the Palestra is known as "the Cathedral of College Basketball." Home to the University of Pennsylvania Quakers men's and women's basketball teams, as well as the university's volleyball and wrestling teams, the Palestra was one of the first steel and concrete arenas in the country and one of the first without pillars to block the view. Renovated in 1955 and again in 2000, it remains an intimate location to watch basketball, seating nearly 1,300 fewer fans than when it first opened. John Feinstein, in his book *A Season Inside,* said "the Palestra is to college basketball what Fenway Park and Wrigley Field are to baseball."

The Big Five magic is not just about the venue. Historic games feature players who have competed against each other since grammar school, while legendary coaches such as Jack Ramsay, Rollie Massimino, and John Chaney lead the drive to victory while still enjoying a unique solidarity. In the world of college basketball, few games rival the power of feeling during games played out in the "Holy War" between Villanova and St. Joseph's, or the North Philadelphia competition between Temple and LaSalle. The intensity of Big 5 games cannot be overstated, as screaming fans, rousing mascots, and deep-rooted rivalries are revived each season, contributing to yet another unique Philadelphia sports experience.

1852: Edwin Austin Abbey, a distinguished illustrator and painter, is born in Philadelphia. His work can be seen in the Pennsylvania State House.

1978: The Trocadero Burlesque Theater holds a final farewell show featuring vaudeville comedians and burlesque dancers before closing after 106 years.

April 2

When the United States Constitution was drafted in 1787, in addition to the power to spend money Congress was also tasked with the power to make it, not by earning but through minting. As a result, the sound of coins jingling in the pockets of American citizens is the direct result of a Congressional Act passed on this day in 1792. Prior to the formation of a central government, the manufacture of coinage and the printing of currency was left to each colony, resulting in nearly impossible-to-decipher exchange rates and a complete lack of monetary value standards. In 1792, Secretary of the Treasury Alexander Hamilton personally devised a plan for a national mint, tasked with enacting Congressional mandates and fulfilling the need for circulating coins, as well as securing the raw bullion reserves. When the three-story building was completed, it was the first federal structure erected under the Constitution.

Located at the intersection of Seventh near Filbert Street, the Philadelphia Mint was placed under the guidance of the nation's first Director of the Mint, David Rittenhouse. Within a year, the mint had produced and released its first coins: 11,178 copper pennies. Over the next several years, the mint produced gold and silver coins as well. Indeed, one of several stories associated with this time suggests that President George Washington contributed some of his own precious metals to the production of coins. This event is commemorated in the John Ward Dunsmore painting *Inspecting the First Coins,* which is on display to visitors at the current Philadelphia Mint.

As the demand for coins grew into the early 1800s, the old mint building was abandoned for a new location at Chestnut and Juniper streets. Ultimately, the mint was moved two more times, each to a larger and more modern facility. Today, the Philadelphia Mint located on Independence Mall is one of five such facilities across the nation and is responsible for all engraving, manufacturing of coin and medal dies, and the production of some circulating and commemorative coins. It is open to the public for tours, and remains one of the primary man-isfestations of the federal government in Philadelphia, an echo of the city's past.

1808: The Schuylkill Falls Bridge Company is incorporated. Within a year the company would build a chain suspension bridge over the Schuylkill River.

1821: The Apprentice's Library Company of Philadelphia is incorporated. It was the first free circulating library in America.

1872: Edwin Forrest closes his dramatic career at the Globe Theatre in Boston, when he appears as Richelieu.

April 3

In the months leading up to the official declaration of war between the states, the Frankford Arsenal based in the Bridesburg neighborhood of Philadelphia provided essential supplies to the United States Army, including thousands of rifles and rounds of ammunition. In January of 1861, local city newspapers noted the shipment of a large amount of supplies southward to Washington, to aid in the preparations for war. The actions of Arsenal Commander Josiah Gorgas on this date in 1861 seemed to belie the assumption that the materials actually reached the U.S. Army. Gorgas, born and raised in Pennsylvania and graduate of West Point, resigned his position as commander in order to cast his lot with the Confederacy. In the weeks following his departure, rumors spread that he had successfully diverted the majority of the supplies at Frankford to the Confederate Army, a betrayal both unexpected and deeply damaging.

As a young man, Gorgas was given the opportunity to attend West Point, the premier training academy for the Army. He chose as his specialty the management of ordnance, and eventually served under General Winfield Scott during the Mexican War. Throughout his career in the U.S. Army, conflicts with his superiors led to missed promotions and undesirable duty assignments. While stationed in Mobile, Alabama, he met and married the daughter of a former governor. This relationship, along with his conflicts within the Army, contributed to his choosing the Southern side in 1861. Following his resignation, the Arsenal at Frankford suffered from depleted supplies and chaotic leadership for nearly a year. Eventually, the Arsenal regained its ability to serve the nation, and as many as 1,000 workers continued to work in support of the war effort.

Gorgas was named Chief of the Confederate Bureau of Ordnance just five days after leaving Philadelphia. The only professional ordnance specialist available to the Confederacy, Gorgas played an essential role in developing ordnance manufacture in the South by acquiring the necessary raw materials and putting the industrial infrastructure into place. Following the war, Gorgas hoped to continue to develop heavy industry, but his initial foray into business soon failed. He was appointed headmaster at the University of the South in Sewanee, Tennessee, and eventually served as President of the University of Alabama, where he died in 1883.

1820: The Chestnut Street Theater burns. It would reopen at Sixth and Chestnut streets December 2, 1822.

1887: The speed record for travel by horseback from New York City to Philadelphia is broken by two brothers from Philadelphia. They arrived in less than six hours, breaking the record by half.

April 4

Alongside the great minds to be found in Philadelphia during the second half of the eighteenth century, few are perhaps more deserving of remembrance or less well known than Episcopal bishop William White, born in Philadelphia on this date in 1748. Inclining to neither political nor military pursuits, White nevertheless played a significant role in the spiritual and intellectual life of Revolutionary Philadelphia. A moderate revolutionary in his own right, his postwar efforts led to the evolution of the Anglican Church in America into the uniquely American Protestant Episcopal Church in the United States.

Educated at what would one day become the University of Pennsylvania, the young clergyman traveled to England in 1770, where he was ordained as an Anglican deacon and priest. By 1772, he was selected to serve as assistant to the rector of the Church of Christ (Christ Church) and its sister congregation, St. Peter's Church. In 1779, White succeeded the outgoing Loyalist rector, a position he held until his death in 1836. Within a few short years, White's reputation as a moderate who supported the American push for independence would place him at odds with many in the Church who remained singularly loyal to the British king. In recognition of the prominent place held by Christ Church within the community, as well as a reflection of his own political leanings, White was appointed chaplain to the Continental Congress in 1777. He continued to serve the young government as chaplain to the Senate from 1790–1800.

In addition to his role as spiritual leader to the political elite, White was instrumental in crafting the 1785 Constitution of the Protestant Episcopal Church in the United States, in which he asserted the radical idea that clergy and laity, rather than bishops, had the right to appoint American bishops. This position, among others, helped define the nature of the Episcopal Church in America. As founder or co-founder of numerous charitable organizations, including the Pennsylvania School for the Deaf, the Magdalene Society (for "fallen" women), and the Prison Society, White further ensured his place as one of Philadelphia's greatest citizens. Though not so well known and perhaps less dramatic than the legacies of Franklin, Jefferson, and Washington, the work and spiritual guidance provided by William White helped to shape Revolutionary Philadelphia and the world beyond.

1902: Wealthy publisher and poet Anthony J. Drexel Biddle and boxing champ "Philadelphia Jack" O'Brien meet in the ring at a match sponsored by the Merion Cricket Club.

1971: Veterans Stadium is dedicated as 35,000 spectators come to watch the Philadelphia Phillies and the Eagles work out on the turf for the first time.

1991: Pennsylvania Senator John Heinz and six others are killed in plane crash over Merion, Pennsylvania.

April 5

In the early decades of the nineteenth century, Philadelphia boasted an unusually large number of institutions devoted to both learning and leisure. The particular stomping grounds of the city's educated elite, these private and semi-private organizations easily combined the seemingly conflicted purpose of providing a place for a relatively small number of Philadelphians to acquire knowledge while passing their leisure hours in a calm, enjoyable atmosphere in the company of others similar to themselves. On this date in 1815, the Supreme Court of Pennsylvania granted a charter for the incorporation of what was to become one of the city's leading institutions, the Athenaeum of Philadelphia. Originally envisioned as a library, museum, and edifying lecture hall, the Athenaeum represented the best that Philadelphia's community of educated professionals could offer to each other in the way of entertainment and social and intellectual engagement.

Among the early founders were prominent sons of Philadelphia's long established and powerful families, including names like Wharton, Smith, Chew, Coxe, and Vaux. Inspired, according to member Thomas Isaac Wharton, by their own "want of a convenient place of common resort in which their leisure hours could be passed," the men first met in February 1814 in hopes of adopting membership rules and identifying a means of acquiring subscribers. The name Athenaeum, derived from the Greek term for a Greek temple of poetry, was selected as inspiration. Shortly thereafter, a newspaper advertisement announced the intent to establish a reading room, a lecture hall, and a museum featuring natural history specimens. Sustained by a steady membership, the reading room was the only long-term success of the Athenaeum when the other components were deemed too difficult to maintain.

In the last fifty years, the Athenaeum of Philadelphia has evolved into more than just a place to read newspapers and discuss the most recent advances in science. Rather, it serves now as one of the premier repositories of archives pertaining to historic preservation and architecture. Under the leadership of architectural historian and Executive Director Emeritus Roger Moss, the Athenaeum evolved into a center for Philadelphia's rich architectural history. Today, the Athenaeum continues to serve as a home to intellectual engagement and stands as a representative of Philadelphia's cultural richness.

1967: Wilt Chamberlin scores an NBA record 41 rebounds in a playoff game versus Boston. The record still stands today.

1968: In reaction to concerns about rioting following the assassination of Martin Luther King, Jr., on April 4, Mayor James H. Tate and Police Commissioner Frank Rizzo declare a limited state of emergency and close all bars in the city.

April 6

In 1789, the first true test of the United States Constitution proved that it was possible to win an election without even trying, and that machinations and manipulations are a natural part of any political system, even one as carefully constructed as that for our fledgling nation. Following the ratification of the Constitution by a necessary nine states in September of 1788, it seemed only natural that General George Washington would be selected to serve as the first leader of the new government. An unenthusiastic candidate who felt it was unseemly to desire the power of such a position, Washington committed no time or attention to campaigning. When all electoral votes were finally counted and George Washington's election as the first President of the United States was confirmed on this date in 1789, he reluctantly assumed a role he seemed destined to enact, regardless of his own personal desire for peace and tranquillity in his final years.

As defined in the Constitution itself, the new president would be appointed by electors, rather than by popular vote in a general election. Only those states which had ratified the Constitution by January 1789 were permitted to appoint electors, resulting in the representation of just ten of the original states in the February election. It was not until April 6, 1789, that the recently elected United States Senate met for the first time and began counting the electoral votes. Of no surprise to anyone, Washington received one vote from each of the sixty-nine electors, giving him a clear and concise victory. What remained unknown was the name of the new Vice President. Unlike today, the Vice President was the presidential candidate who received the second-highest number of votes. In 1789, that man was John Adams, Signer of the Declaration of Independence and one of the most significant advocates for the new government.

But Adams' election was not without intrigue. In the weeks leading up to the election, Alexander Hamilton worked hard to ensure that Washington's victory was clear and pure. While campaigning on Washington's behalf, Hamilton also campaigned specifically against Adams. Of the twelve presidential candidates running, Adams received nearly four times as many votes as third-place John Jay, yet he still received only half as many as Washington. Ultimately, Adams was seen as the successor to Washington's presidential legacy and was himself sworn in as president in March of 1797, a remarkable tribute to the success of the American political experiment.

1879: Fire breaks out in several warehouse buildings near Fourth and Race streets. One man is killed, and the buildings are lost.

1907: Philadelphia businessman and philanthropist P. A. B. Widener offers $10 million to the city in support of the construction of an art gallery on the Parkway. It is the beginning of what would become the Philadelphia Museum of Art.

April 7

One half of the most successful pop duo in American music was born in New York City on this date in 1949. John Oates would ultimately call Philadelphia his home, forging a notable friendship and career while attending Temple University. As a freshman, he met senior Daryl Hall in a freight elevator while both tried to avoid a near-riot at a club where local bands were competing. Realizing their common interest in rhythm and blues as well as rock and soul, the musicians formed Hall & Oates and were eventually signed by Atlantic Records in 1972. Their Philadelphia-influenced form of "blue-eyed soul" would lead them to great success, including 6 number-one records and a remarkable 80 million albums sold.

Growing up in Montgomery County, Oates benefited from the many musical opportunities in the Philadelphia area. At the age of just four, he saw Philly native Bill Haley and his Comets perform at a local amusement park. Exposed to the variety of doo-wop, rhythm and blues, and rock that played on local radio stations and in dozens of clubs and band venues, Oates cultivated a rich understanding of the diversity of American music. Similarly, Daryl Hall found inspiration in the Philadelphia music scene, meeting icons such as Smokey Robinson and the Temptations while working as a session player for the legendary Gamble and Huff. Oates and Hall seemed destined to form a musical alliance when they met in 1969.

As Hall & Oates, the two initially struggled to find their sound and soon switched to the RCA recording label. They also moved to New York City, where they finally hit stride with the release of their 1980 album *Voices,* followed the next year by the album *Private Eyes.* Their self-styled "rock and soul" sound was a mix of rock and roll, rhythm and blues, and new wave music, heavily influenced by their formative musical experiences growing up in Philadelphia. Before the decade was out, they would rack up number-one hits on the Billboard Hot 100, including "Rich Girl," "Private Eyes," "I Can't Go For That (No Can Do)," and "Out of Touch." By 1984, the Recording Industry Association of America reported that Daryl Hall and John Oates had become the most successful duo in the history of recorded music. While working on solo projects, Hall & Oates continue to revisit their partnership, most recently releasing a Christmas album in 2006.

1884: Point Breeze Trotting Park, the city's primary racetrack, is sold at sheriff's auction for $65,000. The 65-acre track and grounds were first used as early as 1855, and after the sheriff's sale continued in use until the early 1910s.

1917: Blues legend Billie Holiday is born at 1409 Lombard Street.

April 8

To be labeled as a "Benedict Arnold" is to be seen as the most heinous of traders, akin to Judas in the mind of Benjamin Franklin and many others. Indeed, the story of the real Benedict Arnold is fraught with betrayals of many kinds, portraying a complexity rarely understood in one of the country's most legendary and least understood narratives. Regardless of which perspective is taken, there is little doubt that it was the marriage on this date in 1779 between General Benedict Arnold and Philadelphia's Margaret "Peggy" Shippen that emerged as a key moment in American Revolutionary War history and gave birth to a legend.

Born to a Connecticut family, Arnold was sixteen when he had his first direct taste of war, enlisting in the local militia during the French and Indian War. He served a mere thirteen days, though the reason for this remains unclear. As an adult, he met with some success in business and was eventually inspired by the fight against the British to join the Revolution, where he served with distinction. At the same time, his aggressive and ambitious personal style made him a number of enemies within the American forces, many of whom were suspicious of his finances and leadership. Cleared repeatedly in several court-martials, Arnold nevertheless began to resent the American military and Congressional leadership. In 1779, while enjoying command of the recently retaken city of Philadelphia, Arnold met and married Peggy Shippen, daughter of a Loyalist judge and skillful correspondent who knew precisely how to communicate with other Loyalists, regardless of battle lines.

It was this talent that supported Arnold over the next year, when he was secretly urged by British general Henry Clinton to acquire a high-level American post and share military secrets with the British. In August 1780, Arnold left Philadelphia and was given command of West Point, a position he immediately used to support his new loyalties to the British. Within two months, British spy Major John Andre (a former suitor to Peggy) was captured by Americans with documents detailing Arnold's betrayal. Arnold escaped to British-occupied New York and continued to serve the British until the end of the war. He died in 1801 in London. In the decades to follow, Arnold's story grew into one of near-mythic significance in the story of the creation of American independence. Portrayed as one of the greatest betrayals in history, Arnold's acts serve to emphasize not only the evils of treason but the complexities of the lives of the treasonous.

1785: The Supreme Executive Council orders the erection of an arsenal, which is eventually sited at 13th Street and Juniper Alley.

1808: The Diocese of Philadelphia is formed. Michael Egan is consecrated as the first bishop two years later.

1861: Oak Hall, Wanamaker and Brown's first department store, opens for business. Sales totaled $24.76 the first day.

April 9

The clouds of discrimination parted for some in the African-American community in Philadelphia on this date in 1816. Under the leadership of Richard Allen, Methodist minister and prominent member of the black community, the African Methodist Episcopal Church in America was formed. As early as 1787, Allen and friend Absalom Jones faced discrimination in the white-led St. George's Methodist Church. Denied their own pulpit and forced to worship in a segregated gallery, congregants sought to change church policy by staging a peaceful protest. While engaged in the simple act of praying in the white-only pews, members of Allen's Free African Society were ejected from the church. The organized mass departure of black congregants from St. George's that followed foreshadowed a larger movement within the black community away from white-led organizations to the creation of their own independent institutions.

In the aftermath of the St. George's protest, Jones chose an affiliation with the Protestant Episcopal Church, while Allen remained active with the Methodists and established the Bethel African Methodist Church in 1794, the first of its kind in the nation. In 1799, Allen was ordained as the church minister by the Bishop of the Methodist Episcopal Church. No longer reliant on white preachers, the church nevertheless continued to encounter prejudice and poor treatment within the Methodist Church. Recognizing that other black Methodist churches were also suffering, Allen called for a meeting in Philadelphia for the purpose of forming a new denomination.

Representatives from black churches in New Jersey, Delaware, and Maryland joined Allen to discuss the value of uniting to counter the discrimination. Together, they founded the world's first fully independent black denomination in the United States, the African Methodist Episcopal Church. After being turned down by another candidate, the A.M.E. offered Allen the position of Bishop, which he accepted. Throughout his lifetime, Allen continued to lead the black community in Philadelphia and beyond, standing as an advocate for slaves and working to end unfair and discriminatory laws. His legacy has continued through the work of the American Methodist Episcopal Church, which today includes more than two million members and seeks to end injustice and oppression in all areas of the world.

1755: William Russell Birch, engraver, enamel painter, and publisher in Warwickshire, England, is born. His *Views of Philadelphia* are known for documenting the Federal Period in the city. Birch died on August 7, 1834, in Philadelphia.

1934: The *Philadelphia Inquirer* newspaper announces it will absorb the *Public Ledger*, which closed after nearly a century in publication.

1951: The Philadelphia Home Show opens, featuring a variety of futuristic appliances, including a cooking range with a television built in and talking dishwashers.

April 10

Committing a crime in early Philadelphia could result in a variety of punishments, the most extreme being death. In cases of heinous crimes such as murder and kidnapping, execution by hanging was virtually guaranteed, but aggressive punishments like public whippings and lengthy imprisonments were still meted out for lesser crimes such as theft and adultery. Under these circumstances, Philadelphia's need for a place to simply segregate all convicted criminals resulted in the creation of dark, dirty, and notoriously inhumane prisons. Plans for a Walnut Street Gaol, or prison, were first enacted on this date in 1773 with the intent of alleviating the crowded conditions in the city's woefully inadequate city jail. After nearly two decades of providing minimal shelter and care for prisoners, Quaker reformers proposed a new system, brought about by enlarging the old Walnut Street Prison. The resulting method of confinement dramatically changed the way in which prisoners were incarcerated, subsequently influencing several generations of prison design.

As envisioned by Quaker reformers in 1790, the enlarged and improved prison served as the first true state "penitentiary," designed to enable prisoners the peace and solitude to properly meditate on their offenses and to feel fully remorseful, or penitent, for their crimes. Individual isolation cells, obstructed views of the outside world, and limited access to visitors were the primary hallmarks of what came to be known as the "Pennsylvania System." Instead of large, communal rooms with little supervision, inmates were held in private cells and given only minimal access to other people, usually only guards and wardens. Unlike earlier jails, prisoners were denied the opportunity to work, since it was decided that labor would only distract inmates from properly pondering their circumstances.

As worse crowding once again necessitated the construction of a new jail, the unique architectural design that grew out of theories enacted at Walnut Street resulted in the creation of a central hub surrounded by cell-block spokes. Prison officials from all over the world traveled to Philadelphia to learn about the "Pennsylvania System," fully realized with the construction of Eastern State Penitentiary in 1836. Unfortunately, the system proved to be even less humane than earlier prisons—isolation and confinement often resulting in desperation and suicide. Prison reformers once again sought to change the treatment of criminals, and the work-based "Auburn System," best realized in a New York prison, led the way into the twentieth-century penal system.

1792: The Delaware and Schuylkill Navigation Company is incorporated. They sponsored the first canal dig in the United States, hoping to connect the Delaware and Schuylkill rivers. Work was halted owing to financial difficulties after fifteen miles of canal were completed.

1816: The Second Bank of the United States is chartered by an Act of Congress.

1880: The last recorded duel is fought in Philadelphia, between William White, M.D., and Robert Adams, Jr.

April 11

By the time William Penn settled in Philadelphia, the area had been home to settlements of Swedish immigrants since 1638. Established under the leadership of Governor Johan Printz, who stood 7 feet tall and weighed over 300 pounds, New Sweden ranged from the falls of the Delaware at Trenton to the mouth of the Delaware Bay. Its capital city, called New Gottenberg, was built on present-day Tinicum Island, and the first Christian church in the region was built there in 1646.

In 1698, construction began on Gloria Dei Church in South Philadelphia. In continuous use since 1700, it is the second-oldest church building in the United States and the oldest church in Pennsylvania. Built primarily in the English style, it features a Swedish-style steeply sloped roof and a semicircular wall (the apse) that is also reminiscent of Swedish church architecture. The bell that hangs in the steeple was recast from a 1643 bell that was used originally at Tinicum. The grounds of the church feature a graveyard that has been in use since 1700. Among the prominent people buried there are the artist James Peale, Alexander Wilson, an authority on eastern birds who preceded Audubon, and General William Irvine, who served as a Congressman after the Revolution.

Designated as a National Historic Site in 1942, Gloria Dei celebrated its 300th anniversary on April 11, 1943. Ceremonies were attended by the Swedish minister to the United States. A chaplain of the Swedish Royal Navy preached the sermon, and there were readings from the church's Gustav Vasa Bible, printed in 1541. A few blocks from the church, the American Swedish Historical Museum was founded in 1926, and continues to preserve and promote Swedish-American history and culture.

1783: Congress officially declares the end of the War for American Independence.

1901: Stockholders in Philadelphia vote unanimously to abandon the Pennsylvania Canal, once a critical means of transporting goods and passengers across the state from Philadelphia to Pittsburgh.

1903: Newly elected mayor John Weaver announces an end to gambling protection by Philadelphia police and government.

1930: Composer Igor Stravinsky's stage ballet, *Le Sacre du Printemps*, has its American premiere in Philadelphia.

1950: Fire damages the old Metropolitan Opera House, site of Enrico Caruso opera performances in the early part of the twentieth century.

1989: The first-ever playoff goal scored by a goalie in hockey is achieved by the Flyers' Ron Hextall.

 April 12 

By the 1780s, there were only two hospitals serving residents of Philadelphia: the Philadelphia Hospital and the Pennsylvania Hospital. Together, these hospitals could not possibly care for all Philadelphians in need. To complicate matters, many poor and disadvantaged people were wary of hospitals. Some were too proud to ask for help, many could not afford treatment, and others erroneously believed that unwarranted experiments were being performed on patients. A means to address this situation and to improve public health in the city was conceived by influential citizens in the form of a dispensary. The Philadelphia Dispensary opened on April 12, 1786, in Strawberry Alley, and was the first of its kind in the United States.

A board of twelve managers oversaw six attending physicians and surgeons, as well as an apothecary, on staff. Four consulting physicians, including Dr. Benjamin Rush, were available to provide advice as needed. Their charitable work was originally funded by 361 contributors (among whom could be counted Benjamin Franklin); each lady or gentleman who paid one guinea annually would be entitled to have two patients under the care of the dispensary. In turn, needy individuals looking for medical assistance would have to seek help and obtain written permission from a contributor before receiving treatment from the dispensary. By allowing physicians to attend patients in the privacy of their own homes, more residents could receive treatment at much less expense to the public. Attending physicians also proved influential in spreading information about proper hygiene to families in need.

The dispensary quickly proved its usefulness as 719 patients were treated during its first year of operation. In 1801, the dispensary moved to a larger, permanent new home on Fifth Street between Walnut and Chestnut. The workload continued to increase, so that the managers instituted two additional dispensaries in 1816. By 1909, it was calculated that almost 1.5 million residents had been assisted by the Philadelphia Dispensary since its founding. Yet the Philadelphia Dispensary eventually declined in importance during the early twentieth century, when the number of hospitals in the city grew and the quality of available healthcare expanded greatly. It finally merged with Pennsylvania Hospital in 1922, because it could no longer provide adequate service to the public as a non-affiliated institution.

1787: The Philadelphia Free African Society is founded by Richard Allen and Absalom Jones. A nondenominational religious mutual aid society for the black community, it eventually grew into the African Church of Philadelphia.

1793: Rickett's Circus at 12th and Market streets opens. The circus featured equestrianship, wire dancers, and clowns.

1909: Shibe Park opens as 31,000 fans watch the Athletics defeat the Boston Red Sox, 8–1.

April 13

Outta Here! With these words, sports announcer Harry Kalas, who called the play-by-play for the Philadelphia Phillies from 1971 until his death on this date in 2009, spoke to the hearts and minds of every Philadelphia baseball fan. Famed for his smooth baritone voice and deep love of Philadelphia and the Phillies, Kalas graduated from the University of Iowa in 1959 and was immediately drafted, ultimately serving two years in the United States Army. His professional career began on the airwaves in Hawaii, where he served as sports director for radio station KGU, calling games for the University of Hawaii. In 1965, he left Hawaii for Houston, Texas, and had his Major League Baseball debut with the Astros. Alongside fellow sportscaster Gene Elston, Kalas called the first game ever played at the Astrodome on April 12, 1965. After just five years, Kalas left Texas and joined the broadcasting team for the Philadelphia Phillies, building a relationship that would continue for twenty-five years.

As he had in Houston, Kalas christened a new sports arena when he called the first Phillies game played at the newly completed Veterans Stadium on April 10, 1971, his first day on the job. Paired with By Saam and former player Richie Ashburn, Kalas developed a mellow, easygoing style frequently interrupted by flights of excitement in response to the plays he called. Initially reluctant to accept Kalas, fans ultimately came to love him, sharing a unique friendship with "Harry the K" grounded in a shared love of the city and the game. Kalas provided memorable descriptions of great Phillies victories, including Mike Schmidt's 500th home run in 1987 and their World Series win in 2008. Indeed, the fact that Kalas was not permitted to call the Phillies' World Series win in 1980 resulted in a successful petition drive to change the rules, allowing local announcers to broadcast from home radio stations. Voted Pennsylvania Sportscaster of the Year a remarkable eighteen times, Kalas was recognized for his achievements in 2002 when he received the Ford C. Frick Award from the National Baseball Hall of Fame, and again in 2004 when he was inducted into the Philadelphia Sports Hall of Fame.

On the morning of April 13, 2009, Kalas worked to prepare for regular season play against the Washington Nationals. Just hours before the game was to begin, Kalas collapsed in the press box, subsequently dying of heart disease. The team debated whether to play, but decided it would have been what Harry wanted; the Phillies went on to defeat the Nationals, 9–8. In a spontaneous show of love and remembrance, fans flocked to Citizens Bank Park to leave flowers and mementos at the base of the Mike Schmidt statue. A few days later Kalas was laid in state at the ballpark, and on April 18 was laid to rest at historic Laurel Hill Cemetery, overlooking the Schuylkill River. The voice has been silenced, but the memories will remain with Philadelphia fans forever.

1847: Waterworks engineer Frederick Graff dies.

1946: The Philadelphia Marriage License Bureau announces a record-breaking number of applications for marriage licenses received in one day: 191.

 # April 14 

The first official step toward institutionalizing the fight to abolish slavery occurred on this date in 1775. Quaker teacher Anthony Benezet, son of a French Huguenot family, called for the first meeting of the Society for the Relief of Free Negroes Unlawfully Held in Bondage, often called simply the Abolition Society. The first organization of its kind in the country, the Society chose as its primary task the defense of blacks and indigenous inhabitants claiming to be unlawfully enslaved. Benezet strongly challenged popular notions of black inferiority and supported education of both the freed and the enslaved. Though it met just four times over the next nine years, the society formed the foundation for the larger and more prominent Pennsylvania Society for Promoting the Abolition of Slavery and for the Relief of Free Negroes Unlawfully Held, also known as the Pennsylvania Abolition Society, which played a significant role in the state's progressive anti-slavery movement.

In addition to Benezet, nine prominent Philadelphia leaders and Quakers met on that day in 1775, including political pamphleteer Thomas Paine. Of the ten men, seven were Quakers who were acting on their belief that slave-owning was not consistent with Christian doctrine. By 1784, the mission of the Abolition Society evolved to include a direct goal of ending slavery, and the new Society was formed. Within three years, under the leadership of Benjamin Franklin and Benjamin Rush, the Pennsylvania Abolition Society worked to expand their membership to include notable Philadelphians of power and fame. During Franklin's term as President of the Society, the state's Abolition Act of 1780 was amended, prohibiting the transportation of enslaved women and young children out of Pennsylvania and ending the Port of Philadelphia's support of the slave shipping trade. In 1790, Franklin brought the issue of slavery to the federal government, which occupied Philadelphia as the Capital City.

Throughout the 1790s and beyond, the Pennsylvania Abolition Society worked to educate, heal, and defend the interests of freed black people. In partnership with the Free African Society and leaders Richard Allen and Absalom Jones, the PAS provided services including schools, vocational support, and social and community opportunities fostering good moral and ethical development. As the first quarter of the century ended, the loss of significant leadership and a growing anti-black sentiment in the city led to a reduction in the size and activity of the society. Other abolition societies benefited from their early legacy, and the goal of ending slavery was ultimately achieved in 1865. Today the Pennsylvania Abolition Society remains active, serving a primarily educational mission.

1835: The earliest rowing club contest between the Imps and the Blue Devil barge clubs is held.

1853: The District of Belmont is created. Within a year, the Consolidation of Philadelphia (February 2, 1854) put an end to its franchises.

April 15 

Philadelphia has been home to many notable sports arenas, but some have found a role in our history by serving as a place for more than athletic prowess. JFK Stadium, originally known as the Sesquicentennial Stadium when it opened on this date in 1926, hosted a significant number of sports teams and events, most notably the Philadelphia Eagles, the Liberty Bowl, and the Army-Navy Game. However, through the 1970s and 1980s, its use as a concert venue is what is most often remembered by Philadelphia's fans.

Designed by the architectural firm of Simon & Simon, the concrete, stone, and brick "horseshoe" open-air stadium was completed in time for the 1926 Sesquicentennial of the Declaration of Independence. Located at the bottom of Broad Street, the stadium was well-placed for visitors coming to the larger exposition. At its peak, the stadium accommodated more than 120,000 seats, including bleachers added later to the open end of the horseshoe. The Eagles played their first game there in 1936, but after just a few years moved to Shibe Park. In 1939, the stadium assumed the role of neutral territory in the decades-old rivalry between Army and Navy, formerly played at Penn's Franklin Field. The game, attracting thousands of cadets, midshipmen, and families, was played annually at JFK until 1979. Boxing, soccer, and track and field have all been featured on the field as well.

As a musical venue, the stadium attracted bands and performers from across the musical spectrum. The Beatles played Philadelphia in 1966, while acts such as the Who, Marvin Gaye, and Michael Jackson followed in the years after. JFK Stadium represented Philadelphia to the world on July 1985 as one of just two venues for Live Aid, a concert that raised millions of dollars for famine relief in Ethiopia, much of which ended up in the hands of a corrupt military junta. Broadcast worldwide, performers included Mick Jaggar, Madonna, and Phil Collins, who played in Philadelphia and Wembley Stadium in England on the same day. By the late 1980s, the stadium was crumbling and had acquired a reputation as distinctly dangerous, following the death and serious injuries of several fans. Less than five days after the Grateful Dead played there on July 7, 1989, Mayor Wilson Goode condemned the stadium, bringing to an end a unique Philadelphia venue. JFK was demolished in 1992, and the site is now part of the South Philadelphia Sports Complex.

1796: Charles-Maurice Tallyrand Perigord, one of the most influential of Napoleonic French diplomats, is made a member of the American Philosophical Society while living in exile in Philadelphia.

1945: Following his death on April 12 from a cerebral hemorrhage, President Franklin Delano Roosevelt's funeral train passes through Philadelphia on the way to the family home in Hyde Park, New York.

1959: Mayor Richardson Dilworth extinguishes the last gas-lit street-lamp in the city, ending a 123-year history.

April 16

The earliest seeds of great ballet in Philadelphia were sowed in early January 1962 by New York Ballet co-founder George Ballanchine and local protégée Barbara Weisberger, who first proposed the creation of a premier ballet school and company to the sponsors of Mrs. Weisberger's ballet school. Within ten months, a core of nineteen Weisberger-trained dancers formed the earliest incarnation of the Pennsylvania Ballet. Following a private performance in July 1963 at the home of Board President C. Colket Wilson III, an unprecedented grant of $295,000 to the fledgling company by the Ford Foundation in December 1963 solidified the future of the Ballanchine-inspired company. On this date in 1964, the first Philadelphia performance of the Pennsylvania Ballet was held at the Irvine Auditorium of University of Pennsylvania, initiating a long history of beauty and success on the stage and small screen.

The first public program included Balanchine's "Concerto Barocco" and "Pas de Dix" among others. When the first subscription series began in October 1964, the Ballet embarked on a creative path known for vibrant performances and a widely diverse repertoire featuring classical, modern, and experimental forms of ballet. Traveling throughout the country in the mid-1960s, the company built a reputation only enhanced by its pedigree and superb performances. In 1968, the company ended a hugely successful season by performing *The Nutcracker,* destined to become one of Philadelphia's most cherished holiday traditions. Appearances on television and landmark partnerships with other premier institutions, such as the Brooklyn Academy of Music, further established the Pennsylvania Ballet among the elite in the country.

Throughout the 1980s and 1990s, the Company continued to pursue excellence in performance and leadership. Under the guidance of now-legendary performers and masters such as Robert Rodham, Roy Keiser, Peter Martins, and Christopher d'Amboise, the Pennsylvania Ballet received numerous honors and acclaim, successfully premiering more than twenty new or rarely performed works. By expanding their mission to include outreach and education through the Pennsylvania Ballet II, the forty-dancer company continues today to influence the quality of dance performance throughout the nation, while representing the deep cultural and artistic roots of Philadelphia.

1927: William Cramp & Sons announces it is closing its shipbuilding facilities in Kensington. Founded in 1830, the 32-acre riverfront Cramp Yard was once the largest ship manufacturing yard in the country. The yard was temporarily reopened for the construction of submarines and other vessels during World War II.

1970: Secretary of the Interior Walter J. Hickel announces that he will halt construction of Interstate 95 until plans are made to create a national wildlife refuge. Tinicum National Wildlife Refuge near the Philadelphia International Airport was subsequently created by an act of Congress in 1972.

April 17

American victories in the early months of the Revolution were few and much valued. On this date in 1776, Captain John Barry, future "Father of the American Navy," met and overcame the British sloop *Edward* off the coast of Delaware while commanding his first American continental vessel, the *Lexington*. Though small, this first victory foretold of Barry's later successes and the eventual might of the United States Navy.

Barry was born in Ireland and immigrated to America as a young man, seeking success in the maritime trade. When war between England and America broke out, Barry volunteered his service to the Continental army under George Washington. In recognition of Barry's extensive captaining experience, he was given command of the newly renamed *Lexington.* Slipping through the British blockade in early April, Barry fought fiercely to overtake the *Edward,* and returned to Philadelphia where it was outfitted for the American fleet. The *Lexington* continued in service, sparring with the British blockade near Cape May. After the smaller cargo vessel *Nancy* ran aground while filled with black powder, Barry ordered her partly emptied under cover of darkness and then exploded using a time-delay fuse that surprised British seamen boarding the ship the next day. In pursuit of privateers and other British-held ships, the *Lexington* proved successful under Barry's command.

After relinquishing command of the *Lexington,* Barry went on to several other opportunities, proving his worth as both captain and strategist for the navy. After the war, Barry returned to private business, but was later chosen by Washington to lead the revived United States Navy. Barry pushed for the creation of the Department of the Navy, and established several training naval yards. His training and excellent preparation of the United States Navy into the early 1800s led to the nickname "Father of the American Navy." He served with distinction until his death in 1803, and is buried in St. Mary's Catholic Churchyard in Philadelphia.

1790: Benjamin Franklin dies. The funeral held four days later draws 20,000 people.

April 18

Much beloved and greatly admired for her elegance and beauty, few Philadelphians are as recognizable as Grace Kelly. Her marriage to Prince Rainier of Monaco on this date in 1956 seemed the culmination of her fairytale life. The first of two ceremonies, the civil service conducted on this date was held in front of a mere 80 guests in the elaborately designed throne room of the Prince's Palace of Monaco. The next day, more than 600 guests attended the religious rite at the St. Nicholas Cathedral, during a high mass celebrated by the Bishop of Monaco. Called by many "the wedding of the century," it marked the beginning of a twenty-six-year marriage known for its whirlwind romance and intense scrutiny.

Known primarily for her career in motion pictures, Kelly began her life the daughter of John "Jack" and Margaret Kelly in the East Falls neighborhood of Philadelphia. Her parents, both notable athletes and fairly driven in their own careers, were dismayed when Kelly announced her intention to pursue acting. She subsequently attended the American Academy of Dramatic Arts, where she launched an early career on stage and screen. Kelly ultimately received acclaim for her roles in *High Noon, Mugambo,* and *Dial M for Murder.* While leading the American delegation to the 1955 Cannes Film Festival, Kelly was introduced to Prince Rainier of Monaco. Apparently taken with her, he traveled to the United States, and within three days of meeting her family he had proposed.

Traditional in many ways, Rainier insisted that the Kellys pay a $2 million dowry, which they did. He also required that Grace quit acting and banned all screenings of her films in Monaco. Her final acting role, in *High Society,* was released in theaters the same year as her marriage. Their years together were marked by philanthropic efforts, as well as initiatives to improve the economy of Monaco, which relied heavily on gambling for its financial stability. Princess Grace established a number of charities, advocating for improved support of local artisans and aiding children in need. The Princess died following a stroke and automobile accident in September 1982. Aware at all times of the intense media scrutiny aimed at her, Princess Grace served as the perfect princess, starring as the lead in a real-life fairytale story.

1898: The city is declared free of typhoid following a three-month epidemic that resulted in the deaths of nearly 200 people.

1960: A Philadelphia-based record distributor said to have ties to disc jockey Dick Clark voluntarily agrees to end the use of payola to encourage record play on the radio.

1966: Philadelphia mayor James H. J. Tate unveils a $75 million plan to quadruple the size of Philadelphia International Airport. One-third of the money was for construction of a new jet-ready runway.

April 19 

The city of Philadelphia was thirsty. One of the first cities in the nation to enjoy running water, its demand for more led to the opening of the Fairmount Water Works on this date in 1819. Twenty years earlier, Benjamin Latrobe's classically designed water works located at Center Square began delivering clean water for drinking and bathing to a select group of taps distributed throughout the city. As the population of the city grew, demand for more clean water grew as well. Latrobe's young assistant, Frederick Graff first proposed the construction of a new water system, based on a reservoir and pumping house to be constructed at Faire Mount on the banks of the Schuylkill River. Beyond providing the water the city needed, the Works would also serve as the starting point of the largest municipal park in the world, Fairmount Park.

While serving as superintendent of the Center Square works, Graff learned of mistakes apparent in the design and implementation of the machinery, which proved very inefficient. Following his recommendation of the Faire Mount site, Graff was entrusted with the construction of a new works. In addition to the elaborately simple but beautifully designed pump house and its inner workings, the plan included the creation of a large reservoir. Within a few years, however, the new system was itself deemed inadequate. A dam was then constructed on the Schuylkill in order to power a series of paddle wheels to pump the water to the reservoir directly.

The new dam worked, and Graff continued to enjoy a forty-two-year career overseeing the works. During this time, the natural and landscaped beauty of the site drew tourists, inspiring the creation of a public park. Recognizing that changes in the quality of the water supply along the Schuylkill River would affect the health and well-being of the citizens, Graff and others pushed to create Fairmount Park in hopes of preserving green space along the Schuylkill River and limiting development of the riverbanks. Formally established in 1867, the park was ultimately unable to fully protect the city, and the Fairmount Water Works closed in 1911.

1813: Benjamin Rush dies.

1835: The Artists' Fund Society of Philadelphia is incorporated and conducted entirely by artists to benefit fellow artists.

Instead of employing optical magnification, an electron microscope bombards a tiny object with electrons in order to create a magnified image. Ernst Ruska made this discovery at the Berlin Technical University in the late 1920s, and he recognized that the implications were tremendous. Theoretically, an electron microscope would allow scientists to see items that were too small to be viewed by an optical microscope, which uses light for illumination. Ruska built the world's first electron microscope in 1931, yet it produced a magnification of only 400x—which was less than that produced by commercial optical microscopes of the time. Two years later, Ruska proved the viability of electron microscopes by constructing one that slightly exceeded the limitations of optical microscopes.

Over the next few years, scientists and corporations quickly took up the challenge to realize the potential of electron microscopy. An electron microscope built at the University of Toronto in 1939 achieved a magnification of 20,000x. But the real breakthrough was achieved later that same year by Vladimir Zworykin, a brilliant scientist and Russian émigré who worked for RCA in Camden, New Jersey. His electron microscope was demonstrated for the first time publicly on this date in 1940, to a group of scientists and researchers attending the closing session of the annual spring meeting of the American Philosophical Society in Philadelphia. The highlight of the demonstration was to show attendees electron microphotographs of the typhoid bacillus, *Streptococcus haemolyticus,* and of the whooping cough germ at 100,000x, an order of magnitude never before seen by the public.

The microscope weighed half a ton, stood more than ten feet tall, and was the first electron microscope to be built in the United States. RCA quickly capitalized on this breakthrough. Commercial versions of Zworykin's microscope took from six to eight months to build and cost $17,500 each, an investment well worth making to many in the industrial and medical fields, considering the research benefits to be gained from such a dramatic and powerful tool in the optical and chemical world. Zworkin's legacy is realized today in the ongoing development of electron microscopes, which can now reach a near-mythological magnification of 1,000,000x, a level of detail only dreamed of in years past.

1778: A state law is enacted declaring that all who voluntarily served the British King during the Revolution would be guilty of treason.

1862: The Cathedral of Saints Peter and Paul opens.

1897: Upon completion of its trolley bridge, the Fairmount Park Transportation Company begins operating its own trolley.

April 21

The biggest news story of the first part of the twentieth century was the sinking of the *Titanic* on April 14 and 15, 1912. Thousands of articles and books and several motion pictures were made about the disaster in ensuing years. Thought to be "practically unsinkable," the luxury liner was on its maiden voyage from England to the United States when it struck an iceberg in the north Atlantic and sank, with the loss of 2,227 passengers and crew. Many prominent Americans were lost on the *Titanic;* the Philadelphia area incurred its losses as well, most notably the deaths of George Dunton Widener and his son Harry Elkins Widener.

Son of P. A. B. Widener, believed to be the richest man in Philadelphia at the time, George Dunton Widener was a rich man himself, running a streetcar business in the city and engaging in a wide variety of charitable enterprises. George, his wife Eleanor, their son, Harry Elkins Widener, and their servants, Emily Geiger and Edwin Keeping, were returning to Philadelphia from Europe on the *Titanic.* On April 14, the Wideners hosted a dinner with Captain Smith and several socially prominent Pennsylvanians, including John B. Thayer, William Carter, and their wives. The gentlemen were still in the dining room when the ship hit the iceberg. George and Harry helped Eleanor, Miss Geiger, and other women into lifeboats but apparently chose not to attempt to board any themselves. Harry reportedly told William Carter "I think I'll stick to the big ship, Billy, and take a chance." Carter managed to board one of the last lifeboats to be launched.

Mrs. Widener and Miss Geiger survived, but the bodies of George and Harry were never recovered. For a time, the body of Edwin Keeping was mistaken for that of George Widener. On April 21, 1912, in her first public appearance since the disaster, Mrs. Widener and members of the family attended a memorial service at the Widener Memorial School, where her husband had addressed the student body prior to leaving on the trip to Europe. Later, Mrs. Widener donated $2 million to establish the Harry Elkins Widener Memorial Library at his alma mater, Harvard University. The Widener family maintains an elegant mausoleum at Laurel Hill Cemetery, where empty places mark the passing of two of Philadelphia's *Titanic* victims.

1895: The first Penn Relays are held in conjunction with the University of Pennsylvania's Spring Handicap Track and Field Games.

1898: Philadelphia Phillies' pitcher Bill Duggleby hits a grand slam on his first at bat.

1937: Twenty-eight sit-down strikers at Artcraft Silk Hosiery Mills forcibly take possession of the plant.

1950: A special grand jury investigating corruption in city offices names twenty-nine present and former city officials as takers of graft.

April 22

One of the most successful architects of Victorian-era Philadelphia, Frank Furness never attended college. Furness was born in 1839, the son of a prominent Unitarian minister whose home served as a stop on the Underground Railroad. In 1857, Furness was apprenticed to architect John Fraser (designer of the Union League building) and then traveled to New York, where he studied with Richard Morris Hunt. Hunt taught him medieval form, which Furness used throughout most of his career. After serving in the Union cavalry during the Civil War and earning the Medal of Honor, Furness returned to Philadelphia where he received his first commission for a new section of Germantown, largely because of his highly respected family connections and his war record. He would go on to become one of Philadelphia's most proficient architects.

In 1872, Furness and his partner, George Hewitt, reworked a version of their design for the Masonic Temple, a commission they failed to secure, and used it to win approval to design and build the new Academy of the Fine Arts on Broad and Cherry streets. The original Academy building on 10th and Chestnut had been destroyed by fire in 1846. Given a great deal of autonomy in the design, Furness and Hewitt created a spectacular structure, incorporating features of Gothic and Second Empire design along with the more modern approach of leaving structural elements like iron girders visible in the interior. The building is richly colored, with rose crystal marble and Jersey granite. At its dedication, on this date in 1876, the chairman of the building committee noted with pride that "the building is fireproof . . . incombustible throughout. . . . we may feel certain that the works placed within our walls will be as safe as human care can render them."

Furness and Hewitt dissolved their partnership and became rivals in Philadelphia's architectural community. Furness went on to build more than 300 structures in the city, among them the library at the University of Pennsylvania, the First Unitarian Church, and the Thomas Hockley house. Many of his buildings would end up being demolished when Victorian style went out of fashion. In the mid twentieth century, his reputation was revived, and the Philadelphia Museum of Art mounted a retrospective of his work in 1973. Many of the surviving examples of his work have been magnificently restored, returning to the city some of its finest and most interesting architectural treasures.

1793: George Washington attends Rickett's Circus at Twelfth and Market streets.

1865: President Abraham Lincoln's funeral cortege passes through the city.

April 23

Pennsylvania's long history as a place of big industry and dramatic business advances often places it at the center of the labor movement. Philadelphia played its own role in the emotionally charged and seemingly endless debate over affirmative action and the use of quotas in hiring practices. As first realized by President Franklin Delano Roosevelt in Executive Order no. 8802 in 1941, the protection of peoples of all races, creeds, colors, and national origins has served as a lightning rod in discussions about fair employment policies. In 1968, the City of Philadelphia proposed the so-called Philadelphia Plan. Limited to the local construction industry and government-sponsored projects, the plan was an attempt to break through membership practices of area construction unions which were overwhelmingly white. Based on demographic studies conducted on the local construction industry, an ultimate goal of 26 percent minority representation in the labor force was established. In 1968, the plan was declared illegal because it seemed to establish quotas, outlawed in the Civil Rights Act of 1964.

However, following a political misstep within the Nixon Administration, the Philadelphia Plan was revived and revised, with support from President Nixon. Initially limited to enforcement on a "pilot" basis in Philadelphia only, the new plan was soon challenged in court. Once again, the quota component was questioned, but in March 1970 Federal District Court Judge Charles R. Weiner found that the plan did not, in fact, violate the earlier Act. A second court challenge from an association of eighty Philadelphia contractors resulted in the April 23, 1971, decision to uphold the plan, declaring it a "valid executive action designed to remedy the perceived evil that minority tradesmen have not been included in the labor pool available for performance of construction projects in which the Federal Government has a cost and performance interest."

In the years since, many have attempted to overturn or otherwise reduce government intervention in fair hiring practices. In each case, however, the earlier executive order has been preserved, and all subsequent presidents have either issued similar orders or continued that of the previous administration. In 1992, Congress amended the Civil Rights Act of 1964 to include protection of affirmative action plans. The Philadelphia Plan remains in effect today, continuing to influence the complex debate over employment rights and anti-discriminatory legislation.

1772: The Society of the Sons of Saint George is founded to assist Englishmen in distress.

1865: Lincoln's body is laid in state at Independence Hall, where an estimated 300,000 people (half the city's residents) come to pay their respects.

1959: During a meeting held in Philadelphia, the National Football League agrees to establish the first-ever noncontributory player benefit plan. The plan gave immediate protection to all active players on the twelve clubs, also paying undefined monthly benefits to former players aged 65 and over.

April 24

In a city known for controversy and conflict, few stories have drawn as much international attention as the murder of police officer Daniel Faulkner and the man tried and convicted for that murder, Mumia Abu-Jamal. Born Wesley Cook on this date in 1954, Abu-Jamal was sentenced to death for the shooting of Faulkner near the intersection of 13th and Locust streets. A journalist and radio personality known for his affiliation with the Black Panther Party and the MOVE family led by John Africa, Abu-Jamal has become a lightning rod for communities as diverse as anti–death penalty activists and the Fraternal Order of Police.

Though versions of the actual events differ, there is little doubt that Faulkner, a seven-year veteran of the police force, was shot and killed during a traffic stop on December 9, 1981. The stopped car belonged to William Cooper, Abu-Jamal's younger brother. While some witnesses placed Abu-Jamal nearby and claimed to have seen him running away after being wounded by Faulkner, others would testify that a second, unidentified man was involved and that Abu-Jamal was an innocent bystander, despite the fact that a .38 revolver belonging to Abu-Jamal, with spent cartridges, was retrieved at the scene. During the trial that followed, prosecutors claimed a hospital-bed confession from Abu-Jamal proved his guilt. Abu-Jamal claimed his public defender was biased, as was the judge; he was denied the right to defend himself or use MOVE leader John Africa as counsel when Judge Albert F. Sabo declared that Abu-Jamal was disruptive to the proceedings. A jury of two black and ten white jurors delivered a unanimous verdict of guilty after less than three hours of deliberations, and Abu-Jamal was subsequently sentenced to death.

In the years that followed, Abu-Jamal achieved national fame as an outspoken activist and writer. Through frequent appeals to courts as high as the United States Supreme Court, Abu-Jamal and his supporters have argued that his trial was not fair, that he is innocent, and that the death penalty is inhumane. Garnering supporters throughout the world and among celebrities and politicians, Abu-Jamal has succeeded in having his death sentence overturned, though his conviction stands. The family and friends of Daniel Faulkner have also continued to fight in his memory, demanding justice and an end to what is perceived by many as the aggrandizement of a convicted murderer.

1767: The first American-written tragedy, Thomas Godfrey, Jr.'s *The Prince of Parthia,* is performed at Southwark Theater on Cedar Street west of 4th Street.

1824: The first concert of the Musical Fund Society is performed at Washington Hall, Third above Spruce Street.

April 25

In the late 1970s the Philadelphia Phillies wanted something that would entertain children and bring families to the games. Earlier, a pair of mascots dressed in colonial garb was introduced during the Bicentennial. "Philadelphia Phil" and "Philadelphia Phillis" were not adequately entertaining, and considered to be too mild a representation for the team known for its passionate fans. The team hired the firm of Harrison-Erickson of New York, the creators of famed Muppet Miss Piggy, to design a costume for a Phillies mascot. At a cost of just $3,900, the costume was provided without copyrights. Less than five years later, the Phillies would pay Harrison-Erikson a quarter of a million dollars to acquire the rights. On April 25, 1978, the Phillie Phanatic made his debut at Veterans Stadium and it was love at first sight for Phillies fans.

The electric green, furry, and feathered character with a big belly, long snout, and curled tongue is allegedly a native of the Galapagos Islands. Riding into the stadium on an ATV, his goal in every game is to delight the fans and put the opposing team off its stride. Whether belly-bumping the umpire, shooting hot dogs with mustard into the stands, dancing on the top of the dugout, taking a dramatic pratfall, or mocking the batting stances of the other team's star hitters, the Phanatic makes even a dull game at the ballpark an experience. From 1978 to 1993, the man in the Phanatic suit was Dave Raymond, who was an intern in the Phillies home office before he got the call to greatness. Raymond invented classic routines and dances for the Phanatic, and helped make him one of the best-known sports mascots in the world.

The Phanatic has been involved in some controversy. When the Los Angeles Dodgers came to town in 1998, the Phanatic ran over a dummy dressed in manager Tommy Lasorda's uniform again and again with his ATV. Tommy complained to the Phillies that children would get the wrong impression from the Phanatic's antics. The next time the Dodgers came to Philadelphia, Lasorda confronted the Phanatic and body-slammed him to the turf on national television. In 2009, when the mascot-free Yankees played Philadelphia in the World Series, the *New York Post* concluded that "the day the Phanatic made his first appearance, Philadelphia lost its last ounce of respectability." For the Phanatic and his fans, that's just the point.

1798: Gilbert Fox first performs Joseph Hopkinson's "Hail Columbia" at the Chestnut Street Theater.

1831: Matthias Baldwin runs a miniature locomotive that seats just four passengers at the Peale Museum.

April 26

The grace and beauty of the natural world as found in America were depicted at their finest in the works of John James Audubon. Born on this date in 1785 in Saint Dominique (now Haiti), he was an illegitimate son to a French naval officer. Introduced to the joys of bird watching and observing nature by his father, Audubon later conducted the first known bird-banding effort in America. As a young entrepreneur, he owned several businesses in Kentucky and spent countless hours sketching birds and their environments before successfully publishing his *Birds of America* in 1827. Unlike any previous catalog of American wildlife, Audubon's detailed prints placed the species in lifelike and lively settings, establishing a new and unparalleled standard.

Upon his arrival in New York City at the age of eighteen, Audubon contracted yellow fever and was nursed back to health by a Quaker family, who taught him to speak English. They helped him travel to Mill Grove, near Philadelphia, where he settled on family-owned land and met and married neighbor Lucy Bakewell. Mill Grove was eventually sold by Audubon so that he could move to Kentucky, where he established a dry goods business. When not working, however, he devoted his time to walking in the woods and sketching the birds he found there. He set as his personal goal the documentation of all American species of birds, and the eventual publication of a fully illustrated catalog. Traveling to Philadelphia in 1824 in hopes of acquiring sponsorship for his publication, he was turned away by experts at the Academy of Natural Sciences, with whom he had an outstanding conflict. Audubon eventually turned to supporters in Britain for the backing to publish his grand work.

With letters of introduction in hand, Audubon arrived in England in 1826. The response was electric, as many in England became fascinated with his images of backwoods America. At a cost of more than $115,000 (approximately $2 million today) the folio was produced. Consisting of 435 hand-colored prints and measuring 39 inches by 26 inches, the volumes were in great demand. Returning to America and a new home in Manhattan, Audubon continued his work for several years and produced a text to supplement his *Birds of America*, and also published a volume on mammals. He died at the age of sixty-five in 1851. Reflecting the significance of his seminal work, a copy of *Birds of America* holds the record for the single highest price paid for a book at auction when it sold for more than $8 million in March 2000.

1918: Fearing anti-American conspiracies, Superintendent of Police William B. Mills bans public meetings in the German language.

1942: Bobby Rydell is born in Philadelphia. A teen idol and still one of the most popular performers of the early 1960s, Rydell inspired the use of the name "Rydell High School" in the film and Broadway musical *Grease*.

1976: The Pennsylvania Academy of the Fine Arts reopens following a $4.3 million restoration.

 April 27 

Unquestionably one of the greatest sports cities in the nation, Philadelphia has often been the birthplace of significant advances in both amateur and professional sports competitions. In the history of track and field, the Penn Relays hold a special place. First run in 1895 as part of the University of Pennsylvania's Spring Handicap Track and Field Games, the Relays are the country's longest-running track meet. In the last century, the meet evolved into the premier event for high school and college-level competition, serving as a proving ground for countless athletes, many of whom have gone on to represent their sports in the World Championships and the Olympics.

In 1893, in hopes of increasing interest in track and field, Penn struck upon the idea of a four-man relay, and invited ivy-league rival Princeton University to compete. Two years later, the organized event drew nearly 5,000 spectators to the newly completed Franklin Field. Built without permanent grandstands or locker rooms, the field was rimmed by lines of festive tents. This tradition continued into the twentieth century, giving the Relays the nickname of "Carnival." In the years that followed, the meet grew in popularity, drawing a growing number of track and field fans and participants. In 1903, the classic horseshoe-shaped grandstand was completed, making Franklin Field the first permanent college stadium in the country. Each year new competitions were added, including varying relay distances, sprints, hurdles, and field events like the long jump and pole vault.

The Relays became an international event as early as 1914, when a team from Oxford joined the competition. Men continued to dominate the events, with the first women participating in 1962. It would not be until this date in 1978 that women athletes were given an entire day to compete, resulting in a three-day event. In recent years, corporate sponsorship has been sought to better defray the costs to colleges and high schools to attend the event, and over 20,000 athletes each year. A significant part of Philadelphia's competitive landscape, the Penn Relays provide a unique opportunity for some of the finest young athletes in the world to meet and compete at the moment when they can achieve their greatest success.

1861: Wanamaker and Brown run their first advertisement in the *Public Ledger.* On the same date in 1978, a final agreement bid of $60 million is announced by Carter Hawley Hale Stores for the purchase of John Wanamaker and Company and the Wanamaker Department Stores. Carter Hawley Hale subsequently invested an additional $80 million in updates and improvements on the stores. Less than ten years later, the stores were sold again to Woodward & Lothrop.

1941: Max "Boo-Boo" Hoff, the city's most infamous bootlegger kingpin, dies.

1963: A new transit plan is announced by the city; it is the beginning of the Southeastern Pennsylvania Transportation Authority, which continues to run the city's transit system.

 April 28

The world of national politics was turned on its head on this date in 2009, when Senator Arlen Specter announced he was switching parties after forty-four years as an elected Republican. By doing so, he brought the Democratic Party just one vote shy of a filibuster-proof United States Senate for the first time since 1979. Born in Kansas but educated at the University of Pennsylvania and Yale University, Specter was a registered Democrat when he ran for and won his first political office as Philadelphia's District Attorney in 1965. After serving the city for two terms, Specter launched two failed campaigns for the United States Senate and Pennsylvania governor, in 1976 and 1978. He was finally elected to the United States Senate as a part of the Reagan Big Tent in 1980, becoming one of the most influential members of Congress with a reputation for moderate perspectives. After nearly 30 years as a senator, Specter rejoined the Democratic Party after facing certain defeat during the 2010 election when a majority of angry constituents protested his support for the landmark Democratic health care bill pending throughout 2009 in Congress. Even so, the eighty-year-old Specter lost the Democratic primary to contender Joe Sestak, effectively ending his political career.

Though controversial, Specter's recent activities are not the first in which his role is particularly notable. As a young lawyer known for his legal acumen, Specter worked for the Warren Commission, charged by Congress with investigating the assassination of President John F. Kennedy. Specter is known for his work with the commission primarily because of his authorship of the so-called single bullet theory, which concluded that both Kennedy and Texas governor John Connally were wounded by a single bullet, negating the possibility of a second shooter. As a senator, Specter is known for right-leaning views on issues like crime, the death penalty, and national security. However, his record shows that he has often voted in opposition to his party in instances involving illegal immigration, environmentalism, and other issues.

In recent years, Specter experienced a drop in popularity among Pennsylvania's Republicans but was still favored by nearly seven points among Democrats in a February 2009 poll. His support for an enormous federal economic stimulus package on top of a voting record frequently at odds with his own party caused support among many of his constituents to waver, ultimately ending in his loss in the 2010 primary.

1941: Barry Sharpless, Nobel Prize winner in chemistry, is born in Philadelphia.

1997: President Bill Clinton addresses the President's Summit for America's Future in Philadelphia.

April 29

Wild rumors gripped the Italian immigrant neighborhood around East Passyunk Avenue. Strange illnesses and a growing number of grieving widows inspired talk of betrayal and greed. Indeed, the case that would later be uncovered remains one of Philadelphia's most scandalous and intriguing crime sprees. By the time the investigation ended and the trial was over, cousins Herman and Paul Petrillo and fifteen additional suspects were believed to be responsible for the deaths of at least twenty known victims. The weapon of choice? Arsenic, delivered in a "love potion" that proved anything but loving.

Herman Petrillo and his cousin Paul arrived in Philadelphia in 1910, and soon established themselves as legitimate businessmen. Paul was a tailor and Herman made pasta. With the crash of the Stock Market and the resulting Great Depression, the two men were drawn to less savory professions. Herman, who already knew a bit about counterfeiting, began selling the fake bills and engaging in loans. Paul sold insurance policies, but often only to the sick or dying, surreptitiously putting himself down as benefactor. In 1938, Herman was the target of an undercover investigation by the Secret Service for his counterfeiting when suspicions arose that he was involved in something more lethal. While the Secret Service focused on a deal Petrillo attempted to make for counterfeit bills in exchange for a "hit" on a local man, a city Assistant District Attorney investigated the mysterious death of Ferdinando Alfonsi. It was soon determined that Alfonsi had died of arsenic poisoning, and that Herman and Paul Petrillo were directly involved.

The investigation that followed uncovered a remarkable story. Paul Petrillo and faith healer Morris Bolber formed a scheme whereby Petrillo would sell insurance policies to women, who would then be persuaded to use an arsenic-laced potion to kill their husbands. They invited Herman to help them. All told, twenty men died in the scheme. The women, who were given the nickname "poison widows" by the local press, varied widely in their expressions of guilt, some claiming not to have known the true nature of the potion. Exhumations proved the extent of the poisoning, and in February a grand jury indicted the Petrillos, Alfonsi's wife Stella, and a second widow, Maria Favato. After Herman and Paul were sentenced to death in March 1939, Bolber and Favato pled guilty and received life sentences. On this date in 1939, Herman Petrillo came clean and implicated himself and a dozen others, mostly widows, in the scheme. All told, the poison ring netted $100,000, and remains to this day responsible for one of the most sensational crime sprees in the city's history.

1747: Franklin writes to Peter Collinson about his chagrin for not yet discovering anything useful in his electrical experiments.

1961: The USS *Kitty Hawk* carrier is commissioned at the Philadelphia Navy Yard.

1970: New York City mayor John Lindsay supports draft resisters at a rally on the campus of the University of Pennsylvania.

April 30

As early as 1891 Rachel Wedell, the daughter of a Dutch immigrant, operated a successful dress shop at 45 North Eighth Street whose specialty was the custom decoration of ladies hats. Joined by her two brothers, Samuel and Jacob Lit, the newly named Lit Brothers Store soon moved to the corner of Eighth and Market in 1893 and expanded the business to include linens and other items for the home. By the turn of the century, Lit Brothers was a complete-service department store. Adding properties surrounding its original Market Street location, Lit Brothers grew to 1 million square feet and in 1907 the ornate Victorian cast-iron facade of the building at 701-707 Market Street was completed. Featuring detailed Italianate arches, the cream-colored iron and stone building was designed by the prominent Philadelphia architect Charles Autenrieth. Above the main entrance, a sign read "Hats Trimmed Free of Charge," reflecting Rachel's signature service.

The Market Street East area was the home to competing Philadelphia department stores for many years. Lit Brothers, Gimbels, and Strawbridge and Clothier each tried to entice customers with special services and attractions. All the department stores owned and operated radio stations beginning in the 1920s, which advertised their wares. Special Christmas displays were also designed to bring families into the stores and create Christmas traditions. At Lit Brothers, an enchanted colonial village was displayed every holiday season from 1962 to 1975. The village was an animated three-quarters-scale representation of eighteen scenes of colonial-era businesses, among them a bakery and a blacksmith shop preparing for the Christmas celebration. The enchanted colonial village was restored and is now on display at the Please Touch Museum in Fairmount Park.

The Lit family sold the business in 1928, but Lit Brothers continued to operate as a department store until changes in the retail market and the decline of Center City retail business forced it into bankruptcy. The store closed on April 30, 1977, and remained vacant for more than seven years. As the building deteriorated, the city contemplated demolition, but a community group organized to save the historic property, which was considered significant because of its cast-iron facade. In a victory for preservationists and after a long battle, the building was renovated and reopened in 1986 as a bank headquarters with retail shops, forming part of the revitalization of the Market Street East shopping district. Lit Brothers Department Store was placed on the national register of historic buildings in 1987.

1887: The first baseball grounds for the Philadelphia Baseball Club (the Philadelphia Phillies) opens at Broad and Lehigh streets to more than 18,000 spectators.

1902: Eight young cigar-factory workers are killed at Tenth and Washington Avenue in a panic caused by false cries of "fire."

1942: The *Philadelphia Herold,* a German-language newspaper, is charged with sedition for publishing anti-war propaganda and barred from using the United States Post Office to mail their publication.

Without question, the assassination of President Abraham Lincoln generated a deeply felt reaction in all who read the first accounts published in hundreds of local newspapers on the morning of April 15, 1865. Whether Northern or Southern, the shocking event evoked unimaginable worries and fears. Public memorials in the form of spontaneous gatherings and displays of mourning drapery and flags helped citizens throughout the country come to terms with the nation's loss. Philadelphia played a special role in the public's grief, as Lincoln's body lay in state in Independence Hall while thousands paid their respects. Sydney George Fisher, author, diarist, and member of the Philadelphia Republican elite, recorded his own reactions and observations to the news in his daily journal, published in 1967 as *A Philadelphia Perspective: The Diary of Sydney George Fisher.*

April 15, 1865

Calamitous news indeed this morning and a sad interruption to the jovial hopes inspired by late events. The national exultation at the prospects of peace & union has been suddenly converted into alarm & grief. Mr. Lincoln and Mr. Seward have been assassinated. Mr. Lincoln is dead and Mr. Seward, it is supposed, mortally wounded. This morning, about 8 o'clock, Sydney knocked at my dressing room door, "Father," he said, "Lincoln is shot." "Nonsense, child how did you hear that?" "It is true, Cornelius heard it at the village. He was shot because he tried to shoot Seward." I was bathing. Bet soon came to the door & said that Cornelius had brought the news from the village that the President had been killed, adding that she thought the story probable enough as he went about everywhere, with the utmost confidence, alone. She had sent to the village for the paper, as ours is not delivered before 11 o'clock. In a little while, when I was half dressed, she brought the paper & read to me, half crying & in a tremulous voice, the sad and terrible story.

I felt for some time a mere dull & stupefied sense of calamity. What disasters, what widespread misfortune may these events produce. A vague feeling of coming ill & real sorrow for Mr. Lincoln, deprived me of the power to think & reason on the subject. I felt as tho I had lost a personal friend, for indeed I have & so has every honest man in the country. . . . His death is a terrible loss to the country, perhaps even a greater loss to the South than to the North, for Mr. Lincoln's humanity & kindness of heart stood between them and the party of the North who urge measures of vengeance & severity. The southern people have murdered their best friend, as they are likely to find ere long.

April 17, 1865

Drove to town with Bet. Festoons of black cloth hanging from the windows of almost every house, shutters closed, flags in all directions with black streamers, portraits of Lincoln draped in crepe in hundreds of windows. The city quiet & has been, except the attempted attack on the Age office, which the police prevented. The windows of the houses of leading Democrats all bowed.

April 24, 1865

The paper full of accounts of the reception of Mr. Lincoln's remains. Windows closed, 30,000 people at the station when the train arrived, a great procession, appropriate ceremonies at the Hall, guards everywhere to preserve order, and a file of people that reached almost to the Schuylkill going in turn to look at his face. This began at 6 o'clock yesterday & continued till evening, thousands waiting patiently for hours.

May

May 1

Like so many other large cities in the late nineteenth century, Philadelphia attracted a wide range of ethnicities and cultures in the form of newly arrived immigrant populations. New immigrants from southern Europe, many from Italy, began to make their mark on Philadelphia and its neighborhoods. South Philadelphia, Germantown, Tacony, and West Philadelphia are but a few of the places where Italians made a home for themselves on the streets of the city. On this date in 1948, local citizens delivered to Pope Pius XII a scroll thanking him for his assistance in defeating fascism in Italy. It was a clear representation of a deep-rooted connection felt by many Americans of Italian descent in Philadelphia. Home was found in two places: Italy and the city that welcomed them as immigrants a generation earlier.

As early as the late 1600s, Italians lived and worked in Philadelphia. Newspaper advertisements from the mid-1750s suggest Italian-American professionals were working in fields such as medicine and music. However, it was not until the 1860s that the largest and most established community of Italian immigrants in South Philadelphia truly blossomed. Drawn by the promise of work and better pay, thousands of men, women, and children left southern Italy and arrived through the immigration station located on the Delaware River at Washington Avenue. Settling within proximity to other family members and folk from their hometowns, these new arrivals established businesses and cultural and social organizations such as churches and beneficence societies. Many individuals and organizations maintained their Italian connections, especially to the religious and cultural leadership in Italy.

Over time, and against many odds, Americans of Italian descent in Philadelphia rose to prominence within political, social, and cultural circles. The Italian fascist movement led by Benito Mussolini in the 1920s further complicated the relationship between these Americans and other Americans concerned about the seemingly conflicted loyalties within the Italian-American community. Although some were attracted by the "Italy first" message from the fascists in Italy, the patriotism felt by many in the Italian communities toward their adopted homeland was ultimately stronger than the pull of a long-past history. Today, Americans of Italian ethnicity play a proud part in Philadelphia's vibrant and manifold environment.

1900: More than 3,000 workers strike in Philadelphia, demanding an eight-hour workday.

1907: All-American singer Kate Smith is born in Greenville, Virginia. Though not a native Philadelphian, Smith's rendition of Irving Berlin's "God Bless America" is associated with the Philadelphia Flyers, who believed they would win any game she opened in song. Smith died on June 17, 1986.

May 2

The power of a single vote is nothing when compared with that of forty thousand voters. It was knowledge of this, as well as lingering prejudice and fear of a potential power shift throughout the state that led to significant changes during Pennsylvania's third State Constitutional Convention, convened on this date in 1837. Known for its overall tolerance of diverse communities including a population of more than fifty thousand free blacks, Pennsylvania was nevertheless in a state of great conflict as the mid nineteenth century approached. Rapid growth, increased immigration, and economic competition resulted in a rise in racial and ethnic tensions. Many whites feared the possibility that blacks within the state might consolidate their power through voting blocks or even violence, and believed the only solution was to change the state constitution in support of white voters. This was necessary because nearly fifty years after the Constitution of 1790 was ratified, it remained entirely unclear whether free blacks even had the right to vote.

As is often the case, the state constitution enacted in 1790 used vague language to define those eligible to vote. They were to be freemen over the age of twenty-one who were state residents for at least two years and paid taxes within six months of the election. The debate, never fully resolved, centered on the definition of "freemen," with some holding that the term applied to any man who was free, while others asserted it applied to whites only. The ability of black men to vote varied widely throughout the state, since some counties fully enfranchised free black men. In Philadelphia, however, a full interpretation of the law was irrelevant, since it was clear in the African-American community that it would be a dangerous folly to even attempt to vote in a city where white animosity against them ran high.

As the convention began, limiting the vote to white men was a key point of debate. Some members of the convention arrived with the immediate intention of categorically disfranchising all free black men. Abolitionists in Philadelphia and Pittsburgh submitted petitions to reverse this trend, but to no avail. During summer break, opponents of black suffrage raised fears throughout the state's white population, describing a future in which hundreds of thousands of supporters might flock to Pennsylvania, the result being a rise in crime and loss of white power in political and economic circles. Ultimately, the new constitution was adopted and ratified in November 1838 by white voters in the state. It would remain to the 15th Amendment to the United States Constitution to reverse the work of the 1838 Constitution, granting all eligible black men equal voting rights in the state once again.

1799: Construction on Schuylkill Water Works begins.

1837: The first convention of the American Institute of Architects is held in the Academy of Fine Arts.

 May 3 

On this date in 1957 John Kennedy, the first African-American to wear a Philadelphia Phillies uniform, played his last game with the team just eleven days after his major league debut at Roosevelt Stadium in Brooklyn. With a record of five games and two at-bats, Kennedy's professional career was too short to be statistically significant. However, his role in the story of desegregation of Philadelphia baseball is unmatched. Ten years earlier, Jackie Robinson broke through the color barrier as a player for the Brooklyn Dodgers. At the time, the all-white Phillies stood at the forefront of public prejudice against black players, the club's manager going so far as to publicly taunt Robinson during play. This dark history was rectified ten years later to the day, when Kennedy's place on the team marked the moment when the Phillies finally joined the rest of the National League in integrating America's game.

Kennedy was born in Jacksonville, Florida, in 1926, where he fell in love with the game of baseball, playing neighborhood stickball and attending as many local games as possible. After college he joined a local baseball league, where his skill on the field was duly noted by scouts for the Winnipeg Buffaloes. Kennedy played shortstop in Canada for several years before joining several teams in the Negro American League. In 1956, Kennedy was invited by the Phillies to work out at spring training in Clearwater, Florida. Living under the remnants of segregation, Kennedy roomed by himself and often ate alone in black-only restaurants. Ultimately, the team signed him, but held off putting him into play until the following season. At the time, Kennedy claimed to be just twenty-one years old; in fact, he was nearing thirty. Chico Fernandez, a black Cuban player signed on after Kennedy, was noticeably younger and was selected to play on opening day.

When Fernandez and Kennedy arrived in Philadelphia for the start of the 1957 season, they were hailed as heroes by many Philadelphians, including many African-Americans desperate to see the game integrated in Philadelphia as it was elsewhere. Overshadowed by Fernandez, Kennedy was soon released by the team. After several years of minor league play, he left the sport to work as a newspaper distributor in Florida. In his late 50s, Kennedy joined a local city baseball league and continued to play his favorite game up to the age of 70. He died, at the age of 71, on April 27, 1998. Gone and forgotten by most, Kennedy's legacy to the city is one of strength, commitment, and love of the game against all odds.

1826: The cornerstone of the Philadelphia Arcade is laid. Completed in September 1827, the grand building on Chestnut between Sixth and Seventh streets featured galleries, a museum, and shops. It was demolished and replaced with a row of modern stores in 1863.

1899: The Triangle Clothing store at 13th and Ridge is consumed by fire. Within one hour, $1.2 million worth of property is destroyed. A documentary film, released in 1903, was made of the fire as it happened.

May 4

The city of Philadelphia is known for its many arts and music institutions. Few, however, are devoted to a single composer or playwright. The Savoy Opera Company, which debuted on this date in 1901, remains the oldest amateur theater company in the nation devoted to the works of one collaborative team, the English operetta masters Gilbert and Sullivan. Following a European tour that included a trip to England and visits to London theaters featuring the immensely popular operettas, Philadelphia doctor Alfred Reginald Allen returned home committed to presenting the operas as they were always intended. Recruiting volunteer performers from among his friends, Allen staged Gilbert and Sullivan's second collaboration, *Trial By Jury*, to great success.

Beginning in the 1870s, librettist W. S. Gilbert and composer Arthur Sullivan enjoyed immense popularity in England and America. At the time of Allen's travel to England, it was estimated that nearly one hundred different productions of *H.M.S. Pinafore* were staged in America, many of them radically altered to appeal to American colloquialisms and local comedic tastes. Allen viewed this as a tragic circumstance demanding action. He assumed the role of conductor and recruited his sister and her friends to manage the first production, staffed entirely by volunteers. After their initial success, additional performances were staged in December 1901 at St. James Hall in West Philadelphia. A labor of love, the performances received many accolades and the company's reputation soon grew.

The Savoy Opera Company continues to offer yearly productions of Gilbert and Sullivan classics, and over the years has featured performers such as Nelson Eddy, Metropolitan Opera soprano Margaret Harshaw, and Broadway star Wilbur Evans. Sponsored by the School of Music of the University of Pennsylvania, proceeds from the all-volunteer performances are given to the school's Alfred Reginald Allen Memorial Fund, which supports the acquisition of books and scores for the university's music library. A true gem among the city's arts community, the Savoy Opera Company holds a special place in Philadelphia's musical heart.

1918: In response to growing anti-German sentiment in the city, the *Philadelphia Morning Gazette* announces it will no longer be printed in German, but in English only. In the late 1700s, nearly one-third of all Pennsylvanians were of German descent.

1978: After a two-year standoff over sanitation and crowding issues, members of the MOVE radical political group surrender to Philadelphia police. Ostensibly a back-to-nature group, MOVE would inspire conflicts that plagued the city for nearly a decade.

May 5

Among the pantheon of American symbols of independence, few hold a place as high or as broadly meaningful as the Liberty Bell. In 1751, members of the Provincial Assembly wished to mark the jubilee (fiftieth) anniversary of the Charter of Privileges and the recent completion of the steeple for the state house in Philadelphia. The bell that ultimately served the city for nearly one hundred years bore witness to great acts of bravery, a national revolution, and the depths of despair. Rising beyond its original use as a state house bell rung to call town meetings and alarms, the Liberty Bell is universally seen today as a physical representation of the promise of liberty and independence to the world.

The bell that arrived from the Whitechapel Foundry in Liverpool, England, on the morning of September 1, 1752, was quickly determined to be unusable, for it immediately suffered a large crack. Local iron workers John Pass and John Stow were engaged to create a new bell, which was soon installed in the steeple of the Pennsylvania State House. For the next twenty-five years, the bell rang for common events such as town meetings and for the more urgent and infrequent need for firefighters and local peacekeeping militia. In 1772, local neighbors petitioned the government to stop using the bell so frequently, because the noise was deemed a nuisance. Throughout the American Revolution, the bell worked steadily, alerting Philadelphians to the progress of war. During the British occupation of the city, the bell was removed and hidden in Allentown for nine months. The second bell also formed a crack, thought to have originated sometime in the nineteenth century.

As the jubilee celebration of the Declaration of Independence neared, the old state house acquired the nickname "Independence Hall." By 1834, the term "Liberty Bell" was first used by abolitionists, who saw the symbolism of the bell's history and inscription, *proclaim liberty throughout the land unto all the inhabitants thereof,* taken from the book of Leviticus, as a call to their own goal of ending slavery. The Centennial Exposition of 1876 further enhanced the bell's place in American memory when it was used as the primary logo for the year-long event. On this date in 1904, the City of Philadelphia agreed to permit the bell to travel by open train car to St. Louis for the World's Fair. It was the sixth of seven remarkable cross-country journeys taken by the bell from 1885 to 1915, giving hundreds of thousands of Americans a once-in-a-lifetime opportunity to gain a glimpse of one of the world's most enduring symbols of freedom.

1853: The American Baptist Historical Society is organized in order to preserve the history of the Baptist Church in America.

1870: The Pennsylvania Anti-Slavery Society is disbanded.

1962: The city's first K-9 police dog joins the force.

May 6

Throughout its history, Philadelphia has witnessed the flow of people into and out of the city. Over time, the earliest settlers faced the arrival of new immigrants, many seeking their own place in an increasingly manifold community. Under certain circumstances, the conflict that arose between old and new resulted in destruction and death. On this date in 1844, a young Protestant apprentice named George Shifler assumed the mantle of "martyr" for a growing number of native-born Philadelphians suspicious of the Irish-Catholic immigrants crowding into the established district of Kensington. In a depressed economy, men from both communities faced a scarcity of work, and the "nativists" blamed the Irish for driving down available wages. Many Irish-Americans sought comfort in their social and familial ties and through their churches, taverns, and businesses. Ignorance, fear, and suspicion would ultimately lead to three days of violence, during which many men died, two churches were burned to the ground, and dozens of homes and businesses were destroyed.

In the 1830s, Kensington welcomed the influx of Irish immigrants, providing homes and jobs in the weaving industry that dominated the district. At times partners in labor disputes and for the most part willing to leave each to his own community, Protestants and Catholics found a way to live together in peace. However, the advent of an economic crisis in the late 1830s and the rapid increase in refugee Irish arrivals in the 1840s led to more intense conflicts over scarce jobs. Some Protestants resented Irish resistance to assimilation and feared the pope's influence. Tensions came to a head when a nativist rally was staged at the predominantly Irish Nanny Goat Market in protest of Catholic opposition to the use of a Protestant Bible in public schools. Shouting and stone-throwing soon escalated to gunfire and arson, each side accusing the other of bringing in new weapons and new combatants.

Over the next two days, several other clashes erupted, each driven by the high emotions of the two opposing sides. The city police, unsure of their jurisdiction within the Kensington district and unwilling to step into the middle of an increasingly violent conflict, stood by as St. Michael's and St. Augustine's Catholic churches were destroyed by angry mobs. Finally, the state militia arrived to end the violence and a truce was called. As a result of the riots, for a time the Irish Catholic community became even more insular, establishing the parochial system of schools. The city police were reorganized, and by 1854 the consolidation of the city into a single municipality standardized protections under the police and fire departments. Though by no means the end of local clashes, the "Bible Riots" of 1844 represent the peak of religious conflict in the city and resulted in significant changes in the relationships among diverse communities.

1732: Ben Franklin publishes the first issue of the *Philadelphische Zeitung*, the first German-language newspaper in America. Only two numbers were issued.

1994: Jeffrey Lurie buys the Philadelphia Eagles from Norman Braman for an estimated $185 million.

May 7

The country's most infamous serial killer was finally brought to justice on this date in 1896. Herman Webster Mudgett, better known under the alias Dr. Henry Howard Holmes, was hanged to death in Philadelphia for murdering dozens of young women, children, and men in Chicago during the 1893 World's Columbian Exposition. Born in Gilmantown, New Hampshire, to a devout Methodist family, Holmes reportedly spent much of his childhood torturing animals. After graduating from the University of Michigan with a medical degree, he moved to Chicago. While there, he embarked on a career fraught with insurance scams, murder, and gruesome dismemberments, many in his home, a three-story home and fortress known as the "Castle." He was captured in Boston in 1894, but brought back to Philadelphia for trial because three of his young victims were from the city.

As a young student at the University of Michigan Medical School, Holmes financed his education with a series of insurance scams whereby he requested coverage for nonexistent people and then presented corpses, which he stole from the university, as the insured. In 1886, Holmes began working as a pharmacist in Chicago. A few months later, he killed his elderly employer but told everyone that the woman was visiting relatives in California. With a new series of cons, Holmes raised enough money to build a giant, elaborate home across from the store. The home featured secret passageways, fake walls and trapdoors, and gas lines that fed into sealed rooms. He frequently changed contractors so that no one would know the true layout of the house. Young women in the area, along with tourists who came to see the 1893 World's Fair in Chicago and rented rooms from Holmes, suddenly began disappearing. Holmes was systematically selecting, torturing, and murdering his victims. Medical schools purchased many human skeletons from Dr. Holmes during this period but never asked how he obtained the anatomy specimens.

Abandoning Chicago following financial troubles, Holmes moved from city to city throughout the United States and Canada. After an insurance scheme to fake his own death failed, he secretly killed Benjamin Pietzel, his assistant and a Philadelphia resident. After talking Pitetzel's widow into letting him take three of her children, Holmes continued his travels before he was eventually captured when a Philadelphia detective began to investigate the children's disappearance. Investigators would later uncover the remains of nearly thirty victims in Chicago alone; he is believed to have killed more than two hundred. Holmes was put to death while an inmate at Moyamensing Prison. He ultimately confessed, saying, "I was born with the devil in me. I could not help the fact that I was a murderer, no more than a poet can help the inspiration to sing."

1754: The Hallam company of actors performs the comic opera *Flora, or Hob in the Well* at the Plumstead warehouse.

1784: The first general meeting of the Society of Cincinnati, with representatives from thirteen states. George Washington is the first president of the association.

May 8

Many of the men known today for their contributions to our nation's birth and subsequent early successes are remembered as men of action like George Washington, men of words like Thomas Jefferson, and men of humor and wisdom like Benjamin Franklin. Robert Morris, English-born but educated and enlightened as a citizen of Philadelphia, can easily be named a man of wealth among the Founding Fathers. Frequently referred to as the "Financier of the American Revolution," Morris fell from the heights of financial success to the abysmal depths of accusations of fraud and debtors' prison, revealing the struggles of one of the nation's greatest supporters.

Morris was born in 1734 in Liverpool, England, but as a young teen moved to Maryland with his family. Dissatisfied with the level of education available in his hometown of Oxford, Morris moved to Philadelphia where he was able to apprentice at the shipping firm of Philadelphia merchant (and later mayor) Charles Willing. Following the death of Morris' father, Robert established his own business in partnership with Charles' son, Thomas. As Willing, Morris & Company, the two men engaged in a highly successful import and export business that placed them among the wealthiest in the colony. As the Revolutionary War approached, Morris was selected to serve on the Continental Congress and later signed the Declaration of Independence. He continued to succeed in business, but also sustained the remarkable loss of more than fifty ships to the perils of war.

War is an expensive undertaking, and the American Revolution would not have been possible without Morris' contribution of nearly $4 million of his personal wealth to finance the Army and other military actions. After the war, Morris served as the Superintendent of Finance and Marine, and as such directed the creation of the first financial institution chartered in the United States, the Bank of North America. Morris also proposed a national mint, and popularized the use of the "$" symbol to denote the American dollar. After several business failures due primarily to European conflicts affecting land deals, Morris was imprisoned for debt for nearly three years, until August 1801. His friends and peers, among them Washington and Jefferson, lobbied for his release. Morris died, sick and generally forgotten, on this date in 1806. Today, he is remembered as one of the Founding Fathers, without whom the nation would not have survived its early years.

1778: General Henry Clinton replaces General Howe of the British occupying army.

1787: The Philadelphia Society for Alleviating the Miseries of Public Prisons is founded by Benjamin Rush and others.

1844: St. Michael's Catholic Church is burned during riots between northern and southern Irish.

1977: A 44-day transit strike ends.

2009: The Philadelphia Phillies hold a victory parade as the 2008 World Series champs.

May 9

Though today it is wide open and frequently negotiated by ships and barges of many kinds, the Delaware River has not always been free of obstacles. Running parallel to the shoreline from Chestnut Street to South Street, a small shoal formed and by 1746 was named Windmill Island, in honor of the miller's power source constructed there for the first time that year. Throughout the city's early history, Windmill Island served multiple purposes, ranging from serving as a home to small businesses to hosting the executioner's noose.

In the years following the city's founding, the as-yet unnamed island offered resources available on shore but with the advantage of less competition. In 1746, an octagonal windmill was built on a point nearly opposite to Pine and Spruce streets. In the years following the American Revolution, the island was suggested as a place to hang pirates and others who committed crimes against the United States, presumably because of its neutral location off the shore between Pennsylvania and New Jersey. In 1780, convicted pirate Thomas Wilkinson was spared the gallows when a petition containing a surprising array of signatures from prominent Philadelphians succeeded in halting his execution. On this date in 1800, three Americans convicted of piracy on the schooner *Eliza* were not so lucky, and were hanged.

In later decades, the island became a popular resort, welcoming city residents to its cooling and relaxing shores. Amenities such as a bathhouse, a restaurant, and even a beer garden and swimming pool eventually opened on the island, renamed Smith Island in honor of the spa's owner. In 1838, a canal was cut through to make way for the Philadelphia-Camden ferry. By the end of the nineteenth century, shipping interests viewed the island as an obstacle to their expansion of the shipping lanes. The island was dredged and more than four million cubic yards of material were taken away and dumped on League Island, where the Navy Yard was located. The work was completed in 1898, removing forever every remnant of a fascinating feature of the Delaware River's past.

1754: The first American newspaper cartoon is published by Franklin in his *Pennsylvania Gazette.* It features a segmented snake with each part named for an American colony and the motto "Join or Die," in a bid to unite the colonies to fight the French and Indian War.

1913: The Department of City Transit is formed. It was ultimately responsible for the construction of the Frankford Elevated line and superseded the Philadelphia Rapid Transit system.

 May 10 

The time for celebrating the greatest industries and the greatest nation in the world was at hand. The 1876 Centennial Exhibition was the first world's fair held in the United States. In the works for a decade, the exhibition opened on May 10, 1876, with unprecedented pomp and circumstance. All told, more than 60,000 exhibitors from around the world participated. Located in Fairmount Park, the exhibition covered nearly three hundred acres with more than seventy acres devoted to specially constructed exhibition halls and buildings. On opening day, a one-hundred-gun salute, parades, concerts, and a speech by President Ulysses S. Grant entertained over 100,000 visitors, most of whom arrived by train to the fairgrounds.

Designed to celebrate the 100th anniversary of the Declaration of Independence and to showcase the industrial and commercial development of the nation, the exhibition included the largest steam engine ever built, a demonstration of the telephone by Alexander Graham Bell, and the cable the Roebling Company devised for constructing the Brooklyn Bridge. The arts were represented at Memorial Hall, the main building constructed for the fair at a cost of $1.5 million and built in the Beaux Arts style. More than seven thousand pieces of art were exhibited there, including a 32-foot painting of the Battle of Gettysburg and works by Thomas Eaton. Popular pastimes and treats were a part of the experience. Root beer and bananas were first introduced at the fair, and "Centennial Cake" is eaten today as shoofly pie.

By the end of the fair in November 1876, more than 10 million visitors had visited Philadelphia for the exhibition, representing almost one quarter of the population of the United States at that time. After the fair, Memorial Hall was used as the Philadelphia Museum of Art until 1928, and served a variety of other purposes until its restoration, completed in 2009, as the Please Touch Children's Museum. The museum also restored and exhibits a 1:192 scale model of the exhibition's buildings and grounds. It remains one of the few standing remnants of Philadelphia's greatest and most elaborate parties.

1752: Franklin first tests the lightning rod.

1775: On opening day of the Second Continental Congress, John Hancock presides as president.

1775: George Washington is named supreme commander of the Continental Army by the Second Continental Congress.

1877: The Pennsylvania Museum and School of Industrial Art opens in Memorial Hall. In 1963, reorganization resulted in the school and museum splitting into what is now the University of the Arts and the Philadelphia Museum of Art.

 May 11 

Georgie Woods—the guy with the goods," a radio fixture for nearly four decades, was born in Georgia on this date in 1927. In 1953, he came to Philadelphia by way of New York City, where he made his debut at WWRL, 1600 on the AM dial. Known for his vibrant and often wild on-air style, Woods was also a passionate civil rights activist who is credited with helping to keep the city calm in the hours following the assassination of Martin Luther King, Jr., in 1968. For the majority of his forty-year career, Woods worked for two of the city's most successful radio stations: WHAT-AM and WDAS-AM. He died in Florida on June 18, 2005. He is remembered by many for his bold and clever personality and his commitment to his adopted home.

After a brief stint in New York, Woods accepted a position with WHAT-AM in Philadelphia in 1953. The station today has the distinction of being one of the longest-running radio stations in the country. He remained there for just three years and in 1956 moved to WDAS-AM. For the next decade, Woods built a following and served as a catalyst to a number of performers, including Sam Cooke and the Beatles, both of whom he supported and introduced to local listeners. He also worked within the civil rights movement, organizing "Freedom Shows" at the Uptown Theater and sponsoring busloads of Philadelphians to travel to join Martin Luther King, Jr., on his Alabama and Washington, D.C., protest marches. In 1968, he ran for City Council but was defeated in a recount by future Representative Tom Foglietta.

Originally nicknamed "the man with the goods," Woods changed "man" to "guy" when the phrase "the man" took on a different meaning within the black community. Woods once again returned to WHAT-AM for two years before settling back with WDAS at a moment when the city needed him most. Following King's assassination on April 4, 1968, Woods and his fellow jockeys offered constant reminders of King's teachings of nonviolence, working to keep the peace in a city on the verge of chaos. Woods remained at WDAS-AM for the next twenty years, devising a talk-show format and earning the title of Program Director, before moving on once again back to WHAT and then joining fellow WHAT alumnus Jerry Blavat at WPGR, Geator Gold radio. Following his death, Woods was recognized for his outstanding professional and personal commitment to diversity and peace by the Broadcast Pioneers of Philadelphia, who inducted him into the pantheon of legends, their Hall of Fame.

1751: A bill is signed into law establishing the Pennsylvania Hospital.

1752: The first American fire insurance policy is issued in Philadelphia by the Philadelphia Contributionship.

1959: The new Vertol helicopter, named for its ability to achieve a vertical takeoff and landing and featuring a 24-person seating capacity and twin turbine engine, is tested in Philadelphia. The Vertol Aircraft Corporation would later be acquired by Boeing.

May 12

Horse racing has been part of Philadelphia's history almost from its founding. William Penn is credited with bringing the first horse bred for racing to America in 1699. While Quaker Philadelphians did not gamble or engage in violent sports, horse racing was a common pastime. William Penn is said to have raced his horses on Sassafras Street. This thoroughfare was so well known for this activity that a century later it was formally renamed Race Street. Interest in horse racing grew in the 1700s as German and other ethnic groups came to Philadelphia, leading to a well established industry by the late nineteenth century.

In 1766, the Philadelphia Jockey Club was founded specifically to sponsor and promote horse racing in the city. But by 1820, reformers succeeded in having the legislature ban thoroughbred racing in the state. Horse enthusiasts turned to trotting horses, which were exempt from the ban. In venues across the state, including Hunting Park Racecourse in Philadelphia and at annual agricultural fairs, trotting horse competitions attracted large crowds. New immigrants from countries with gambling traditions arrived in the city, and in 1866 the first bookmaking business was established. By the turn of the nineteenth century, trotting horse racing was a society sport. The Philadelphia Country Club, founded in 1890 as one of the earliest country clubs in the nation, was organized for riding and driving. Its logo features a horse head. A sixty-acre property adjoining Fairmount Park included a polo field; golf followed in 1892.

On May 12, 1894, the fourth season of racing began at the club with 2,000 people attending. That year, flat racing and steeplechase events took place, with one jockey hurt and a horse killed in a fall. In 1959, the legislature legalized horse racing again in the state. The modern era in Philadelphia racing, primarily at Philadelphia Park, has featured a number of prominent horses. The most popular was Smarty Jones, a Pennsylvania horse who won two of the three Triple Crown races in 2004. Interest in horse racing and its profitability has waned in recent years and Philadelphia Park is now a "racino" offering racing and 3,000 slot machines to attract patrons.

1875: The Philadelphia branch of the Young Men's Hebrew Association, the second in the country, is organized.

1917: Ground breaking for the Central Library of the Free Library of Philadelphia takes place.

May 13

If asked what single event holds the strongest personal memory for them, many Americans would reply the assassination of President John F. Kennedy in 1963, or the explosion of the space shuttle *Challenger* upon takeoff in 1986. For many Philadelphians, a single event on this date in 1985 stands with equal significance in their memories: the bombing by Philadelphia Police of the MOVE compound at 6221 Osage Avenue in West Philadelphia, resulting in the deaths of eleven members of the "back to nature" movement.

Founded in 1972 by John Africa, MOVE took a radical position on environmentalism and directly opposed science in medicine and technology. Known for wearing their hair in dreadlocks and for living communally, MOVE quickly established a rancorous relationship with their neighbors in the Powelton Village community. As early as 1978, members of the John Africa–led MOVE organization (not an acronym, but a self-defined name) clashed with Philadelphia police and local neighbors over issues that included sanitation and noise pollution. That year, one police officer was killed and fifteen others injured in a shoot-out, for which nine members of MOVE were found guilty of third-degree murder, and remain incarcerated.

By 1983, the Philadelphia Police once again faced a confrontation with MOVE, now living on Osage Avenue. Responding to complaints by local residents, the police attempted to remove the MOVE residents from their home, but met with resistance. An attempt was made to drive them out with tear-gas and water-cannons, which drew gunfire from within the house and resulted in nearly ninety minutes of return fire from the police. Finally, a police helicopter dropped a four-pound bomb on the roof of the house in hopes of destroying a bunkerlike structure there. The resulting explosion and fire consumed the entire block of homes in a fire that was visible throughout the city.

Mayor Wilson Goode appointed a commission to investigate the bombing, which determined that the city used excessive and "unconscionable" force in the raid. A subsequent civil lawsuit required the former fire and police commissioners to pay $1.5 million to a survivor and families of two people killed. The homes destroyed by the fire were rebuilt but were found to be of extremely poor construction, condemned, and rebuilt again. In the years since the MOVE incident, the question of right or wrong has been debated, with many simply remembering it as one of the worst days in Philadelphia's modern history.

1684: The Provincial Council, chaired by Governor William Penn, orders a dispute between two men settled in part by having them shake hands and forgive each other.

1909: The Bellevue Stratford Hotel announces it is opening an aerial garage on its roof where airships can be repaired while flyers enjoy refreshments in the rooftop garden.

May 14

Composed on Christmas Day, 1896, the song that would become America's national march was first performed in front of an audience in Philadelphia on this date in 1897. John Philip Sousa, who was inspired to write *Stars and Stripes Forever* while on a ferry in Europe, began his career as an apprentice to the United States Marine Band at the tender age of thirteen. Of the countless musical pieces he created during his lifetime, including ten operettas and a variety of musical suites, his most popular works resulted in his name being synonymous with the broad, uplifting themes of marching music.

Following his honorable discharge from the Marine Band in 1874, Sousa sought new opportunities to earn a living as a musician. As a young man, he developed a deep connection to Philadelphia playing with orchestras in the city, including the Centennial Exposition Orchestra and with the stage band at Mrs. Drew's Arch Street Theater. In 1889, he married a young Philadelphian, Jane van Middlesworth Bellis and shortly afterward returned to the U.S. Marine Band, remaining as its conductor until 1892. In his role as leader of the President's Own band, he served under five presidents and performed at two inaugural balls. Following his departure from the Marine Band, he established his own touring performance band, and traveled around the world, performing a remarkable 15,623 concerts until 1931.

From 1901 to 1926, Sousa served as the summertime conductor-in-residence at Willow Grove Park, an amusement park located just outside the city. Regularly trying out new music on the appreciative audiences at Willow Grove, he resisted all efforts to record his band, arguing that the social aspects of music far outweighed any advantages given by the mass production possible with modern recording technology. In addition to music, Sousa was a versatile writer, producing works of fiction as well as an autobiography, *Marching Along,* in 1928. He died in Reading, Pennsylvania, on March 6, 1932, just hours after rehearsing his best-known march, *Stars and Stripes Forever.*

1787: Delegates begin gathering in Philadelphia for a convention to draw up a new United States Constitution.

1865: The Union League opens on Broad Street.

1888: Temple College (now University) is incorporated.

May 15

Philadelphia's long and emotional relationship with the oldest franchise in the National Basketball Association began on this date in 1963, when the Syracuse Nationals were purchased by Irv Kosloff and brought to the city. Formed in 1946, the Nationals played in the National Basketball League until joining with six other league teams to combine with the Basketball Association of America in 1949, organizing the NBA. When the Nationals arrived in Philadelphia, they restored the game of pro ball to the city, which had bid farewell to the Warriors just one year earlier. Beginning with the return of Philadelphia-born superstar Wilt Chamberlain in 1964, the newly named "76ers" would experience the absolute heights of success as well as sinking to the lowest levels in the sport.

The ability to shut down the Boston Celtics, the city's long-standing rivals, seemed the greatest advantage to the return of Chamberlain. The Sixers won the Eastern Division championship his first year back. Though they lost the NBA championship that year, the Sixers went on to build on their potential and had what has become universally accepted as the best season in league history in 1967-68, with a record of 68-13 and their first national championship. Over the next decade, the team suffered a decline, posting the league's worst season ever in 1972-73, with a remarkable 73 losses. In 1976, the team was rescued by new ownership and the arrival of Julius "Dr. J" Erving, who remains today one of the most beloved players in the game.

The ultimate success, a second national championship for the city, remained elusive until 1983 when the remarkable talent of Erving, Moses Malone, Mo Cheeks, Andrew Toney, and Bobby Jones led them to victory once again. Another period of decline followed, but as the twentieth century drew to a close, rookie point guard Allen Iverson seemed to promise a new beginning. Falling just shy of the championship, the 2000-2001 season nevertheless brought more accolades, including the NBA's MVP (Iverson), Coach of the Year (Larry Brown), and Defensive Player of the Year (Dikembe Mutumbo). In the past decade, rancorous coach-player relationships and financial challenges have lingered, but the franchise remains strong, as always looking to the future while retaining a close connection to its storied past.

1775: The Second Continental Congress places the colonies in a state of defense.

1897: President McKinley unveils the statue of George Washington in Fairmount Park in a celebration that included speeches, a parade, a salute from warships, and an evening banquet.

1957: The Walt Whitman Bridge is dedicated with 3,500 people in attendance.

1996: A Zagat survey cites Philadelphia as home to the nation's best restaurant tippers.

May 16

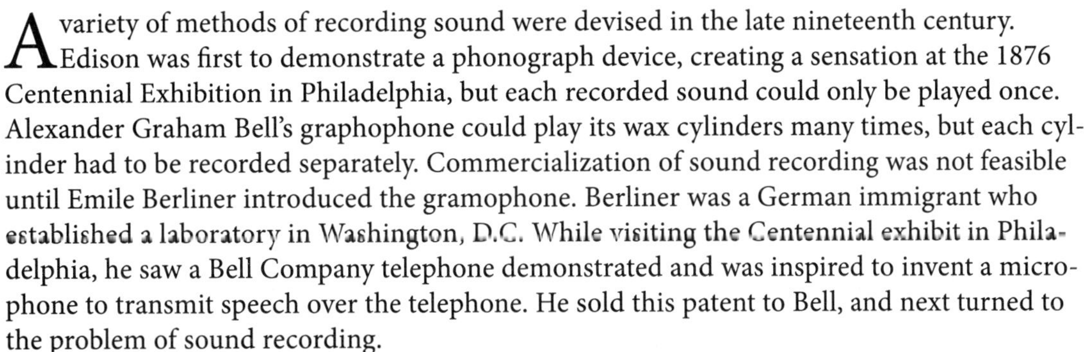

A variety of methods of recording sound were devised in the late nineteenth century. Edison was first to demonstrate a phonograph device, creating a sensation at the 1876 Centennial Exhibition in Philadelphia, but each recorded sound could only be played once. Alexander Graham Bell's graphophone could play its wax cylinders many times, but each cylinder had to be recorded separately. Commercialization of sound recording was not feasible until Emile Berliner introduced the gramophone. Berliner was a German immigrant who established a laboratory in Washington, D.C. While visiting the Centennial exhibit in Philadelphia, he saw a Bell Company telephone demonstrated and was inspired to invent a microphone to transmit speech over the telephone. He sold this patent to Bell, and next turned to the problem of sound recording.

In 1887, he patented the "gramophone," which used zinc discs instead of cylinders. Later that year, he improved the gramophone by adding a reproducer mounted on a pivot arm. On May 16, 1888, he demonstrated this model in public for the first time at the Franklin Institute in Philadelphia. Berliner commercialized sound recording and manufactured the first devices and reproducible discs in Germany in 1889-90. In 1894, he opened a factory in Baltimore and produced gramophones with electric motors and discs on the Berliner Gramophone label. Technical improvements, including his invention of the stylus, led to increased sales; in 1898 Berliner's company sold more than 700,000 discs.

Berliner also made an important contribution to the history of advertising. Following several mergers, Berliner Gramophone became the Victor Talking Machine Company. In 1908, Berliner used a painting of a dog listening to a gramophone. "His Master's Voice" became the trademark of the company (later absorbed by RCA) and remains one of the world's most recognizable and classic advertising logos. Three major record labels can claim ancestry in Berliner's company: Sony Music Entertainment, EMI, and the Universal Music Group. Driven by technological improvement, Berliner's success helped lay the foundation for an entire industry.

1931: Louise Pellegiano, sixteen years old, is found operating a fifty-gallon still when police raid a house on Pashall Avenue near 72nd Street.

1971: In a track and field race held at Franklin Field, Marty Liquori beats Jim Ryun in the mile run for the third time. Liquori wins the Dream Mile race by a foot with a time of 3:56.

May 17

In the midst of a decade fraught with racial conflict, the night of May 17, 1838, stands as one of the most public expressions of anti-abolitionism and fear of the power of blacks in Philadelphia history. On the last of four planned days of a reform movement conference featuring anti-slavery and women's groups, the newly completed Pennsylvania Hall was attacked by a mob and burned to the ground. The next evening, rioters set fire to the Friends Home for Colored Orphans and attacked two black churches. Throughout the rioting, the police and fire brigades refused to act to protect the men and women of the reform groups, standing back and allowing the rioting to continue. Faced with such drastic and violent opposition, many within the reform movement were forced to reassess their approach to women's suffrage and abolitionism, choosing to proceed with great caution toward the ultimate goal of freedom and independence for all Americans.

Earlier that spring, tensions were running high in Philadelphia. The state constitutional debates of the previous fall suggested that blacks within the state would soon be suffering a reversal of their right to vote. Anti-slavery and pro-women's groups were greatly limited in their ability to gather in meetings because very few public venues wanted to bring such potentially divisive activities to their theaters or clubs. A group of developers sympathetic to the need for a venue to support public reform meetings built Pennsylvania Hall. Its first public event, held on May 14, 1838, was a gathering of national abolitionist leaders, including William Lloyd Garrison, Theodore and Angelina Grimke Weld, and Maria Weston Chapman. Each day, a growing mob gathered at the Hall to protest the meetings. In addition to the anti-slavery agenda, the prominence of women struck the protesters as an abomination. Rumors quickly spread throughout the city, suggesting that interracial couples were seen at the meetings.

For the first few days, the rioters threw stones and verbally abused the attendees. However, on the night of May 17, tensions escalated. Mayor John Swift attempted to calm the nearly three thousand rioters, but to no avail. Following the destruction of the hall, rioters turned their attention to other black organizations, including the orphan's home and two churches. In the end, a grand jury exonerated the rioters, asserting that the reform groups had fostered promiscuous audiences and promoted the socialization of black men and white women. Over the next decade, many anti-slavery groups lost what little public support they had, as the opponents of equity increasingly raised their voices in anger.

1905: The birthplace of famed comedic actor Joseph Jefferson, located at Sixth and Spruce streets, is sold at auction to a speculator for $8,125. He was best known for his portrayal of Rip Van Winkle.

1955: Owen J. Roberts, associate Justice of the United States Supreme Court, dies at eighty years of age.

May 18

At a time of war, civilians and soldiers alike frequently suffer extreme hardship and deprivation. Most Americans know the story of George Washington and his army struggling to survive the cold winter months at Valley Forge in 1777. However, while Americans shivered and sickened, many of the British who occupied Philadelphia enjoyed only the finest of food and shelter, living a life of comfort complete with leisurely meals and theatrical distractions. When British general William Howe was called back to England in the spring of 1778, there were many who wanted to show their fondness for him and his cause. The resulting grand event held on this date in 1778, known as the Mischianza, remains an unparalleled exercise in extravagance in Philadelphia's long history.

Organized under the direction of British captain John Andre, the Mischianza was intended to mimic the grandness of a kingly court of centuries past, complete with processionals, a jousting tournament, and pursuit of the favors of fair young maidens. The party began in the early evening hours with the departure of almost thirty galleys and barges from Knight's Wharf, located at the foot of Vine Street on the Delaware River, each carrying military and civilian guests of honor. The party-goers debarked at the wharf near Old Swedes' (Gloria Dei) Church and proceeded to Joseph Wharton's estate near what is now 5th and Wharton streets. The path was lined with two hundred fully uniformed grenadiers, and nearly as many full-sized painted wooden figures. Passing through two triumphal arches adorned with statues, feathers, and burning torches, the four hundred invited attendees soon enjoyed a jousting tournament complete with knights and horses, an elaborate buffet, and gaming tables. The evening ended with a rare and extremely extravagant display of pyrotechnics.

In the wee hours of the next day, the party dispersed and General Howe prepared to leave the city within the week. Those who supported the American cause decried the wasteful celebration and eagerly awaited the return of American control of the city. General Howe returned to England to explain why he never attacked the vulnerable Americans at Valley Forge, choosing instead to live in peaceful comfort and luxury. John Andre, known for his elegance and popularity among his fellow officers and the American ladies he socialized with, was later hanged for his part in the spy ring that forced Benedict Arnold into exile. For just a few months, these men had enjoyed only the best that Philadelphia had to offer. The Mischianza was their last great *huzzah!* before they finally faced the brutal realities of war.

1784: The first meeting of the Pennsylvania Society of the Cincinnati is held at the State House.

May 19

The Philadelphia Flyers were created in 1967 during the first expansion of the National Hockey League since its founding twenty-six years earlier. A long shot among numerous cities vying for a team, its petition was strengthened by a pledge to build a facility for the team's home ice. The Spectrum was constructed in South Philadelphia on Broad Street, one of several large sports venues in that neighborhood. The Flyers played their first home game at the Spectrum in 1967 against the Pittsburgh Penguins and continued at that location until they moved to the Wachovia Center in 1996. Known for their physical style of play in the 1970s, that decade saw the team's greatest success. Anchored by legendary players such as goalie Bernie Parent and forward Bobby Clarke, and helped by the tough play of Dave "the Hammer" Schultz and others, the "Broad Street Bullies" won the Stanley Cup in both 1974 and 1975.

Perhaps the Flyers' success in those golden seasons of 1974 and 1975 had something to do with the remarkable relationship of the team and its fans, and the singer Kate Smith. In 1969, Flyers Vice President Lou Schienfield ordered that her recording of Irving Berlin's "God Bless America" be played in place of the national anthem. That night, the Flyers beat Toronto 6–3. Subsequently, Schienfield played the song for important games and when he thought the team or its fans needed a boost.

Kate Smith first sang in person at a Flyers game in the 1973-74 season. Embraced by the fans, she sang before the critical sixth game of the 1974 Stanley Cup against the Boston Bruins, and the Flyers won the cup that night. The following year, a live performance in game seven of the semi-finals helped spur a victory over the New York Islanders and put the Flyers in the championship series for the second straight year. In the first three years of this tradition, the record with Kate's song was 19-1-1 as compared with about even wins and losses without "God Bless America." Kate's final record with the Flyers was 77-21-4. While the team has been competitive since that time, and played in several Stanley Cup championship series, they have been unable to bring home the cup to Philadelphia since their triumphs of the mid-seventies.

1962: Demolition begins at the Schuylkill Arsenal, a compound of twenty-three buildings along the eastern shore of the Schuylkill River, to make way for a new Philadelphia Electric Company building. Originally established by the federal government in 1799, the arsenal later served as a primary outfitter for the government and supplied the Lewis and Clark Expedition of 1803.

May 20

Much of the urban landscape of Philadelphia was first crafted in the mind of a single man. Edmund Bacon, the Executive Director of the Philadelphia City Planning Commission from 1949 to 1970, brought his own unique vision to the process of planning for the future of Philadelphia's built environment. During his tenure with the commission, Bacon personally envisioned and oversaw the completion of defining projects such as the Penn Center–Suburban Station complex on Market Street, vast developments in the Far Northeast and most famously Interstate 95 and Society Hill. On this date in 1976, his seminal text on urban design, *The Design of Cities,* was released in popular paperback version, an indication of the universal power of Bacon's perspective and his ability to engage the world in his debate about the nature of urban progress and its impact on the landscape we live in.

Born in 1910 to a Quaker family in West Philadelphia and raised in Delaware County, Bacon was interested in architecture and urban design from a young age. After graduating from Cornell University in 1932, he traveled Europe and worked in China with several leading American architects before returning to the States in 1934. Under the tutelage of Finnish architect Eliel Saarinen, Bacon developed his skills while working for the planning board of Flint, Michigan. After facing opposition to his commitment to affordable housing from among local businessmen, Bacon joined in the early efforts to establish a planning commission in Philadelphia. In 1949, when he was selected to head the agency, he provided a strong vision of Philadelphia's future, which he articulated with equal success among fellow professionals and the average citizen. Partnering with mayors, community leaders, and developers, Bacon inspired others to follow his lead. In 1964 at the peak of his success, Bacon was featured on the cover of *Time* magazine in a nod to the international reputation of the city's planning office.

Under his direction, large projects were seen as both a boon to the city and a challenge to its established neighborhoods, many of which dated back to the eighteenth and early nineteenth centuries, in particular Society Hill. Ultimately, Bacon proved to Philadelphia and the world that an eighteenth-century city could be reborn to meet the needs of a modern century. When asked to identify his greatest success, Bacon answered simply, "Philadelphia." He died on October 14, 2005, leaving a remarkable legacy to his beloved city.

1688: The annual date is designated by the Provincial Council as the day for holding fairs in the city.

1766: News of the repeal of the Stamp Act reaches Philadelphia.

May 21

As the nation descended into the difficult throes of the Civil War, Philadelphia faced the unusual challenge of managing the presence of thousands of young men passing through the city's essential transportation hubs. Soldiers traveling alone or with their regiments frequently arrived by boat or train on their way south from points to the north and west of the city. As the war progressed, just as many men made their way back home through Philadelphia, often injured or simply exhausted from their difficult service to the country. On this date in 1861, the Union Volunteer Refreshment Saloon opened its doors at Washington Avenue near Swanson Street in southeast Philadelphia. By war's end, nearly half a million young men had benefited from the food, drink, and rest provided by one of the nation's most effective Civil War charities.

In the weeks following the official declaration of war in April 1861, citizens in the southern wards along the Delaware River saw a dramatic increase in the number of young men arriving in the city without plans for food or shelter, and attempted to help whenever they could. The number of men was more than could be easily accommodated, however, resulting in ominous consequences. Crime was increasing, and many Philadelphians expressed concern that the city would decline into dangerous disorder. Barzilai S. Brown, a local grocer, set up a coffee cart on a local corner but quickly realized more was needed. With no government funding or official support, Brown and a committee of nearly two-dozen men and women established the Saloon in a former boat-rigger's shop. In addition to coffee and food (1,200 men could be fed at one sitting), the Saloon offered opportunity to bathe, wash their clothing, and write letters, with free postage provided. These small civilities meant a great deal to the thousands of soldiers experiencing the dehumanizing effects of war. In addition to healthy men, the Saloon provided medical care in a 500-bed hospital.

In tandem with the similarly managed but separate Cooper Shop Volunteer Refreshment Saloon, the two organizations helped unify Philadelphians and the traveling soldiers in the common effort to win the war. Through their immediate care for the men, as well as highly successful fund-raising fairs and events, the Saloon helped in no small way to bring success for the Union. With gestures both grand and small, Philadelphia's unique care of American soldiers established a precedent for great patriotic charities throughout the Civil War and beyond.

1895: More than 100,000 people attend the dedication of the $1 million Temple of the Independent Order of Odd Fellows, at Broad Street on the southeast corner of Cherry Street. The building would be demolished in 2008 to make way for expansion of the Convention Center.

May 22

Few Americans can imagine a day fully enjoyed without the refreshing carbonated beverages that occupy so many of our pantry shelves, shopping carts, and advertising billboards. For millennia, naturally fizzy or mineralized water was viewed as medicinally helpful, if not so very pleasing to the taste. As early as 1741, Englishman William Brownrigg created the first manufactured mineral water. But it was the work of chemist and Pennsylvania resident Joseph Priestley that first brought truly carbonated water to the world in 1767 when he found that suspending a bowl of water over a beer vat produced the slightly salty-tasting but refreshing beverage. On this date in 1807, Philadelphia druggist Townsend Speakman improved upon Priestley's work and changed the world by introducing flavored juices to carbonated water. His "Nephrite Julep" soon became the first marketed soft drink in history.

While still in Europe, Priestley discovered that gases put off during the beer brewing process could be captured and infused into water to create something which mimicked the healthful waters of natural spas such as those in Bath, England. By 1783, German-Swiss jeweler Jacob Schweppe had improved upon the manufacturing process and began to produce aerated waters on a commercial scale. In each case, however, the flavor was a detriment to the full realization of the value of carbonated water as a desirable beverage. It was Philadelphia doctor Philip Syng Physick, intrigued by the medicinal potential of Priestley's original idea, who asked Speakman to prepare carbonated water for his patients.

Following Speakman's improvement, other inventors strove to build upon the idea that mineral waters were curative by adding their own supplements. These included birch bark, ginger, sarsaparilla, and lemon. Most famously, Dr. John Styth Pemberton first sold his Coca-Cola formula at a pharmacy in Georgia in 1886. Inspired by the singular success of Townsend Speakman's simple improvement, a global industry was born.

1821: The cornerstone is laid to Eastern State Penitentiary.

1875: The City of Philadelphia becomes successor to the property of the Banneker School by deed. Founded in 1789 by Quakers, the school educated African-American children until it closed in the early 1890s.

May 23

Philadelphia bid farewell to a beloved cornerstone of the local retail industry when Strawbridge's, the final incarnation of the Strawbridge and Clothier Department Store, closed the doors of its flagship store at 8th and Market streets for the last time on this date in 2006. A family-owned and run company known mostly for its genteel atmosphere and strong relationship with its employees and customers, Strawbridge and Clothier was founded by Quaker merchants Justus Clayton Strawbridge and Isaac Hallowell Clothier in 1868. Remaining under family control for the next 138 years, the last of the great department stores was sold in 1996 to the May Company, which eventually closed many of the remaining thirteen stores because of declining revenue and increased competition.

Shortly after its founding, Strawbridge and Clothier opened up shop in a three-story building at the busy intersection of 8th and Market, the former office for Secretary of State Thomas Jefferson in the 1790s. Within ten years, new retail rivals Wanamaker & Brown's and Gimbels helped establish the east end of Market Street as a premier shopping destination. By 1930, Strawbridge and Clothier opened their new, modern flagship store on the site, just one of more than a dozen department stores along Market Street. Over the next century, the business grew, but leadership among members of the Strawbridge and Clothier families limited expansion and maintained the local flavor of the stores. Not afraid of innovation, in 1929 the company opened one of the first suburban branch department stores in the nation at Suburban Square in Ardmore, followed quickly by a branch in Jenkintown.

Additional innovations in the early 1970s resulted in the creation of the Clover discount store chain, which eventually outnumbered Strawbridge and Clothier in the number of store locations. A series of attempted takeovers, as well as declining revenues, led to the families' decision to sell to the May Company. In the years since the closing, the grand building on Market Street has served as a Macy's Department Store and is currently a controversial option for an urban casino. For many Philadelphians, however, Strawbridge and Clothier will remain firmly in our memories as one of Philadelphia's greatest shopping destinations and a unique reflection of the city's splendid retail past.

1890: Spitting is prohibited for the first time in horse-drawn streetcars run by the Philadelphia Traction Company. The action was deemed necessary owing to the unusually high rate of tobacco users on the lines.

May 24

Philadelphia's soul diva, Patti Labelle, has been a successful singer and recording artist for more than forty years. Born Patricia Holte on this date in 1944, Patti grew up in the city and formed her first singing group, the Ordettes, in 1960 with Sandy Tucker, who was replaced by Cindy Birdsong within a year. Nona Hendryx and Sarah Dash joined the group at the same time, and were collectively renamed the Bluebelles, recording a top twenty hit in "I Sold My Heart to the Junkman." In 1970, Birdsong left to join the Supremes, and the group LaBelle was born. By this stage in the group's career, it was moving away from traditional popular soul and moving toward more hard-driving rock and roll and rhythm and blues.

Following a stint opening for the Who, the group went on to perform at the Apollo Theater in New York City, as well as the Metropolitan Opera House, where they became the first African-American and contemporary pop group to perform there. A powerful vocalist, with a four-octave range, Patti and the group achieved their greatest success with the single "Lady Marmalade" in 1975. LaBelle in this era featured extreme glam costumes and high energy performances. The group disbanded in the late 1970s and Patti LaBelle pursued a successful solo career. She scored a hit with "New Attitude" in 1984, her duet "On My Own" with Michael McDonald topped the charts in 1986, and she won Grammy awards twice during the 1990s for her albums.

Tragically, Patti's sisters had all died young from cancer and diabetes, and Patti reared her own child and the children of her late sisters. Diagnosed with diabetes herself in 1995, she has become a spokesperson for the American Diabetes Association and the American Cancer Society, published four books, and has also pursued an acting career. Always in tune with trends in music, she has collaborated with local hip hop artists and continues to tour nationally.

1935: The first Major League baseball night game at Cincinnati's Crowley Field is played. The Reds beat the Phillies 2–1.

May 25

From its earliest days, citizens and political leaders in Philadelphia sought to protect homes and businesses throughout the city from a dangerous and significant threat: fire. William Penn, remembering the devastating Great Fire of London in 1666, specified a grid plan for the layout of city streets, a plan implemented by surveyor Thomas Holme in 1682. On this date in 1695, residents successfully petitioned Governor William Markham and the Provincial Council to pass a law to provide them with ladders and buckets for firefighting. Half a century later, Benjamin Franklin returned from a trip to his native Boston with the observation that Philadelphians were oddly ill-prepared for the possibility of fire, and had little to no measures in place to respond if such a disaster struck. From these seeds of concern grew the first organized firefighting club in 1736.

In the mid-1600s, fire remained a leading cause of the destruction of neighborhoods and entire cities throughout Europe. The 1666 Great Fire of London grew from a small blaze in a baker's shop to the ruin of nearly 70,000 homes. Philadelphia founder William Penn, himself a resident of London at the time, understood that the disordered street layout and the prevalence of wooden structures contributed to the resulting damage. In addition to providing firefighting equipment, a provincial law that passed in 1696 prohibited cleaning chimneys by burning them out, while having a dirty chimney could result in a fine of 40 shillings. Residents were also required to maintain a fire bucket in their home. The province purchased its first fire engine in 1718, but still required unorganized private citizens to provide the majority of firefighting labor. By 1735, a series of near disastrous fires had drawn attention to the need for better protection.

Franklin's call for organized firefighting resulted in the first volunteer fire company, the Union Fire Company, in 1736. Within a few months additional clubs were formed, including the Heart in Hand Fire Company, the Britannia Fire Company, and the Fellowship Fire Company. Functioning as associations for mutual assistance, members of the clubs each agreed to provide six leather buckets and two bags, which he was expected to bring to any fire. By 1750, six fire companies protected the city. Volunteer companies continued in service to Philadelphia until the creation of the Philadelphia Fire Department, the city's first fully professional firefighting agency, in December 1870.

1755: Gustavus Hesselius, who lived on Market Street below Fourth and is recognized as the earliest painter in America, dies. He arrived from Sweden in 1710 or, more reliably, on May 1, 1711, in Christina (Wilmington, Delaware).

1787: In response to calls for a stronger central government, a Constitutional Convention comes to order at the State House. George Washington is elected President of the convention, whose first act is a vote to keep the proceedings secret.

1824: The American Sunday School Union is formed to unite similar societies under one banner.

May 26

The search for a murderer consumed the city Police Department. Roy Wilson White, a young and highly popular law professor at the University of Pennsylvania, was brutally assaulted near the train station in Powelton Village on the night of May 19, 1900. Beaten and robbed, he would soon die of his injuries, triggering one of the most reported and avidly followed murder cases in city history. Assuming the most likely suspects to be vagrants traveling along the railroad, police initiated the largest dragnet in department history within hours of White's death. All told, more than forty men were rounded up and subjected to an identity line-up where the sole witness, a local railroad messenger, claimed to recognize just one man, Henry Ivory of Wilmington, Delaware.

Ivory, subjected to intense interrogation techniques, pointed the finger at a second man. Captured in Trenton on May 25, Amos Stirling, alias "William Field," was brought to Philadelphia on this date in 1900. Arriving unannounced at the Broad Street Station, Stirling was nevertheless greeted by a crowd of 300 waiting passengers who cheered as he was escorted off the train in full shackles. A few weeks later, a third man, Charles Perry, was arrested after attempting to pawn the victim's watch. Perry and Ivory were eventually tried and convicted at the same time, the trial and jury deliberation completed in a remarkable two days. Stirling, sick with tuberculosis, was several times deemed unfit for trial before he, too, was found guilty.

A rare and shocking story, the apparently random and senseless violence so horrifyingly relayed through the press coverage revealed a yellow journalism found in many large cities, which repeatedly drew on fears among law-abiding citizens. Little attention was paid to the truth of evidence, while unidentified reporters repeated rumors and supposition as fact. As was true in many dramatic crime cases reported at the time, the untimely and violent death of one of the city's brightest educators became less about the victim and more about the act of murder and the guilty parties. Ivory and Perry were hanged on October 8, 1901, the first double-hanging in the city in more than fifty years. Stirling, claiming innocence to the end, was put to death on February 27, 1902, bringing to an end a Philadelphia "crime of the century."

1781: The Bank of North America is incorporated.

1861: The Cooper Shop Volunteer Refreshment Saloon opens on Otsego Street below Washington Avenue.

1941: The home said to be that of Betsy Ross is given to the City of Philadelphia. In 1876, the building was touted as the Ross home by her descendants and first opened to the public in 1898.

William Penn's reign over the heights of Philadelphia came to an end on this date in 1987, when the official topping-off of Liberty Place, a 61-story skyscraper located at 17th and Chestnut streets, was held with great excitement and some local dismay. Superseding the statue of William Penn atop City Hall as the tallest structure in the city, Liberty Place developers initially faced great opposition as its mere existence threatened a decades-old "gentleman's agreement" to honor the city founder by never obstructing his symbolic view of his domain. The vision of real estate developer Willard G. Rouse, the postmodern tower would eventually gleam a bright electric blue, outshining Philadelphia's grand architectural past with its showy presence.

Planned as the first of a pair of towers, One Liberty Place was designed by Helmut Jahn of Murphy-Jahn Architects to echo the spire of New York's Chrysler Building. Generally seen as a successful addition to the architectural landscape, the 945-foot-tall Liberty Place stands nearly twice as high as Penn's hat, spectacularly breaking tradition. Beyond its height, Liberty Place also challenged established notions of the relationship between tall tower and pedestrians by refusing to incorporate the more traditional "open plaza" street-level design. Notably opposed by Philadelphia's most powerful urban planner, Edmund Bacon, Rouse and Associates aggressively lobbied for approval of their project, focusing on the potential for jobs and economic rejuvenation of the city. Faced with these possibilities, many Philadelphians supported the project, and construction was permitted.

Within three years, the second tower was also completed, though it stands slightly shorter than the original. One Liberty Place retained its place as the city's tallest building until June 2007, with the completion of another Rouse and Associates project: the Comcast Center, which reaches skyward to 975 feet. In a uniquely Philadelphia twist to the story, superstitious Philadelphia sports fans looked to the breaking of the gentleman's agreement as the start of the "Curse of Billy Penn," the hard-to-take drought among the city's professional sports teams. The curse remained unbroken until October 2008, with the Phillies' World Series victory. Regardless of its impact on local sports, there is little question that Liberty Place remains a significant presence on the city skyline.

1962: Mrs. Flora Morris Vare, the first woman to serve in the Pennsylvania State Senate, dies at the age of 88.

A. Philip Randolph, co-founder of the Committee Against Jim Crow in the Military Service and Training, brought his particularly successful form of civil disobedience, the "March of Silence," to Philadelphia on this date in 1950. Described by Randolph as "a mighty protest against the cynical disregard of Negro rights in America," the march was attended by thousands and followed a route from North Philadelphia down Broad Street to City Hall. There, veterans staged a silent vigil in commemoration of the service personnel lost in a time of war, and their ongoing battle for equal rights. This march, along with several others led by Randolph in the 1940s and 1950s, were precursors to the civil rights marches used to great effect in the 1960s.

Born in Florida in 1889, Randolph moved to New York City where he hoped to start an acting career. Instead, he soon joined the socialist movement, inspired by the labor rights efforts of famed socialist leader Eugene Debs, who had served time in prison for his role in the Pullman Strike of 1894 and again in 1919 for sedition during World War I. In 1925, Randolph organized the Brotherhood of Sleeping Car Porters and led their efforts to improve working conditions and pay. In 1941, he turned his attention to the potential for job discrimination in the growing military industry as America prepared for war. Ultimately, in response to Randolph's threat of a large and significant march to Washington in protest of job discrimination, President Franklin D. Roosevelt signed Executive Order 8802, which permitted African-Americans to fill the newly available lucrative jobs.

Randolph called off the march, but was dissatisfied with the limitations of the executive order. He believed it was necessary to end Jim Crow within the military itself. He once again pursued civil disobedience as a mechanism, frequently seeking meetings with President Truman in 1947 and 1948. At the Democratic National Convention held in Philadelphia in 1948, Randolph marched with black veterans in protest, enjoying a small victory when Truman called for a congressional session in order to act on his previously submitted civil rights legislation. On July 26, 1948, Truman signed Executive Order 9981, essentially ending discrimination within the military. Randolph continued to see a need for change, and staged a number of additional protests, including the one in Philadelphia in 1950. By 1963, Randolph's position as an "elder" civil rights activist was firmly established when he led the March to Washington for Jobs and Freedom, known primarily for the hundreds of thousands who attended and the "I Have A Dream" speech so effectively delivered by Martin Luther King, Jr.

1698: Construction of the present-day Gloria Dei (Old Swedes) Church is begun.

1975: After the Philadelphia Flyers win their second Stanley Cup on May 27, a parade down Broad Street to JFK Stadium is held on this date to celebrate.

May 29

American Bandstand is the most famous Philadelphia-based television program, but the *Mike Douglas Show* was also produced in the city. Mike Douglas began his career as a singer and started a syndicated television variety show in 1961 in Cleveland. In 1965, the show moved to Philadelphia, finding a home at KYW TV in a studio at 1619 Walnut Street. A combination talk and variety show, it featured a song by Douglas as the opening act and attracted many of the top performers of its time. A wide range of musical tastes were accommodated; performers ranged from Barbra Streisand and Ray Charles to KISS and the Rolling Stones.

Each week, Douglas had celebrity co-hosts, including comics such as Billy Crystal and Totie Fields. Initially broadcast live, in 1965 the show adopted a one-day delay following an on-air profanity by Zsa Zsa Gabor. Perhaps the most unusual co-hosts were John Lennon and Yoko Ono, who co-hosted for a week in 1972 during their campaign to establish permanent residency for John in the United States. On May 29, 1970, co-host of the week Louis Armstrong ended his appearances with a singing performance of "Blueberry Hill," and a duet of "Hello Dolly" with Pearl Bailey participating electronically from Atlanta. On two other songs that evening, "Basin Street Blues" and "When the Saints Go Marching In," Sammy Davis, Jr., played the drums with Pete Fountain on clarinet and Stan Kahn on the organ accompanying the house band.

The show's run spanned 21 years and more than 6,000 episodes, and was consistently the top-rated daytime talk show during its reign. Production moved to Los Angeles in 1978 and the final show was broadcast on November 30, 1981. Douglas earned five Emmys for the show and leading talk-show hosts of today, including Jay Leno and David Letterman, have acknowledged Douglas' mild, chatty style as inspiration.

1775: The Continental Congress, meeting in Philadelphia, sends a letter to the Inhabitants of Canada urging them to join the Americans against the British.

From its earliest days, Philadelphia's place along the Delaware River contributed to the city's role as a significant home to shipbuilding and shipping industries. Throughout the 1700s, Philadelphia's economy grew along with the rapidly expanding number of cargo and passenger ships entering the wharves along the banks of both the Schuylkill and Delaware rivers. In the 1790s, the first commissioned American frigates were built and set sail from the Wharton & Humphreys shipyard. The success of Philadelphia's shipbuilding industry continued through the nineteenth century, reaching a peak in the wake of the first great war of the twentieth century.

Hog Island, nearly one thousand acres of boggy land just south of the city, was first established in November 1917 to serve the needs of a country newly at war. By 1921, the American International Shipbuilding shipyard at Hog Island would successfully launch 122 "hog islanders," well-built and highly practical cargo ships and troop transport ships. The largest shipyard in America at the time, Hog Island boasted fifty ship ways and a workforce of nearly 30,000. The yard also featured a hospital, a Y.M.C.A., a dozen cafeterias and mess halls, a trade school, and a hotel. It was said that the plant's telephone traffic matched that of a city of 140,000 residents. Primarily Italian and Irish immigrants, employees worked relentlessly to meet the demand for completed ships.

The first ship, the *Quistconck,* was launched on August 15, 1918, but with only 65 percent of the riveting complete, it wasn't until November that the ship was truly ready for service, by which time the war itself had ended. Construction at the yard continued nevertheless and on this date in 1919, in the fastest time recorded at Hog Island, five ships were launched in just forty-eight minutes and forty-eight seconds. The last keel was laid on December 8, 1919. The plant was eventually broken down and the land purchased by the city in 1930 for development as the new Philadelphia Municipal Airport, now the greatly expanded Philadelphia International Airport.

1783: The first American daily newspaper, the *Pennsylvania Evening Post,* begins publication in Philadelphia.

May 31

One of the greatest disasters in American history occurred on this date in 1889 in the western Pennsylvania city of Johnstown. A steel company town of about 30,000 inhabitants, Johnstown was located downstream from the South Fork dam. Formerly owned by the State of Pennsylvania, the abandoned dam had been purchased by a number of prominent Pittsburgh-area industrialists, who then made repairs to the dam and used the lake created by it for their hunting and fishing club. Unfortunately, the dam did not hold. After rains of up to ten inches in one day, the dam failed, sending 20 million tons of water at forty miles an hour down the valley and into Johnstown.

Residents tried to escape the sixty-foot wall of water, but more than 2,200 people died, and the town of Johnstown was largely destroyed. Many of those who were not caught in the initial rush of water died when debris caught on fire or they were trapped by barbed wire from a manufacturing plant in the path of the flood. Bodies were recovered for months after the event, and many were never found.

As soon as word of the tragedy spread, aid workers, including many from Philadelphia, rushed to the scene. Clara Barton, who had founded the American Red Cross to assist primarily in times of war, set up operations in Johnstown. Staff from the Philadelphia Children's Aid Society, whose headquarters in Johnstown was destroyed with much loss of life, traveled to the city to assist orphaned children. The Philadelphia Red Cross, a separate organization from the American Red Cross, took a great share of the responsibility for providing medical assistance to the survivors.

Many survivors pursued lawsuits against the hunting and fishing club. Most were dismissed when a judge ruled the event an act of God, but as a result of the incident, many state courts began to apply the British common law concept of liability when natural land has been modified. A great American tragedy of epic proportions, the Johnstown flood helped forge the role of disaster relief in America, and also led to a change in American law that continues to influence court cases today.

1926: The Sesquicentennial International Exposition opens during an unusually rainy spring. The exposition ran through November and featured an eighty-foot replica of the Liberty Bell covered in 26,000 lightbulbs that straddled South Broad Street. Organizers expected 30,000,000 visitors, but just 10,000,000 came.

1976: Team America soccer plays a match against England as part of the USA Bicentennial Cup Tournament, during which England defeats America, 3–1.

May

A culmination of nearly a decade of planning, the morning of May 10, 1876, brought with it an extravagant public display during the opening ceremonies of the Philadelphia Centennial Exposition, participated in by thousands of Philadelphia citizens. Hundreds of thousands more Americans experienced the rich pageantry in the pages of the *Public Ledger,* the most successful newspaper published in Philadelphia. Featuring elaborate woodcut illustrations and highly detailed descriptions of the exhibition displays, the fairgrounds, and celebrity attendees, the *Public Ledger* offered daily observations and event listings, many of which were distributed throughout the country in dispatches and updates. For over a year, the *Public Ledger* served as the primary source of information on the exposition, feeding the public's hunger for news to be proud of, as the nation celebrated one hundred years of American ingenuity and success.

Philadelphia *Public Ledger* (May 11, 1876)

Patriotism had full possession of Philadelphia yesterday. Never in the history of our city has there been so brilliant a scene, such an assemblage of distinguished and illustrious visitors, such as a unanimous outpouring of the people. We have had memorable days in Philadelphia, when the population has been strongly moved, when all the principal streets have been thronged, when the highest manifestations of popular favor and respect have been paid to living presidents, soldier and statesmen, when profound homage has been paid to the memory of the patriotic dead, when the city has been gaily decorated and the people have surged through the thoroughfares, impelled by all manner of motives, from mere curiosity to the most intense feeling; but never have we had such a day as yesterday. Notable days were those which witnessed the ovation to Lafayette, the centenary celebration of Washington's birthday in 1832, the reception of General Jackson, the welcome home of our soldiers after the Mexican war and the war of the rebellion, the funeral solemnities of General Meade, the incoming of New Year's Day of the present year, and the observance of the last 22d of February—but none of those (rivaled) yesterday, and the 10th of May; 1876, will now stand as the great day in Philadelphia until equaled, if not surpassed by the Centennial Fourth of July, now so near at hand.

This is due to the exalted character of the great event, of which all this is commemorative. It is this which has brought here the grand array of representatives of nations, kingdoms, States, empires, and peoples; it is this which has led to the impressive procession of historic characters, eminent and illustrious men, accompanying the President of the United States, his cabinet, the foreign embassies, the Justices of the Supreme Court of the United States, the distinguished leaders of the army and navy, the Legislature of the nation; it is this which made the walls of all houses brilliant with the colors of all countries; it is this which has its hold deep in the hearts of the people, and which packed the streets with multitudes in mass.

June

June 1

Stretching more than fifteen miles from the Schuylkill Expressway to the far Northeast, Roosevelt Boulevard maintains an essential place in the hearts and minds of many Philadelphia motorists. First proposed in 1902 by Mayor Samuel H. Ashbridge to connect northern and central Philadelphia with the growing population in the northeastern neighborhood of Torresdale, the Boulevard has evolved into a primary artery serving the most densely populated areas of the city. As historical as it is frustrating and notorious, the boulevard nevertheless continues to pose both successes and challenges to Philadelphians on the go.

Beginning at the Schuylkill Expressway in Fairmount Park, Roosevelt Boulevard runs in the form of a freeway through North Philadelphia, after which it becomes a divided twelve-lane highway. The full-length Boulevard is Philadelphia's contribution to the historic Lincoln Highway, the first road across America, which ran from Times Square in New York City to Lincoln Park in San Francisco for a total of 3,389 miles. Shortly after its initial completion to Torresdale in 1914, more extensions were planned with the highway reaching neighboring Bucks County in the years following World War II. Today, the boulevard, named for President Teddy Roosevelt, is one of the most traveled inter-city roadways in the country and as a result poses a variety of traffic-related complications, including accidents, pedestrian injuries, and congestion.

In 2001, State Farm Insurance Company designated two intersections along the boulevard as the second and third most deadly in the country. On this date in 2005, the first red-light cameras installed in the city became operational at three infamous intersections along the boulevard: Red Lion Road, Grant Avenue, and Cottman Avenue. Over the last five years, a total of thirty-four cameras have been installed at thirteen intersections, the majority of them along the boulevard. Though plans have been proffered to expand and improve the Roosevelt Boulevard, they have met with little public support. Always a challenge, frequently a danger, the boulevard nevertheless maintains a careful balance within Philadelphia as a link from residential to commercial areas, providing 100,000 vehicles with a bridge from home to work every day.

1833: The first successful omnibus line in Philadelphia (by James Reesides & Company) begins operation between the Merchant's Coffee House at Second and Walnut and the Schuylkill River. The first bus was named "Jim Crow."

June 2

On the banks of the Schuylkill, a green oasis sits in the midst of a heavily industrialized and urban setting. The garden and home of John Bartram, one of the earliest and most important American botanists, it remains the oldest botanical garden in America. Born on this date in 1699 in Darby, Pennsylvania, Bartram developed an interest in native American plants early in life. Poorly educated but inspired by the unexplored natural world around him, Bartram hired a tutor to teach him Latin and enable him to read the works of the era's most famous botanist, Carl Linnaeus. Years later, Linnaeus described Bartram as the finest "natural botanist" of his time.

Bartram traveled widely in the colonies collecting specimens for his patron, Peter Collinson, a wealthy cloth merchant who arranged contracts with other Europeans for Bartram to supply them with unique seeds and plants. Bartram collected and recorded hundreds of native American species in trips through Pennsylvania, Georgia, the Carolinas, the lake Erie region, and even Florida. An original member of Benjamin Franklin's American Philosophical Society, he performed the first hybridization experiments in the new world and discovered a flowering tree in the Carolinas he named the *Franklinia alatamaha.* Saved from extinction by Bartram, the Franklinia survives in Bartram's garden and other botanical gardens around the world.

Because he was so poorly educated and found writing so difficult, Bartram published few works during his lifetime. His son William accompanied him on many of his trips, and achieved his own recognition as a botanist and writer with the publication in 1791 of *Travels through North and South Carolina, Georgia, East and West Florida, the Cherokee Country, etc.*, a record of their pioneering travels. John Bartram was highly respected for his work and was appointed Royal Botanist by King George III in 1765. Bartram died in 1777, leaving his garden for succeeding generations to enjoy.

1897: President McKinley presides at the opening ceremonies for the International Commercial Conference at the Academy of Music.

1927: The main building of the Free Library of Philadelphia officially opens.

1930: The Hog Island property is sold to the City of Philadelphia for construction of a municipal airport.

June 3

David Rittenhouse was an accomplished clockmaker, inventor, mathematician, surveyor, and astronomer who is credited with building the first telescope used in the United States. Born in Rittenhouse Town near Germantown in 1732, he was self-taught, and established a workshop for the development of scientific instruments at the age of 19. Clock working was his first commercial enterprise. His interest in astronomy led him to construct a telescope and a plan to observe the transit of Venus on June 3, 1769, at the observatory he had built on the family farm. The transit of Venus occurs rarely, when Venus passes between the Sun and the Earth, and is visible across the face of the Sun. After nearly a year of planning, the excitement of the moment overwhelmed Rittenhouse and he fainted during the observation itself.

Among his pioneering observations, Rittenhouse calculated the Sun to be 93 million miles from Earth, and was the first American to sight Uranus in 1781. In 1768, Rittenhouse was elected a member of the American Philosophical Society, and became its president following founder Benjamin Franklin's death in 1790. Over the course of his life, Rittenhouse published many mathematical papers and treatises, and was greatly admired by Thomas Jefferson and John Adams for his scientific achievements. Skilled as a surveyor, his 1763-64 survey of the Delaware and Pennsylvania border was adopted without change by Mason and Dixon in their survey of the Pennsylvania-Maryland border. In 1784, Rittenhouse completed the survey of the famous Mason-Dixon Line to the edge of southeastern Pennsylvania.

Active in the government of the new nation, Rittenhouse served as the treasurer of Pennsylvania from 1777 to 1789 and was appointed the first Director of the United States Mint in 1792. The first prototype coins to be made at the mint were hand-struck by Rittenhouse. Rittenhouse died in 1796, but his accomplishments were long remembered by Philadelphians. In 1825, one of the original Penn squares in Philadelphia was named Rittenhouse Square in his honor.

1930: The U.S. shipping board signs an agreement to sell the city of Philadelphia Hog Island for $3 million.

June 4

Individual responsibility, personal liberties, and a pacifist approach to conflict are the hallmarks of the Quaker ideals held by founder William Penn and the subsequent legislative and cultural leaders in Pennsylvania. Their great Holy Experiment, defined by a peaceful approach to military and diplomatic conflicts, dominated Pennsylvania politics and the structure of government for over seventy years before violence and anger on the western frontier forced a change. For all intents and purposes, the Holy Experiment was abandoned on this date in 1756 when six leading Quaker assemblymen handed in their resignations, forever altering the future of American Quakers and the structure of Pennsylvania's government.

Nearly twenty years after he first established a colony here, William Penn enacted the basic principles of Pennsylvania governance in the Charter of Privileges of 1701, grounded in the concept of liberty of conscience. Pacifist in nearly every way, the Quaker leadership often refused to acknowledge the need for military intervention and avoided support of the defense of settlers in the far-reaching western lands. By mid-century, however, tensions arose in the western fringes of Pennsylvania between settlers and local tribes, encouraged by France and Spain in hopes of weakening the colony. Violence broke out and hundreds of deaths within the settlements were blamed on attacks by native tribes. The settlers on the western frontier felt isolated and betrayed by the inaction of the Quaker-led Assembly. Anti-Quaker sentiment flourished as more and more Pennsylvanians called for military action and the removal of Quaker political ideals. The French and Indian War was under way, and conflict spread across the northern and middle colonies.

Benjamin Franklin, long a critic of the Penn family and its Quaker practices within government, led the charge to force a change by waging political war in the pages of his newspaper. At the same time, London-based Quakers pushed for Pennsylvania Quakers to give up power and avoid the blame for European deaths and French victories. Finally, the last Quaker leaders resigned, making way for a more defense-minded government. Anti-Quaker attitudes continued, however, carrying over to the American Revolution when many Quakers chose the unpopular position of political and military neutrality. Over the next two centuries, Quakers remained an important aspect of Pennsylvania's cultural identity, even as their numbers dwindled and their political power ended. Launched with the best of intentions and in hopes of bringing peace and liberty to the world, a Holy Experiment found the reality of conflict to be too great a challenge to overcome.

1845: The first American opera, William H. Fry's *Lenora,* is performed for the first time at the Chestnut Street Theater.

1944: Two submarines are launched by the Cramp Shipbuilding Company, dedicated to the first policeman from Philadelphia to die in World War II. Eight thousand people attended.

June 5

Life in eastern Pennsylvania and all along the Interstate-95 highway from Maryland to northern New Jersey seemed to come to a standstill at 10:18 A.M. on this date in 1967. Potentially less dangerous than the historic November 1965 blackout that occurred overnight across four states, the daytime event nevertheless left 13 million people across 15,000 square miles without electrical power. The blackout began when a spike in demand for power across the eastern half of Pennsylvania led to an overload, resulting in the simultaneous breakdown of three power stations. Traffic lights, household appliances, and office buildings alike went dark on what was a typical Tuesday in early summer.

In Philadelphia, the power was temporarily restored within thirty minutes, but the system staggered once again and a secondary blackout ensued. For the next few hours, city residents struggled to move on with their day. For 1,500 passengers on the subway, their journey ended with a flashlight-led exodus from the depths of the underground system. Air traffic, halted by the sudden breakdown of control communications in Philadelphia and Newark airports, came to a standstill while the simple act of crossing the street acquired life-threatening status as traffic lights went dark across the city. Power was finally restored in all affected communities at 7:30 P.M., almost ten hours after the lights first went out.

For many outside the primary areas affected, such as Trenton, Camden, and communities in Delaware and Maryland, the secondary blackout indicated the weaknesses in what was already identified as an outdated and inadequate power grid. Ultimately, the blackout was attributed to a variety of factors, including an aging infrastructure and a minor heat wave that placed a heavy demand on electrical supplies. Though not the most significant blackout in local history, it nevertheless resulted in the recognition that the power grid needed to be expanded and strengthened to meet the needs of a growing, and power-hungry, population.

1793: Congress passes an act licensing the retail sale of liquor.

1855: The Know Nothing Party holds its first political convention in Philadelphia.

1876: Bananas are sold for the first time at the Centennial Exposition; they had been rarely eaten by any American up to that date.

1957: The Philadelphia Free Library opens a special unit for the blind, with more than 50,000 volumes.

1964: Ten religious leaders from the Roman Catholic, Protestant, and Jewish faiths issue a statement condemning racial discrimination as immoral and asserting that it "can in no way be justified."

June 6

Competition for control of meeting the burgeoning demand for quick transportation of people and freight was fraught with quick starts and early failures. Railroad companies, many inspired by the success of technological advances overseas in England and Germany, began laying claim to a variety of routes in and out of Philadelphia. Many of these routes were centuries-old footpaths that had evolved into toll roads and thoroughfares. The northwest path leading out of Philadelphia through the communities of Germantown and Norristown was not the first route to be chosen for development, but it did beat the competition when it opened to great fanfare on this date in 1832.

As early as 1829, small, independent railroad companies sprang up and were incorporated by the dozens long before any construction began. Often named after the terminus points along the route, these early companies included the Delaware and Schuylkill Railroad in 1829, the Philadelphia, Germantown and Norristown Railroad in 1831, and the Philadelphia and Trenton Railroad in 1832. In each case, advance shares of stock were sold, often selling out in the face of great demand. If enough investors were secured (not a guarantee), work was begun on the actual rails. Ultimately, the Philadelphia, Germantown and Norristown Railroad line was the first to formally open, as horse-drawn cars departed the corner of 9th and Green streets for points northwest and arrived in Germantown forty-five minutes later. Fare was twenty-five cents and cars were scheduled to depart every two hours.

The PGNRR served a vital purpose in the early expansion of local industry by providing a consistent and easy connection between the city markets and manufacturers of goods and raw materials coming in from outside Philadelphia. The line also permitted an increase in suburban residential development, as businessmen were able to commute daily to and from their jobs. Within six months of the line opening, horse-drawn cars were abandoned as the new steam locomotives manufactured by industry pioneer Matthias Baldwin pulled as many as four passenger cars at a time and cut travel time in half. Although the company did not survive the great rivalry between the Pennsylvania Railroad and the Reading Railroad, the PGNRR nevertheless proved that even the smallest can compete given opportunity, and timing.

1931: Four high officials of the Philadelphia Police Department narrowly escape death when a mysterious explosion demolishes a former rum-running boat, which had been converted into a police harbor patrol launch.

1944: The sound of the Liberty Bell is broadcast over radio in recognition of the pending landing of United States troops on Normandy, France. The Bell is said to have last been rung in 1835.

With grace and great solemnity, one of Philadelphia's most important religious leaders was laid to rest on this date in 1951. Cardinal Dennis Joseph Dougherty, leader of the Catholic Archdiocese of Philadelphia for thirty-three years, was interred under the high altar of the Cathedral of Saints Peter and Paul in the presence of 2,000 mourners, many of them from among the highest levels of government, religion, and culture. Born in Ashland, Pennsylvania, on August 16, 1865, Dougherty was the first native-born son to rise to the level of cardinal. Educated in public schools, he chose as one of his most essential goals the creation and implementation of Catholic education from first grade through college. By realizing his goals, Cardinal Dougherty forever influenced Philadelphia Catholics and set an example for archdioceses throughout the country.

The fourth of ten children, Dougherty worked during summer vacations as a breaker boy next to his father in the coal mines of Schuylkill County. At the age of fourteen, he passed exams for admission to the St. Charles of Borromeo Seminary but was ultimately denied because of his young age. After studying in Canada for two years, Dougherty returned to enter the seminary and ultimately received a doctorate in theology from the Pontifical Urbanian Athenaeum *De Propaganda Fide* in Rome. He was ordained a priest while in Rome and returned to Philadelphia to teach at the Seminary. In 1903, Dougherty was appointed the thirtieth Bishop of Nueva Segovia, in the Philippines. Facing a splinter group known as the Philippine Independent Group, Dougherty nevertheless regained control of the cathedral and reopened and reconsecrated a number of churches. His success after twelve years led to his being selected as Bishop of Buffalo, New York. While there, he reorganized the Catholic schools and charities and stabilized finances. On May 1, 1918, Dougherty was named Archbishop of Philadelphia. Within three years, he was made the city's first cardinal.

Cardinal Dougherty quickly exhibited managerial controls that explained his reputation for ruling with an iron fist. Deeply interested in overseeing all aspects of diocesan functions as a means of understanding and meeting the needs of Philadelphia Catholics, the cardinal completely reorganized the administrative structure to ensure he always knew every detail. Dougherty continued to serve for the next thirty-three years, during which he established more than 100 new parishes, 75 churches, 146 schools, and a dozen nursing homes and orphanages. For his great work toward creating both a physical and theological infrastructure in which thousands of Philadelphia Catholics lived, learned, and worshiped, Cardinal Daugherty will forever be remembered as "the Great Builder."

1712: The Pennsylvania Assembly bans the importation of slaves.

1848: Abraham Lincoln first visits Philadelphia as a delegate to the Whig Party National Convention.

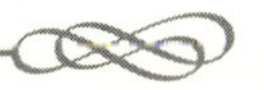

June 8

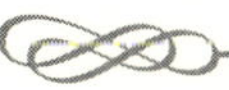

Philadelphia has long enjoyed the benefits of a quantity and quality of newspapers unmatched in any other city. While the vast majority succeeded for just a few months or years, some found great support and established a long-term niche that only they could fill. Founded in 1870 as a two-cent daily, the *Philadelphia Record* was one of those singular publications. Within its first quarter century, the paper was received as one of the best in the country, selling 57 million copies in 1893 alone. Successful for many years, ultimately it lost out to both intense competition with the city's other grand newspaper, the *Philadelphia Inquirer*, but also to an extended strike. It shut down forever in 1947.

The paper's first owner-publisher, William Swain, was also founder of the *Public Ledger*, the city's most prominent newspaper at the time. Swain's intent was to overtake the *Ledger* in sales and popularity, but he never attained this goal. He sold the paper in 1877, one of several significant changes of leadership throughout the paper's history. The new owner, William Singerly, cut the *Record*'s cost by half and ordered the design to be spruced up, resulting in its popularity soaring. Investigative, sensationalistic stories about graverobbers and exposés on bogus medical colleges added to the paper's success. The paper also served as one of the few Democratic voices among the city's publications, at a time when all others supported the Republican agenda. In 1902, after Singerly suffered extensive financial losses in his other investments, the *Record* was purchased by Rodman Wanamaker, son to the department store mogul.

After managing the paper for more than twenty-five years, Wanamaker sold the paper to New Jersey newspaperman David Stern on this date in 1928. Stern continued the Democratic editorials, frequently making the case for labor and progressive politics. Facing competition from Walter Annenberg's *Philadelphia Inquirer*, the two newspapers waged political and journalistic war from across the street, based in buildings that were within sight of each other. In November 1947, a Newspaper Guild strike slowed the presses across the city. Stern, a strong supporter of labor, felt betrayed when his workers walked off the job. Ultimately, the *Record* could not withstand the financial pressures of the strike and Stern shut down permanently on February 1, 1947.

1885: Councilmen of the City of Brotherly Love resort to fisticuffs during a tour of inspection by the Joint Committee on Railroads over proposed routes of the Baltimore and Ohio's branch lines through the city.

1931: The Municipal Auditorium at 34th and Vintage Avenue (opposite the Philadelphia General Hospital) is formally opened when the American Medical Association begins its sessions there.

June 9

With the slow recital of a countdown, Philadelphia experienced the end of the pioneering Philadelphia Naval Hospital when it was demolished on this date in 2001. The nation's first high-rise hospital building constructed for the United States Navy in 1935, the hospital provided state of the art prosthetic and orthopedic care, as well as general care, to thousands of service personnel. At its peak, the hospital featured 650 beds and a total of over 350,000 square feet of floor space. Ultimately, a decline in the use of the hospital's services and difficulty in upgrading its facility and technology led to the decision to close and ultimately demolish the building.

A remarkable and acclaimed example of the Art Deco form of architecture, the hospital was a shining beacon of beauty and high-quality care in its early years. Constructed of yellow brick and brown terra cotta, the fifteen-story hospital featured specially designed elements reflecting its naval relationship, among them heater grates shaped like sailing ships and air intakes in the form of dolphins. Located on forty-nine acres of land, the entire complex comprised more than fifty buildings and included office buildings, a gas station, and residences for the hospital staff. Surrounded by residential neighborhoods, the dedicated military medical mission of the building and its physical height made it an icon on South Broad Street.

After nearly two decades of decline, the Base Realignment and Closure Act of 1988 brought the Naval Hospital to its end. The building was vacated in 1993, and it remained abandoned for the next eight years, guarded only by a small security and maintenance staff. Under the direction of Controlled Demolition, Inc. and Geppert Brothers, two hundred pounds of dynamite was inserted in more than 600 locations throughout the partially gutted main building. Watched by thousands both in person and on television, a part of Philadelphia's great naval and medical history was imploded at 7:02 A.M. Today, the site is the location of the NovaCare Complex, home to training and administrative offices of the Philadelphia Eagles football team.

1790: The *Philadelphia Spelling Book* is copyrighted, the first in the United States.

June 10

Travel by train was the major form of transportation from city to city in the nineteenth and early twentieth centuries. Philadelphia's Broad Street Station was built in 1881 and expanded in 1893 by the Pennsylvania Railroad to bring train travelers directly into center city. Trains would enter the Gothic-style, ornate station by way of a raised stone viaduct known as the "Chinese Wall," because of its supposed resemblance to the Great Wall of China. Debarking at Broad and Market, across from City Hall, passengers could take trolleys and other public transportation to all parts of the city. At the height of its operation, Broad Street Station handled more than 600 arrivals and departures a day, and as early as 1886, a million passengers a month used the station. Consisting of a number of train sheds and multiple tracks, the station's main train shed with its glass roof became the latest engineering leap with the largest single span of any shed in the world at 306 feet.

On this date in 1923, fire broke out in the middle of the night under the shed, the thick black smoke rousing sleeping passengers in Pullman cars. Soon, the entire train shed was on fire, including the baggage room and an underground mail room. Post Office employees attempted to save the mail before being driven out by the flames. As the fire progressed, it went to seven alarms bringing out most of the firemen and firefighting equipment in the city. Within two hours of the start of the fire the great roof of the shed collapsed, sending broken glass and embers flying. One locomotive and its coaches crashed through the floor of the shed, narrowly missing firemen below. Despite their best efforts, the shed and much of the infrastructure under it were destroyed.

After the fire, the Pennsylvania Railroad brought in 3,500 employees to clear the wreckage and reopen the station. This was accomplished in only five days, but within a few years, a new main station at 30th Street was built and the transportation dominance of Broad Street Station ended. The station was torn down in 1952, but a mural from the station, *The Spirit of Transportation,* was preserved and is still viewed daily by thousands of train passengers in the main waiting room at the 30th Street station.

1922: The cornerstone is laid at Franklin Field.

1925: Three amphibious planes take off from the Philadelphia Navy Yard on the first lap of the journey to the North Pole with the MacMillan expedition.

1972: Hank Aaron passes Willie Mays' record with his 649th career homer as the Atlanta Braves rout the Philadelphia Phillies, 15–3.

June 11

Religious liberalism and a trend toward modernism in the Presbyterian Church was soundly rejected on this date in 1936 when John Gresham Machen and several of his conservative colleagues founded the Presbyterian Church of America, now known as the Orthodox Presbyterian Church, at a conference in Philadelphia. Born in Baltimore, Machen was raised within the Presbyterian Church by his mother. At points questioning his faith, he ultimately found answers through his association with the Princeton Theological Seminary. As a Professor of the New Testament at the historically conservative seminary, Machen felt that changes enacted by the Seminary Board in 1929 threatened the correctness of his approach to basic Christian tenets. In protest, he and several other educators from Princeton founded the Westminster Theological Seminary. Machen initially approached the larger General Assembly of the Presbyterian Church of the United States of America in hopes of reestablishing a more orthodox doctrine within the Church, but was rejected. In reply, Machen struck out on his own and organized the Independent Board for Presbyterian Ministers.

Within a few years, the PCUSA deposed Machen and his followers, removing them from the ministry of the PCUSA, which ultimately resulted in the formation of the Orthodox Presbyterian Church. Grounded in the strong Calvinist, evangelical doctrines of the Princeton theology, the OPC was also entirely committed to Reformed Theology. Machen argued for the intellectual truth of the Bible in Christian lives, rather than the more humanist approach of modern liberalism. Often seen as a representation of the Christian Fundamentalist movement of the time, Machen was in fact opposed to fundamentalism's strict adherence to issues involving abstinence from alcohol, anti-communist activism, and a doomsday view of the future. His views led him to an anti-war stance, even as he served in a nonmilitary capacity during the First World War.

Sensitive to the impact of the "social gospel" on members of minority religious groups, Machen and his followers opposed the blending of religion and politics. Opposed to prayer in school as well as the assertion of governmental powers over the individual, he believed in the separation of church and state to the point of arguing against the creation of a national education system. Machen also stood against Prohibition, which he saw as yet another intrusion of the government into private lives. Unable to enjoy the fruits of his beliefs for more than a year after the founding of the OPC, he died, at the age of 55, on January 1, 1937.

1781: A Peace Commission is appointed by Congress. Members include Benjamin Franklin, Thomas Jefferson, John Jay, and Henry Laurens.

1905: The Pennsylvania Railroad debuts the fastest freight train in the world, traveling from New York to Chicago, by way of Philadelphia, in 18 hours. The next day, the Pennsylvania Special (later called the Broadway Limited) set a passenger train speed record from New York City to Chicago of 127.2 M.P.H.

June 12

Fast food is everywhere in America today, some tracing its origin to the first Horn and Hardart automat, which opened on Chestnut and Eighth streets on June 12, 1902. Founded by Philadelphian Joseph Horn and German immigrant Frank Hardart, the chain brought factory concepts for the preparation and delivery of inexpensive, fresh food to the restaurant industry. Food was prepared at a central location under strict quality-control procedures and delivered daily to the outlets. The founders ate lunch every day from a different chain site to ensure the consistency of the food.

Horn and Hardart was especially renowned for its coffee, which was prepared by the French-drip method brought from New Orleans by Hardart. Coffee was prepared on a rigid schedule with new brews every twenty minutes, and meticulous attention was paid to the cleaning of the pots. Irving Berlin's song "Let's Have Another Cup of Coffee" celebrated the beverage and became the theme song of the chain. From 1912 to 1950, a cup of Horn and Hardart coffee cost a nickel. The most distinctive feature of the Horn and Hardart automat was the adoption of vending technology. Instead of being served by waiters, customers put nickels into vending machines and served themselves with sandwiches, pie, rice pudding, and other cold foods. Hot foods, such as the signature macaroni and cheese, creamed spinach, and baked beans, were served cafeteria-style. The restaurants and their "help-yourself" style were hugely popular, and the chain spread to New York and other cities. At its peak the chain served 800,000 people a day.

Horn and Hardart also popularized take-out food, opening outlets primarily in the suburbs and advertising their products as "Less Work for Mother." By the time of Horn's death in 1941, New York City boasted more than fifty Horn and Hardart restaurants. As tastes changed and other fast-food enterprises grew, Horn and Hardart faded into restaurant history. The last automat closed in New York City in April 1991. Today a 35-foot piece of the ornate 1902 Philadelphia eatery is preserved at the Smithsonian Institution in Washington, D.C.

1909: The cornerstone to the new John Wanamaker store on Market Street and Juniper is laid.

June 13

The opportunity to stand witness to a great moment or to be close to a person of fame or fortune comes rarely to most average citizens. Whether one-on-one or en masse, to touch, see, or even hear a revered idol can be a significant experience. On this date in 1927, Philadelphians of all walks of life shared a unique and entirely twentieth-century event when Charles Lindbergh and an escort of twenty-one planes flew over the city on their way to New York. Hundreds of thousands of people stopped everything to cheer the aviators, flanking rooftops and sidewalks all over the Philadelphia region, each seeking his own moment to be close to one of the most famous men in the world.

Less than a month before, Lindbergh had completed his astounding flight across the Atlantic Ocean from New York City to Paris, France, piloting his specially designed airplane *Spirit of St. Louis.* Just before 8:00 A.M. on May 20, Lindbergh took off from Roosevelt Field and landed in Paris a mere thirty-three and a half hours later. He had completed the first solo flight across the Atlantic Ocean, one single event that raised him to the level of miracle worker in the hearts and minds of most Americans. Lindbergh returned to Washington, D.C., aboard the USS *Memphis,* traveling up the Chesapeake Bay and Potomac River. After being welcomed home by President Coolidge, Lindbergh took off for a major tickertape parade planned for June 13 in New York City.

News of Lindbergh's flight through the Delaware Valley on his way to New York spread like wildfire, and thousands waited with baited breath to catch sight of the bright-yellow U.S. Navy plane piloted by Lindbergh. At approximately 11:30 A.M., Lindbergh and his convoy of planes flew over the city. Thousands of Philadelphians literally stopped in their tracks, bringing businesses and city activity to a halt. They were ultimately only a fraction of the total number of Americans who witnessed his triumphant journey. In New York, a remarkable four million Americans were said to have lined the streets during what may well have been the largest parade in city history up to that time. Lindbergh visited Philadelphia again in October as part of a 22,000-mile tour of the country, giving local fans one last chance to be a part of history.

1782: Congress asks Charles Thomson to create a Great Seal.

1963: The U.S. Navy provides its first public demonstration of a boat that rides on an air bubble. It was a success after five failures.

June 14

That the flag of the United States shall be of thirteen stripes of alternate red and white, with a union of thirteen stars of white in a blue field, representing the new constellation." With this resolution, the Continental Congress on June 14, 1777, in Philadelphia established the design for our national flag. At the siege of Boston in 1776, it is believed General George Washington ordered the Grand Union Flag to fly over his headquarters. This flag, also known as the Congress Flag, had thirteen alternate red and white stripes with the British Union Jack appearing in the upper left-hand corner. Much to the annoyance of the Americans, the Grand Union Flag was interpreted by the British as a sign of surrender. Washington was determined to adopt an American flag that would clearly represent the emerging nation.

Though the true history of the birth of the iconic first flag with a circle of stars in a blue field and thirteen stripes is unknown, the apocryphal story of Betsy Ross and her role in the design is well known. Ultimately, the new flag first appeared in battle on September 11, 1777, at the Battle of the Brandywine south of the city. Over the years, the design of the flag was altered to accommodate new states, but it was not until a century later that efforts toward establishing an observance of Flag Day began.

Early celebrations took place in other states, but in 1893, Elizabeth Duane Gillespie, a direct descendant of Benjamin Franklin and the leader of the Society of Colonial Dames, succeeded in having the City of Philadelphia adopt a requirement to fly the flag at all public buildings. The Colonial Dames also tried to have June 14 declared Flag Day, but it was not until May 7, 1937, that Pennsylvania became the first and still the only state to establish Flag Day as a legal holiday. In August 1949, President Harry Truman and Congress approved a national observance of Flag Day on June 14 of every year, honoring one of our most revered symbols of American independence and democracy.

1951: UNIVAC I (Universal Automatic Computer I), the first computer developed for commercial use, is delivered to the United States Census Bureau, its first customer.

June 15 

Philadelphia history includes many examples of people overcoming adversity; one of the most unlikely success stories is the life of John Carlin. John Carlin lost his hearing in infancy, soon after his birth on June 15, 1813. In 1820, David Seixas, a Philadelphia philanthropist, took Carlin in as one of sixteen students in the first class of the Mount Airy School for Deaf (now the Pennsylvania School for the Deaf). There, Carlin learned reading, writing, and sign language from Laurent Clerc, a pioneer in teaching the deaf. In 1834, he established a painter's studio at Queen Street specializing in miniature portraits. After an extended trip to Europe to study art, he established a studio in New York, where he painted miniatures of prominent people.

As the camera destroyed the market for miniatures, Carlin turned to larger works, mostly landscapes and topical paintings. His work was exhibited at the Pennsylvania Academy of the Fine Arts and the American Art Union. His art career proved what he believed, that deaf and hard of hearing people could, and should, live lives of equal challenge and accomplishment as those lived by others. In addition to his talent as an artist, Carlin gained fame as a deaf poet, something that most people thought would be impossible. He published his most famous poem "A Mute's Lament" in the first issue of the *American Annals of the Deaf* and also was published in such mainstream publications as *Harper's New Monthly Magazine* and various newspapers. His ability to write poetry was attributed partly to his intensive reading of Shakespeare, Milton, and other poets, and his use of pronunciation and rhyming dictionaries. The editor of the *American Annals of the Deaf* said of his achievement that "we should almost as soon expect a man born blind to become a landscape painter, as one born deaf to produce poetry of even tolerable merit."

Active in the deaf community, Carlin had an influence on Edwin Galludet in the founding of the first college for the deaf and raised funds for schools and homes for the aged deaf. Carlin was conflicted about the value of sign language, and encouraged deaf people to learn to read lips in addition to sign. In an 1854 essay in support of a college for the deaf, Carlin said that "there can be found no difference between speaking persons or deaf mutes, of the higher class, in imagination, strength, depth of thoughts, and quickness of mind." In 1864, he was awarded the first honorary degree from Galludet University. He died in 1891.

1752: Benjamin Franklin tests the relationship between electricity and lightning by flying a kite in a thunderstorm.

1769: Birth of Adam Eckfeldt, first coiner of the U.S. Mint and likely coiner for the first United States half dime.

1775: The Second Continental Congress unanimously votes to place Washington as general and commander-in-chief of the new Continental Army.

June 16

Philadelphia was known among the colonies as a center of music performance and publishing. Although few people today know his name, Francis "Frank" Johnson was an important figure in early-nineteenth-century music in the city, the Northeast, and abroad. Originally thought to have emigrated from the West Indies, recent scholarship confirms that he was born in Philadelphia on June 16, 1792, a free African-American. Virtually nothing is known of his childhood, but by 1819 he was an established bandleader in the city and during the 1820s he and his band played extensively at dancing schools, balls, and parties. His group was versatile, incorporating string or wind instruments as appropriate for the music and the event. Highly skilled on the keyed bugle, Johnson was among the first to introduce this instrument to band work in America.

A composer of more than two hundred pieces, Johnson was the first African-American to have his music published. His work included marches, cotillions, popular songs, quadrilles, and arrangements of classical music. In 1824, he composed most of the music played in the many celebrations surrounding Lafayette's return to Philadelphia. He also received numerous commissions from military groups in the city, including the First Troop Philadelphia Cavalry. Playing primarily in the city in winter and on tour in the summer, his band ranged from Toronto to Mount Vernon, where he participated in the 100th anniversary of Washington's birth. In addition to his performances, Johnson operated a music school in the city.

In 1837, Johnson took four of his band members to England, where they played everything from Mozart to popular American tunes. After a command performance, the recently crowned Queen Victoria gave Johnson the gift of a silver bugle. This European trip exposed Johnson to Viennese waltzes and made him famous internationally as the first American bandleader to tour overseas. Johnson continued his teaching and performances until his death in April 1844. At his funeral march, his band and hundreds of others paid tribute as his casket led the procession, topped with his silver bugle.

1863: Mayor Henry issues a proclamation calling on the citizens to close their places of business and prepare to defend the State. The State House bell tolls at 3:00 P.M. A large assembly is convened in Independence Square.

1864: President Lincoln visits the Sanitary Fair and asks that Americans be ready to respond to emergencies of war.

June 17

The Republican Party began in 1854 in Ripon, Wisconsin. Founded by former Whigs, Democrats, abolitionists, and members of the Free Soil Party, its formation was spurred by opposition to the Kansas-Nebraska Act. The Act opened the territories of Kansas and Nebraska to slavery, reversing the provisions of the Missouri Compromise of 1820. By the start of the first Republican national convention in Philadelphia on June 17, 1856, violence in "bloody" Kansas between pro- and anti-slavery proponents had led President Franklin Pierce to send in federal troops. The nation was in crisis, and the *Philadelphia Evening Bulletin* newspaper spoke for many when it stated that "a more important convention . . . has not been assembled in our city, perhaps not the country, since the days of 1776."

Six hundred delegates attended the convention, which was held at the Musical Fund Hall on Locust Street. The hall seated 1,200 and its acoustics were excellent. More than 100 reporters covered the convention from prime seats at the front of the auditorium. The convention adopted a platform calling for prohibiting slavery and polygamy in the Territories, and admitting Kansas to the union as a free state. It also called on the federal government to support construction of a railroad to the Pacific, and "restoring the action of the Federal Government to the principles of Washington and Jefferson."

When the convention turned to the selection of candidates for President and Vice President, the contenders were Senator Salmon Chase of Ohio, Senator William Seward of New York, and retired Army officer John C. Fremont. Seen as a national hero for his multiple crossings of the Rockies and his military service, Fremont was the choice of the convention. For Vice President, Abraham Lincoln was one of fifteen candidates, with the convention ultimately selecting William L. Dayton, a former senator from New Jersey. The convention of 1856 did not lead to an electoral victory that year, but by 1860 Lincoln prevailed as the Republican Party's candidate for President, and the nation soon entered the Civil War, which tested American democracy, preserved the union, and ended slavery.

1862: An ordinance is passed to purchase League Island for $310,000 with the intent to present the land to the United States government for the construction of naval ironclads.

June 18

"Last week, I went to Philadelphia, but it was closed." This famous W. C. Fields movie line represents the view of Philadelphia as a somewhat staid and conservative city, certainly as compared with Chicago or New York. Blue laws, prohibiting a wide variety of Sunday activities, were the foundation of this reputation. As early as 1682, William Penn's "Great Law" as adopted by the Pennsylvania Assembly, prohibited any work or social activity on the Sunday Sabbath. Quaker Philadelphians read the scriptures and attended church services on that day. Temperance and moderation were expected during the rest of the week, with prohibitions against cards, dice, stage plays, cockfighting, and "rude and riotous" sports.

As Philadelphia grew and Anglicans and others came to the city, restrictions were lifted. By early in the eighteenth century, dances, theatrical performances, and a variety of sports, including horse racing, ice skating, and swimming, were popular. Taverns were also growing in both number and customers, much to the displeasure of Quaker residents. Keeping the Sabbath was still seen as highly important, and in 1794 it became a crime for businesses to operate on Sunday in the city. As the nineteenth century progressed, tensions arose as the temperance movement kept liquor sales on the Sabbath out of the city, but the growing economy demanded Sunday work hours. In a unique case reflecting the conflict between blue laws and industry, the United States Supreme Court ruled that a railroad could not evade responsibility for damages to a ship just because it was traveling on a Sunday.

Blue laws continued into the twentieth century, with Sunday professional baseball becoming legal only in 1934. Four days after the end of Prohibition, the Pennsylvania Liquor Control Board was established, prohibiting the sale of bottled wine and liquor except in "state stores." In the city, liquor by the drink could be served on Sunday only in private clubs. In 1961, five Jewish businessmen challenged the Sunday closing laws, but the United States Supreme Court stepped in once again and ruled that the blue laws did not violate individual freedom of religion. On this date in 1967, Sunday sale of liquor was legalized in the city for the first time in 167 years. Sunday business restrictions have been lifted, but the "state stores" remain, opening on Sundays for liquor sales for the first time in 2002. Philadelphia is no longer "closed," but the legacy of blue laws continues.

1778: Led by General Henry Clinton, the British evacuate Philadelphia. American forces enter the city.

1971: Schools in Philadelphia and Pittsburgh are ordered to "eliminate" racial imbalances in public school districts today by the Pennsylvania Human Relations Commission.

June 19

As a nation, the United States can claim less than ten American Saints of the Catholic faith. Philadelphia, long a home to a significant number of Catholics resulting from a combination of early policies of religious tolerance and a later role as point of entry for thousands of immigrants, is home to two saints—Katharine Drexel and John Nepomucene Neumann. While Drexel was American-born, Neumann is more typical of American saints, born in Europe and drawn to service in the United States. As a missionary, Neumann lived and traveled across the country, but it was in Philadelphia where he made his most significant impact and here that he is most strongly remembered today.

Born the son of a mill owner, in Prachatitz, Belgium, in 1811, Neumann did not commit to the priesthood until he was twenty years old. After training in Prague, Neumann found that there was a surplus of priests and he was unable to be ordained. Looking to the pioneering opportunities available as a missionary in America, Neumann applied to the Diocese of New York, from which he served in churches in Buffalo, Baltimore, and Pittsburgh. Particularly skilled at languages, Neumann worked with German, Italian, and Irish students, teaching them catechism and striving to improve educational opportunities. Finally, in March 1852, he was consecrated in Baltimore as Bishop of Philadelphia.

In Philadelphia, Neumann continued his work in education as bishop, developing the first Catholic diocesan school system in the country and ultimately increasing the number of Philadelphia parochial schools from one to one hundred. In addition to schools, Neumann built a number of churches, at an estimated rate of one a month, some of which were specifically meant to serve Italian, Irish, or German immigrants. Challenged by the anti-Catholic Know Nothings, Neumann nevertheless worked to stabilize and support the Catholic Church in Philadelphia. He died suddenly of a stroke on January 5, 1860. A century later, Neumann was canonized on this date in 1977 in recognition of his role in building the Archdiocese of Philadelphia. He lies at rest in a glass reliquary at the National Shrine of Saint John Neumann at the St. Peter the Apostle Church in Philadelphia.

1778: George Washington's troops leave Valley Forge in hopes of intercepting the British on their way to New York City.

1778: General Benedict Arnold reenters Philadelphia and takes over command as Town Major after the British withdraw.

1787: The Constitutional Convention votes to completely reinvent the government rather than revise the current Articles of Confederation, resulting in the United States Constitution.

June 20

They say that three's the charm, and in the case of the design of the Great Seal of the United States, nothing could be truer. As early as July 4, 1776, the Continental Congress established a committee for the sole purpose of designing a national emblem, to be used primarily in the signing of international treaties and agreements. Elements as varied as eagles, Hercules, chariots, crowns, and clouds vied for favor. Finally, six years, three committees, and countless designs later, a final version of the Great Seal of the United States was both proposed and adopted on this date in 1782.

The first committee, with members Benjamin Franklin, Thomas Jefferson, and John Adams, looked to artist Pierre Eugene du Simitiere for assistance in designing what they thought of as a traditional herald in the form of a shield in six sections. Each section represented a country of origin for the people of the United States and ringed by state names. A female figure representing Liberty and an American soldier stood to the side, supporting the shield, with an anchor of hope, the Eye of Providence (a radiant triangle) and a spear, rifle, and tomahawk. Franklin urged the motto *E Pluribus Unum,* Latin for "Out of Many, One," as well as a depiction of the parting of the Red Sea by Moses for the reverse of the seal. The design was unpopular in Congress and was soundly rejected. A second committee, this time led by Francis Hopkinson, kept several motifs and resubmitted a design that included red and white stripes and thirteen stars. It too, was rejected, as were the suggestions of yet another committee formed a few months later.

Finally, on June 13, 1782, Secretary to Congress Charles Thomson was asked to compile a final design drawing from all three previous submissions. Basing much of his work on the third design, Thomson depicted an American bald eagle supporting a shield of thirteen stripes. In the eagle's claws were an olive branch and a bundle of thirteen arrows. Franklin's motto was also incorporated. For the reverse, Thomson combined the Eye of Providence and a thirteen-step pyramid. The seal was approved and remains today the primary symbol of the United States government. Variations have been created for use as the Seal of the President of the United States and numerous government agencies.

1775: Thomas Jefferson arrives in Philadelphia for the first time to attend the First Continental Congress as a delegate for Virginia.

1918: The Beam-Fletcher Transportation Company is organized in Philadelphia to operate a fleet of motor trucks between cities within a radius of 100 miles.

1940: The Philadelphia Municipal Airport opens.

June 21

Political trends in anti-government or anti-establishment protests are often the result of conflicts between public opinion and the policies of a governing power. Anti-war, anti-tax, and anti-violence are all versions of protests frequently seen in Philadelphia and across the country. Historically, Philadelphia experienced many significant protests, perhaps most notably those enacted against the British rule that eventually led to American independence. Within just a few years of gaining victory over the British, Philadelphia was also the scene of a more extreme form of protest, a military mutiny that eventually forced the temporary relocation of Congress and inspired the creation of Washington, D.C.

On June 17, 1783, Congress, seated in Philadelphia under the Articles of Confederation, received a letter from locally stationed Continental Army soldiers demanding back pay for their service during the war, which had officially ended just two months earlier. At the time, Congress held no direct authority over the military, relying instead on local and state militia. Congress made no response to the demands, choosing to ignore the threat made by the soldiers that they intended to take action if ignored. Two days later, Congress was informed that eighty soldiers had abandoned their posts in Lancaster and were en route to Philadelphia. Upon their arrival, they joined with soldiers stationed at the city barracks, bringing the number to more than 500 disgruntled and armed men.

On June 20, the men stormed the State House, barricading the doors and refusing to let the congressional delegates leave. Alexander Hamilton, future Secretary of the Treasury under Washington, successfully negotiated a temporary peace, but also secretly urged the Pennsylvania Executive Council to intervene. Hamilton threatened the state with the likelihood that Congress would be forced to leave Philadelphia if help was not provided. On June 21, the Pennsylvania Executive Council refused again to protect Congress, fearing that the local militia would side with the mutinous soldiers and perhaps feeling a bit supportive themselves of the stated grievances. Without assurances of their own safety and that of the government, Congress left that day for Princeton.

Eventually, Congress paid the soldiers their due and the conflict was resolved with no legal proceedings enacted. For several years Congress continued to move, with Annapolis, Maryland; Trenton, New Jersey; and New York City each serving at various points as the nation's capital. Congress would not return to Philadelphia again until 1787, in response to the call for a new government structure and the eventual creation of the U.S. Constitution. In hopes of avoiding a similar situation where Congress was left unprotected, the creation of a new national District was included in the new Constitution, the direct result of a single mutiny.

1884: The first public swimming pool opens in Philadelphia.

1948: The Republican National Convention opens. Democrats open their own convention in Philadelphia on July 12.

1995: Wanamaker Department Store is sold to May Department Stores.

 June 22 

Singer, songwriter, and producer Todd Rundgren is known for a diversity of sounds and musical styles. Born on this date in 1948, Rundgren is frequently represented on compilations of music from the 1970s for his single "Hello It's Me," while his later work with artists as varied as MeatLoaf, Foghat, and XTC suggests his success in the music field is not limited to just a few hits. Today, Rundgren travels the country and continues to perform the music that best represents his early life in Philadelphia and the musical influences he experienced in the city of his birth and beyond.

As a teenager, Rundgren lived and went to school in Upper Darby Township, located in Delaware County just to the west of Philadelphia. As a student at Upper Darby High School, he formed his first band, called Money. In proximity to music venues such as the Tower Theater and many smaller clubs downtown, Rundgren soon realized his interest in the sounds of psychedelia and formed the Nazz in 1967, with which he performed as opening act for the Doors that same year. With band manager John Kurland's guidance, the band turned toward the more marketable sound of pop, producing their first album and the hit "Hello It's Me." Relationships within the band broke down soon after and in 1969 Rundgren left the Nazz to start a new band, Runt. With Runt, Rundgren joined the Bearsville Records label and maintained more control over the sound, resulting in a less commercial but more critically acclaimed album, titled *Runt.*

By the mid-1970s, Rundgren once again changed bands and organized Utopia, a somewhat experimental musical exploration of psychedelic rock instrumentals. Balancing his progressive work with pop-centric productions, Rundgren found a way to employ a diversity of interests and talents. At the same time, Rundgren was increasingly in demand as an engineer and producer, and was invited to work with acts such as Bette Midler, Hall and Oates, Patti Smith, and the Ramones. In 1983, he released a solo album of pop music, *The Ever Popular Tortured Artist Effect,* which included the song "Bang on the Drum All Day," now ubiquitous for its use at sporting events and on Friday end-of-work radio broadcasts. In the last two decades, Rundgren has continued to produce and explore through interactive music releases and limited-engagement tours, often featuring musicians drawn from all music styles.

1865: George Moore, a Philadelphia Seaman in the U.S. Navy, is awarded the Medal of Honor for his efforts in rescuing officers and the crew of the USS *Monitor* in December 1862.

1948: United States senator Edward Martin steps out of the Republican race for president and endorses Dewey.

1978: Mayor Rizzo officiates at the ground breaking of the commuter tunnel and calls it the greatest day in Philadelphia history. The tunnel finally opens on November 10, 1984.

June 23

For a quarter of a century, Philadelphia has been home to one of the most important professional bike races in the country: the Philadelphia International Championship. This pro cycling event has hosted some of the most famous names in the sport, and is known internationally for the difficulty of the course. Until 2005, it served as the official national championship of American pro cycling. Two Philadelphians, current Pro-Cycling President David M. Chauner and Chief Operating Officer Gerard F. Casale, sought to develop a 156-mile race course that would rival European courses in difficulty, while introducing the cycling world to the charms of their native city. They chose a route along the Ben Franklin Parkway, up the Schuylkill, and into the Manayunk neighborhood.

Manayunk, with its narrow cobble-stoned and steep streets lined with nineteenth-century row houses, was a part of the city that the race founders thought would seem familiar to European riders. Its suitability for a pro cycling event was capped by the presence of what became known as the Manayunk Wall. In cycling terms, a "wall" is a steep gradient, and in this race cyclists go up the half-mile, 17 percent–grade on each of ten laps, cheered on by the thousands that line the streets of Manayunk to enjoy the cyclists' efforts.

The first race was won on this date in 1985 by Eric Heiden, who turned pro cycler after his Gold Medal speed-skating performances in the 1980 Winter Olympics. Lance Armstrong won his first professional race by beating the "Wall" in 1993, earning a million dollars for winning a triple crown of races that year. Manayunk has changed from the first years of the race, going through a re-gentrification that brought new retail businesses, restaurants, and revitalized housing to the area. Parts of the neighborhood were placed on the National Register of Historic Places in 1984, and a plaque honors the Wall's place in cycling history.

1683: William Penn signs the friendship treaty with Lenni Lenape.

1936: The Democratic National Convention opens.

June 24

One of the most important characteristics of William Penn's new world colony was the religious freedom it offered to dissident European groups. Driven by Penn's own writings and the publication of several volumes describing both the natural and cultural advantages of the colony, word spread very quickly about the opportunity for religious freedom for settlers in Pennsylvania. On this date in 1694, only a decade after the founding of the colony, Johannes Kelpius and his followers arrived from Germany. They were among the most unusual religious sects to settle in Philadelphia for they had come to await the end of the world.

Kelpius was a university-educated religious mystic, musician, author, and heretical Christian who also studied botany, astronomy, and the occult. His analysis of the book of Revelation in the Bible led him to believe the world would end in 1694. Seeking a place in the wilderness to wait for the end, Kelpius and his followers came to Philadelphia and settled in the beautiful valley of the Wissahickon Creek. Committed to celibacy and a life of contemplation, the group lived in small huts or caves supplemented by a large meetinghouse. Although they were known as the Hermits of the Wissahickon, they interacted with others in the community, opening a school for children, organizing study groups, and providing medical care. Music was an important part of their lives and Kelpius wrote a hymnbook that is thought to be the earliest music book written in America. The mystics also had a pipe organ built by an English convert. Also known as the "Society of the Woman in the Wilderness," the group was alleged to have been interested in numerology, with the number forty having special significance.

As the years went by without the world ending, the sect slowly dissolved. Kelpius died in 1708. Deep in the Wissahickon, which is now part of Fairmount Park, there is a cave that is purported to be Kelpius' home. A marker indicates that Kelpius is considered to be the first Rosicrucian master in America. The Rosicrucians (from rose and cross) are a brotherhood of persons whose mystical philosophy and beliefs are said to have begun in ancient Egypt, but which spread as far as the side of a creek in northwest Philadelphia by way of one of the region's most interesting residents.

1731: The first Masonic Lodge in the Americas, Libre B, or the St. John's Lodge of Philadelphia, meets for the first time.

1783: Congress leaves Philadelphia for Princeton in hopes of avoiding the wrath of protesting army veterans, whose back wages Congress eventually pays.

1817: Governor and Signer of the Declaration of Independence Thomas McKean dies.

1940: The Republican Convention opens in Philadelphia; on June 28, delegates nominate Wendell Wilkie and Charles L. McNary.

June 25

Modernist architecture is characterized by little or no ornamentation, an emphasis on function, and the use of man-made materials such as concrete. A leading modernist architect, Mies van der Rohe described the approach as "less is more." Postmodernism in architecture is a reaction to the austerity of modernism. Its ground-breaking proponent, Robert Venturi, is a Philadelphia architect, who with wife and partner Denise Scott Brown, devised an approach to architecture using decoration and classical elements that argues "less is a bore."

Robert Venturi was born in Philadelphia on June 25, 1925, the son of a fruit grocer. He studied architecture at Princeton and spent two years in Rome, especially experiencing the art and architecture of the Baroque period. Returning to the United States, he established a partnership with John Rauch in 1958. In 1966, Venturi married Scott Brown and she joined the firm. Their theories and designs were not popular among potential clients and Venturi spent many years teaching at the University of Pennsylvania. During this period, he designed a house for his mother in the Chestnut Hill neighborhood that expressed his vision. The Vanna Venturi house, with its distorted symmetry and hints of classical styles, was alternately praised and derided by public and critics alike.

In the late 1960s, Venturi published two books that revolutionized thinking about architecture. *Complexity and Contradiction in Architecture* argued that architects should reject the stark and impersonal forms of modernism and look to classical architecture with its ornamentation, and hybrid elements. In it he wrote, "I am for messy vitality over obvious unity. I am for richness of meaning rather than clarity of meaning." His subsequent book on Las Vegas commercial architecture, written with Denise Scott Brown and Steven Izenour, treated the architecture of the "strip" seriously, arguing that it was a vernacular art form and offering lessons for architects about what engages people and helps them relate to their environment. Ultimately, these works and the buildings that Venturi and the firm designed according to their philosophy were recognized as important in the history of architecture. Venturi was awarded the Pritzker Prize in Architecture in 1991. He and Denise Scott Brown continue the firm and live in Philadelphia.

1798: President John Adams approves and signs into law an Act Concerning Aliens.

1856: Mademoiselle Delon makes a balloon ascent in Philadelphia, and is believed to be the first female aeronaut to appear here. She arose from an enclosure at the corner of Seventh and Callowhill streets, and landed safely on a farm about a mile and a half north of Tacony.

June 26

Philadelphia is no stranger to the peculiar relationship between Americans and the lucrative soft drink industry. Birthplace to the first application of carbonated water to a sweetened beverage in 1807, the city inspired a soda fountain craze following the Centennial Exposition in 1876. One of several beneficiaries of the growing American interest in fizzy drinks was Charles E. Hires, who first introduced his "root beer" to visitors to the Centennial. By the end of his first year selling root beer, Hires claimed to have poured more than 115,000 glasses of the drink. On this date in 1906, the word "Hires" was registered as a company trademark, securing forever the name's association with the sweet, dark treat.

Charles Elmer Hires, born to a farming family in rural Pennsylvania in 1851, early on decided to establish himself in the big city and moved to Philadelphia by the age of fifteen. An unofficial student at the Philadelphia College of Pharmacy, Hires established his first pharmacy in 1869 and quickly achieved success by virtue of his hard work and creative product development. In addition to traditional remedies and cures, Hires devised a dried clay product used as a wool and flannel cleaning agent, dramatically increasing his annual revenue. He married in 1875 and on his honeymoon acquired the recipe for a traditional "root tea," used for generations by tribes indigenous to the area.

Returning to Philadelphia, Hires experimented with the recipe and devised his unique formula for the tea. Inspired by his friend Russell Conwell, founder of Temple University, Hires marketed his drink at the 1876 Centennial Exposition to great acclaim. Conwell, a devout Christian and advocate of the temperance movement, recommended the name "root beer" in hopes of appealing to the many hard-drinking laborers in the city. The Hires Company went on to great success, expanding their product line to include condensed milk, later sold to the Borden Company. Though never benefiting as sole owners of the root beer patent, the company name continues to inspire thoughts of one of America's first soft drinks.

1977: Tens of thousands of Philadelphians gather at an outdoor mass to honor newly canonized Saint John Neumann.

June 27

In the early part of the nineteenth century, naturalists and explorers expanded our knowledge of the geography, flora, and fauna of America. One of these was Thomas Say of Philadelphia, known as the father of descriptive entomology (the study of insects) and also an expert on mollusks. Born on June 27, 1787, Say was the great-grandson of the botanist John Bartram. Trained as an apothecary, Say was a self-taught naturalist and in 1812 he became a charter member of the Academy of Natural Sciences in Philadelphia, where he served as a curator from 1812 to 1826 and a professor of zoology from 1821 to 1825.

In 1818, Say and William Maclure, who is known as the father of American geology, traveled to islands off Georgia and to Florida, then a Spanish colony, to collect specimens. Say would also join the Major Stephen H. Long expedition to the Rocky Mountains in 1820, serving as the zoologist. The expedition traveled through Nebraska, Colorado, and Oklahoma, collecting specimens of plants, animals, and fossils. The collared lizard, which is now the official lizard of the State of Oklahoma, was first collected and described by Say on this trip, and the accounts of his travels provide the first descriptions of the coyote, Say's phoebe, and the western kingbird, among many other birds and animals.

Accompanying Maclure and other scientists, Say joined the experimental communistic settlement established by Robert Owen at New Harmony, Indiana, in 1826. Owen was one of the founders of socialism and sought to establish a utopian community. Once there, Say married Lucy Way Sitare, who was an artist and illustrator of specimens and the first woman member of the Academy of Natural Sciences. The community failed two years after its founding, but Say and others remained in New Harmony where Say wrote two classic works of science and nature, on the insects and shells of North America. In his career, Say described more than 1,000 new species of beetles and more than 400 species of insects. Inspired by his remarkable drive and desire to learn about the natural world, a number of zoologists have named birds and animals in his honor. Thomas Say died of fever in New Harmony at the age of 47 in 1834.

1796: David Rittenhouse dies.

1936: Franklin Roosevelt accepts the nomination of his party for a second term as president on the closing day of the Democratic National Convention in Philadelphia. The president's unprecedented four terms in office would lead to the 22nd Amendment in 1951, which limited a president to two terms.

June 28

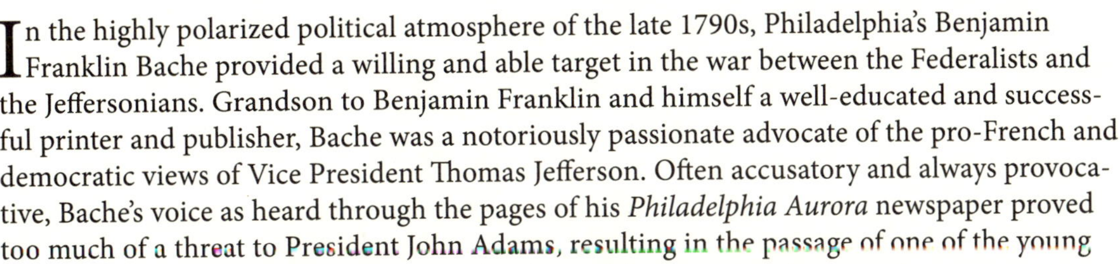

In the highly polarized political atmosphere of the late 1790s, Philadelphia's Benjamin Franklin Bache provided a willing and able target in the war between the Federalists and the Jeffersonians. Grandson to Benjamin Franklin and himself a well-educated and successful printer and publisher, Bache was a notoriously passionate advocate of the pro-French and democratic views of Vice President Thomas Jefferson. Often accusatory and always provocative, Bache's voice as heard through the pages of his *Philadelphia Aurora* newspaper proved too much of a threat to President John Adams, resulting in the passage of one of the young nation's most restrictive laws involving freedom of the press and free speech.

As a young man, Bache enjoyed the benefits of a European education while his grandfather served as American envoy to France. He also endured the loneliness and isolation of a boarding school education, gaining a reputation as a shy, insular young man. Following his grandfather's death in 1790, Bache acquired a printing press and shop as well as many of Franklin's books. Bache quickly established himself as a strong supporter of Jefferson, frequently writing taunting and aggressive editorials criticizing the Adams administration for its anti-French stance and a decidedly militaristic stance. In 1798, Adams supported passage of the Alien and Sedition Act, which would make illegal anything the government deemed false, scandalous, and malicious, severely limiting the ability of newspapers to include anti-government editorials. On this date in June, a full two weeks before the official vote to pass the law, Bache was arrested and charged with sedition, a clear indication that ending Bache's actions was a primary reason for enacting the law.

Bache was released from jail on $4,000 bail on June 29, 1798. His trial was set for October, but Bache merely returned to his newspaper and continued his written attacks against the president and his administration. In his own words, "prosecution no more than persecution" could keep him from fighting for the cause he believed in. Bache argued that the Sedition Act itself was unconstitutional, and a violation of all that was truly patriotic. Unfortunately, he never had an opportunity to defend himself in court. Bache died of yellow fever on September 10, 1798, and is buried in Christ Church Burial Ground, just a few feet from his famous grandfather and within sight of Independence Hall.

1948: President Harry Truman signs a bill authorizing the creation of Independence National Historical Park.

June 29

The history of great American cities is often reflected in the history of their leading newspapers. In Philadelphia, the *Inquirer* and the *Bulletin* reported the news, got involved in the issues of the day, and pursued interests and ideas for generations. Founded on June 1, 1829, the *Philadelphia Inquirer* is the third-oldest surviving newspaper in the United States. In its early years it was published from a shop on Bank Alley, between Front and Second streets. In the 1840s, it not only published Edgar Allan Poe's "The Raven" for the first time, but was the first American paper to obtain serial rights to several novels by Charles Dickens.

During the Civil War, the *Inquirer* was known for its objective reporting. It was circulated widely among Union troops and also read by Confederate forces trying to track the movement of Union forces. In 1863, it was one of the first papers to use a web feed rotary press, allowing printing on both sides of the paper. By the start of the twentieth century, the Elverson family owned the newspaper, which was characterized as the "Republican Bible of Pennsylvania." The *Inquirer* maintained a rivalry with several local competitors, but primarily with the continued Democrat-leaning *Bulletin,* which closed its presses for good in 1982. In 1925, the Elverson family moved the paper to its current location at Broad and Callowhill streets, just across the street from the *Bulletin* offices. The paper was taken over by the Annenberg family in 1936, which remained its owners and adopted the slogan "an independent newspaper for all the people." They continued to publish the newspaper until 1969.

The *Inquirer* was one of the leading daily papers in the last part of the twentieth century, winning many editorial and reporting awards. In 1995, Knight-Ridder, publishers of the *Inquirer,* began making content available through a Web site. The twenty-first century has witnessed a deepening decline in the fortune of newspapers, many of which have suffered from competition by the Internet and a market increasingly polarized by their content. On June 29, 2006, the paper was sold to a group of Philadelphia businessmen led by Brian Tierney, CEO of Philadelphia Newspapers, LLC. That group filed for bankruptcy in February 2009, leading to an auction sale of the paper to its creditors on April 28, 2010. As is the case with many big city papers, the future of the *Inquirer* remains uncertain.

1863: A general mustering for defense of the advance of Confederate General Robert E. Lee and his forces is called. Earthworks are constructed on roads leading to the city in hopes of keeping the Confederates at bay.

June 30

As early as 1887, a ballpark in North Philadelphia served as the home of the Phillies. After fire claimed the first wooden stadium, it was replaced in 1895 by what was later named the Baker Bowl in honor of Phillies owner William F. Baker. The stadium is considered by some sports historians to be the first modern ballpark built for baseball, featuring cantilevered concrete supports that eliminated many of the wooden columns which had created "obstructed view seats." A railroad tunnel ran under the outfield, leading to the nickname "the Hump." The Phillies played their last game at the Baker Bowl on June 30, 1938, losing to the New York Giants, 14–1. The Baker Bowl was demolished in 1950.

For more than forty years, the Baker Bowl was the scene of lively action and baseball history. Its unusual dimensions, with a short right of only 280 feet, led some to describe it as a "cigar box." Always a hitter's park, many believed teams enjoyed a 25 percent increase in runs because of the layout. For example, the 1920 Phillies had 50 home runs at home, while managing only 14 on the road that year. Despite its reputation as a hitter's park, Grover Cleveland Alexander's 1916 season record of 16 shutouts still stands today. In 1915, the Baker Bowl hosted the World Series, with the Boston Red Sox defeating the Phillies in four games. Throughout its history, the stadium was home to teams other than the Phillies. Negro League games were frequently played there during the 1920s and 1930s, featuring the Hilldale Daisies from Darby, Pennsylvania. Between 1924 and 1926, the Negro League World Series was held there. The Baker Bowl was also home to the Philadelphia Eagles football club between 1933 and 1935, making it the first dual-use stadium in Pennsylvania.

One small part of the legacy of the Baker Bowl can be felt at every baseball game played today. Anyone who has caught a baseball in the stands and taken it home has a young Philadelphian named Reuben Berman to thank for the privilege. From the earliest games, baseball team owners would force fans to return foul balls hit into the stands. This continued until 1923, when eleven-year-old Reuben spent a night in jail for refusing to return a ball. The judge ultimately sided with the young fan, and baseball fans ever since have enjoyed these souvenirs of the national pastime.

1990: A historical marker for Benjamin Franklin is dedicated at Chestnut Street between 3rd and 4th.

Among his many famous experiments, few garner such fame and recognition as Benjamin Franklin's lightning experiment. What makes his effort unique is the fact that Franklin, a man well known for documenting every aspect of his life in letters, maxims, and an autobiography, never directly described the event that took place, by all accounts, on June 15, 1752. Often described by young children as Franklin "inventing" electricity, the experiment in actuality allowed Franklin to prove the theory that lightning was a form of electricity. From this observation, Franklin was able to invent electricity-related objects such as his version of the lightning rod, which was designed to deflect lightning strikes, leaving buildings unharmed and drawing the electricity into the ground. The steps taken to conduct the experiment were not described by Franklin until December 1752, in a letter written in October and publicly read at the Royal Society two months later. Indeed, it was not until 1777 that Joseph Priestley's description of the night of June 15, 1752, was finally made public.

Letter Concerning the Kite Experiment

Read at the Royal Society, December 21, 1752
Philadelphia, 19 October, 1752.

Sir:—As frequent mention is made in public papers from Europe of the success of the Philadelphia experiment for drawing the electric fire from clouds by means of pointed rods of iron erected on high buildings, &c., it may be agreeable to the curious to be informed that the same experiment has succeeded in Philadelphia, though made in a different and more easy manner, which is as follows.

Make a small cross of two light strips of cedar, the arms so long as to reach to the four corners of a large thin silk handkerchief when extended; tie the corners of the handkerchief to the extremities of the cross, so you have the body of a kite; which, being properly accommodated with a tail, loop, and string, will rise in the air, like those made of paper; but this being silk is fitter to bear the wet and wind of a thunder-gust without tearing. To the top of the upright stick of the cross is to be fixed a very sharp-pointed wire, rising a foot or more above the wood. To the end of the twine, next the hand, is to be tied a silk ribbon, and where the silk and twine join, a key may be fastened. This kite is to be raised when a thunder-gust appears to be coming on, and the person who holds the string must stand within a door or window, or under some cover, so that the silk ribbon may not be wet; and care must be taken that the twine does not touch the frame of the door or window.

As soon as any of the thunder-clouds come over the kite, the pointed wire will draw the electric fire from them, and the kite, with all the twine, will be electrified, and the loose filaments of the twine will stand out every way, and be attracted by an approaching finger. And when the rain has wetted the kite and twine, so that it can conduct the electric fire freely, you will find it stream out plentifully from the key on the approach of your knuckle. At this key the phial may be charged; and from electric fire thus obtained spirits may be kindled, and all the other electric experiments be performed which are usually done by the help of a rubbed glass globe or tube, and thereby the sameness of the electric matter with that of lightning completely demonstrated.

B. Franklin.

Joseph Priestley (*The History and Present State of Electricity, with Original Experiments,* 1775, excerpt)

As every circumstance relating to so capital a discovery as this (the greatest, perhaps, that has been made in the whole compass of philosophy, since the time of Sir Isaac Newton) cannot but give pleasure to all my readers, I shall endeavor to gratify them with the communication of a few particulars which I have from the best authority. The Doctor, after having published his method of verifying his hypothesis concerning the sameness of electricity with the matter of lightning, was waiting for the erection of a spire in Philadelphia to carry his views into execution; not imagining that a pointed rod, of a moderate height, could answer the purpose; when it occurred to him, that, by means of a common kite, he could have a readier and better access to the regions of thunder than by any spire whatever. Preparing, therefore, a large silk handkerchief, and two cross sticks, of a proper length, on which to extend it, he took the opportunity of the first approaching thunderstorm to take a walk into a field, in which there was a shed convenient for his purpose. But dreading the ridicule which too commonly attends unsuccessful attempts in science, he communicated his intended experiment to nobody but his son, who assisted him in raising the kite.

The kite being raised, a considerable time elapsed before there was any appearance of its being electrified. One very promising cloud had passed over it without any effect; when, at length, just as he was beginning to despair of his contrivance, he observed some loose threads of the hempen string to stand erect, and to avoid one another, just as if they had been suspended on a common conductor. Struck with this promising appearance, he immediately presented his knuckle to the key, and (let the reader judge of the exquisite pleasure he must have felt at that moment) the discovery was complete. He perceived a very evident electric spark. Others succeeded, even before the string was wet, so as to put the matter past all dispute, and when the rain had wetted the string, he collected electric fire very copiously. This happened in June 1752, a month after the electricians in France had verified the same theory, but before he had heard of any thing that they had done.

Besides this kite, Dr. Franklin had afterwards an insulated iron rod to draw the lightning into his house, in order to make experiments whenever there should be a considerable quantity of it in the atmosphere; and that he might not lose any opportunity of that nature, he connected two bells with this apparatus, which gave him notice, by their ringing, whenever his rod was electrified.

July

 July 1 

On July 1, 1874, Philadelphia became the site of the first American kidnapping for ransom. Charles Brewster Ross, just four years old, and his five-year-old brother, Walter, were enticed into a buggy by two men who promised candy and fireworks. The men took the children to a store and sent Walter in to purchase the fireworks. When he returned, his brother and the men were gone. Charley's father, Christian K. Ross, a well-to-do resident of the Germantown neighborhood in Philadelphia, began receiving a series of ransom demands from the kidnappers. The ransom was $20,000 for the safe return of Charley, about $400,000 in today's currency, an enormous sum. Ross, not as wealthy as many believed, went to the police against the warning of the kidnappers and a massive search for Charley began. Over time, numerous attempts were made to meet the kidnappers' demands, but each time the kidnappers failed to appear at the appointed time and place.

The case was widely reported and the Pinkerton National Detective Agency, a nationally famous private security agency, was brought in to aid in the search. Pinkerton printed millions of flyers and posters, many featuring Charley's likeness. Charley's disappearance was national news, and even a popular song was written titled "Bring Back Our Darling," reflecting the public's interest in the case. In December 1874, two men were shot in a burglary at the home of a local judge on Long Island, New York. As he lay dying, Joe Douglas admitted that he and his partner, Bill Mosher, who was killed instantly during the burglary, had kidnapped Charley. Witnesses could not agree whether Douglas said Charley was dead, or that he would be returned. Walter Ross later confirmed the identity of the two kidnappers.

In 1875 William Westervelt, a former Philadelphia policeman and brother-in-law of Bill Mosher, was convicted of conspiracy in the case and sentenced to prison. He maintained his innocence and continued to claim that he did not know the whereabouts of Charley. Two years after the crime, Christian Ross published a book titled *The Father's Story of Charley Ross, the Kidnapped Child* and spent the proceeds searching for Charley over several decades. Charley was never found, and many believe that the warning "don't take candy from strangers" is a legacy of this case.

1874: The Philadelphia Zoo opens as the first in the country. Chartered on March 21, 1859, the Civil War delayed construction.

1926: Completion of the Delaware River Bridge, now known as the Benjamin Franklin Bridge. It was the longest suspension bridge in the country at the time, a record held for only three years when it was overtaken by the Ambassador Bridge in Detroit.

2010: Officials announce June 2010 to be the hottest June in more than 135 years, with an average temperature of 78.2 degrees.

July 2

It is not common for disagreements to arise in identifying the specific date on which a particular event occurred or an occasion is to be commemorated. Many holidays have been designated "official" by acts of Congress or through repeated ritual. One of the most important and celebrated American holidays is Independence Day on July 4, when parades, memorials, picnics, and fireworks bring people across the nation together to remember the moment when America declared independence from a tyrannical British king. Founding Fathers such as George Washington, Thomas Jefferson, and John Adams are also remembered for their individual role in pursuing independence and for their combined representation of American freedoms. For Adams, however, Americans have spent the last two centuries celebrating on the wrong day.

Indeed, Adams declared in a letter written to his wife, Abigail Adams, on July 3, 1776, that "the Second Day of July 1776 will be the most memorable Epoch in the History of America. . . . It ought to be solemnized with Pomp and Parade, with Shows, Games, Sports, Guns, Bells, Bonfires and Illuminations from one end of this Continent to the other from this Time forward forever more." While Adams was correct in predicting the manner in which Americans would celebrate their independence, he was wrong about the date. He viewed the moment when a single phrase within the Declaration of Independence was adopted by the members of the Continental Congress as the defining moment in American history. The specific resolution, proposed by Virginian Richard Henry Lee months earlier, proclaimed among other things "that these United States are, and of right ought to be, free and independent states."

With the adoption of these words, the members of the Continental Congress officially and quite firmly declared America to be free of British rule. Adams understood the true nature of the American insistence on freedom, and assumed the resolution would be remembered most. Two days later, the full text of the declaration was adopted, and the date of July 4, 1776, was eventually inscribed on the final, signed version of the document. Since then, the official version has been reproduced in countless newspapers, books, and posters, a resounding image for all Americans. Adams never changed his mind about the significance of July 2, though in a great coincidence, both he and Jefferson died on the fiftieth anniversary of the celebration of the Fourth of July, in 1826.

1778: Congress returns to Philadelphia from Lancaster when the occupying British army leaves.

1788: Congress announces that the United States Constitution is now in effect, having been ratified by the necessary nine states.

July 3

By 1863, Philadelphians were becoming weary of the war and opposition to Lincoln was growing. The elections of 1862 saw the Democrats take control of the Pennsylvania legislature, but Republican mayor Alexander Henry was reelected handily in Philadelphia. Popular support for the war continued to decline as casualties mounted, the leadership of the Union forces appeared to be in complete disarray, and the purpose of the war seemed less clear. But in the summer of 1863, a direct threat to Pennsylvania and the city of Philadelphia energized Union supporters and changed how the city experienced the fears of war.

Confederate president Jefferson Davis and General Robert E. Lee devised a plan to invade the north designed to distract Union attention from the western campaigns and achieve a major victory that could end the conflict. Their target was Gettysburg, in Adams County, roughly 70 miles west of Philadelphia. In the meantime, Philadelphia Democrats planned for a huge rally on June 1 protesting the arrest of Confederate supporters in the North and opposing the restrictions on civil liberties imposed by the Lincoln administration. But the associated Democratic calls for violence against the government were rejected by most Philadelphians, who also suspected that the prominent wealthy businessmen who were part of the Democratic opposition were primarily interested in the protection of their financial interests.

By mid-June, news of Lee's invasion led to recruiting booths opening all over the city in response to Lincoln's call for 100,000 troops. Residents in the northwestern corridor of the city were convinced Lee's troops would soon be marching down Germantown Avenue. The Union League led the recruitment effort, forming three regiments mustered into service on July 1. George Fahnestock wrote in his diary that "nothing but drum and fife is heard, and companies are forming and marching in every direction. . . . The people are aroused at last, and I hope it may not be too late." On July 3, 1863, the third day of the Battle of Gettysburg, Lee mounted a last attack on Cemetery Ridge, but the Union forces prevailed in what was the military turning point of the Civil War. On July 4, as church bells rang and Philadelphians celebrated, it was clear that Philadelphia would remain devoted to the Union cause, but the memory of such a close call would remain for many years to come.

1940: Radio DJ Jerry Blavat (a.k.a. the Geator with the Heater, and the Boss with the Hot Sauce) is born in South Philadelphia.

July 4

Midway through the twentieth century, New York and Chicago became famous for their skyscrapers, but between 1901 and 1908 Philadelphia's City Hall held the record as the tallest building in the nation. On July 4, 1874, the cornerstone was laid for this impressive structure at Broad and Market streets, marking the beginning of a quarter-century of conflicts and construction before the building was finally completed in 1901. City Hall, standing at the center of five public squares laid out by William Penn in 1682, remains today the tallest occupied masonry building in the world.

Designed by Philadelphia's own John McArthur, the ornate French Second Empire style of City Hall has led some to compare it to a wedding cake. The 548-foot-tall building, which features massive stone and brick walls up to 22 feet thick, is capped by a tower and a thirty-seven-foot statue of William Penn. The tower features four clock faces on each side with diameters of 26 feet that are illuminated at night. Richly decorated with 250 works of sculpture by Alexander Milne Calder, the complex covers a city block and is anchored by a large public inner courtyard. By 1901, the cost of design and construction was estimated at a remarkable $75 million, nearly $2 billion in today's currency.

City Hall's construction was controversial with regard to style, cost, and attempts by Philadelphia political boss Boies Penrose to take control of the project. Because it took so long to complete, the building design had to be modified mid-construction when electrification and the installation of elevators became possible. Over the years since its completion, there were several times when demolition was urged by one group or another, but the building has persevered, and significant rehabilitation efforts have restored its exterior. With its 700 rooms, City Hall houses the mayor's office, the city council, and civil courts. For most of the city's history, a "gentleman's agreement" prohibited constructing any other building taller than Billy Penn's hat. In 1987, that tradition ended with the construction of One Liberty Place. After more than a century, the building is now treated with the respect it deserves.

1776: The fully amended Declaration of Independence is adopted by members of the Continental Congress.

1829: The cornerstone is laid for the United States Mint on the corner of Chestnut and Juniper streets.

1833: The cornerstone is laid for Girard College, designed by Thomas Ustick Walter, architect of the United States Capitol.

1938: The Philadelphia Phillies play their first game at Shibe Park, during which the Braves defeat the Phillies, 10–5.

July 5

Unlike so many other early American cities founded over three hundred years ago, Philadelphia benefits from the early efforts of William Penn and surveyor Thomas Holme to bring order to the chaos of a true American wilderness. Holme was born in England in 1624 but after serving in Cromwell's army moved to County Wexford, Ireland. It is presumed that while he was there he met members of the Quaker faith, among them Philadelphia founder William Penn. In 1682, Penn hoped to develop the land in Pennsylvania granted to him by King Charles II and needed to establish a large town where the Delaware and Schuylkill rivers met. Penn had met with some resistance from the Swedish settlers already occupying the land, and decided instead to purchase one square mile of land along the Delaware River. He invited Holme to Philadelphia to conduct a full survey and establish the lot lines that are still reflected today in the city's grid design.

Penn was dissatisfied with the initially cramped city plan and purchased the land westward to the Schuylkill River, creating the original two square miles of the city of Philadelphia now popularly called Center City. At Penn's urging, Holme drafted a clean urban grid, oriented northeast to southwest, in hopes of avoiding the overcrowding and dangerous health conditions of old European cities like London. The plan featured a large central square and four smaller squares, one in each quadrant. The north and south axis streets of Broad Street and High (now Market) Street were laid out as well. Initially, east-west streets were named after trees, and north-south streets were numbered First through Thirteenth in from each river to meet at Broad Street. Large lots were drawn, and advertised as attractive and available for subdivision. The plan was completed on this date in 1682.

As Surveyor-General for the colony, Holme also traveled throughout the region, documenting and surveying the many waterways, ancient native paths, and existing property boundaries. In 1687, he produced the first detailed map of the area, titled *A Mapp of the Improved Part of Pensilvania in America, Divided Into Counteys, Townships and Lotts.* Penn used this map, along with a print of the city plan, as illustrations in marketing pamphlets sent back to England and Germany in hopes of attracting investors and new colonists. Alongside Penn's glowing descriptions of the rich natural resources available in Pennsylvania, Holme's maps provided the proof of Pennsylvania's great potential, attracting hundreds of thousands of new and pioneering colonists.

1776: The first printing of the Declaration of Independence is completed by John Dunlap.

1844: Anti-Catholic riots rage in Southwark.

1915: Philadelphia bids good-bye to the Liberty Bell as it heads west by train to the Panama-California Exposition in San Francisco.

 July 6 

The availability of high-quality medical care has long been a key feature of life in and around Philadelphia. From its earliest days, medical schools and hospitals have provided the most progressive and successful medical technology and techniques to citizens and those who travel from abroad seeking aid. Evolving from among several of the city's neighborhood hospitals and training schools, a merged hospital care center in Philadelphia was envisioned in the early 1950s to provide medical teaching, research, and community health all within a single organization. On this date in 1951, the world's greatest scientist and humanitarian was announced as the namesake of the new center, and the Albert Einstein Medical Center was born.

As early as 1866, the Jewish Hospital on 56th Street in West Philadelphia served Philadelphians seeking affordable or free health care. Founded specifically to aid the suffering poor of all religions, the hospital initially boasted just twenty-two beds. Throughout the city, other organizations formed to meet the medical needs of the city, including the Mount Sinai Hospital in 1905 and the Northern Liberties Hospital in 1925, among others. Although each met the needs of its immediately surrounding community, pockets of the city remained without a centralized health care provider. In addition, patient and doctors were often limited by their hospital affiliation, unable to move beyond their neighborhood boundaries to seek new technologies or care.

In 1950, at the behest of the Jewish Hospital, a study was conducted to consider the feasibility of a merger. The study's author, Dr. Henry B. Makover, showed that there was an opportunity to consolidate resources while also expanding services, in particular opening the system to a much broader city population. Local attorney Joseph M. First, representing Mount Sinai Hospital, was the first to approach Albert Einstein, who agreed to the use of his name. The merger was finalized in 1952, and the Center, now called the Albert Einstein Healthcare Network, continues to serve hundreds of thousands of patients each year. Known for its excellent rehabilitation and surgical practices, the Network remains a shining example of the city's best and brightest medical services.

1776: The Declaration of Independence is first published, on the front page of the *Pennsylvania Evening Gazette.*

1835: Chief Justice John Marshall dies.

1860: The Public Buildings Commissioners decide on Penn Square as the location of the new city court houses.

1926: Daily air service for Philadelphia is established, as ten passenger planes to and from Washington start flying today as an adjunct to the Sesquicentennial Exposition.

 July 7 

Shipbuilding along both sides of the Delaware River was important to the defense of America from before the Revolution. Warships built in Philadelphia played a role in all of the major military conflicts up to World War II. Many of these ships engaged in significant battles; some survived and some did not. Perhaps the most dramatic fate of a Philadelphia warship was the tragic story of the *Indianapolis,* whose sinking caused the greatest single loss of life in the history of the American navy.

The *Indianapolis* was a cruiser commissioned at the Philadelphia Navy Yard on November 15, 1932. During peacetime, the *Indianapolis* served as flagship, carrying President Franklin Roosevelt to his camp at Campobello Island and taking him to South America for state visits. After the start of World War II, the ship engaged in battles in the South Pacific and off the coast of Alaska. The ship was among those attacking Tokyo and it transported part of the atomic bomb to Pearl Harbor. On July 30, 1945, the ship was struck by two Japanese torpedoes, causing it to sink within twelve minutes and killing about 300 of the 1,196 sailors on board. The rest of the crew went into the ocean with few lifeboats and waited for rescue during four days of horror.

Of the 880 men who went into the water, only 321 came out alive. Dehydration, hypothermia, starvation, and dementia took their toll, with the survivors constantly under the threat of shark attack. A seaplane that was the first to arrive at the scene saw men being attacked by sharks and landed against orders, taxiing to snatch men from the water and tying them to the wings of the plane. Ships finally arrived on the scene, shining searchlights, which for most survivors was the first indicator of rescue. After the rescues, the ship's captain, Charles McVay III, became the only captain court-martialed after his ship sank in World War II. He was convicted in a controversial trial for "failure to zig-zag" but returned to active duty until 1949. The captain, who committed suicide in 1968, was exonerated in 2000 by resolution of Congress. On July 7, 2007, the USS *Indianapolis* Museum opened at the War Memorial Plaza in Indianapolis, with the diminishing number of survivors as honored guests.

1780: The Pennsylvania Bank begins business on Front Street, two doors above Walnut.

1864: The Great Central Fair on Logan Square opens.

1989: The Grateful Dead play JFK Stadium. It was not known at the time, but the concert would become the last concert held at the crumbling stadium.

July 8

The age-old philosophical question asks: When a tree falls and no one is there to hear it, does it really make a sound? In Philadelphia in 1776, a powerful and seemingly invincible assumption fell when faced with the revolutionary ideas of America's greatest political and civil minds. But at what point was that momentous event really heard? At what moment did the Declaration of Independence move beyond thought and theory to reality for the thousands of American colonists affected by its proclamations of independence? On this date, a crowd of several hundred Philadelphians experienced the first public reading of the complete Declaration of Independence. The city, and the world, would never be the same.

In the days following the adoption of the radical idea that the American colonies were free and independent states, Thomas Jefferson finalized his own great work as one of several members of the Continental Congress assigned to articulate the many grievances against the British crown. On July 4, 1776, the final wording of the document was approved and Congress ordered that copies be sent "to the several Assemblies, Conventions, and Committees or Councils of Safety, and to the several Commanding officers of the Continental Troops, that it be proclaimed in each of the *United States,* and at the head of the Army." By the next day, the first newspaper version appeared in the German-language *Pennsylvanischer Staatsbote,* soon followed by the *Philadelphia Evening Post.* However, a large percentage of Americans could not read and in a long-standing tradition, a public reading was arranged.

A local government printer named John Dunlap was selected to produce an unknown number of broadsides, or posters, of the full text. After a few tries, his work was approved and provided to Colonel John Nixon of the Philadelphia Committee of Safety, a local militia. The State House bell (now known as the Liberty Bell) was tolled to notify citizens of a significant event in the public square in front of the State House on Chestnut Street. With great seriousness and grace, Nixon stood up to read aloud the words that firmly declared a state of war and a bid for independence, enumerating a long list of grievances. The secret was finally out; a nation was born as the call for freedom and independence was heard around the world.

1885: Mayor Smith approves an ordinance giving permission for the Baltimore and Ohio Railroad to build lines through Philadelphia to the Delaware River and to connect with the Reading system.

1958: Actor Kevin Bacon is born in Philadelphia.

 July 9 

At the center of the history of American constitutional law stands a single man, Chief Justice John Marshall. Born in 1775 along the Virginia frontier, Marshall went on to become the longest serving Chief Justice in Supreme Court history. More notably, he served at a time when the intricacies of the Constitution were repeatedly tested for the first time, giving Marshall the unique opportunity to guide and in many ways define how the laws of the land affect the daily lives of all Americans. He died on July 6, 1835, and three days later, his passing was commemorated with the extended tolling of the Pennsylvania State House bell, now known as the Liberty Bell. In an unlikely reflection of his impact on American society, it is believed that the tolling led to the distinctive crack in the Liberty Bell, one of the most recognizable objects in American mythology.

Marshall, the son of a private agent and surveyor for one of Virginia's wealthy elite, benefited from a large family of substantial means. Well educated in literature and history, Marshall was frequently given the opportunity to use the library of his father's employer. Later, he was sent to an academy in Washington, Virginia, where he studied with classmate James Monroe before the American Revolution intervened, during which Marshall served in the army up to 1780. Subsequently, he studied with George Wythe in Williamsburg and was admitted to the bar. For the next twenty years, Marshall continued to serve as lawyer and judge, participating in both state and federal debates, often taking the Federalist position. Finally, in recognition of his long experience, President John Adams appointed Marshall to the United States Supreme Court in 1801. As a member of the court, Marshall spent much of the year in Philadelphia, seated at a revolving court.

Just a decade removed from the creation of the United States Constitution, Marshall and his fellow judges faced little precedent and a position as a lesser of the three branches of government. Under Marshall's guidance, the Supreme Court established itself as an equal branch, securing the role of the court within the checks and balances system of government central to the Constitution. Among their most significant rulings were *Marbury v. Madison,* in which judicial review was established as an expected process with government; *McCulloch v. Maryland,* which prevented states from passing laws deemed unconstitutional by the Court; and *Gibbons v. Ogden,* which overturned a monopoly established by the New York legislature. Following a carriage accident in 1835, Marshall traveled to Philadelphia seeking medical care. He died here on July 6, 1835.

1703: Edward Shippen, patriarch of a significant and influential Philadelphia family, is born in Boston.

1933: The NFL grants an expansion franchise to Bert Bell and Lud Wray and awards them the remains of the Frankford Yellow Jackets organization. They name their team the Philadelphia Eagles, after the symbol of Franklin Roosevelt's New Deal.

July 10

During the Second World War, life on the home front was often defined by the need and desire to support the battles being waged across the sea. In addition to the direct production of the tools of war, Philadelphians by the hundreds also organized knitting circles and pen pal clubs to provide tangible reminders of what the war was intended to defend. Like all Americans, Philadelphians also faced one of the most difficult aspects of life on the home front: rationing. Designed to conserve scarce resources and emphasize the role of the home front in achieving victory, rationing was viewed as both an essential effort and a challenging hardship.

Worthy of observance but difficult enough they inspired unusual efforts to bypass or avoid entirely the restrictions they enacted, rationing laws came to represent a unique kind of warfare between creative and crafty citizens and the officials charged with enforcing the rationing. A variety of goods were rationed, ranging from food to energy and even modern products that used materials deemed necessary to the war effort, such as nylon for parachutes, iron and steel for weapons, and rubber for tires. Rationing cards were distributed by the government to ensure that everyone got their fair share. Energy conservation was also primary to rationing, as the coal used to produce electricity, or the fuel used to move cars and trucks, was needed to fuel the industries supporting the war effort. Fuel rations in particular were used to reduce wear and tear on rubber tires, since the rubber supply to American manufacturers was cut off by the war waging in Asia.

Some sought to get around these restrictions, attempting to hoard goods or otherwise avoid limitations. Some planted Victory gardens or raised chickens and pigs, both efforts endorsed and encouraged by the government. Others chose less credible ways. On this date in 1943, one such effort was found to be legal, if not actually ethical. William C. Fox, an auto mechanic, had successfully developed his own fuel to be used in his truck. Accused of violating rationing laws, he was investigated by the Office of Price Administration, which oversaw rationing. Based on the written laws, however, the government was unable to stop Fox from using his own invention to drive as much as he wanted. In a small way, Fox proved that ingenuity and creativity could solve immediate problems, but the reality of the national effort to defend the nation through rationing meant he risked condemnation by doing so.

1797: The *United States* is launched at Philadelphia, the first ship built under the new organization of the Navy. The command is given to Commodore John Barry, who supervised its construction.

1940: Chairman Martin Dies of the House committee to investigate un-American Activities says today that he has information that a plot to sabotage a battleship under construction in a Pennsylvania Navy Yard has been uncovered. Officials at the Philadelphia Navy Yard (the only naval yard in Pennsylvania building a battleship) deny knowledge of said plot.

July 11

On this date in 1797, the first of six great frigates designed by Joshua Humphreys was commissioned. Launched from the Humphreys and Wharton Shipyard at Christian Street on the Delaware River on May 10, the USS *United States* and its fellow frigates formed the core of the United States Navy and were born of the Naval Act of 1794, which allotted nearly $700,000 to the cost of designing and constructing the first American-made frigates. Administered by the Department of War, the creation of newly constructed warships was a change from earlier plans, which intended to convert merchant ships into fighting vessels. President George Washington and Secretary of War Henry Knox knew the value of a strong navy, and chose Humphreys to lead the design work.

Joshua Humphreys, born in Haverford in 1751, trained as a young apprentice under shipbuilder Thomas Wharton. During the American Revolution, Humphreys and Wharton were given the opportunity to build frigates, though they only completed the 32-gun *Randolph.* Following the war, Humphreys purchased the shipyard and built a reputation as a skilled designer and builder. In 1794, working with several others, among them captains John Foster Williams and John Barry as well as shipbuilder Josiah Fox, Humphreys envisioned a 44-gun vessel that was long and narrow and featured an innovative diagonal scantling, or rib, design. As a result of his recommended improvements in ship design, it was anticipated that the American frigates would be stronger and faster than their European counterparts.

In hopes of speeding up production and spreading the economic boon to several cities, shipyards in Boston, New York, Baltimore, and Philadelphia were engaged, as well as Portsmouth, New Hampshire, and Gosport, Virginia. The USS *United States* was the first to launch, followed quickly by the USS *Constellation* and the USS *Constitution,* which is the only surviving frigate of the period. All six frigates went on to great military and maritime success, particularly during the War of 1812. The USS *United States* was decommissioned in 1849 and later seized by the Confederate States Navy in 1861 and scuttled. A year later, the United States Navy raised the ship and used her for the remainder of the war. The USS *United States* sailed for the last time in 1865, after which she was dismantled, bringing to an end her service to the nation.

1681: William Penn issues conditions and concessions to his agents to lay out a large town or city, the first written mention of what would become Philadelphia.

1838: Department store founder John Wanamaker is born in Philadelphia.

July 12

A major event that helped to define the mid-century civil rights movement occurred in Philadelphia during the Democratic National Convention of 1948, which opened on this date. Faced with a weakened national leadership, the Democratic Party seemed destined to lose to the stronger Republican Party which just weeks earlier had nominated New York governor Thomas E. Dewey for president at their own Philadelphia-based convention. Further, incumbent president and Democrat Harry S. Truman seemed perpetually overshadowed within his own party: first by predecessor Franklin Delano Roosevelt and during the convention by the more traditional southern Democrats. Prepared to stay the course, Truman was urged by the liberal-minded Americans for Democratic Action to incorporate a progressive human rights initiative into the increasingly irrelevant Democratic platform.

Philadelphia was chosen because of its central location along the newly emerging television broadcast coaxial cable lines, allowing both Republican and Democratic conventions to be televised for the first time in history. Democratic Senatorial candidate Hubert Humphrey seized the opportunity and on July 14 delivered an impassioned address on behalf of the ADA. He urged his party to "get out of the shadow of states' rights and walk forthrightly into the bright sunshine of human rights," a message which ultimately prompted a walkout by southern delegates when the liberals won a close vote to include a human rights statement in the platform. Many southern delegates who remained ultimately supported Georgia senator Richard B. Russell as a protest presidential candidate. Truman, however, stood firm and delivered a rousing and deeply felt speech in the early hours of July 15, declaring that he would call Congress back into session with the sole purpose of passing the liberal-leaning legislation proposed by the controlling Republican Party. This new message energized many delegates and appealed to the growing number of African-American Democrats.

Within the Democratic Party, the Convention proved to be a public airing of ongoing conflicts surrounding issues of race, employment, human rights, and justice. Two weeks after the convention closed, Truman signed an executive order integrating the United States military and federal service. In response, the States' Rights, or "Dixiecrats" Party united under the leadership of Senator Strom Thurmond with the goal of maintaining mostly Southern states' rights to regulate race relations. Unable to get Congress to act on many of Truman's liberal initiatives, the Democratic Party nevertheless built on its public declaration of the significance of the fight for civil rights, paving the way for more successful initiatives among Republicans and Democrats in the 1960s and 1970s.

1937: Actor and comedian Bill Cosby (William Henry Cosby, Jr.) is born.

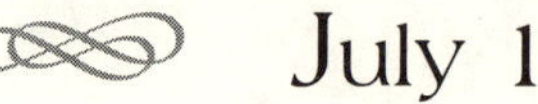

July 13

The tradition of organizing rock concerts for charitable fund raising began with George Harrison's Concert for Bangladesh in 1971. On July 13, 1985, Philadelphia and London were the locations for the Live Aid concert aimed at famine relief in Africa. Organized by Bob Geldorf of the rock group Boomtown Rats, the concert was held simultaneously at Wembley Stadium in London and JFK Stadium in Philadelphia, and broadcast around the world. An estimated two billion viewers watched the broadcast in sixty countries.

Almost 100,000 people attended in Philadelphia, enduring temperatures into the 90s. The Philadelphia venue featured some of the most popular rock stars and bands of the time. Joan Baez started the concert around ten in the morning with "Amazing Grace," telling the crowd that "this is your Woodstock." Madonna, Tom Petty, the Rolling Stones, Bob Dylan, Tina Turner, and Duran Duran, appeared, among many others. Philadelphia native son Teddy Pendergrass sang in his first public appearance after surviving a debilitating car accident. British singer Phil Collins performed at both Wembley and JFK, utilizing the Concorde for a fast transatlantic flight. The Philadelphia concert concluded around 11:00 P.M. with a group rendition of "We Are the World," in which the main performers were joined by other stars such as Cher and Peter, Paul, and Mary.

Now that teenagers can use a Web camera to send video and sound cross-country instantly and without difficulty, the complexity and impact of technology for the concert is easily underappreciated. The concert broadcast used live feeds by way of satellite hook-ups from two locations, and was a dramatic technological breakthrough. The BBC handled the London feed using a stereo radio feed to simulcast the performances. In Philadelphia, ABC was responsible for the broadcast, with an entirely separate and simultaneous feed supplied for cable MTV viewers. The entire concert was televised from London; ABC televised only the final three hours of the Philadelphia concert, mixing live events with taped segments from earlier performances in Philadelphia and London. To date, the Live Aid concert remains one of the largest television broadcasts of all time, a proud part of Philadelphia history.

1976: Demolition begins on Shibe Park as the Major League Baseball All Star game is played at Veterans Stadium.

July 14

Without question, Americans love their Westerns. Iconic stories of the lone hero, riding the plains with only a pistol and a horse for company, populate our memories and our popular culture. Many of the earliest examples of the frontier novel were born in the mind of a sickly Philadelphian, Owen Wister, who was born in Germantown on this date in 1860. The son of a physician and grandson to the infamous actress Fanny Kemble, Wister grew up surrounded by the benefits of wealth and comfort. As a young lawyer, he suffered a series of health crises and eventually toured areas of Wyoming in hopes of a restful recovery. Wister drew from those experiences to craft short stories and novels that continue today to define the image of the western hero.

Well educated and creative, Wister attended schools in Switzerland, England, and the United States before graduating from Harvard University in 1882. Attracted to the arts rather than to the legal career he seemed destined for, Wister briefly studied music in Paris but soon gave it up and returned home to begin work in a local law firm. Unfortunately, he began to experience horrific headaches, dizziness, and hallucinations and suffered a breakdown of unknown cause in 1884. On the recommendation of his doctor, Wister traveled to a ranch in Wyoming to recover. While there, he befriended the local ranch hands, intently observing their way of life and listening with great interest to their long stories about life on the range. Wister returned to Philadelphia but continued to spend summers in Wyoming for the next fifteen years.

In 1891, Wister began writing short stories about the cowboys he knew. Published in *Harper's Weekly,* the tales were hugely popular and spurred Wister to write his best-known novel, *The Virginian,* in 1901. Published a year later to great acclaim and popularity, *The Virginian* went on to sell nearly 200,000 copies the first year. Since then, it has been adapted into several films, television shows, and plays. Wister disliked the attention, and felt particularly conflicted about his role in popular fiction when he himself admired most of the complex and elite authors of the time, among them Henry James. Wister never wrote another western novel, focusing instead on general themes in fiction and nonfiction. His legacy, however, lies in his creation of the prototype to all great western stories, forever influencing America's vision of the western frontier and the men who made it great.

1798: President John Adams signs into law the federal Sedition Act.

July 15

Among the many fine food delights to be found in the city, few are as essentially "Philadelphia" or have as storied a history as ice cream. First eaten as shaved ice and flavoring as many as several millennia ago, the modern concept of ice cream made with milk was first brought to America from France late in the eighteenth century. The earliest available ice cream could be found in New York City and Boston, but it was in Philadelphia that the cold treat was first experienced by the elite in society, politics, and culture. On this date in 1782, the Chevalier Luzerne gave a fete at the French embassy in Philadelphia in honor of the Dauphin. Featuring a pyrotechnic display and other special delights, the honored guests, among them George Washington, were served ice cream. The treat became immediately and intensely popular.

Originally a treat for the wealthy because it was costly to produce, ice cream became available to ordinary citizens in the 1820s when a black chef, Augustus Jackson, brought to Philadelphia new recipes, perfecting techniques which made enjoying ice cream at numerous "pleasure gardens" in the city affordable to more of its citizens. Philadelphia's love of the sweet dessert inspired other local inventors, among them Nancy M. Johnson, who in 1843 obtained a patent for the first hand-cranked ice cream machine. In 1874, the ice cream soda was invented in the city by Robert Greene, and in 1876 a patented ice cream scoop was manufactured on South 11th Street. Because the Philadelphia area had an abundant supply of dairy farms and milk with a high fat content, the city became the ice cream capital of the nation in the nineteenth century.

Philadelphia-style ice cream was made without egg yolks, as compared with the traditional French custard-based recipe. At one time, Philadelphia had four dozen ice cream companies. The most famous of these still in operation today in the city is Bassett's, originally founded in 1861. In 1885, Lewis Bassett began selling ice cream at 5th and Market streets. When the Reading Terminal Market opened in 1893, Bassett's was manufacturing ice cream in the market's basement and established its retail store at that location, where it remains today. In 1973, Bassett's moved production to 20th and Fairmount streets, continuing the long history of ice cream in the city.

1964: The first tenants move into Society Hill Towers.

2007: The Philadelphia Phillies lose their 10,000th game to the visiting St. Louis Cardinals with a score of 10–2.

July 16

Two-term mayor Frank Rizzo was one of the most colorful and controversial politicians in Philadelphia history. Born to a Philadelphia police family in 1920, he joined the city police department in 1943 and rose through the ranks to become police commissioner in 1967. Known as a man who did not shy from action, he once left a dinner with a police truncheon tucked into his tuxedo cummerbund to help break up a riot. Tough-talking and tough-acting, he expanded the police force and kept the crime rate low in the city. At the same time, he and members of the force were heavily criticized, by the African-American community in particular, for racism and police brutality.

In 1971, Rizzo won his first term as mayor, and continued to oversee police activities. He was an avid supporter of Richard Nixon and was quoted as defining a conservative as "a liberal who was mugged the night before." In 1979, the U.S. Department of Justice brought suit, charging that the mayor and eighteen high-ranking city and police officials were responsible for police brutality, including shooting and beating suspects, and guilty of racial discrimination within the force. Rizzo contended that the tactics were necessary to combat crime in the inner city, and argued that he had integrated the Philadelphia police force. Ultimately, the federal district court dismissed the charges for lack of evidence.

Barred by law from serving a consecutive third term, Rizzo never gave up his quest to return to the mayor's post. Defeated in the Democratic primary in 1983, he ran as a Republican in 1987 but lost the general election. On this date in 1991 he was running for mayor again in a close race against future governor Ed Rendell when he unexpectedly died after suffering a massive heart attack. Respected and revered by members of the police force and many in the public, he is honored today by a mural in South Philadelphia and by a life-sized statue at the Philadelphia Municipal Services building.

1787: At the Constitutional Convention, delegate Roger Sherman proposes the creation of a House of Representatives to be determined by population, with equal representation for all states. This results in the creation of the "three-fifths rule," which determined that an African-American citizen would count as only three-fifths of a full person for the purposes of limiting their impact on such a body in the Southern states.

2005: Philadelphia celebrates the 200th anniversary of Oliver Evans' Orukter Amphibolos. This was the first known self-propelled amphibious vehicle—a steam-powered, wheeled dredging barge.

Faith and conflict often go hand in hand, especially in instances where one person's convictions are challenged by the thoughtless conformism of mainstream opinion. In 1787, African-American lay preachers Absalom Jones and friend Richard Allen protested the policy of racial segregation among the pews at St. George's Methodist Church staging what might be called a "pray-in." Forcibly ejected from the church, Jones and Allen were forced to choose their paths in faith. On this date in 1794, Jones realized the resolution of his own greatest conflict in faith with the opening of the African Church, now known as the African Episcopal Church of St. Thomas.

Born into slavery in southern Delaware in 1746, Jones was able to teach himself to read by studying the Bible. At the age of sixteen, he was brought to Philadelphia to work and allowed to earn an independent wage in the hours after his regular work was done. By 1784, Jones was able to purchase his own freedom, as well as that of his wife. During this time, Jones joined St. George's and met and befriended Richard Allen. In 1787, they founded the Free African Society, a religious and benevolent society for freed blacks in the city. Together, the men led the African-American community through their service and sacrifice to the city as thousands grew sick and died during the great Yellow Fever Epidemic of 1793. Their care for the sick and dying was widely noted, but also universally attributed to incorrect and ignorant assumptions about blacks and their vulnerability to the disease. Nevertheless, Jones and Allen remained committed to their mission to aid as many people as possible.

Following their ejection from St. George's, Allen chose to remain with the Methodist Church and founded the Bethel African Methodist Episcopal Church in 1794. Jones, however, felt betrayed and chose instead to join the African Church to the Episcopal Church. With the support of Bishop William White, Jones and his congregation were ultimately welcomed to the diocese that same year, with Jones as deacon. Renamed the African Episcopal Church of St. Thomas, the church continued to experience segregation, though of a lesser form, when they were denied access to the Diocesan Convention until 1864. Jones, however, rose to the highest level within his church when he was ordained a priest in 1804, becoming the first African-American Episcopal priest in the country. Conflicts and prejudices aside, Jones proved through his care and service to others that faith can overcome any conflict.

1784: Peter Carnes, a justice of the peace from Baltimore, attempts the first balloon ascension in the country at the prison yard at Sixth and Prune streets. The aerostat struck the prison wall and Carnes was thrown out of the balloon. Shortly thereafter the balloon caught fire from the furnace and burned.

1836: Episcopal bishop William White dies.

July 18

In the decade prior to the outbreak of the Civil War and the emancipation of slaves, many Philadelphia abolitionists were active in the Underground Railroad, the secret routes used by fleeing slaves to escape Southern states. Philadelphia was the home of a significant number of free people of color, many of whom were successful business owners. One such man was William Still, the prominent president of the Vigilance Society, a local abolitionist group. Under the Fugitive Slave Act of 1850, escaped slaves who fled to Free states like Pennsylvania could be captured and returned to their owners. Still, along with many others, frequently risked his life in opposition to this federal law.

On this date in 1855, Colonel John Wheeler of North Carolina arrived in Philadelphia accompanied by his slave, Jane Johnson, and her two sons. Wheeler was passing through the city on his way to New York to travel to Nicaragua. Johnson was determined to be free, and managed to communicate this desire to William Still through several hotel workers. Acting quickly, Still and his white co-abolitionist Passamore Williamson, accompanied by several dockworkers, confronted the Wheeler party at the docks and took Johnson and her children to safety at Still's house. Wheeler complained to the authorities, and federal judge John Kintzing Kane issued a writ of habeas corpus against Williamson demanding he produce Jane and her children, incarcerating him when he professed not to know her whereabouts. Williamson spent more than three months in Moyamensing Prison, giving newspaper interviews and receiving visits from prominent abolitionists of the day, including Harriet Tubman and Frederick Douglass.

William Still and the dockworkers were arrested by order of Judge Kane and tried for rioting and assault and battery. Johnson appeared at the trial as a surprise witness, accompanied by Lucretia Mott and a large group of abolitionists. Johnson testified that she had not been abducted against her will, and the jury acquitted Still and most of the dockworkers. After her testimony, Jane fled the courthouse and was followed by several federal marshals, intent upon arresting her. State and local authorities assisted in a second escape, and Johnson and her family eventually settled in Boston. Only two years later, the Supreme Court of the United States ruled in the Dred Scott case that no American of African descent, enslaved or free, could be a citizen and that slave owners had legal rights to their property, even in free territories.

1786: Charles Willson Peale opens his first public museum.

1837: The USS *Pennsylvania* is launched at the Navy Yard. It is described as the largest and most heavily-armed man-of-war in the world.

July 19

The future of rail travel along the Northeast Corridor was unveiled in Philadelphia for the first time on this date in 1966, more than two years before the official start of the use of the Budd Company's Metroliner by the Pennsylvania Railroad. A self-driven electrical multiple unit, the Metroliner featured a more streamlined interior design and was intended to more efficiently carry a larger number of passengers to and from Washington, D.C., and New York City. Traveling through Philadelphia and Baltimore at an estimated speed of 110 M.P.H., the trip was ultimately shortened by over thirty minutes. Born of a government initiative to reduce air flight and automobile use within the congested corridor, the first forty-four cars ultimately cost local and federal governments $45 million.

When the government passed the High Speed Ground Transportation Act of 1965, it was the beginning of an extended effort to reestablish the role of rail travel in the United States, with particular attention paid to the burgeoning demands along the Northeast Corridor. In collaboration with the rail companies, the government worked with manufacturers to identify and implement pioneering technological advances in electric passenger trains. Budd, based in Philadelphia, had successfully developed earlier generations of electric cars for the Pennsylvania Railroad known as the Silverliner. Additional work was done to improve railbeds and train over 4,000 railroad employees. By 1966, a new prototype was revealed and the company continued to develop and test until service started in 1969.

Within a year of the first unveiling, the Pennsylvania Railroad merged into the Penn Central Line, which itself went bankrupt in 1971. The newly formed Amtrak assumed control of the Metroliner lines and cars, and continued to use them through the early 1980s. Undergoing a full overhaul and paired with the newer Amcoaches, also produced by Budd, the old Metroliner cars were slowly phased out of use along the Corridor, as well as along other Amtrak lines. Only a few complete Metroliners exist today, though a preserved example is on display at the Railroad Museum of Pennsylvania in Lancaster County. Others, relegated to storage on Amtrak yards in Delaware, tell of a recent past and a significant initiative in regional rail transportation.

1990: Baseball legend Pete Rose is sentenced in Cincinnati to five months in prison for tax evasion.

July 20

The city of Philadelphia has struggled with the typically urban problem of garbage and refuse removal for countless generations. The question of how to manage waste removal and the government's role in that process has engaged city politicians and citizens for centuries. Located in a premium spot along several water courses, the city has historically relied on the availability of flowing water to manage the elimination of a wide variety of household and industrial wastes. Often blamed for disease and illness in the city, trash was seen as primarily a health issue. Long before a municipal plan was in place, private citizens relied on their own labor (or that of servants and slaves) to cart away or burn the foul and unpleasant products of living and working in a heavily populated city.

By the early twentieth century, citizen complaints about the city's poor sanitation efforts were loud and frequent. New advances in waste management theoretically made the work of government a bit easier, as railroads and emerging gasoline-powered vehicles permitted garbage to be hauled away from the more populated areas. In Philadelphia, however, deep-rooted corruption and control of the government by party-driven bosses resulted in a distinctly uncaring approach to the care and maintenance of the city streets by those in charge. Across the city, higher-income neighborhoods enjoyed the attention of the limited sanitation resources available to the citizenry. Streets were kept clean and garbage hauled away to be burned in open dumps. In the poorer or emerging neighborhoods, however, the streets were frequently filthy and neglected. Private companies, many of them run by small-time farmers, picked up trash on an irregular schedule.

The city, forced by growing demands for reform and proper accountability from the residents, enlarged the city's streets agency and standardized trash pickup in the early 1940s, using larger, more modern trucks. Ironically, a protest was waged on this date in 1940 when residents of more than thirty streets in the West Oak Lane neighborhood blocked their rear-access alleyways and streets with baby playpens, denying garbage trucks access because the heavy vehicles were loud and damaged the cement streets and driveways. The conflict was eventually resolved as the residents came to terms with the consequences of not having trash pick-up. Philadelphia government continued to expand and manage the sanitation services for the city, and it wasn't until the 1970s and 1980s that the debate over trash removal erupted once again as the city's financial health decayed.

1893: The will of the late Anthony J. Drexel is probated, disposing of about $30 million.

1956: A fire attributed to negligence engulfs the coal pier of the Philadelphia Coke Company.

July 21

The Bicentennial summer of 1976 was an exciting time for the city and its businesses. Hotels and convention sites were booked; everyone wanted to meet in Philadelphia that year. The American Legion of Pennsylvania hosted its 58th convention from July 21 to July 24 with more than 4,000 legionnaires and their families in attendance. But very quickly, people who attended the convention and returned home began to get seriously ill. Soon, more than 230 people came down with coughing, high fever, and breathing problems. At first, many believed the illness was part of a swine flu outbreak that struck the United States earlier that year. But then, inexplicably, people began dying and doctors did not know why.

Because the conventioneers had returned to their homes all over the state, public health officials did not at first recognize that something medically unusual was happening. Doctors were unable to find either a cause or a cure. Many of the Legionnaires had stayed at the Bellevue Stratford, a historic hotel located in Center City on South Broad Street since 1904. In some cases, one roommate at the convention died, while the other never became ill. Over the next several months, the search for a cause centered at the hotel as fear of the epidemic mounted. Survivors relate that friends and family were afraid to come near them for fear of catching the disease. All told, thirty-four conventioneers died.

In January 1977, doctors finally determined that the illnesses and the deaths were caused by a particular bacterium found in water. Named *Legionella pneumophila* and popularly known as Legionnaire's disease, it was thought to have been spread through the air conditioning system of the hotel. The hotel closed and never regained its glory and reputation as the best place to stay in the city. As research continued over the years, a blood test was developed and more has been learned about the prevalence of the bacteria in water. Though Philadelphia was the first, it is not the last place to experience an outbreak. Over the last thirty years, victims have been claimed in Great Britain, the Netherlands, Australia, and Spain. But how and why the bacteria are transmitted to people and make only some of them deathly ill has yet to be conclusively established.

1953: An estimated 200,000 persons line Camden's streets for two-and-a-half miles to roar tribute to new heavyweight champion Jersey Joe Walcott as he returns to an official celebration by his hometown of Camden in honor of his retirement from boxing.

July 22

Alexander (Sandy) Calder, third in a line of internationally recognized and highly successful Philadelphia artists, was born on this date in 1898 in the northeastern Pennsylvania town of Lawton. Known primarily for his energetic and kinetic sculptures, Calder was strongly discouraged by his family from pursuing art as a career even as they frequently provided him studio space to explore his creative talents. Rarely in one place for longer than a year or so, Calder attended schools in Philadelphia, Arizona, New York, and California before graduating from the Stevens Institute of Technology in Hoboken, New Jersey, in 1919. For the next few years, he held down jobs as varied as hydraulics engineering and as a crewmember on board a freighter before he finally moved to New York City to try his hand as a professional artist. From there, he went on to challenge traditional expectations in sculpturing, inventing unique forms along the way.

The Calder family's connection to Philadelphia was well established when Sandy Calder joined the "family business." His grandfather, Alexander Milne Calder, is best known for his work on City Hall, including the William Penn statue atop that same building's masonry tower. Father Alexander Stirling Calder, whose best-known work is likely the Swann Fountain in Logan Circle, was a constant source of support and inspiration. After several years in New York, Calder moved to Paris, where he joined the arts community that included Marcel Duchamp and Joan Miro, among others. As a child, Calder made small trinkets and toys, many of them with articulated arms or parts that bobbed or moved at the slightest touch. A visit to abstractionist Piet Mondrian inspired him to combine the abstract with the engineering of precision balancing. His "mobiles" (so coined by Duchamp to signify their movement) proved both intriguing and mesmerizing.

In contrast to the seemingly free-floating mobiles, Calder's work with "stabiles" (so called by Jean Arp to signify their immobility) gave him the opportunity to place his art within the realm of the grounded. His largest work, the 60-foot stabile *El Sol Rojo* was constructed for the Olympic Games in Mexico City. His *WTC Stabile* was destroyed along with the World Trade Center towers in 2001. Calder's influence on modern art was recognized through several major exhibitions, most notably at the Metropolitan Museum of Art in 1943 and at the Whitney Museum in New York shortly before his death on November 11, 1976.

1823: William Bartram, traveler, naturalist, and son of John, dies at the age of 85.

1884: The American Catholic Historical Society is founded.

 July 23 

The presidential election of 1948 is remembered as an upset and for the singular photograph of Harry Truman, holding up a newspaper with the headline "Dewey Defeats Truman." It was also an unusual campaign because of the presence of two independent parties: the States Rights Party and the Progressive Party. Strom Thurmond was the presidential candidate of the "Dixiecrat" or States Rights Party, which split from the Democratic Party over Truman's civil rights platform. The Progressive Party, to the left of the Democratic Party, began its national founding convention in Philadelphia on July 23, 1948, just eleven days after the Democratic National Convention in the same city.

After the death of President Franklin Delano Roosevelt, many of the progressive "New Deal" cabinet members left the Truman administration while others found themselves in conflict with the president. Henry Wallace of Iowa, who had served as secretary of agriculture, vice president (1941-45), and commerce secretary under Roosevelt, was fired by Truman because of his opposition to American foreign policy regarding the Soviet Union. Wallace feared that the cold war would ultimately lead to a third world war that would destroy both America and the Soviet Union. The Progressive Party's convention, which was dominated by labor unions and the Americans they represented, nominated Wallace for president.

The platform adopted by the convention called for the end of the peacetime draft, opposed the Marshall Plan for the reconstruction of Europe, called for negotiation with the Soviet Union to find areas of agreement, supported equal rights for women, demanded a minimum wage of $1 an hour, proposed national health insurance, and condemned segregation and discrimination in all its forms. Although the party's platform was alluring to many Americans and reflected many initiatives that an advancing progressive ideology in government has since adopted, Wallace's endorsement by the Communist Party, which he refused to renounce, and his staunch, uncritical support of the Soviet Union resulted in only 1.1 million votes (matching the result for the States Rights Party) and no electoral votes. The Progressive Party was on the ballot in every state and enjoyed an active national organization, but it was unable to persevere against the anti-Communist sentiments of most Americans. After the defeat and Truman's unexpected election, the party dissolved.

2002: Historical marker for Tomas Garrigue Masaryk is installed at Independence Hall. He presented the Mid-European Union's Declaration of Common Aims at Independence Hall on October 26, 1918.

July 24

Within walking distance of all of Philadelphia's sixty-three neighborhoods, the 9,300-acre Fairmount Park is the largest urban park in the world. The yellow fever epidemics of the late eighteenth century led city officials to develop the Fairmount waterworks along the Schuylkill River in 1812; landscaping along the riverbank was installed to protect it from industrial pollution, and residents began to enjoy the parklike setting. Laurel Hill Cemetery, located on bluffs overlooking the river, was a popular site for strolling and enjoying the fresh air in the mid nineteenth century. It was also one of the earlier attempts at manipulating the landscape to craft a pleasant getaway from the crowded city. City planners and their benefactors soon looked to that model in thinking about a larger park for the city.

On this date in 1824, the city purchased the Lemon Hill estate from the defunct Bank of the United States as the foundation for the new park. Originally owned by Robert Morris, a signer of the Declaration of Independence, the house was built in 1800 by financier Henry Pratt, who used the house and estate as a summer retreat and the location of legendary gardens. Over time, the city purchased many other historic estates and properties to add to the park, including John Bartram's house and garden. Beginning in the late nineteenth century, the park began to offer more recreational opportunities besides quiet contemplation of nature.

Today Philadelphians can enjoy 368 athletic fields, horse trails, 215 miles of scenic hiking trails, fishing, picnic areas, six golf courses, a public boathouse, and a skate park. The Philadelphia Zoo is located in the park, as are the Philadelphia Museum of Art, the American Swedish Historical Museum, the Mann Music Center, the Academy of Natural Sciences, and the Franklin Institute. Historic homes within the park are open to visitors as are the azalea garden and the Japanese house and garden. Significant pieces of sculpture, including works by August Saint-Gaudens, Daniel Chester French, and Frederic Remington, dot the landscape. Fairmount Park was the site of the Centennial Exposition of 1876, and its Memorial Hall is now an interactive children's museum. A key attraction and benefit to living in Philadelphia's urban environment, Fairmount Park welcomes several million visitors a year who take advantage of Philadelphia's unique urban park.

1683: A group of thirteen Mennonite families depart from London aboard the *Concord;* following their arrival in Philadelphia in October that year, they settle and establish the community of Germantown.

1921: In a daring robbery allegedly funded by an international smuggling ring, over $50,000 in liquor is stolen from a warehouse and carted away in four trucks in the company of two dozen robbers.

July 25

With the Philadelphia Museum of Art, the Barnes Foundation, and the Academy of Fine Arts, the city is well known to art museum patrons. But one of the most important Philadelphia artists of the last two centuries never had a painting purchased by a museum until after his death. Thomas Eakins was born in Philadelphia on July 25, 1844. His father Benjamin was a writing master and teacher who was known for embellishing and decorating manuscripts and formal documents. After graduating from Central High School, the first public high school in the city, Thomas Eakins traveled to France to study art at the Ecole des Beaux-Arts in Paris, a leading art school.

Returning home on Independence Day 1870, Eakins began his career as a painter. He focused at first on portraits, bringing to his work realism and attention to expressions on faces that was uncommon at the time. An outdoorsman and sportsman by nature, he also produced a series of paintings featuring scullers on the Schuylkill River. Always fascinated with the structure of the human body, he studied anatomy by observing autopsies and medical procedures in an effort to understand how the interior foundation of the body was reflected in its exterior. In 1876, his most famous painting, *The Gross Clinic,* was rejected for exhibition in the main art gallery at the Centennial Exhibition because of its portrayal of a surgeon at work in a bloody operation. The painting was displayed for many years at Jefferson University Hospital, but in 2006, the hospital sought to sell the painting to museums in Washington and Arkansas for $68 million, the highest price ever paid for an Eakins painting and for an American portrait. A public outcry arose, and a group of donors matched the selling price to keep the painting in the city.

Eakins continued his interest in realism as a painter and as a teacher at the Academy of Fine Arts. Eakins was also one of the first artists to utilize photography as a basis and inspiration for painting, inspired in part by the pioneering motion-capturing work of Eadweard Muybridge. Eakins' controversial use of male nudes in both painting and photography eventually led to his dismissal from the Academy of Fine Arts. Eakins continued to paint and live a modest life until his death in 1916.

1951: Dr. Albert C. Barnes, noted art collector and inventor, dies in an automobile crash.

July 26

As early as the thirteenth century, a medieval guild was organized for the welfare of carpenters living and working in London. In the seventeenth century, when the first of Penn's settlers came to the Philadelphia area, they brought the concept of a builders' association with them. James Portues, a carpenter who arrived on the ship *Welcome* with Penn in 1682, was one of the original founders of the Carpenters' Company of the City and County of Philadelphia in 1724. A skilled craftsman, Portues built Penn's house on Second and Walnut streets, later known as the Slate Roof House.

The members of the Company were builders and early architects, many of them trained not in a formal school but as apprentices. On this date in 1792, the Company was chartered with the purpose of "obtaining assistance in the science of architecture, assisting such of their members as should by accident be in need of support, or the widows and minor children of members; and for the furtherance of the said charitable and useful designs." One of the most important activities of the Company was the establishment of a "rule book," which set the cost of tasks associated with building. These standards emerged from the Quaker concepts of fairness in the payment of laborers for work of good value, and contributed to the generally excellent quality of construction in colonial Philadelphia. High standards led to the use of superior brick produced locally, rather than reliance on inferior imported brick.

In 1770, the Company constructed its headquarters, Carpenters' Hall, on Chestnut and Third, which it still owns and operates. A notable example of Georgian architecture, the two-story hall features a Flemish bond brick pattern, a cupola, and tall twenty-paned windows. Five Carpenters' Company emblems are incorporated into the interior of the building. Company members also designed or built Christ Church, created much of the woodwork in Independence Hall, and in the nineteenth century, built Victorian mansions for newly rich industrialists. Modern innovations designed by Company members include the first Philadelphia skyscraper with an interior steel frame, and the nation's first baseball stadium built with reinforced concrete. The Company's current 150 members include many of the city's most prominent architects, continuing the legacy established by Portues at the birth of Philadelphia.

1689: After lack of action from the Provincial Council, the Monthly Meeting of Friends decides to act on William Penn's call to create a public grammar school. A school is approved by Meeting on August 20, 1689. It is the beginning of the William Penn Charter School, still located today in Germantown.

1775: Benjamin Franklin becomes postmaster general.

July 27

Philadelphia has served as the birthplace of many great musicians. It has also proven to be a place that welcomed those born elsewhere. Jazz great John Coltrane grew up in North Carolina, the son of a tailor and the grandson of a preacher. In 1943, he settled in Philadelphia with his extended family and after service in Hawaii during World War II returned to the city to pursue music. Originally an alto saxophonist, he switched to the tenor sax and played with a variety of jazz bands around the Philadelphia area. In 1951, he joined Dizzy Gillespie's big jazz band. Later, he was hired by Miles Davis and his career as a valued sideman took off. Around that same time, Coltrane became a heroin addict, which greatly interfered with his career and led to a break with Davis.

By 1957, Coltrane quit heroin and signed with the Prestige label as a solo artist. Critics were never in agreement about his work; some described it as "angry" or "noise," while others such as the critic Ira Gitler praised it as "sheets of sound." By this point in his career he had switched to the soprano saxophone. Coltrane was never afraid to experiment, and his extended solos became known as "free" jazz. In 1965, his album *A Love Supreme* was nominated for two Grammy awards, in composition and performance. The album became his biggest seller, although his 1961 album *My Favorite Things* featured his jazz version of the Rodgers and Hammerstein song and became his signature tune.

John Coltrane died suddenly of liver cancer on July 27, 1967, at the young age of 40. Numerous posthumous albums were released and helped cement his reputation. Twenty-five years after his death, he won a lifetime achievement Grammy. John Coltrane's house in the Strawberry Mansion neighborhood was placed on the National Register of Historic Places in 1999, but the home is now vacant and badly deteriorated. The Philadelphia Preservation Alliance is working on a plan to restore the house where significant American jazz music was created.

1777: The Marquis de Lafayette arrives in Philadelphia. Inspired by the leadership of George Washington, he volunteers to serve without pay and is later appointed Major General in the Continental Army by Congress.

July 28

As early as 1705, Philadelphia Quakers established means for the care of the poor and indigent among their community. In 1731, the Philadelphia Almshouse was constructed, becoming the first government-sponsored facility for the care of the poor, sick, and insane in America. In 1767, the facility was moved to Tenth and Spruce streets under the name of the "Philadelphia Bettering House." Under the oversight of elected Overseers of the Poor, the facility was a hospital and a workhouse, a combination that was to continue in the city for many years. Nearly 300 persons were admitted in 1767, many of whom were the wives and children of debtors. It was common for family members of debtors to be employed producing goods made of wool, flax, and later, cotton. In 1784 a new corporation, the "Guardians of the Poor of the City of Philadelphia," was formed to take over the duties of the Overseers. Investigations of unhealthy food, lack of clothing, and the mixing of diseased patients with "honest, decent, and cleanly" paupers took place as early as 1784.

The Bettering House population soon grew too large for the facilities, and there was also a problem with inmates frequenting the bars and other unsavory establishments around Tenth Street. On July 28, 1834, the old facility was closed and the new suburban hospital, insane asylum, orphanage, and poorhouse, known as Blockley, opened at 34th Street near the University of Pennsylvania. Appalling conditions were the rule in the four main buildings, which by 1876 housed more than 3,000 persons. Mortality rates among infants in the orphanage were 95 percent, and financial scandals plagued the institution. The University of Pennsylvania medical school provided medical care, and thousands of students received training at Blockley.

One of the enduring debates surrounding the institution was the use of the bodies of the dead for autopsy by medical students. Beginning in the 1840s the dead were stolen or sold from Blockley for this purpose. By the twentieth century, the institution was renamed the Philadelphia General Hospital. Reforms and improvements led to the establishment of a nursing school and a more traditional medical facility until it closed in 1977. In 2001, construction in the area revealed the remains of more than 1,000 people, including the partial remains of autopsied cadavers, and the remains were respectfully interred in Woodland Cemetery.

1720: Andrew Bradford runs the first full page of advertisements in his newspaper. All but two regard absconding slaves or redemptioners; the remaining two are the first ever "lost and found" notices.

July 29

After achieving victory as an independent state, Pennsylvanians turned to the development and further settlement of the western regions in the years immediately following the American Revolution. Finding a means of compensating the Commonwealth's Revolutionary War veterans was also a priority. In 1785, the Pennsylvania legislature set aside 600,000 acres of land west of the Allegheny River near the northwest corner of present-day Pennsylvania to allot to veterans. A scheme of allotment was devised that awarded a minimum of 200 acres to those with the rank of Private, with increasing allotments dependent on rank. A Major General could receive as much as 2,000 acres. To identify land for this program, the Commonwealth selected a fellow veteran, Brigadier General William Irvine.

Born in Northern Ireland, Irvine served as a ship's surgeon in the Royal Navy but immigrated to the colonies in 1764 to practice medicine. Sympathetic to the American cause, in 1775 he raised and commanded the Seventh Pennsylvania Regiment and was captured and imprisoned for a time in an expedition against Canada. He saw action in Staten Island and performed well at the Battle of Monmouth, where a former Irvine family servant, "Molly Pitcher," gained a place in history. In 1781, through the recommendation of his friend General George Washington, he was given command of the northwest frontier at Fort Pitt. He remained at that post until the end of the war, and served in other military capacities in later years, including commanding the troops during the Whiskey Rebellion in 1794.

In 1785, Irvine traveled in Western Pennsylvania to identify land and recommended to the Commonwealth that it should purchase the Erie Triangle, which would give it frontage on Lake Erie. For his service, he received a large land grant in what is now Warren County. Irvine also engaged in political activity, serving as a delegate to the Continental Congress of 1786-88 and was a delegate to the Pennsylvania Constitutional Convention in 1790. In 1800, he moved to Philadelphia, to take charge of the arsenals, supplies, and ordinance of the Army, and died on July 29, 1804.

1794: Mother Bethel African Methodist Episcopal Church is founded by Richard Allen.

1889: St. Peter Claver is founded by the Archdiocese of Philadelphia to serve the African-American Catholics of the city.

1999: The state historical marker honoring the Church of the Advocate in North Philadelphia is dedicated.

July 30

Immediately after the end of World War II, the United States and the Soviet Union began a "cold war" to determine world political and economic dominance. Especially after the Soviet Union proved it had nuclear weapons, concern about espionage and attacks on the American way of life were reflected in adoption of loyalty oaths for federal employees, black-listing of people in the motion picture industry with "red" connections, hearings and accusations of communist influence in government, and legislation prohibiting the advocacy of communist violence. This social and political environment led to the arrest and conviction of nine Philadelphians for violating the Smith Act in 1954.

Despite the attention paid to anticommunism, the Communist Party in the United States had an estimated membership of as few as 10,000 in 1954. In Philadelphia, a small group of nine men who were admitted members of the party, were arrested on July 30, 1954. Specifically, they were charged with "unlawfully, willingly, and knowingly organizing and helping to organize, as the Communist Party of the United States, a society, group and assembly of persons who teach and advocate the overthrow of the United States by force and violence." Although no overt acts of espionage or other criminal offenses were alleged by the prosecution, *The Communist Manifesto* by Karl Marx and other documents fundamental to the communist ideology were brought to bear as evidence. A fine and up to ten years in prison were the maximum possible penalties. Defended by a group of prominent members of the Philadelphia Bar Association, the nine defendants were convicted on August 13, 1954, after a trial that lasted seventy-one days. Government informants testified against the men, while the defense was based on American civil liberties rights to free speech and assembly.

In 1956, the United States Supreme Court restricted the Smith Act to instances in which there was proof of advocacy for concrete acts of violence, as opposed to merely teaching such acts as a concept. The convictions of four of the Philadelphia defendants were later overturned on appeal, with the Justice Department free to proceed with a new trial. On May 16, 1958, all charges against the remaining defendants were dropped by the federal government. Nationwide, more than 100 persons were charged and convicted under the Smith Act, some serving terms in prison. One of the lasting contributions of the case was the establishment of a process in Philadelphia to provide legal counsel to unpopular defendants; that process was later employed in cases involving the civil rights and peace movements.

1718: William Penn dies in England.

1935: On a small television screen built into a radio cabinet, a group of chorus girls, an orchestra, and Mickey Mouse perform for an invited audience at the Television Laboratories in Chestnut Hill.

July 31

Following the establishment of a government and laws to guide them, the newly formed United States Congress turned its attention to a variety of other needs, among them public defense and civil rights, addressed with the Bill of Rights and the creation of a military service. However, before the nation could fully engage in another important function, domestic and foreign trade, it needed a banking system, and that banking system needed money. In Article 8, Section 1 of the United States Constitution, the government was granted the right to coin currency and regulate its value. Beyond issues of credit, the creation of a national bank in 1791 addressed the management of the national money. On this date in 1792, the cornerstone was laid to the nation's first mint, fulfilling the first necessary component of unifying and regulating American finances.

Even as the Constitution was ratified in 1787, many people remained suspicious of the idea of consolidating certain powers into a federal government. Issues of states versus federal rights touched debates as varied as the structure of Congress and the creation of an American currency. Led by Federalist advocate Alexander Hamilton, a unified financial system was designed. On March 3, 1791, Congress finally authorized the creation of a United States Mint and less than a month later the legislation was passed. Authority was also granted to construct a new special-use building, to be located near Seventh and Filbert streets. David Rittenhouse was appointed director by President Washington, and assayers, coiners, and engravers were also hired. The first circulating coins, more than 11,000 copper pennies, were struck in early 1793. A common (but undocumented) story suggests that silver flatware owned by George and Martha Washington was used in the manufacture of the first silver coins.

In addition to circulating coins, the Philadelphia Mint also produced a number of significant Peace Medals used in behalf of the United States Government during Thomas Jefferson's presidency. The current mint near Independence Hall was completed in 1969. It is a popular tourist attraction, drawing thousands of visitors each week, but it also strikes coins at a rate of up to one million coins in thirty minutes. It is the only mint facility in the country that engraves all dies and strikers, and as such continues in service to the country as the origin of all American coins, many of them carrying a small "P," for Philadelphia.

1777: The Marquis de Lafayette and George Washington meet for the first time.

1790: The first patent in the United States is issued to inventor Samuel Hopkins for an improved method of making potash, used in the manufacture of soap.

2000: The Republican National Convention convenes in Philadelphia and ends four days later.

For more than two centuries, Americans have celebrated the Fourth of July as the most significant date in the history of our national freedom. That date marks the commemoration of the Declaration of Independence, the document that delineated American colonial grievances against the King of England and boldly stated the intention to become independent of the king's rule. Indeed, the actual timeline of events surrounding the Declaration of Independence has proven far more complex than a single date could denote. While the final wording of the complete document was indeed adopted on July 4, 1776, a fully engrossed version was not prepared until early August, and the last signature was not applied until five years later, in 1781. For patriot and future president John Adams, it was yet another day that would be remembered for all time by grateful Americans, for that was the date of adoption for the congressional resolution "that these united colonies are, and of right ought to be, free and independent states."

Letter from John Adams to Abigail Adams, July 3, 1776 (excerpt, Adams Family Papers)

Had a Declaration of Independency been made seven Months ago, it would have been attended with many great and glorious Effects. . . .

. . . But on the other Hand, the Delay of this Declaration to this Time, has many great Advantages attending it.—The Hopes of Reconciliation, which were fondly entertained by Multitudes of honest and well meaning though weak and mistaken People, have been gradually and at last totally extinguished.—Time has been given for the whole People, maturely to consider the great Question of Independence and to ripen their judgments, dissipate their Fears, and allure their Hopes, by discussing it in News Papers and Pamphlets, by debating it, in Assemblies, Conventions, Committees of Safety and Inspection, in Town and County Meetings, as well as in private Conversations, so that the whole People in every Colony of the 13, have now adopted it, as their own Act.—This will cement the Union, and avoid those Heats and perhaps Convulsions which might have been occasioned, by such a Declaration Six Months ago.

But the Day is past. The Second Day of July 1776, will be the most memorable Epoch, in the History of America.

I am apt to believe that it will be celebrated, by succeeding Generations, as the great anniversary Festival. It ought to be commemorated, as the Day of Deliverance by solemn Acts of Devotion to God Almighty. It ought to be solemnized with Pomp and Parade, with Shows, Games, Sports, Guns, Bells, Bonfires, and Illuminations from one End of this Continent to the other from this Time forward forever more.

You will think me transported with Enthusiasm but I am not.—I am well aware of the Toil and Blood and Treasure, that it will cost Us to maintain this Declaration, and support and defend these States.—Yet through all the Gloom I can see the Rays of ravishing Light and Glory. I can see that the End is more than worth all the Means. And that Posterity will triumph in that Days Transaction, even although We should rue it, which I trust in God We shall not.

August

August 1

On this date in 1944, in the midst of the Second World War, Philadelphia witnessed one of the most significant race-related labor disputes in American history. The city's all-white transit operators began a strike in protest of the hiring of eight black trolley drivers. Within hours, the impact of the strike was felt throughout Philadelphia's wartime industries, where nearly one million war workers labored to support the military overseas. George White, an African-American angered at the disregard for blacks serving in the military and the blatant racism of the strike and strikers, struck the Liberty Bell with a paperweight and uttered the words "Liberty Bell. . . . That's a lot of bunk!" His emotional protest drew attention to the inequities of the wartime labor market and brought to light tensions felt across the country.

As more and more Philadelphians left to serve overseas in the military, essential industries came to rely on women, the aged, and people of color to fill roles on the home front left vacant. The Philadelphia Transit Company was not alone in considering integration as a solution, and employed nearly 600 blacks in low-level positions. But at the suggestion that African-Americans be hired for the more prestigious driver positions, the 10,000 white employees resisted and ultimately went out on strike. Beginning as early as 4:00 A.M., PTC employees arrived for work but soon went home "sick." Over the next five days city officials grew increasingly concerned about violence, ordering bars to close by 3:00 P.M. and canceling large public gatherings, including a Phillies baseball game.

After three nights of general calm, striking workers were asked by President Roosevelt to return by 5:30 A.M. the next day as a sign of shared concern for the well-being of the nation during a time of war; however, none agreed to do so. After five days, Roosevelt ordered the United States Army to the city to take over 2,500 PTC streetcars and the subway. Overall, nearly 7,000 armed troops were called in to keep the peace. Trolleys began to run again, some manned by African-American employees, as two soldiers escorted each car. Strikers were warned that if they continued the walkout, they would lose their jobs and their certificates of availability for other jobs, or be subject to the draft. Under these terms, most strikers returned to work, grudgingly accepting the presence of black co-workers. The strike was broken, and the city once again settled into the business and industry of war.

1932: The Philadelphia Savings Fund Society building at 12th and Market officially opens.

August 2

Contrary to most popular films, books, and art, the famed group signing of the Declaration of Independence neither occurred on July 4, 1776, nor did it include all of the men who could lay claim to their participation in declaring the American states free and independent of the King of England. Rather, the formal, or engrossed, version of the Declaration we are all familiar with was in fact not completed until nearly one month after the vote which made its language official. On this date in 1776, fifty of the fifty-six men who would ultimately affix their names to one of our most significant American documents gathered in the first floor assembly room of the Pennsylvania State House to forever pledge their lives, their fortunes, and their sacred honor for the good of all Americans.

July 4, 1776, will forever be remembered as the moment when the United States was born. However, the document reviewed and accepted by Congress that day was a draft by the hand of author Thomas Jefferson. After the vote, Congressional Secretary Charles Thomson began arrangements for the preparation of a formal calligraphic copy. He looked to Timothy Matlack, the official scribe for Congress who was already entrusted with the daily responsibility of recording and formalizing acts of Congress. Matlack began work immediately but required nearly a month to complete the carefully drawn, parchment copy. On August 2, Congress reconvened with the expectation of signing the completed document. All but five representatives were in attendance, led by Congressional president John Hancock, still known today for the grand signature he hoped would be clearly seen by King George. Over the next four months five more men signed, but the final signature, that of Thomas McKean, was not inscribed until 1781.

During the American Revolution, the Declaration traveled with Congress, most likely rolled into a tube. In 1789, following the creation of a new government under the United States Constitution, the Declaration was placed in the custody of the newly created Department of State. During the War of 1812, it was evacuated from Washington, D.C., along with countless other government archives. As the fiftieth anniversary of the Declaration approached in 1826, national interest and nostalgia regarding the document led to its growing place as an American icon. Exhibited for more than thirty years in the Patent Office, the ink was badly faded before it was pulled from public display at the end of the nineteenth century. Under the care of the National Archives, the Declaration has been restored and is currently encased in a maximum security, environmentally neutral display, available for viewing by all who wish to once again relive the moment when fifty-six men signed their names and risked their lives to form a new nation.

1957: Eighty-one passengers on a crowded Broad Street subway train are injured in a panic that occurs after an electrical explosion beneath the first car.

August 3

In the history of civil activism and advocacy, few figures can match the passion and commitment of Margaret "Maggie" Kuhn, who died in the Philadelphia neighborhood of Germantown on April 22, 1995. Born in Buffalo, New York, on this date in 1905, as a young adult Kuhn embraced many of the progressive ideas of the first half of the twentieth century. Later, after a life of professional service and activism, Kuhn faced forced retirement at the age of 65 in 1970. Believing in her own potential and that of all aged people, Kuhn and seven friends went on to found the Consultation of Older Adults (later renamed the Grey Panthers) on April 17, 1970. Driven to eradicate "ageism" and address global issues such as the war in Vietnam and elderly abuse, Kuhn and her colleagues redefined societal views of the aged in ways that continue to resonate into the twenty-first century.

After graduating from Case Western Reserve University in Cleveland, Kuhn soon moved to Germantown to join her parents. In 1930 she accepted a position with the Germantown Y.W.C.A. as head of the Professional Department of Business for young women, working to provide training and social support in order to empower young women. Kuhn continued living and working in Germantown through World War II, serving as program coordinator and editor for the Y.W.C.A.'s United Service Organizations until 1948. In 1950, Kuhn began working for the Social Education and Action Department of the Presbyterian Church's headquarters in Philadelphia. It was from this job she was forced to retire in 1970, believing her work undone and her life still left to live.

The underlying mission of the Grey Panthers was to address the specific needs of the aged, but also to seek opportunities for creating a more intergenerational and accepting society. Communal housing, job-sharing, and universal preventive health care were just a few of the group's goals as envisioned by Kuhn and her fellow activists. Early meetings were held in Kuhn's home on Greene Street, but the organization grew and soon developed branches throughout the country. The first national convention was held in 1975, a culmination of their efforts. The Grey Panthers currently boast a membership of over 40,000 people of all ages. Health care, job equity, and housing remain their priorities, a tribute to the remarkable vision of Maggie Kuhn.

1885: A terrifying tornado sweeps up the Delaware River causing an immense amount of damage to property and killing or injuring eighty-one people.

1965: Dr. Martin Luther King, Jr., leads 5,000 chanting and singing demonstrators in protest of the segregated policies of Girard College.

August 4

The trial of John Peter Zenger in 1735 was one of the most famous legal cases in the early history of America. Zenger, a newspaper publisher in New York, wrote numerous articles criticizing the actions of that colony's governor, William Cosby. The governor had established his own newspaper to praise himself, leading his detractors to strike back with their own newspaper, with Zenger as its printer and publisher. Zenger's continuing articles against Cosby eventually resulted in Zenger's arrest on November 17, 1734, for seditious libel. During eight months of incarceration before his trial, lawyers who volunteered to defend Zenger were barred from practice by Cosby. Finally, Zenger turned to Andrew Hamilton of Philadelphia to provide his defense. Hamilton agreed to defend Zenger *pro bono,* believing in the significance of the case to all American subjects of the British crown.

Andrew Hamilton was a Scottish immigrant who settled in Virginia in 1697 and moved to Philadelphia in 1716. He served as attorney general of Pennsylvania and was for many years a member of the assembly, in addition to maintaining his law practice. At the beginning of Zenger's jury trial, he astounded the court by admitting that Zenger had written and published the material against Cosby that had led to the arrest. Begging the indulgence of the court, he argued that British libel law should not be followed, and that truth could be considered as a defense to libel by the jury. He also argued that, contrary to the practice at the time, the jury could rule on the law and not only on the facts of the case. The jury returned a verdict of "not guilty" and an important foundation of freedom of the press was established in the colonies. Hamilton was widely celebrated, and the term "a Philadelphia lawyer," meaning a very clever and capable attorney, was said to have emerged from Hamilton's victory in the Zenger case.

In addition to his service to law, Andrew Hamilton and his son, James, left a mark on Pennsylvania. As founders of Lancaster, the Hamiltons created the fourth county in the commonwealth in 1732. That same year, the Hamiltons granted land near present-day Fifth Street on Chestnut Street for the construction of a new state house, now known as Independence Hall. In 1740, the elder Hamilton built an estate on 153 acres near the present-day 17th and Fairmount streets, which he called Bush Hill. He died there on this date in 1741, and is buried at Christ Church.

1821: The *Saturday Evening Post* is first published in the city as a four-page newspaper without illustrations.

1937: A citywide trucker's strike, which has idled more than one-third of the truck drivers in the city in support of striking A&P truckers, ends.

August 5

Strength in industry matters most at moments of great need and demand. Philadelphia, benefiting from a range of both natural and manmade resources, once enjoyed high stature among the large urban manufacturing centers across the country and was frequently called upon during time of war to provide goods and services to the nation. As early as the American Revolution, the region's position along water routes and its central location between the northern and southern states placed it at the heart of the importation of goods and raw materials used to outfit soldiers. Indeed, the success of the city's textile industry exemplified a long association between industrial and wartime success.

While weaving mills in New England often claim the attention of historians seeking the stories of American textile manufacture, Philadelphia far surpassed the milling towns of Massachusetts by the mid-1850s. Just prior to the Civil War, the city claimed more textile companies than any other American city. Fed by cheap coal, high-quality machine-manufacturing shops, and the availability of specialty labor in the form of recent immigrants, Philadelphia's clothing and textile industry thrived. During the Civil War, companies such as William Horstmann and Sons and Stetson worked long shifts to make the hats, socks, blankets, and jackets worn by the Union Army. World War I and World War II proved equally demanding, and on August 5, 1940, over a full year before the official start of World War II, the United States Army ordered more than half a million woolen undershirts and drawers, and a remarkable 1.5 million pairs of cotton underwear.

Unfortunately, the peak rate of textile production reached in the city just prior to World War I was soon eclipsed by the draw of cheap raw materials and labor in the new textile mills of the South. Additional economic stresses and the growth of overseas factories resulted in a devastating loss of companies as varied as Botany 500, After Six, and Stetson. Today, fewer than 200 residents work in textile manufacturing in the city. Unlike many early companies which relied on mass production, however, a more promising future for the Philadelphia textile industry appears to lie in fine and specialty work, which makes newer and more refined demands on one of the longest-running forms of manufacture in Philadelphia.

1918: The first ship is christened after construction at the Hog Island shipyard. The USS *Quistconck* was contracted in 1917 as part of the nation's war effort.

August 6

As backdrop to compelling stories and striking visuals, Philadelphia has long enjoyed a special place in the motion picture industry. Whether offering a unique view into the elite world of the Main Line as in *The Philadelphia Story* (1940), or as title character in a groundbreaking depiction of the pain and triumph associated with the AIDS epidemic in *Philadelphia* (1993), the city is no stranger to the excitement of filmmaking. Director, screenwriter, and actor M. Night Shyamalan in particular has taken many opportunities to feature his adopted home as a significant player in his storytelling. On this date in 1999, the city was once again introduced to the world through the vision and art of film in *The Sixth Sense*. Addressing themes of love, faith, and personal challenges framed within a decidedly spooky tale, *The Sixth Sense* remains his most successful and critically acclaimed work.

Born to two physicians in Pondicherry, India, on this date in 1970, Shyamalan was raised in the affluent suburb of Penn Valley just outside Philadelphia. Educated in private Roman Catholic and Episcopal schools (his family were Hindus), Shyamalan discovered an interest in filmmaking early on when he was given a Super-8 film camera. As a student in New York University's Tisch School of the Arts, he borrowed money from family and friends to film his first real movie, titled *Praying with Anger,* which is the only one of his films not shot in Philadelphia. *Wide Awake* soon followed in 1996 and by 1999 he had completed and released *The Sixth Sense,* which held its world premiere in Philadelphia on August 2, 1999. The film, with a $40 million budget, earned more than twelve times that amount and brought Shyamalan many accolades, including nominations for Best Picture, Best Director, and Best Original Screenplay.

Locations throughout the city are heavily featured in the film, among them St. Albans Street in South Philadelphia, Pierce College on Pine Street, St. Augustine's Church on Fourth Street, and the Dream Garden mosaic by Tiffany in the Curtis Building on Independence Square. In his subsequent films, Shyamalan has continued to draw from his love of Philadelphia and the surrounding countryside, filming in Bucks County and Lancaster County, as well as in more urban settings downtown. His work continues a long history of Philadelphia on film.

1787: Delegates to the Constitutional Convention begin debating the first complete draft of the proposed Constitution of the United States.

1903: In the top of the fourth inning of the second game of a double header at the Baker Bowl (Phillies vs. Boston Braves), fans hear a brawl on the street outside. Hundreds rush to the top of the stands, and their collective weight cracks rotten timbers. The stadium collapses to the street, killing 12 and injuring 232.

1911: Lincoln Beachey wins the first long-distance cross-country aeroplane race ever held in the United States when he flies from New York to Philadelphia.

August 7

Independence Hall has been the site of many citizen demonstrations throughout its history. On July 4, 1965, the first national demonstration by gays and lesbians took place there. Inspired by the historical precedents established by civil rights and women's rights activists, the city's homosexuals pursued their cause, ultimately to win approval for a number of shifts in city policy.

Through the 1970s, Philadelphia saw an increase in the number of gay citizens and the establishment of institutions geared specifically to them. Businesses, support organizations, and a community center opened, many in the neighborhood known as Washington Square West, located between Seventh and Broad streets along Locust Street. Parades and festivals were also established, including the Gay Pride March in 1972, which now attracts more than 25,000 people annually as Pride Day. Mark Segal was a teen-aged gay activist when he interrupted the *CBS Evening News* with Walter Cronkite in 1973 to display a sign that read "Gays protest CBS bigotry." He went on to found the *Philadelphia Gay News* in 1976. Barbara Gittings and Dr. John E. Fryer, a Philadelphia psychiatrist who testified at a hearing in a mask, succeeded in 1973 in getting the American Psychiatric Association to remove homosexuality from its official list of mental illnesses. Dr. Walter J. Lear, the regional health commissioner for the Pennsylvania Health Department, publicly revealed he was gay in 1976.

By the 1980s, gays and lesbians were successfully pushing significant changes in Philadelphia laws and opinion. On this date in 1980, the Philadelphia Police Department ended its ban on openly gay persons serving on the police force. Two years later, the city passed an ordinance prohibiting discrimination based on sexual orientation. Opposition on the basis of religion, fiscal policy, and other concerns, however, remained firm.

In the early 1990s, tensions between the city and gay activists arose over issues including neighborhood disturbances attributed to illegal gay activity and alleged police brutality. However, due in part to the city's Democratic leadership, Philadelphia enacted a domestic partner's law in 1997. The law, which provides a tax break for gay and lesbian couples, is still in effect but is frequently challenged in court. Today, the gay, lesbian, transgendered, and bisexual cause remains a politically and culturally active part of Philadelphia, influencing a diversity of cultural, social, and business organizations throughout the city.

1918: The city marks its highest recorded temperature of 106°F.

1961: Beer is sold at Connie Mack Stadium for the first time.

1964: A homeowner and a real estate dealer are ordered by a city agency today to sell a dwelling to Lawrence M. Moy, an American of Chinese descent, after he complained he had been denied the purchase because of his race.

August 8

Religious tolerance and freedom of worship stand as primary principles throughout Pennsylvania history, seen in the early acceptance of religions considered less than desirable among most colonies. In particular, Catholicism has long been a presence in the city. On this date in 1976, 100,000 worshipers gathered at JFK Stadium for the third and final day of prayer, song, and communion featured in the 41st International Eucharistic Congress, a massive expression of Catholic faith and unity. Held every quarter century, the event in Philadelphia was only the second of its kind in the United States, after the 1926 Congress in Chicago. Guided by the theme of "Hungers of Mankind" and directed by Philadelphia archbishop John Cardinal Krol, it was deemed a wild success by the nearly one million attendees. The event at JFK Stadium served as the culmination of a gathering marked by diversity, community, and an appeal by the Catholic Church for a return to compassionate worship.

The first modern Congress was held in Lilles, France, in 1881. Intended to offer Catholics from around the world an opportunity to share their faith and culture with one another and renew their commitment to the Church, the Congress in Philadelphia featured a new openness and desire to emphasize the rich cultural strengths of global Catholicism. Convention Hall, at 34th Street in West Philadelphia, served as the center of many activities, including displays by over 400 exhibitors and religious orders. Appeals to alleviate hunger and injustice throughout the world were met with support, while efforts were made to meet the needs of minority groups through special services. An African American–centric mass was said at the Spectrum, while a much smaller service served the 200 attendees of Native American descent.

On the final day, most attendees crowded JFK Stadium to hear two speakers—one live and one beamed by satellite. President Gerald Ford, in attendance, called for deeper understanding between peoples. Pope Paul VI, in Bolsena, Italy, called for unity of faith, worship, and charity. In addition to the speakers, attendees included 2,500 clergy and several hundred attendants. At the end of President Ford's speech, the priests sprinkled holy water onto the crowd, many of whom had traveled from around the world to attend the conference. A singular moment for Philadelphia's Catholic community, the Congress stands as a reflection of the significant role the Church plays in Philadelphia's religious history.

1803: The Philadelphia Bank is founded, with George Clymer as president.

1906: Five marines are put in double irons on board the receiving ship *Lancaster,* at the League Island Navy Yard, and ten sailors placed under arrest, after a mutiny in which two of the mutineers were badly injured.

1978: A Philadelphia police officer is killed in the first storming of the MOVE house in West Philadelphia. The death is a precursor to the tragedy of May 13, 1985, when police once again storm the home and a police-thrown bomb kills eleven members of the radical group.

August 9

Philadelphia's relationship with cars and parking changed forever on this date in 1951 when the newly formed Philadelphia Parking Authority purchased its first plot of land with the intention of building a city-run parking garage. Organized by Mayor Bernard Samuel in March 1950, the Authority was charged with relieving central city traffic congestion and immediately began seeking appropriate locations throughout the downtown area. With the purchase of the 29,500-square-foot lot on Walnut Street near Rittenhouse Square, the city's love-hate relationship with ticket writers and traffic overseers began.

Throughout its three centuries, the streets of Philadelphia have always been crowded with the vehicles of choice, ranging from the earliest carts and carriages to horse-drawn trolley cars and still later automobiles. By the mid twentieth century, a rapidly growing postwar population demanded relief from the congestion caused by too many cars and trucks. Initially focused on the development of off-street parking, the Philadelphia Parking Authority looked to multi-level parking garages as the solution. The first project was four stories tall and would eventually accommodate 500 cars. Other garages quickly followed, but the city continued to struggle with the lack of easy-access, affordable parking.

In 1982, in hopes of improving parking in general and centralizing control of both on-street and off-street parking, a law was enacted transferring various functions to the Authority. This included management of parking meters, parking regulations, towing for violations, and the issuing of parking tickets. It is these last few responsibilities that have generated tremendous resentment toward the Authority in recent years, inspiring the selection of the city agency as a feature of a reality television show, *Parking Wars.* Though for many Philadelphians the Parking Authority stands as a representation of much than can be irritating or overbearing about city government, the role it continues to play in managing a primary urban problem cannot be overstated, and there is little question its work will continue for many years to come.

1775: An advertisement appears in the *Pennsylvania Journal* newspaper calling for skilled spinners and weavers to support the manufacture of American cloth.

1946: After almost four years of effort, Public Law 711 is enacted calling for the creation of a seven-member commission, known as the Philadelphia National Shrines Park Commission, to investigate the establishment of a national park "to encompass within its area the buildings of historical significance in the old part of the city of Philadelphia."

August 10

Today's television entertainment gossip shows cover new Hollywood scandals every week. People seem never to tire of hearing about the marital troubles of movie stars and recording artists. In the 1950s, fan magazines covered the most scandalous divorces of the day, with the Eddie Fisher–Debbie Reynolds–Elizabeth Taylor divorce and marriage saga perhaps the most publicized of that era.

Eddie Fisher was born in Philadelphia on August 10, 1928, the fourth of seven children of Russian Jewish immigrants. Known as "Sonny" to his family, he exhibited singing talent early in his childhood and successfully competed in singing contests in the Philadelphia area. In 1949, Fisher was performing at Grossinger's Resort in the Catskills when he was "discovered" by Eddie Cantor and joined Cantor's radio show. A singing star by the time he was twenty-one, Fisher soon had his own radio show sponsored by Coca-Cola, and started releasing hit records. Seventeen of his pre–rock and roll hits made the Top 10 on the music charts, and several, including "Oh My Pa-Pa" and "I Need You Now" reached the number-one spot.

Fisher married movie star Debbie Reynolds in 1955; they were known as America's Sweethearts and their presumably happy marriage was followed closely by the media. In 1958, Mike Todd, Fisher's best friend and the husband of actress Elizabeth Taylor, was killed in a plane crash. Soon after, Fisher was seen spending time with Taylor; their affair led to a bitter and public divorce from Reynolds. Taylor went from being a pitied widow to being characterized as a home-wrecker. Fisher received as many as 7,000 letters a week denouncing his behavior. Fisher and Reynolds divorced in 1959, and Fisher married Taylor immediately.

The Fisher-Taylor marriage lasted only four years. Fisher continued appearing in Las Vegas shows in the 1960s and 1970s, but his style of singing was out of favor, and he never again released popular hits. Fisher was married three more times, including to actress Connie Stevens. His 1991 autobiography caused its own scandal when he revealed he had been addicted to drugs and alcohol most of his life. Famed primarily for the scandals in his life, Fisher was recognized for his early music success when he was inducted into the Philadelphia Walk of Fame in 1988.

1753: Benjamin Franklin and William Hunter of Virginia become joint postmasters general for the British Crown in the colonies.

1910: The Witching Wave Company is chartered for operating a witching wave amusement device, invented by Theophilus Van Kannel of Philadelphia, who also invented the revolving door.

August 11

An extensive and progressive marketing and retail project finally came to fruition on this date in 1977, when the Gallery I, Philadelphia's downtown shopping mall, opened to the public for the first time. Extending from 8th Street to 10th Street along the historic Market Street, the Gallery I offered a variety of retail opportunities set in a decidedly urban environment. Within its first year, the mall exceeded expectations, achieving per-square-foot profits that were greater than most suburban shopping malls. However, in conflict from the very start with local citizens and undermined by larger urban and economic challenges, the Gallery I (and II, opened in the mid-1980s) has proven to be both a symbol of success and a target for much that is said to be wrong about the Center City retail industry.

Historically, Market Street has served as a retail center for the city, though it began life as the more traditional High Street. Home to an extensive open-shed market from its earliest days, Market Street was the place to go for many of the fresh produce, meats, and goods available for sale in the bustling eighteenth and early nineteenth centuries. By the 1850s, however, the sheds were condemned and a new variety of retail attraction emerged: department stores. Names like Wanamaker, Gimbels, and Strawbridge and Clothier set up shop. The farmers markets moved to 12th Street, and were later incorporated into the Reading Railroad's Terminal Market. Less than a century later, flagging sales and the departure of thousands of citizens for suburban communities resulted in a run-down and generally failing retail strip.

As early as 1953, City Planner Edmund Bacon envisioned a multi-level shopping destination along Market Street. Community retailers resisted until the early 1960s, when they finally agreed to a below-street-level plan. That plan was not realized until the first phase of the Gallery opened. When the second phase was completed, the mall extended from 8th Street to 10th Street, and was paired with the extensive commuter rail development known as Market East. The disconnect with the pedestrian lifestyle (and local residents) was felt, however, in the immense blank-wall components of the mall design. Bolstered in part by the development of the Convention Center and associated hotels, the area along East Market Street continues to struggle in a challenging economy and a divisive urban landscape. In contrast, the Gallery enjoys a rare occupancy rate of 95 percent, making it one of the most successful malls in the country.

1943: Kenny Gamble, producer and songwriter, is born. Gamble and business partner Leon Huff became the principal architects of the Philly Soul sound, one of the most popular and influential music developments of the 1970s.

August 12

Though many would argue that the events reportedly witnessed by Al Bielek on August 12, 1943, in the Philadelphia Navy Yard could not possibly have occurred, there are others who believe his remarkable tale as truth, one of many moments when government actions were kept from the American people. Regardless, the experiments described by Bielek have since been incorporated into the larger mythology of Philadelphia, have been memorialized in television and film, and remain one of the most interesting and unlikely moments in Philadelphia history. Specifically, Bielek describes an effort by the United States Navy to cloak, or make invisible, the USS *Eldridge* in what is commonly called the Philadelphia Experiment.

As early as 1955, the story of a naval military experiment emerged following Morris K. Jessup's publication of a book about UFOs and the potential of nonrocketry propulsion, proposed by none other than Albert Einstein as the "Unified Field Theory." Jessup was contacted by Carlos Allende, also known as Carl Allen, who reported that he had witnessed the *Eldridge* disappear, then reappear, in October 1943 in an event marked by utter chaos and multiple injuries on board the *Eldridge.* Jessup ultimately dismissed Allen's claims, but in 1957 the story was revived by the Office of Naval Research, which published an Allen-annotated version of Jessup's book.

In 1984, following the publication of several retellings of the Philadelphia Experiment story, a motion picture loosely based on the accounts and directed by Stewart Raffill was released. Six years later, Alfred Bielek, a self-proclaimed member of the USS *Eldridge* crew, claimed the movie version was close to his experience. He claimed that at the moment when one try at the experiment was enacted on August 12, 1943, he and his brother jumped overboard and were instantly transported to the year 2137. He also claimed to be involved with other secret military experiments, most having to do with time travel. With the advent of the Internet, Bielek's story has spread throughout conspiracy-minded Web sites and blogs. Skeptic Web sites have also addressed the claims of Bielek and a number of others, refuting the possibility of such a conspiracy of experimentation in an active naval shipyard at a time of war. Whether one believes or not, the Philadelphia Experiment holds a unique place in the tales told about Philadelphia.

1769: Benjamin Franklin Bache, publisher and grandson to Benjamin Franklin, is born.

1872: Work begins on the monumental City Hall at Penn Square.

August 13

Universally remembered as a shameful and tragic part of the country's history, lynchings and related violence against African-Americans in the late 1800s and early 1900s are not normally associated with Mid-Atlantic states like Pennsylvania, and certainly not extended metropolitan regions like Philadelphia. However, on this date in 1911, one of the most violent and memorable lynchings in American history took place in the small town of Coatesville, just miles outside Philadelphia in Chester County. Zachariah Walker, a black steel worker accused of killing a white security guard, was publicly hunted down and burned to death in front of a reported 1,600 townspeople. Regional and national anger at the event and its particularly soulless nature ultimately led to Pennsylvania's anti-lynching law of 1923 and serves today as a reminder that justice is not always achieved, even under the most extreme need.

The racial atmosphere across the country in the years just before the First World War was fraught with tensions and prejudices. Fears of economic inequities, an increase in competition for jobs, and a general fear of the role of blacks and whites in a changing world fostered violence and an increase in attacks against African-Americans. Walker, an outsider, had come to Pennsylvania from rural Virginia specifically to work in the Coatesville steel industry. One evening, after a night of drinking, he shot and killed Edgar Rice, a well-respected former borough policeman working as a security guard. Walker fled the scene, escaping up a tree, where he shot himself in the mouth in an attempt at suicide when he was cornered by pursuers. The men took him to the hospital, but in the early hours of the morning a mob of masked men dragged him from his hospital bed and forced him to a semi-remote area outside town.

Over the next few hours, Walker's torture and death by fire was watched by hundreds of people, none of whom attempted to provide aid. Ultimately, fifteen local men and an underage boy were indicted for murder, but were subsequently acquitted because of lack of interest in achieving conviction among local Chester County residents. Reported in newspapers across the country, Walker's death and the trial and acquittal of his murderers were widely known, inspiring the NAACP to launch an anti-lynching campaign and directly influencing both state and federal laws intended to protect all people from racially motivated violence. In the years since, residents of Coatesville have worked to redeem their town by acknowledging the crime and apologizing for their role in a bleak moment in Pennsylvania history.

1979: The United States Justice Department files a civil rights lawsuit accusing the Philadelphia Police Department of police brutality. The first of its kind in the nation, the suit specifically accuses Frank Rizzo of initiating many illegal practices as Commissioner from 1967 to 1971.

August 14

President Andrew Johnson was in political trouble. With an unpopular incumbent and at risk of losing many of the significant mid-year Congressional elections of 1866, Johnson's supporters called for a national convention of pro-South politicians and persons of influence. The National Union Convention, also known as the Loyalist Convention, opened on this date in 1866 and continued for two more days. Housed in a massive temporary structure on Girard Avenue between 19th and 20th streets, thousands of notable attendees flocked to the city. Their primary goal of establishing a new political party was never met, however, and Johnson was forced to seek new opportunities for making his case.

Known as the Great Wigwam, the National Union Convention was organized in the wake of increasing resistance to Johnson's pro-South and anti–civil rights Reconstruction policies. Accused of corruption and increasingly challenged by Congress and the electorate, Johnson's administration was on the defensive against a broad spectrum of Republicans. Ultimately, more than 7,000 attendees arrived in Philadelphia, including many from the United States House of Representatives, the publishing world, and business and industry leaders. In many cases, supporters feared the growing influence of the African-American community, bolstered by the freeing of hundreds of thousands of slaves following the war. For others, their support of Johnson was based on their desire to benefit from an economically stable South, in contrast to many others who hoped to adequately punish the South and its strongest supporters for daring to turn against the federal government. Widely publicized in newspapers across the country, it was clear by the end of the three-day event that Johnson had been unable to convince most Americans to follow his lead.

Johnson next turned to a cross-country speaking trip, known as the "Swing Around the Circle," in which he regularly spoke to crowds in opposition to the growing Republican approach to the problem of recovery in the South. Flanked by heroes of the Civil War, among them George Custer and Ulysses S. Grant, the president pushed his agenda. Johnson did not help his cause however, frequently sounding belligerent in his bid to overcome opponents. Ultimately, Johnson was impeached by Congress in 1868, as the nation stumbled forward to deal with the aftermath of the war. The Great Wigwam, seen as a precursor to Johnson's success, became instead the first death knell for the Johnson administration.

1929: The Tacony-Palmyra Bridge opens.

August 15

Equestrian tricks and daring acts are often viewed as the earliest examples of what would later become the modern-day circus. In England, famed show riders such as Philip Astley and Charles Hughes introduced the exciting and complex single-man acts that included leaping on and off galloping horses, riding full speed while juggling, and training horses to engage in dog-like tricks. In America, New York City first hosted similar acts in the early 1780s, to the delight of many. In Philadelphia, the announcement of the start of Thomas Pool's equestrian show first appeared in the *Pennsylvania Packet* on this date in 1785. Advertising the first performance of his self-named "Menage" for August 20, Pool hoped to attract a crowd with his remarkable antics.

Indeed, Pool enumerated several highlights of the show in his advertisement. These included standing on a saddle with the horse at full speed, and throwing an orange and catching it on the tines of a fork. In another striking trick, Pool mounted two horses at full speed, a foot in each stirrup. He then jumped a crossbar and landed back on the two horses. Pool continued in this way twice weekly, every Wednesday and Saturday. Universally appealing, Pool invited men, women, and children to his shows, making a point of asking the ladies to leave their dogs at home. To his diversity of equestrian tricks, Pool added a clown, presaging one of the most defining elements of the circus.

After performances for just a few weeks, a notice appeared in the newspapers indicating that Pool had "met with an unfortunate accident" and was unable to continue with the act. He hoped to return to the show, but never did. Almost a year later, Pool reappeared in Boston, where he was given permission to stage a similar performance. In Philadelphia, Pool was succeeded by the great John Bill Ricketts, whose equestrian show attracted the cream of Philadelphia society. In April 1793, President George Washington attended his first Ricketts show, returning there several years later to celebrate retirement following his presidency in 1797. In the years to come, high-wire acts, animals, and a diversity of clowns and jugglers would evolve into the circus we know today, complete with daring tricks and enticing displays of skill.

1860: John E. Heenan, the famed "Benecia Boy," gives a boxing exhibition in Camac's Woods near 9th Street and Columbia Avenue.

August 16

Violet Mary Klotz, born in Philadelphia on this date in 1910, was almost certainly never recognized by her given name. Nor is her stage name, Mae Clarke, known by most moviegoers today. However, it is almost certain that anyone who has a love for great 1930s films would know her work. The daughter of a theater organist who began her career in vaudeville, Mae Clarke's most famous work was completed in 1931 when, with the release of both *Frankenstein* and *The Public Enemy,* she was rocketed to brief stardom, which eventually gave way to small parts and general obscurity.

Performing in vaudeville and in nightclubs throughout Philadelphia and New York, Clarke began her career as a dancer. As a teenager she left Philadelphia for Hollywood, and was soon hired by Universal Pictures, which was incorporated in 1925 and was newly under the leadership of Carl Laemmle, Jr. Between 1929 and 1930, Clarke was featured in five films, none of them particularly successful. At the same time, Universal Pictures began to produce a series of monster movies, among them *Frankenstein* and *Dracula,* both completed in 1931. In *Frankenstein,* Clarke played the role of Henry Frankenstein's fiancée, who is attacked by the monster on her wedding day. That same year, Clarke was an uncredited bit player in the James Cagney vehicle *The Public Enemy.* In a scene now considered iconic, it is Clarke who has a grapefruit smashed into her face by an angry Cagney. A hugely popular movie, *The Public Enemy* played on a 24-hour rotation in New York City. It was said Clarke's ex-husband knew exactly at what time the scene occurred in the film and would frequently return to see it played.

For the next few years, Clarke was featured in five or six films a year, in many instances serving as leading lady. Married and divorced three times, she was also romantically linked with Humphrey Bogart and Howard Hughes. For reasons that remain unclear, by the mid-1930s, Clarke's popularity had waned and work dropped off dramatically. She continued to act, but found it more and more difficult to find work in film. Clarke found some work in television through the 1960s and 1970s, but made her last film in 1970, *Watermelon Man.* She died in California on April 29, 1992. Once headlined beside names like Boris Karloff, James Cagney, and Hedda Hopper, Clarke's work today is largely unknown, even as her contribution to American film history is substantial.

1942: Children's author Eileen Spinelli is born.

1966: The Beatles play at JFK Stadium.

1971: The first football game is played at Veterans Stadium, a pre-season game pitting the Eagles against Buffalo Bills.

2005: The Phillie Phanatic is inducted into the Mascot Hall of Fame.

August 17

Once described by a U.S. District Attorney as "the most dangerous woman in America," Mary Harris Jones, known to everyone as "Mother Jones," spent her life fighting for workers rights. Born in Ireland in 1837, she immigrated to North America to escape the potato famine. Settling in Chicago, she married and had four children, only to lose her family in the yellow fever epidemic of 1867. After suffering more personal loss with the destruction of her dressmaking business in the great Chicago Fire of 1871, she began traveling the country to organize mine workers and workers in other industries into unions, advocating for improvements in labor laws and working conditions. Her ability as an orator and her fearlessness made her a driving force in the union movement.

Working conditions in the late nineteenth and early twentieth centuries were severe. Mineral mining was particularly dangerous, but textile manufacturing was equally risky, with many factories in Philadelphia reflecting the industrywide dangers. Lack of adequate ventilation, low wages, poor safety conditions, and no government regulation in the textile mills led to a high rate of injury, illness, and death. Pennsylvania law forbade employment of youth under the age of twelve, but these laws were poorly enforced and children as young as ten worked long hours in the mills under appalling conditions.

In 1903, Mother Jones decided to bring the condition of these children to the attention of President Theodore Roosevelt and the American people. She organized a children's march from Philadelphia to Long Island, hoping to meet directly with the president. Starting from Independence Hall, and conducting meetings and rallies along the way, Mother Jones would point out the poor nutrition and health of the children, displaying the permanent, maiming injuries suffered by children working around textile machinery. When the group finally reached the home of President Roosevelt, Oyster Bay in Long Island, Mother Jones was refused entrance. Temporarily defeated, the group returned to Philadelphia, arriving back at Independence Hall on this date in 1903. Although the immediate goal of the march was not achieved, within three years Pennsylvania, New York, and New Jersey adopted laws restricting the employment of children under fourteen. Mother Jones lived a long life, continuing her work until her death in 1930 at the age of 94. She is buried in Union Miners Cemetery in Mount Olive, Illinois.

1787: Debate at the Constitutional Convention leads to the power of Congress to "declare war" rather than "make war," to give the executive branch the ability to respond to military attacks.

1876: At the Centennial Exhibition, an international convention for the amendment of English orthography meets, and the American spelling reform association for the simplification of English spelling is organized. Mark Twain is a founding member.

August 18

Recognized as a national hero in multiple countries, Polish-Lithuanian Thaddeus Kosciuszko represents for many the finest in military success while also standing for the universal ideals of liberty and independence. Combining both intellectual and moral strengths, Kosciuszko's life was devoted to the pursuit of justice for all people as exemplified in his service to both the American and Polish armies, as well as a deep commitment to abolitionism and independence of thought. On this date in 1798, he returned to Philadelphia for the last time, fresh from personal and military losses but still seeking opportunities to ensure equality and representation for both nationalities.

Born in 1746 into a long-established Belarusian family in what was then a part of the Grand Duchy of Lithuania and the Polish-Lithuanian Commonwealth, at a young age Kosciuszko determined to pursue military training while also seeking a general education. Between 1769 and 1775, he traveled to and from France but was unable to secure a military position. In 1776, he arrived in Philadelphia for the first time and soon was commissioned a colonel of Engineers for the Continental Army. In this capacity, he fortified protections around Philadelphia before moving to Fort Ticonderoga. Against his recommendations, fortifications were not completed there and the Americans were forced to flee. Kosciuszko continued to show strong leadership and in 1780 was transferred to the Southern Army.

At the end of the war in 1784, Kosciuszko returned to Poland, but not before selecting friend Thomas Jefferson as executor to his will, which specified a large quantity of estate funds be used for the manumission of slaves. After Kosciuszko's death, Jefferson stated that he was unable to honor his role as executor, and the U.S. Supreme Court eventually awarded the funds to Kosciuszko's descendants. In Poland, Kosciuszko once again engaged in a battle for independence, this time with the Poles against the Russian tsar. Militarily successful, he was nevertheless defeated by the king's own concessions. Kosciuszko returned again to France, where he received many accolades, but none overcame his desire for an independent Poland. Homeless for several years, he eventually settled in Switzerland, where he died in 1817.

1863: J. L. G. Ferris, noted painter of scenes from American history, is born.

1883: The Young Ladies Baseball Club plays its first game in front of 500 spectators, many of whom laugh much of the time to see women playing a sport traditionally reserved for men.

August 19

Philo T. Farnsworth, a significant participant in the refinement of television and broadcasting images, was born in Utah on this date in 1906. A natural in mechanical and electrical engineering, Farnsworth showed an aptitude early on of his later skill and success as an inventor and innovator. During his service in the United States Navy, he realized that inventions patented during his service would belong to the government and acquired an honorable discharge. After several years of working toward completing an electronic resolution to the transmission of television images, in 1927 Farnsworth unveiled his "image dissector camera tube" in his San Francisco laboratory. His first image, in a nod to his backers, was of a dollar sign. He continued to develop his electronic television system, featuring both transmission and reception of signals.

In 1931, Farnsworth turned down an offer from RCA to transfer his patents to their control and work for them. Within a few months he agreed to work for Philadelphia-based Philco, which manufactured radios. After less than a year, however, the relationship ended amicably. Farnsworth remained in Philadelphia and established Television Laboratories, with headquarters in Chestnut Hill in northwest Philadelphia. For the next few years, Farnsworth worked to improve his television system, taking opportunities to publicize his successes whenever he could. On August 24, 1934, he demonstrated his electronic system by broadcasting a tennis game at the Franklin Institute in front of an amazed public audience. A year later, improvements in the clarity of his television picture were featured at a press event. In 1938, Farnsworth left Philadelphia to return to the West Coast, where he announced the formation of a new company, Farnsworth Television.

As happened to many inventors before and after him, Farnsworth spent many of his professional years pursuing ownership of his ideas and patents. He variously battled RCA, AT&T, and Bell over patent rights, in many cases engaging in extended court cases. Finally, in 1939, he resolved his conflicts with industry-giant RCA, and his all-electronic television system was mass manufactured for the first time. Farnsworth continued to work in his basement laboratory in Indiana, generating designs for projects as varied as sweep-control radar, submarine detection, and nuclear fusion; in all, he acquired more than 300 patents in his lifetime. He died of pneumonia in 1971.

1905: At an auction, collectors pay high prices for pieces of the historic elm and white hawthorne trees, which had stood for years in front of the Lippincott mansion at Broad and Walnut streets. The elm was said to have dated from 1665.

1925: The epitaph penned by Benjamin Franklin as a young printer is found in the collection of William Mason, a Chicago businessman.

1961: To start its third century with all accounts settled, St. Peters Protestant Episcopal Church bills the British government for $769,555.20.

August 20

The Philadelphia Phillies were victorious in two World Series, in 1980 and 2008. In contrast to these victories, they also hold records for some of the most impressive losing streaks in professional sports. The Phillies have lost more than 10,000 games in their history, the worst record of losses in modern athletics. A fair number of these came in the years 1933-48, when the Phillies had 16 consecutive losing seasons, a Major League baseball record. On August 20, 1961, the Phillies beat Milwaukee 7–3 to end the longest losing streak in modern baseball history: 23 games. This sad record was only "surpassed" by the 1899 Cleveland Spiders, who managed to lose 24 in a row.

The most excruciating record loss occurred in the year 1964, remembered by all Phillies fans as "the Phlop." The team had been slowly improving in the early 1960s and for the 1964 season featured the eventual Rookie of the Year Richie Allen at third base, shortstop Bobby Wine, and future Hall of Fame pitcher Jim Bunning on the mound. The Phillies started the season well, and by the All-Star game they were in first place. Bunning had pitched a perfect game against the Mets in June, and the team kept winning into September. Phillies fans, always hopeful of victory and famous for their passionate loyalties (often tinged with brutal criticisms) got ready to buy their World Series tickets.

On September 20 the team returned from a road trip with a six-and-a-half game lead over the second-place Cincinnati Reds, with only twelve games remaining in the season. All they needed was to win another four or five games to claim the pennant. But when the Cincinnati Reds played the next game against the Phillies, the Reds won 1–0 by stealing home. Subsequent losses to Cincinnati, Milwaukee, and St. Louis sent the manager and the fans into a panic. The losing streak lasted ten games, and although the Phillies did win the final two games, it was too late to save the season. Through the ups and downs of the many seasons since, some observers still believe that Phillies fans have never really recovered from the trauma of "the Phlop," one of many painful losses in team history.

1971: After standing unused and empty for nearly a year, Shibe Park is severely damaged by fire. It was eventually demolished, in 1976.

August 21

Wilton Norman Chamberlain was born in Philadelphia on August 21, 1936. As "Wilt the Stilt," he was to become one of the greatest players in professional basketball history. At Overbrook High School, he led the team to near perfect records in three varsity seasons. Six feet eleven inches tall in high school, he dominated other players, and eventually grew to stand seven feet one inch tall. His height was matched by his agility and made him a force on offense that could not be denied.

Recruited by more than 200 colleges, Chamberlain attended the University of Kansas, scoring a school-record 52 points in his first varsity game. Leaving college a year early to go pro, he spent a year playing for the Harlem Globetrotters and was drafted by the Philadelphia Warriors. In his first pro season he was named Rookie of the Year, All-Star Game Most Valuable Player, and NBA Most Valuable Player. In the 1962-63 season, he became the only NBA player to score 4,000 points in a season. In one game against the New York Knicks, Chamberlain scored 100 points, a record that many believe will never be broken.

After moving with the Warriors to San Francisco, he joined the 76ers in 1965. In 1967, he matched up against his longtime rival, Bill Russell of the Celtics, in the division championship, and the team went on to win the NBA championship against the Warriors. Wilt's offensive dominance led to NBA rule changes, including widening the lanes and creating the rules for offensive goaltending. He achieved incredible stats in his career: 23,924 rebounds, 31,419 points, led the NBA in scoring for seven years in a row, and held the record at .727 for the highest field goal percentage. Traded to the Los Angeles Lakers in 1968, he helped his new team get to the NBA finals four times in five seasons, winning the championship in 1972. After retiring in 1973, he was devoted to volleyball, tennis, and even polo. Chamberlain died at his California home in 1999, leaving behind the memories of his Philadelphia fans and the respect of basketball fans worldwide.

1899: The Park Commission adopts a resolution to prohibit the admittance of automobiles in Fairmount Park.

August 22

Like so many early American inventors before him, John Fitch began his professional career as a clockmaker and silversmith, but through unique innovation and persistence, he became one of the most influential transportation pioneers in the country. Born in a small town in Connecticut in 1743, Fitch was apprenticed to a clockmaker, who provided his only education. During the American Revolution, Fitch produced guns for the New Jersey militia, even as his small Trenton, New Jersey, shop was being destroyed by British troops. After serving to support General Washington's troops in Valley Forge, Fitch found himself heading south for Kentucky, where he tried his hand at surveying. Following a brief imprisonment by the British, Fitch finally settled in Buck County, Pennsylvania, where his ideas for a steam-powered engine would bring him some fame but little fortune.

Using his persuasive powers, Fitch successfully lobbied Pennsylvania leaders to allow him a monopoly for steamboat traffic on several sections of the Delaware River and related waterways. This gave him ample opportunity to raise financial support for his real interests. Inspired by several British designs for steamboats, Fitch reworked the basic constructs and devised his own version in a Philadelphia workshop. Propelled by oars and driven by Fitch's own engine design, the first successful run of his forty-five-foot steamboat took place on the Delaware River on August 22, 1787. Within a few years, Fitch and partner Henry Voight had refined their designs to the point where, in 1791, they received a U.S. patent.

To Fitch's dismay, he did not receive a monopoly patent from the Patent Commission; as a result, many of Fitch's financial supporters withdrew their investments, weakening Fitch's position. Other inventors eventually utilized Fitch's innovations, adding their own to create new and successful advances. Most notably, Robert Fulton designed and successfully marketed a steamboat almost twenty years after Fitch received his own patent. Consumed with legal difficulties and facing a seemingly doomed effort to secure rights to his inventions, Fitch died by his own hand on July 2, 1798. His legacy, however, remains as certain as the eventuality of steamboat success in America.

1786: Charles Willson Peale collects a swordfish beak stuck in a ship in the harbor to add to his collection of "curiosities."

August 23

An intense and brilliant observer of the natural wonders of his adopted home, Scottish-born poet, illustrator, and "Father of Ornithology" Alexander Wilson succumbed to years of the rigors of pioneering travel when he died of dysentery on this date in 1813. Born in 1766 to an illiterate distiller, Wilson spent much of his life seeking both fame and reputation, first by way of the literary world and then as one of the country's greatest naturalists. By the age of fourteen, Wilson was apprenticed to his uncle, a local weaver. After five years, he left to become a traveling peddler, frequently recording his experiences and observations through verse. Inspired in part by his experiences as an apprentice and wanderer, he wrote poetry about the struggles of everyday life, including work, conflict, and relationships. Ultimately unsuccessful as a poet, Wilson eventually sought new opportunities, leaving Scotland at the age of twenty-eight in hopes of beginning a new chapter of his life in Philadelphia.

Wilson was initially hired as a schoolteacher near Philadelphia, but soon left to accept a position in New Jersey. After several years he moved back to Pennsylvania, to Grey's Ferry along the Schuylkill River. In nearby Kingsessing, he met the brilliant and famous naturalist William Bartram. Bartram, noted horticulturist and author, inspired Wilson to explore the joys of the natural world through drawings and illustrations. Desiring once again to shift his profession, Wilson built on his interest in birds specifically and began to travel the countryside locating, studying, and illustrating the birds of America. In his travels, he walked from Grey's Ferry to Niagara Falls, as well as various points beyond Pennsylvania.

After compiling a portfolio of two dozen illustrations, Wilson sought the opportunity to have them made into prints to be sold, but found it difficult to acquire the funding to move forward. Finally, after working as illustrator to *Rae's Encyclopedia,* Wilson succeeded in publishing the first of nine volumes of his *American Ornithology.* Untrained and lacking in published sources, Wilson based his detailed captions on his own observations, including information on appearance, song, and habitat. The volumes were both popular and highly respected and were a singularly unique addition to the best libraries in the country. Wilson died in Philadelphia while at home working on his ninth volume, which was ultimately completed by Wilson's friend, George Ord. He is buried at Old Swedes Church in Southwark. Twenty-six of the 268 species in the volumes were newly described by Wilson, a small measure of his immense contribution to the science of American ornithology, and his commitment to documenting the natural resources of his adopted country.

1832: The Girard Bank (later the Girard National Bank) opens in the old First Bank of the United States building on 3rd near Chestnut. The building was originally constructed in 1797.

August 24

Conflicts in Europe throughout the seventeenth and eighteenth centuries inevitably affected life in the colonies. English disputes with France and Spain, among others, often began as land disputes in the New World. In the American colonies, these threats often resulted in fears of invasion or attack from outside groups as well as from the indigenous inhabitants already in residence. Colonial governments looked to England for protection, and in all colonies except Pennsylvania, British troops were occasionally mustered to serve as protectors during times of crisis. Pennsylvania's unique history as a Quaker settlement meant that its peaceful, diplomatic government policies rejected the use of military force, and so British troops and Pennsylvania citizens were not permitted to form military units.

By the mid-1740s, the lack of protection seemed dire, especially as Philadelphia faced a particular threat from French privateers sailing up the Delaware River. Benjamin Franklin, in opposition to Quaker colonial leaders, urged the formation of a militia in a pamphlet titled *Plain Truth.* Finally, on December 7, 1747, the Philadelphia-based militia known as the Associators was formed. Intended to specifically protect the interests and safety of Philadelphia residents, the Associators were made up of local volunteers outfitted privately. Finally, on this date in 1748, the city learned of the Treaty of Aix-la-Chapelle, signed in France on October 18, 1748. By signing the treaty, England resolved a number of conflicts with France and Austria and relieved tensions, and threats to Philadelphia were reduced.

The Seven Years' War, also known as the French and Indian War, resumed concerns about defending Philadelphia in the 1750s, so the Associators continued to serve the colony until 1777, when the Continental Congress enacted a militia law designed to fulfill a similar mission. In the meantime, Associators formed the basis of the Marine Corps, founded in 1775, as well as serving with great distinction in Washington's Army. The Associators were remustered for the War of 1812, during which the foundation of the Pennsylvania National Guard was established with the creation of what would later become the First Brigade, First Division of the 111th Infantry and 103rd Engineers. Today, protection of the state of Pennsylvania is left to federal service personnel, who every day honor those who began their great legacy more than 270 years ago.

1759: *Beggar's Opera,* the first opera performed in Philadelphia, is staged at Southwark Theater.

1907: The *Ben Franklin,* the biggest balloon ever built in America up to that point, makes a successful flight from Philadelphia in front of thousands of spectators.

1934: A new television instrument, said to be capable of broadcasting not only close-ups but entire football and baseball games and tennis matches, as well as news shots, is demonstrated at the Franklin Institute.

August 25

William Penn received a charter for the lands we know as Pennsylvania from King Charles II, but Penn believed the land belonged to the indigenous inhabitants and purchased it from the tribes. In 1682, the Treaty of Friendship between Penn and the Lenni Lenape was established. At the treaty ceremony, Penn declared that "no advantage shall be taken on either side but shall be openness and love." Chief Tamanend of the Delaware nation replied that "we will live in love with William Penn and his children as long as the creeks and rivers run and while the sun, moon, and stars endure." Penn and the Lenape kept their promises. Unfortunately, Penn's children did not adhere to the spirit of the agreement.

After Penn's death, his sons John and Thomas accumulated significant debt and needed new sources of income. The population of the colony was increasing and settlers were moving into areas north and west of the city. Acting governor James Logan and Thomas Penn, using a previously incomplete treaty, convinced the Lenape to agree that all lands in the upper Delaware and Lehigh river valleys as far as a man could walk in a day and a half would belong to the white men. Since the Penn brothers owned the proprietorship, they would be able to sell the land to settlers. On August 25, 1737, the Walking Purchase agreement was signed; the next step was to measure the land.

The Lenape had traditionally used the "walking" measurement and thought they knew how much land they had agreed to surrender. But Penn had sent scouting parties ahead to determine the easiest route, cleared obstacles, and hired three of the fastest runners in the colony to run the "walk" at a fast pace. Only one of the three completed the race, but at the end the Lenape learned that the 1,200 square miles of land was more than three times what they had estimated, including some of their best traditional hunting grounds. By breaking the spirit of the Treaty of Friendship, the Penns repudiated the policy of fairness established by their father and their actions eventually led to warfare with the tribes. Ultimately, the Lenape were forced out of Pennsylvania, and the remnants of the tribes settled in Oklahoma more than a hundred years later.

1860: The People's Wigwam formally opened with a political rally for Abraham Lincoln.

John Adams was in Philadelphia in 1775 when his wife, Abigail, wrote him to "remember the ladies" in the work of forging a new nation and its laws. Adams treated her comments as humorous, replying that men would fight "despotism of the petticoat." He was right that achieving women's rights, including suffrage, would be a struggle, one that ultimately took almost a century and a half. Quaker Philadelphia had a tradition of equal participation of women in the church, and abolitionists like Philadelphia resident Lucretia Mott emerged from that tradition. Nevertheless, in 1840 she and other women were barred from full participation in the World Anti-Slavery Convention in London. In 1848, Mott and Elizabeth Cady Stanton would organize the first Women's Rights convention in Seneca Falls, New York, where a Declaration of Sentiments, calling for the right of women to vote, was adopted.

During the Civil War, most women suspended pro-suffrage activities, but when the Fourteenth Amendment freeing slaves excluded women, activist women objected and the national Woman Suffrage Association was formed. Carrie Burham of Philadelphia tried to vote, arguing that under the Pennsylvania Constitution of 1838 she had that right. Burham did not succeed. In 1876, women were largely excluded from the official proceedings of the Centennial, leading the Woman Suffrage Association to open a special Philadelphia center to make their presence known. Denied a right to speak at Centennial proceedings, Susan B. Anthony read a Declaration of Rights for women on the steps of Independence Hall on July 4, 1876.

Early in the twentieth century, American women began to adopt the tactics of British suffragists using public marches and demonstrations, arrests, and jailings. Alice Paul, a Swarthmore College and University of Pennsylvania graduate from New Jersey, formed the National Woman's Party, emphasizing efforts toward a federal constitutional amendment for suffrage. Local Philadelphians, including Carolyn Katzenstein, were also instrumental in these efforts. On this date in 1920, the Nineteenth Amendment to the Constitution was finally ratified, giving women the right to vote. Paul, Katzenstein, and others turned their attention to an Equal Rights Amendment and although feminists continued through the 1970s to labor on its behalf, it has never been ratified.

1940: Following eighteen months of investigation, nineteen State troopers and three city detectives in two raids expose what Colonel Lynn G. Adams, Commissioner of the State Motor Police, describes as a $15,000,000 lottery scam.

1975: A fire at Gulf Refinery in Philadelphia is officially declared out after nine days and the deaths of seven firemen.

August 27

The New York Armory Show of 1913 featured works of avant-garde artists and is considered a turning point in art history. Marcel Duchamp's *Nude Descending a Staircase* caused a sensation and influenced forever a young artist, Emmanuel Radnitzky, who was born in Philadelphia on this date in 1890. Soon after, his family moved to New York City where his father and mother worked in the garment industry. At an early age, Radnitzky decided to pursue art and by 1912 had adopted the name "Man Ray." Man Ray became friends with Marcell Duchamp and experimented with cubism, holding his first gallery exhibition in 1915.

In addition to his paintings, Ray experimented with art photography, focusing on manipulations of the technology to create his own unique form, which he called "rayographs." In 1921, he won an award in John Wanamaker's exhibition of photography. Soon after, Ray moved to Paris where he joined the community of artists and writers known as the Lost Generation, which included Jean Cocteau, Gertrude Stein, James Joyce, Salvador Dali, F. Scott Fitzgerald, Erik Satie, and others. Ray's photographs of the people in this community were featured on the covers of magazines as he worked as a graphic artist. In succeeding years, he and Duchamp were leaders of the Dada movement in New York, the philosophy of which was to reject the economic and social forces that they believed led to world war.

By the 1930s, Ray was an established fashion photographer and filmmaker, working in film with Pablo Picasso, among other artists. Influenced by surrealism, he became famous for his unusual photographs of nude women, many of whom were his lovers or wives. When World War II broke out, Ray left Paris and moved to California where his work in fashion photography continued. He also photographed a number of movie stars such as Ava Gardner. In 1951, Ray returned to Paris where he lived until his death in 1976. Dadaism and the work of artists like Ray influenced not only modern art and photography, through the use of found objects, shadow and light, and innovative composition, but are thought by some critics to have been the precursors of performance art.

1867: Philanthropist Rebecca Gratz dies.

August 28

In the "great migration" of African-Americans to the North during the Second World War, many who came to the Philadelphia area settled in North Philadelphia. During the nineteenth and early twentieth centuries, North Philadelphia was an important center of manufacturing. Huge factories and row houses built for workers were served by subway lines, and major freight lines passed through the North Broad Street Station. The lower part of the neighborhood featured the large, luxurious homes of industrialists, and the shopping areas along Columbia, Susquehanna, Dauphin, and Erie streets served a broad cross-section of North Philadelphia residents. Among African-Americans, North Philadelphia was the home of doctors, lawyers, businessmen, and factory workers alike.

The growth of suburbs in the 1950s and a rapid decline in manufacturing led to severe decline in the neighborhood. As whites moved out and employment opportunities dwindled, the neighborhood became more racially segregated and the population included a much larger proportion of the poor. By the 1960s, many parts of North Philadelphia suffered from poverty, drugs, and gang violence. On August 28, 1964, an incident and its effects accelerated the decline of the neighborhood. An African-American woman, Odessa Bradford, got into an argument with two Philadelphia police officers, one white and one black, over her inability to move a stalled car at the corner of 23rd Street and Columbia Avenue. The officers attempted to remove her from the car and a bystander intervened by attacking the officers, leading to the arrest of Bradford and the man. That night, rumors spread that a pregnant black woman had been killed by white police officers.

By midnight, as many as 300 people, mostly black young men, began breaking windows in mostly white-owned businesses, attacking police officers with rocks, stopping a city bus and beating passengers, and setting fires. Limited reinforcements from the police were brought in, but the police essentially withdrew. Civil rights leaders walked the streets urging people to disperse, but most of the business district along Columbia and Ridge avenues was destroyed. Rioting and looting continued the next day, and Mayor Tate ordered a quarantine of 125 square blocks of the neighborhood. Most businesses were never restored or reopened. In the succeeding decades, redevelopment has occurred in some areas, but North Philadelphia remains troubled, economically and socially in a lasting legacy of Philadelphia's twentieth-century decline.

1963: Martin Luther King, Jr., gives his "I Have A Dream" speech in Washington, D.C.; thousands of Philadelphians take a bus to the rally.

1995: The Wanamaker Store closes for the last time; though no longer run by family, the name had continued in use up to this point.

August 29

Colonial Philadelphia is known for its revolutionary patriots, but it was also home to supporters of the British Crown. Joseph Galloway was speaker of the Colonial Assembly from 1766 to 1775, and during that time was one of the most powerful politicians in Pennsylvania. He and Benjamin Franklin joined forces to propose a bill that would make it a crime for whites to murder Indians, a reaction to the increasing tensions along Pennsylvania's western frontier. Rising violence and a growing distrust of the native populations resulted in the defeat of the bill, and Galloway and Franklin both lost their next elections. Nevertheless, in recognition of his significant service to Pennsylvania, Galloway was elected by the Assembly to serve as a member of the First Continental Congress in 1774, but ultimately could not reconcile himself to a break with England.

Joining the British forces in New York, he returned to Philadelphia with General Howe's army when it occupied the city in 1777. Howe put Galloway in charge of the police, and of imports and exports. These duties were especially important since a key strategy of the occupation was to counteract revolutionary activity and prevent supplies from reaching Washington. Galloway was an effective and efficient administrator, improving trade and successfully limiting the goods that could reach Washington at Valley Forge. His preferred method of dealing with revolutionaries was to spy on them and disrupt their operations. Galloway was bitterly disappointed when the British abandoned Philadelphia in June 1778 and then refused to allow him to negotiate directly with Washington.

After the British withdrew, Galloway fled to London with his daughter, leaving his wife behind in an attempt to protect his property. She remained in Philadelphia until her death in 1792, writing in her diary of her attempts to protect her daughter's dowry rights, her fear of being hanged as a Tory traitor, and her distress at the lack of communication from her husband. Galloway was placed on a small pension by the British, and while he served as a voice for other exiles, he was never completely trusted by the British. In 1783, his property in Pennsylvania was seized, and in 1793 the Pennsylvania government rejected his petition to return to America. Galloway died in exile on this date in 1803, remaining forever a symbol of conflicted loyalties.

1780: Notice is published in a broadside that German Hessian deserters will be welcomed into Rochambeau's American command.

August 30

Philadelphia immediately preceding the Civil War was a community divided. Long a stronghold of abolitionist sentiment, merchants in the city were also involved in lucrative business pursuits with Southern states. These merchants counseled caution, and there were several pro-Southern newspapers in the city. But once the attack and defeat at Fort Sumter occurred, Philadelphians patriotically supported the union cause.

When Abraham Lincoln called for volunteers in April 1861, the Philadelphia area responded. Eventually more than fifty infantry and cavalry regiments were formed in the city. The Eighty-eighth Regiment was formed in August 1861 by two brothers, George P. McLean of Philadelphia and Joseph A. McLean of Berks County. The regiment was composed of men from both areas, with many of the troops coming from Philadelphia, Manayunk, and Conshohocken. The regiment trained without guns on land located where the Wissahickon Creek meets the Schuylkill, frequently accompanied by the Berks County marching band. The 831 men of the Eighty-eighth Regiment finally left for the Washington, D.C., area in October, joining thousands of other United States troops for points southward.

The first major battle for the Eighty-eighth was the second battle of Manassas. Confident of victory, the troops under General Tower engaged in heavy fighting on August 30, 1862. Joseph McLean was shot and mortally wounded. General Tower lost a leg to gunfire while Captain Belsterling was killed instantly, six days before the birth of his daughter in Philadelphia. The Eighty-eighth fought well, but could not succeed against the secessionist artillery and ground forces, and the battle became the greatest victory of the war for the South. Of the more than 14,000 Union troops killed, fifteen men from the Eighty-eighth lost their lives.

The Eighty-eighth went on to fight in many of the most significant battles of the war, including Antietam, Chancellorsville, Gettysburg, and the Siege of Petersburg. The Eighty-eighth was at Appomattox when Lee finally surrendered and were mustered out of the army in June 1865 having lost a total of 181 men. Two of the members of the Eighty-eighth earned Medals of Honor for their actions at Gettysburg while as a whole the Eighty-eighth were recognized for their service to Philadelphia and a tired but reunified nation.

1983: Philadelphia-born Guion Stewart "Guy" Bluford becomes the first African-American to go into space with his flight on Space Shuttle *Challenger.*

August 31

The late 1960s may have been the time of "peace and love," but it was also a time of conflict. Philadelphia experienced one of the first race riots of the era in 1964, when false rumors about a police killing sparked confrontations that led to three days of destruction in North Philadelphia in which more than 300 people were injured and 225 stores were damaged or destroyed. Relations between the African-American community and the Philadelphia police department were tense, with continued allegations and complaints about police brutality continuing through the end of the decade. The Black Panther Party, founded in California in 1966, had established a chapter in Philadelphia by 1968. Committed to the defense of the black community and evolving into a philosophy strongly influenced by Maoist Marxism, the Black Panthers were the dominant radical political group of the African-American community.

In August 1970, the Panthers announced plans for a national conference to be held at Temple University and declared war on police officers nationwide. Over the weekend of August 27, violent shooting acts against Philadelphia police resulted in the death of one officer and the wounding of several more. Police Chief Frank Rizzo ordered emergency measures, including 12-hour shifts for police, and announced that Mayor Tate had authorized the hiring of an additional 600 officers to bring the city's force to 7,500. On August 31, separate teams of 45-50 police officers conducted raids on the three Panther headquarters in West Philadelphia, on Columbia Avenue in North Philadelphia, and on Queen Lane in Germantown.

Gunfire was exchanged at two of the raids until tear gas drove the Panthers out. Fifteen people were taken into custody on charges of assault with intent to kill and weapons offenses. The police strip-searched the suspects, and the photograph of the Panthers leaning up against the wall under police guard was distributed by the Associated Press nationwide. Commissioner Rizzo announced that the raids had been based on information connecting the Panthers with the murder of a police officer earlier that weekend. More than 1,000 rounds of ammunition and 13 guns were confiscated in the raids, but no charges were subsequently brought against any of the Panther suspects in the police murder and shootings. The raid added to Commissioner Rizzo's reputation as a tough cop standing up against radicals. Rizzo later served two terms as Philadelphia mayor.

1949: Actor Richard Gere is born.

One of the worst epidemics in Philadelphia history, yellow fever raged through the city in the late summer and fall of 1793. A medical mystery attributed to a variety of causes, including malodorous piles of garbage, the presence of refugees from Santo Domingo (Haiti), and even bad water, yellow fever seemed an undefeatable foe. The earliest symptoms began in August of that year, with a rise in cases of fever, nausea, skin eruptions, severe vomiting, jaundice, and eventually certain death. Soon, citizens began to flee the city, seeking refuge in outlying areas; indeed, President George Washington and his Cabinet spent several months in Germantown, in order to avoid the disease. All tallied, by the end of the epidemic, more than 5,000 Philadelphians were dead.

In the midst of the epidemic, Mayor Matthew Clarkson desperately sought help. Many people feared any contact with the sick and dying, incorrectly believing that the disease was contagious (in fact, it was transmitted by mosquito bite). With bodies accumulating in the streets as citizens increasingly feared handling them enough to simply bury them, Clarkson knew the city was approaching the worst crisis of its history. Clarkson turned to the one community he believed was unaffected by the disease: African-Americans. His assumption was incorrect, but under the direction of community leaders Richard Allen and Absalom Jones, blacks in the city answered the call, provided unswerving service to the city.

After the epidemic passed, Clarkson and others betrayed the black community by accusing them of not adequately assisting the citizens. Allen and Jones quickly published a refutation of Clarkson's accusations. The excerpt that follows suggests the great hurt, and pride of accomplishment, felt by many of the blacks who had helped to alleviate the crisis:

In consequence of a partial representation of the conduct of the people who were employed to nurse the sick, in the late calamitous state of the city of Philadelphia, we are solicited, by a number of those who feel themselves injured thereby, and by the advice of several respectable citizens, to step forward and declare facts as they really were; seeing that from our situation, on account of the charge we took upon us, we had it more fully and generally in our power, to know and observe the conduct and behavior of those that were also employed.

Early in September, a solicitation appeared in the Public papers, to the people of color to come forward and assist the distressed, perishing, and neglected sick; with a kind of assurance, that people of our color were not liable to take the infection. Upon which we and a few others met and consulted how to act on so truly alarming and melancholy an occasion. After some conversations, we found a freedom to go forth, confiding in him who can preserve in the midst of a burning fiery furnace, sensible that it was our duty to do all the good we could to our suffering fellow mortals. We set out to see where we could be useful. The first we visited was a man in Emsley's alley, who was dying, and his wife lay dead at the time in the house, there were none to assist but two poor helpless children. We administered what relief we could, and applied to the overseers of the poor to have the woman buried. We visited upwards of twenty families that day—they were scenes of woe indeed! The Lord was pleased to strengthen, and remove all fear from us, and disposed our hearts to be as useful as possible.

In order the better to regulate our conduct, we called on the mayor next day, to consult with him how to proceed, so as to be most useful. The first object he recommended was a strict attention to the sick, and the procuring of nurses. This was attended to by Absalom Jones and William Gray; and, in order that the distressed might know where to apply, the mayor advertised the public that upon application to them they would be supplied. Soon after, the mortality increasing, the difficulty of getting a corpse taken away was such, that few were willing to do it, when offered great rewards. The black people were looked to. We then offered our services in the public papers, by advertising that we would remove the dead and procure nurses. Our services were the production of real sensibility;—we sought not fee nor reward, until the increase of the disorder rendered our labor so arduous that we were not adequate to the service we had assumed.

September

September 1 

One of Philadelphia's most famous artists of the eighteenth century spent much of his adult life abroad. Benjamin West was born in Springfield, outside Philadelphia, in 1738. Encouraged early in life by his parents, he began as a portrait artist, turning to historical and biblical paintings on the advice of a client. Dr. William Smith, the first provost of the University of Pennsylvania, was so impressed by West's painting of the death of Socrates that he invited West to study art, literature, and history in Philadelphia. In 1760, Smith arranged for West to study in Italy, where he learned the neoclassical and Romantic style of painting. With his wife and children, West settled in London and never returned to his native land, though he grew to be particularly revered in America.

In London, West taught art to other American painters who traveled to England to train with him, including Charles Willson Peale of Philadelphia. West also continued to paint his own larger-than-life works. His success led to his appointment by King George II to the Royal Academy of Arts in 1769. Two of West's historical works, *The Death of General Wolfe* and *William Penn's Treaty with the Indians*, led the king to designate him as the royal historical painter and have since become icons of early historical painting. A skilled portraitist, West also painted portraits of the British royal family.

On September 1, 1800, the president of Pennsylvania Hospital in Philadelphia wrote to West requesting that he contribute a "suitable" historical painting to the hospital. West completed *Christ Healing the Sick in the Temple* in 1811, and it made such an impression in England that West was persuaded to sell the painting to the new British National Gallery as its first acquisition. West kept his promise to the hospital by painting a second version of the painting, this time including visual references to the treatment of the mentally ill, an area of medicine particularly associated with Pennsylvania Hospital. The painting arrived in Philadelphia in 1817, accompanied by a letter in which West dedicated its donation to his late wife, who was a Philadelphia native. More than 30,000 people viewed the painting during the first year it was displayed and it still hangs at the hospital today.

1752: The first Whitechapel Bell (later known as the Liberty Bell) arrives in Philadelphia.

1781: George Washington and the French commander Rochambeau arrive in Philadelphia following their victory at Yorktown and the surrender of the British.

1884: The International Electrical Exhibition, the first international electrical exhibition in the world, opens in Philadelphia under the auspices of the Franklin Institute.

September 2

Patrick Lyon was a Philadelphia blacksmith who specialized in creating locks. A successful and respected craftsman of the city, Lyon was engaged by the Bank of Pennsylvania to put new locks on the bank's vault in Carpenter's Hall. In 1798, when Lyon did the work for the bank, a yellow fever epidemic was spreading in the city. Lyon's young apprentice became ill and Lyon took him to Delaware early in September in an effort to save his life. Shortly after the apprentice died, Lyon learned from a friend that on September 2, 1798, bank officials discovered that the enormous sum of $162,821.61 (an estimated equivalent of $3 million today) was stolen. He also learned that he was a primary suspect and returned to Philadelphia to clear his name.

Despite his unassailable alibi, bank officials accused him of being an accomplice and had him imprisoned for three months in the Walnut Street Gaol, as well as imposing an impossibly large bail. Soon after his imprisonment, the actual thieves, a bank porter and a carpenter who had used the porter's keys to get into the vault, were identified. The porter died of yellow fever and the carpenter foolishly deposited some of the proceeds of the theft back into the Bank of Pennsylvania and other city banks. Almost all of the funds were recovered from the carpenter, who confessed and swore that he and the porter had been the only ones responsible. But Patrick Lyon remained in jail, losing his livelihood and his good name and risking his life as the yellow fever epidemic continued.

After he was finally released, Lyon sued bank officials, arguing that they had acted out of malice in keeping him imprisoned without probable cause and harming his reputation and business. The jury ruled in favor of Lyon and awarded him $12,000 in damages. One of the judges in the case gave the opinion that the bank officials had suspected Lyon for his ingenuity, which doctrine if admitted in a court of law would encourage stupidity and punish genius. Before an appeal could be heard, the parties settled out of court for an award to Lyon of $9,000. Accused of masterminding the largest robbery in American history up to that time, Lyon ultimately regained his position in society and went on to build fire engines, acquiring considerable wealth by way of hard work rather than theft.

1964: The Beatles make their first Philadelphia appearance at the Philadelphia Convention Center.

September 3

A unique form of popular entertainment, the "dime museum," made its formal debut in Philadelphia on this date in 1883 when Hagen and Campbell opened their establishment at 9th and Arch streets. Formerly the American Museum and the Colonel Woods Museum, the building was perfectly suited for the wide variety of entertainments available at Hagen and Campbell's. Known for their exhibitions of natural wonders, short theatrical productions, and tantalizing views of human oddities, dime museums offered cheap entertainment for the masses, reaching out to the thousands of immigrants, factory workers, and women newly employed and ready to spend both leisure time and money on seeking pleasure.

From the late 1700s, Philadelphia had been home to museums and "curiosity closets," collections of natural and man-made wonders privately owned but open to the paying public. Intended to serve as educational, these early museums were orderly explorations of the newly discovered world. One of the earliest, Charles Willson Peale's collection of natural diorama displays and portraits of famous Americans, drew hundreds of visitors each year. Museum owners and promoters based in New York, among them Colonel Woods and P. T. Barnum (in his pre-circus days), set up shop in Philadelphia as well. By the second half of the nineteenth century, however, the growing trend in museums was toward entertainment and away from education, and the new demand for entertainment among women and families newly enjoying leisure time led to the establishment of the dime museum.

Theatrical in nearly all ways and often quite disorderly, dime museums featured exotic oddities, stage productions, and traveling circus acts like sword swallowing and high-wire feats. Following in the footsteps of Barnum, the great promoter, Hagen and Campbell also displayed curiosities of nature such as unusual animal specimens or human freaks. With the advent of minstrelsy and vaudeville at the turn of the century, the broad attractions of the dime museum would give way to a focus on stage acts. In 1911, Frank Dumont purchased Hagen and Campbell's Dime Museum and set up shop with minstrels in blackface and vaudeville comedy. Today, many aspects of the old dime museum concept can be seen in small traveling circuses, on television, and even on the Internet, as people continue to find ways to entertain while sharing the oddities of the world with interested and enchanted viewers.

1783: The Treaty of Paris officially ends the American Revolutionary War.

September 4

Among members of Philadelphia's African-American community striving for equal rights after the Civil War, baseball was viewed as a means to encourage acceptance. As early as 1866, two black teams were organized: the Excelsior, and a club affiliated with the Quaker-founded Institute for Colored Youth, the Pythians. Octavius Catto, activist and educator, served as the shortstop and captain of the team and sought admission of the team to the Pennsylvania Association of Amateur Base Ball Players in 1867. The team withdrew its application after it became clear that it would not be admitted, and later that year, the association voted formally against admitting any clubs that included black members.

Despite difficulty in gaining access to playing fields in the city, the team played to enthusiastic crowds including members of the Republican Party and social activists. Pre-game and post-game social events, dances, and banquets were organized, giving the community opportunities to meet and discuss issues larger than baseball. The team also traveled to other cities to play, including Washington, D.C, where Frederick Douglass attended a game. As part of the team's social and political agenda, it sought to play against white teams. On September 4, 1869, a large crowd witnessed the first recorded contest between a black team and a white team. The Pythians, in their blue-and-white uniforms, played against the city's oldest ball club, the Olympics. Colonel Thomas Fitzgerald, later founder of the Philadelphia Athletics and the publisher of the *Item* newspaper, served as umpire. Although the Pythians lost to the Olympics 44–23, it was an important moment in Philadelphia and national sports history.

A few weeks later, the Pythians defeated a white team sponsored by Fitzgerald and also played a game against the white Masonic Club of Manyunk. Over the next two years, following the passage of the Fifteenth Amendment in 1870, members of the team were engaged in organizing black voters. In 1871, the team played and won its last game against a strong black team from Chicago. Octavius Catto continued his social and political activism, but on Election Day 1871, he was assassinated at the age of thirty-two near his house at Eighth and South streets. City offices closed for his funeral, and thousands of Philadelphians, both black and white, lined the streets to pay their respects. A small part of his legacy, however, lived on in the decades to follow as African-Americans sought and succeeded in playing a part in America's favorite pastime.

1999: The Cincinnati Reds set a National League record of nine home runs in a single game against the Phillies at Veterans Stadium.

September 5

The American colonies were unhappy. As early as the late 1760s, taxes imposed by the British Parliament rankled and irritated Americans, many of whom felt that taxation without their full representation in Parliament was a violation of their rights as British citizens. Indeed, dissatisfaction with the tax laws resulted in a boycott against British goods. The resulting effort to break the boycott by the British Crown led to the most famous raid in American history, known today as the Boston Tea Party. Angered by the Americans' direct attack on British trade, Parliament enacted a series of orders and stipulations. Known collectively as the Intolerable Acts, these steps eventually led to the organization of the unified effort among the American colonies to express their grievances and consider their collaborative response. The First Continental Congress, attended by representatives of twelve of the thirteen colonies, met for the first time in Carpenters' Hall in Philadelphia on this date in 1775.

It was clear that in passing the Intolerable Acts, many of which were targeted specifically at Massachusetts, the British Parliament intended to force the other colonies to abandon the more radical colony. To the contrary, the extreme circumstances established by the Acts, including forced quartering of British troops in American homes, high taxes on goods, and the complete shutdown of the Boston Port, led to a growing sense of unity among the colonies. In the Congress, representatives called for discussions on a variety of options, ranging from a continuation of the boycott to expressing their grievances to outright dissolution of the relationship with Britain. Patrick Henry, John and Samuel Adams, and George Washington were among the men sent by their respective legislatures to navigate differences of opinion and gauge the nature of the unified American response.

Ultimately, the more cautious desire to reconcile with Britain was overruled by the emotional resolutions proposed by communities near Boston. The Congress chose to continue the boycott, which proved an effective measure, forcing a 97 percent drop in British imports over the previous year. The Congress also asserted that if the King and Parliament continued their aggressive actions against the colonies, a second congress would be called in Philadelphia the following year. It was that group of men, many of whom had served in the First Congress, who went on to declare independence from Great Britain, bringing to fruition the efforts begun just a year before.

1937: The first printed copy of the Federal Constitution is found in the archives of the Historical Society of Pennsylvania.

September 6

Shortly after the December 1941 attack on Pearl Harbor, Commissioner of Baseball Kenesaw M. Landis wrote to President Roosevelt, asking advice about whether professional baseball should continue while the country was at war. In his January 15, 1942, "green light" reply, Roosevelt concluded that eligible Major League players should go into the service, but that "I honestly feel it would be best for the country to keep baseball going." Ultimately, more than 400 Major League players, including stars like Joe DiMaggio, Hank Greenberg, and Bob Feller, would serve in World War II. Travel restrictions led to staying home for spring training and equipment was hard to come by, but Major League baseball continued throughout the war, relying largely on retired players and new young recruits. One of these was sixteen-year-old Carl Scheib from the small Pennsylvania town of Gratz, who became the youngest pitcher in American League history when he played his first game for the Philadelphia Athletics on September 6, 1943.

The Athletics had an especially difficult time recruiting wartime replacement players. Unlike other Major League teams, the Athletics did not operate a farm team system. The team's legendary owner and manager, Connie Mack, preferred to rely on personal contacts among old ballplayers, high school and college coaches, and others. Mack first heard about Carl Scheib from a traveling salesman who had come through Gratz and got a recommendation about Scheib from a local grocer. Over 6 feet tall and weighing 190 pounds, Scheib had pitched at age 15 for an American Legion team. He first tried out with Mack late in the season in 1942, but Mack advised him to go back to school and return the following year, which he did to some success.

Scheib played for the Athletics until he turned eighteen and was drafted into the Army. Because the armed services thought baseball was good for the morale of the troops, many professional players were assigned to play ball in the service. In January 1946, Scheib shipped out and played an important part in winning the "G.I. World Series" of occupied Germany for his 60th Infantry Regiment. Scheib returned to the Athletics for the 1947 season and enjoyed a career in baseball until his retirement in 1957. His lifetime record was 45-65, and he was known as a very good batter for a pitcher, hitting .298 in 1948. Interviewed in 2006, he said, "The main thing I regret was not being able to meet and thank the salesman who wrote the letter [to Connie Mack] and gave me my chance."

1846: The cornerstone of the Cathedral of Saints Peter and Paul is laid. The structure is not completed until 1864.

September 7

In the post–World War II years, the city of Philadelphia seemed to offer personal and professional success to anyone who sought them. New affordable housing developments grew in the far northeastern and southwestern areas of the city, while new jobs in health services, education, and industry provided the potential for long-term job stability. A keen observer of the urban landscape and its residents, Leon Sullivan arrived in Philadelphia in 1950 to serve as pastor to the Zion Baptist Church. Contrary to expectations, Sullivan found that many of his congregants were jobless, even as thousands of jobs went unfilled. He believed discrimination contributed to this inequity, and committed much of his life to righting what he believed was a terrible wrong.

Born in Charleston, West Virginia, in 1922, Sullivan experienced prejudice firsthand as a young man when he was denied service in a local drugstore. As an adult in Philadelphia, he believed racism existed in a more subtle way—discrimination in education and jobs. Believing that jobs were the key to improving the lives of African-Americans, Sullivan organized a boycott of city businesses that were unwilling to agree to hire blacks. With the support of other ministers, Sullivan's "Selective Patronage" boycott worked in part because 20 percent of the city population was African-American. Sullivan later estimated that more than four thousand jobs were created as a direct result of their efforts.

Hoping to further advance training opportunities for the African-American community, Sullivan founded the Opportunities Industrialization Center in Philadelphia in 1964. With funding provided in part by the Ford Foundation, the OIC provided job and life skill training while also working to match graduates with prospective employers. On this date in 1966, Sullivan announced the expansion of the OIC to eight additional cities to train more than six thousand more people. Sullivan went on to serve as Pastor to Zion Baptist Church until 1988, growing the congregation from a few hundred to six thousand. In the 1970s, he developed the *Sullivan Principles,* an ethical code of conduct for businesses operating in South Africa. Later in life he expanded his activism to include the fight against apartheid, and respect for human rights on a global scale. He died on April 21, 2001, but his legacy continues today through the work of the Sullivan Foundation, which works to establish opportunities in Africa and the Unites States for learning and success for all peoples.

1784: Publisher Mathew Carey sets sail for Philadelphia from Dublin.

1889: The new steel cruiser *Philadelphia* is launched at Cramp's shipyards at 11:42 A.M.

September 8

A long and bitter teacher's strike that began on this date in 1981 consumed city politics and denied nearly a quarter of a million schoolchildren and 18,000 teachers access to their classrooms. Driven by a $223 million deficit, the Philadelphia Board of Education had cut 3,500 teaching jobs and canceled a scheduled 10 percent increase in teachers' pay the previous May. Simmering beneath the surface through the summer, tensions and anger among the Philadelphia Federation of Teachers rose to the forefront as schools prepared to open for the new school year. Believing the city and school board to have purposely broken a contract established just one year earlier, the teachers' union resolved to strike in hopes of forcing thc mayor and city council to meet its demands and honor the contract. By the fiftieth day, however, fist fights in council, accusations of aggressive picketing, and a slew of court orders marked one of the longest and most contentious strikes in city school history.

As the first day of school loomed, the stage was set for the battle between the teachers and the city. A court decision declaring the school board to have acted within its rights inflamed teachers and impeded talks for resolution. Mayor Green proposed a 10 percent increase in real estate taxes to help cover part of the deficit and reduce the impact on the school board budget, but also required concessions from the union. Further complicating the situation was vocal opposition to Mayor Green's taxation plan within City Council. Following an emotional Special Session, two Councilmen came to blows, including future mayor John F. Street, over the extent to which funds budgeted elsewhere should be redirected to the educational needs of the city.

Picketing continued in front of most schools and the District headquarters for several weeks, as negotiations broke down and other local unions were recruited to help the teachers. With little movement in resolving the differences, and with the court ruling that the city was acting within its rights, there seemed little hope of a quick or easy end to the strike. Indeed, on October 27, the Philadelphia Council of the AFL-CIO announced a mass strike for the next day, in hopes of showing solidarity and forcing the hand of Mayor Green. Before that could occur, however, the three-member Commonwealth Court ordered teachers to return under their original contract. Relieved and partly validated in their position, the teachers' union voted to end the strike after fifty days, permitting teachers and students to return to school on October 29, 1981.

1819: Vauxhall Garden, a public theater and garden at Broad and Walnut streets, is destroyed by a mob following the cancellation of a special balloon ascent.

1862: Independence Square is first used as recruiting camp.

1947: The Better Philadelphia Exhibition opens.

September 9

Philadelphia loves its sports heroes, perhaps none more than Richie Ashburn, who had a forty-seven-year relationship with the Phillies and the city. Ashburn, also known as "Whitey" for his blond hair, was a center fielder with the Phillies from 1948 to 1959. At the end of his active career, he played for the Cubs and the Mets. Never a slugger, Ashburn had a .306 lifetime average built primarily on singles. He could hit to any part of the field and held the record for the most hits (1,875) in the decade of the 1950s. Winning the National League batting title twice, he was also known as a superb fielder. In 1950, he threw a runner out at the plate to preserve a tie and help the team win the pennant.

In 1963, Ashburn began a second career as a radio and television baseball commentator with the Phillies. First working with Phillies announcers Bill Campbell and Byrum Saam, he worked for twenty years with Harry Kalas and the two enjoyed respect and ratings in the Philadelphia market. Ashburn was known for his dry humor and wit, once commenting about a young player that "the kid doesn't chew tobacco, smoke, drink, curse, or chase broads. I don't see how he can possibly make it." Traveling to away games, he characterized Houston as "the only town where women wear insect repellent instead of perfume." In 1962 at the birthday party of "Marvelous" Marv Throneberry (sometimes called the worst fielder in baseball history), he told him, "We were going to give you a cake, but we thought you'd drop it."

In 1995, Ashburn was elected to the Baseball Hall of Fame, joining Mike Schmidt in that year's class. More than 25,000 Philadelphia fans traveled to Cooperstown for the ceremony. Philadelphia baseball honors him through the "Ashburn's Alley" section of Citizen's Bank Park, and the Richie "Whitey" Ashburn broadcast booth. The Richie Ashburn Foundation provides a free baseball camp to more than 1,000 needy children in the Delaware Valley each summer. Fans were shocked when Ashburn died suddenly on September 9, 1997, in New York after a Phillies-Mets broadcast. In 2004, he was posthumously elected to the Philadelphia Sports Hall of Fame and is remembered as one of the city's greatest sports treasures.

1776: The Second Continental Congress makes the term "United States" official, replacing "United Colonies."

1823: Joseph Leidy, the Father of American Vertebrate Paleontology, is born.

1843: Nancy Johnson receives a patent for an ice-cream freezer.

September 10

Considered by some to be the first American cult leader, Father Divine was a controversial figure in the first half of the twentieth century. Although he was never forthcoming about his origins, he was thought to have been born to freed slaves in Maryland in 1879. By 1919 when he moved to Sayreville, New York, with some of his followers, he had established a faith movement based on his divinity and a commitment to desegregation, positive thinking, economic self-sufficiency, celibacy, and racial justice. He established an interracial Peace Mission which spread across the country and attracted both black and white followers. Known variously as "the Messenger" and "the Reverend Major Jealous Divine," he promoted a utopian vision.

During the Great Depression, his missions in Harlem and across the nation grew, and he established numerous successful businesses, which provided needed goods and services such as gas stations, hotels, and restaurants. By the mid-1930s, it is estimated that the Peace Mission had more than $1.5 million in assets. During that time, his followers also mounted an anti-lynching campaign and promoted desegregation, frequently buying houses in white neighborhoods. In 1943, his first wife died and soon after he and his second wife moved to Philadelphia so that "the inhabitants of this City might be contagionized with the spirit of honesty, competence, and truth such as I have established among you."

In Philadelphia, the Peace Mission owned and operated three hotels, among them the "Divine Lorraine" in North Philadelphia. The 10-story Lorraine was one of the first high-rise buildings in the city and had served as luxury apartments in the late nineteenth century. Men and women occupied separate floors at the Lorraine and guests had to follow the rules against smoking, drinking, profanity, and "undue mixing of the sexes." The Lorraine became the first major desegregated hotel in Philadelphia. Father Divine and his wife lived in an estate outside the city called Woodmont. Father Divine largely withdrew from public activities and died at Woodmont on September 10, 1965. Although the Peace Mission has many fewer followers than in the past, his widow continues to lead the movement.

1798: Benjamin Franklin Bache dies of yellow fever.

Stephen Girard emigrated from France in 1776 to Philadelphia, where he made a fortune in international shipping and banking. At the time of his death in 1831, he was the richest man in America. Long active in philanthropic activities, the childless Girard left most of his fortune to the City of Philadelphia, specifying that it was to be used for building and operating a free, residential school for white, male orphans. Girard College opened in 1848 on a 43-acre campus in the Fairmount neighborhood, and it has since educated more than 20,000 students in grades 1-12. In the 1950s, city officials, including Mayor Joseph Clark, tried to persuade the other Girard College trustees to admit African-Americans, but the majority of the trustees believed that the will of Stephen Girard superseded *Brown v. Board of Education* and the Fourteenth Amendment to the Constitution. The trustees refused to integrate the school.

Beginning in 1965, local residents, church groups, NAACP president Cecil B. Moore, and Marie Hicks, a widowed African-American mother who sought admission for her sons, organized neighborhood protests. The tall stone walls and the gates of Girard College were the scene of large demonstrations, some of which ended in arrests. Mrs. Hicks marched at the wall every day for a year, and Martin Luther King, Jr., spoke at a demonstration in 1965. Mrs. Hicks was one of the plaintiffs in a suit finally resolved by the United States Supreme Court in May 1968 when it ruled that the terms of the will could not be sustained in light of the decision in *Brown v. Board of Education.*

On September 11, 1968, four African-American boys, including Theodore Hicks, were admitted to Girard College. His older brother Charles was admitted four months later and became the first African-American graduate of Girard. Theodore became the first African-American valedictorian. In the 1980s the Girard trustees voted to admit girls. The school enrollment of 600 students is now about equally divided between girls and boys, and is about 85 percent African-American, a demographic shift due in part to larger changes in the city population.

1777: The Continental Congress flees to Lancaster as the British army under the command of General William Howe approaches Philadelphia.

1964: Philadelphia begins its first public school busing program designed to transfer 1,480 black students to predominantly white schools.

1970: Philadelphia is formally announced by President Richard Nixon as the center of the Bicentennial celebration of 1976.

September 12

Great literature is often born of the imagination; but so, too, is great pulp fiction. Born in Germantown on this date in 1897, Walter Brown Gibson, who wrote under the pen name of Maxwell Grant, may very well be Philadelphia's claim to fame in the world of popular adventure fiction. For more than twenty years, Gibson crafted novel-length stories featuring wealthy playboy and vigilante Lamont Cranston, who as the Shadow fights crimes with his psychic powers. Gibson, an astoundingly prolific writer, is believed to have written more than three hundred stories for the Shadow in addition to countless newspaper articles, books on magic, and juvenile fiction.

After attending Colgate College, Gibson returned to Philadelphia seeking work as a newspaperman. In addition to short articles, Gibson became a skilled crossword and puzzle writer. In the late 1920s, the character of Lamont Cranston was featured as a mysterious radio narrator for Street & Smith Publishers radio show, *Detective Story Hour.* The character was so popular the publishers approached Gibson and asked him to create an adventure series for publication. Gibson assumed his pen name and the first issue of *The Shadow Magazine* was released on April 30, 1931. Within six months, Gibson's character had his own radio show, and the onetime quarterly magazine was increased to twice monthly. Gibson continued to write for *The Shadow,* providing storylines for comic books, strip cartoons, and games.

Gibson cultivated a variety of interests in his lifetime in addition to puzzles and pulp fiction. An avid magician, he was influential in the founding of Philadelphia's chapter of the Society of American Magicians, and served as a ghost writer for prestidigitation superstars like Harry Houdini, Harry Blackstone, and Joseph Dunninger. Among some of his own, unique contributions to magic are the introduction of the "Chinese Linking Rings" trick, as well as the "Nickels to Dimes" trick that is a staple in magic stores even today. Gibson's interest in psychic phenomena, séances, divination, and fortune-telling led him to a writing partnership with his wife, Litzka R. Gibson, a writer herself. Gibson died at the age of eighty-eight on December 6, 1985, in Kingston, New York.

1848: The Sharps Rifle is patented by the Sharps Rifle Manufacturing Company of Philadelphia.

1958: Filmed primarily in Downingtown and Phoenixville, the B-movie sci-fi thriller *The Blob,* starring a youthful Steve McQueen, opens nationwide.

September 13

In 1935, Lit Brothers and Strawbridge and Clothier merged their two radio stations into a single broadcast. Eleven years later, in 1946, the station was sold to Triangle Publications, leading to the establishment of WFIL television. Triangle was owned by Walter Annenberg, who also owned the *Philadelphia Inquirer* and *Daily News* newspapers. The first studio building in the nation devoted solely to television was built by Triangle at 46th and Market streets, and on September 13, 1947, WFIL-TV began telecasting. Its early broadcasts featured a daily newsreel program, the first in the United States, and it was the first affiliate station of the American Broadcasting Company network. In 1963, the station moved to City Line and Monument avenues.

The station's most famous locally produced show was *American Bandstand*. Begun in 1952 with host Bob Horn, the show was first telecast locally. In 1956, Dick Clark became the host, with local programming over seven hours a week. Network broadcast of some of the hours of *American Bandstand* began in 1957 and continued until 1963. In 1966, the station began locally televising the annual Philadelphia Thanksgiving parade, which is the oldest such parade in the nation. The station continues to broadcast the majority of local parades, among them the Pulaski Day, Puerto Rican Day, and July 4th celebrations. From the beginning, the station often chose its own local programming over network fare. In 1975, the station ran the *Captain Noah and His Magical Ark* children's program in the morning instead of ABC's new show, *Good Morning America*.

In 1971, the Federal Communications Commission forced the sale of the station after Governor Milton Shapp complained that the Annenberg-owned stations across the commonwealth had waged a smear campaign against him. New owners Capitol Communications subsequently changed the call letters to WPVI-TV. The early 1970s also saw the development of the innovative "Action News" format, which presented much shorter and snappier news reports than those of other stations. The "Action News" theme song, "Move Closer to Your World," by Al Ham, has been used unchanged and continuously since 1972 and sparked a grassroots protest during an attempt to modernize the arrangement in 1997. In 1996, the station was acquired by the Walt Disney Company. Action News today retains its number-one share of the Philadelphia television news market and is an evening ritual in hundreds of thousands of Philadelphia homes each night.

1803: John Barry, "Father of the American Navy," dies in Philadelphia.

1907: Frank Shuman incorporates the Sun Power Company in Camden, New Jersey. He invented and operated his first solar engine in Tacony.

1977: Orchestra conductor Leopold Stokowski dies in England.

September 14

Tensions in the city mirrored those across the country as the United States joined the war effort in April of 1917. Philadelphia's special place in the history of Americans of German descent and as home to thousands of German immigrants gave way to what may have been an exaggerated concern over the loyalties of those citizens, and the general fear that spies and operatives lived among them. Early neutrality soon gave way to acts of vandalism against German-owned stores, historical monuments, and individuals. On September 14, another step in the treason and conspiracy trial of five editors of a German-language newspaper took place with the setting of a $10,000 bond. By the end of the trial, all five editors would be found guilty and a part of the proud German history of the city deeply changed.

On the evening of September 10, the offices of *Tageblatt,* one of several German-language newspapers still published in the country, were raided by federal agents. Herman Lemke, business manager, and Dr. Martin Darkow, managing editor, were promptly arrested. Three other editors later surrendered. Each was initially charged with conspiring to violate the Espionage Act, and intentionally undermining the American position in the war through pro-German propaganda. The agents claimed to have found a money trail through Mexico alleged to be a German source, while unopened American government news releases and dispatches were seen to indicate a decidedly anti-American bent. The men were soon indicted and awaited trial.

In March 1918, the five editors were put on trial for treason, a more serious charge, in addition to the previous accusations of an anti-American policy. Within days, however, the men were acquitted of treason. Nevertheless, each resigned from the newspaper while the owner, C. J. Henning, vowed to ensure a significantly pro-American viewpoint from that day on. Finally, on September 28, 1918, all five editors were found guilty under the Espionage Act and sentenced for between two and five years in prison. Though the end of the war brought a lessening of public suspicion toward German-Americans, the next few decades proved even more challenging as international politics influenced the daily lives of thousands of German-American Philadelphians and their neighbors, customers, and friends.

1908: Thousands of unemployed Philadelphians clamor for work on demolishing the old Wanamaker building at Thirteenth and Chestnut streets. Mr. Wanamaker requests that contractors give preference to Philadelphia workers whenever possible.

1953: Crown Prince Akihito of Japan tours historic sites during a visit to the city.

1957: The Cruiser Olympia Association wins a three-year battle to save from the scrap heap *Olympia,* the flagship of Admiral Dewey at the Battle of Manila Bay. As of June 2010, the ship is once again at risk for being lost, despite its status as the only surviving naval vessel of the Spanish-American War.

September 15

In the early decades of the nineteenth century, the role of free African-Americans in the life of the country was an issue that engaged whites and blacks alike. Concerned that free men of color could never achieve equality in the United States, a young free black man named Hezekiel Grice of Baltimore wrote to a number of prominent black leaders proposing a convention where mass emigration to Canada would be discussed. On September 15, 1830, a ten-day National Negro Convention began in Philadelphia at Mother Bethel African Methodist Episcopal Church. Forty black men from nine states attended, including Mother Bethel Bishop Richard Allen.

Opposition to the African colonization effort was a primary impetus for the call for a National Negro Convention. The American Colonization Society was formed in 1816 to implement a plan to establish a colony for free blacks in Africa. Dominated by slaveholders, the Colonization Society also included some African-Americans and abolitionists. Ultimately, that group sent 13,000 blacks to establish Liberia in 1821. In contrast, the result of the National Negro Convention was a new association, the American Society of Free People of Colour, dedicated to improving the condition of blacks in North America, by purchasing land and by encouraging free blacks to emigrate to a new settlement in Canada. Members of the American Society of Free People of Colour argued that civic freedoms were already available in Canada. Further, its customs, language, climate, and soil were similar to those in America, and land could be purchased cheaply.

Richard Allen was elected president of the society, calling on free men "to aid each other by all honorable means, and to plant and support one in that country." Allen also appealed to "our colored brethren, and to all philanthropists here and elsewhere, to assist in this benevolent and important work." Conventions similar to the first national meeting in Philadelphia in 1830 were held through the 1840s in New York and other states, but the movement eventually faded. Although many African-Americans immigrated to Canada, particularly after the Fugitive Slave Act was enacted in 1857, a specific colony in Canada was never established.

1792: President George Washington issues a proclamation denouncing opposition to the whiskey excise tax.

1794: Forty-three-year-old James Madison marries Dolley Payne Todd and resides in Philadelphia for the next three years.

September 16

America's entry into World War II began in December 1941 as a result of the bombing of Pearl Harbor, but the federal government had been preparing for military action earlier. It turned, as it has so many times before, to the historic facilities and expertise available in Philadelphia. The Cramp Shipyard, begun in 1830 by William Cramp with profits from his family's shad fishery business, was a leader in ship-building during the age of the clipper ship. When the shift to iron took place after the Civil War, many of the area's shipyards closed, but the Cramp company invested in new technology and expanded its business. By 1890, the shipyard stretched more than a quarter mile on the Delaware and employed 5,000 workers.

In a significant building campaign by the Navy in 1890, Cramp shipyards produced the battleships USS *Indiana* and USS *Massachusetts* and the cruisers USS *New York* and USS *Columbia.* Ships built at the Cramp yards distinguished themselves in the Spanish-American War. By 1895, the Cramp shipyards were the largest in America, employed 6,000, and continued to produce ships for the Navy through the end of World War 1. In 1919, Cramp Shipbuilding was sold to American Ship and Commerce Corporation, but the facilities closed in 1927.

As the country prepared for involvement in World War II, the Navy made arrangements to renovate the facility and its equipment. A contract called for the shipyard to produce six cruisers at an estimated cost of $12 million. Twelve Philadelphia banks cooperated in making loans totaling that amount to the shipyard to fund its renovation and begin work on the ships, to be repaid when federal funds arrived. This arrangement made it possible to bring the shipyard back to life in less than a year, scheduling the opening for September 16, 1940. The yard employed more than 18,000 during the period of war production, building submarines in addition to surface vessels. After the war, it closed permanently, having made an important contribution to American victory.

1948: Newscaster Vernon Odom is born.

1977: Musiq Soulchild is born.

September 17

In the years immediately following the Second World War, many in the country continued to struggle with the larger meaning of the war and its impact on the American concepts of liberty and independence. Within the context of great evil and tremendous personal sacrifice, American ideals of peace, justice, and the rights of individuals were challenged by the realities of war. President Harry S. Truman hoped to help all Americans reconnect with those essential beliefs by supporting the Freedom Train of 1947-49. Over a two-year period, the nation's most significant and irreplaceable framing documents traveled the country, allowing average citizens the opportunity to read for themselves the inspiring words of the Founding Fathers, as well as revisit the principles that guided American freedoms and the objectives of war.

Initially proposed by Attorney General Tom Clark, the Freedom Train was a play on Truman's own favored form of campaigning, the "whistle-stop tour." The program was not, however, a government initiative; rather, it was entirely funded with private donations through the American Heritage Foundation. A specially outfitted American Locomotive Company diesel engine was completed in August 1947 and pulled seven cars: a baggage car, three display cars, and three passenger cars for the associated staff. All told a total of 127 American documents and 6 historical flags were displayed, including some of the most important in American history. Originals of the Magna Carta, the Declaration of Independence, the Bill of Rights, the Emancipation Proclamation, and the Gettysburg Address were just a few seen by more than three million people at over three hundred stops.

On several occasions, the deeper meaning of the documents was tested as the train journeyed more than 37,000 miles in all forty-eight of the contiguous states. In Birmingham, Alabama, city officials intended to maintain regional segregation protocol and require "white only" times during which African-Americans would not be permitted aboard. The American Heritage Foundation refused to permit the train to stop in the city under those circumstances, firmly asserting the rights of all Americans to fully participate in the Train and its meaning. A true representation of the country's desire to seek the foundation of purpose and intent behind American ideals of freedom and liberty, the Freedom Train that departed Philadelphia for the first time on this date in 1947 would ultimately do just that for millions of Americans of all races and creeds.

1787: The United States Constitution is approved and signed by the Constitutional Convention in Philadelphia.

1918: The first cases of the influenza pandemic are reported in Philadelphia; however, interventions (school closings, shut-down of large public events, etc.) are not implemented until October 3.

September 18

The early 1960s saw the creation of a long series of teenaged singing idols. Frankie Avalon was the first of these manufactured stars. Born in Philadelphia on September 18, 1939, Francis Thomas Avallone was a trumpet player in the South Philadelphia neighborhood. At the age of twelve, he and drummer Robert Ridarelli, who became an idol himself under the name Bobby Rydell, performed with Rocco and the Saints. This neighborhood dance band played at the CR Club, a private club associated with Palumbo's restaurant, and at the Sons of Italy, high school sock hops, and all along the Jersey shore.

The success of *American Bandstand* encouraged a number of Philadelphians to go into the music business, and Dick Clark served as a mentor to many area musicians and music entrepreneurs. Chancellor Records was founded by Peter DeAngelis and Robert Marucci, who signed the renamed Frankie Avalon to a singing contract. The first of their recording efforts were minor hits, but in 1959 Avalon recorded "Venus" by Ed Marshall. With its soft beat reminiscent of the calypso, the record sold over a million copies. Avalon's next recordings, "Bobby Sox to Stockings," "Just Ask Your Heart," and "Why" sold more than a million copies each. But by 1961, Avalon's time as a hit recording artist were over.

With his engaging smile and good looks, Avalon next built a career in the movies. He starred with Annette Funicello, formerly of Disney's Mouseketeers, in a series of lighthearted surfer movies. *Beach Party, Muscle Beach,* and *Beach Blanket Bingo* were big hits for the duo. Later in his career he appeared as Teen Angel in the film version of *Grease.* In 1985, he and two of the other Philadelphia teen idols, Fabian and Bobby Rydell, went on a fifty-city tour as the Golden Boys of Bandstand, and in 1987 he teamed with Annette again in a parody of their early beach movies called *Back to the Beach.* Avalon continues to make appearances at nightclubs and concerts.

1873: Jay Cooke & Company's Northern Pacific Railroad Company fails, leading to the Panic of 1873. Jay Cooke, a Philadelphian, was a fiscal agent of the United States government during the Civil War.

September 19

In a dubious first for the city, Philadelphia mayor Thomas B. Smith was accused of conspiracy in the murder of a city policeman on this date in 1917. Smith, a strong Republican affiliate with ties to one of the state's two party factions, was accused of willfully knowing and allowing a reign of terror within the city's Fifth Ward that resulted in the death of special officer George A. Epperley. Known as the "Bloody Fifth" for over thirty years of contentious and often violent political theater, the ward lived up to its reputation during the 1917 elections for city councilman. Smith was ultimately tried by a grand jury and indicted for trial by jury, along with the incumbent ward councilman, a police lieutenant, and five other policemen.

In the few years leading up to the election in 1917, the Republican Party experienced dramatic shifts in loyalty and a split that waged two sides against each other. The Vares, Congressman William S. and State Senator Edwin H., ruled large areas of the state and the city of Philadelphia. In opposition to them were Senator Boies Penrose and State Senator James McNichol. In the Fifth Ward, as with all city wards, election to Council also entailed choice over ward leadership, an unpaid yet highly powerful position in city politics. In 1916, Smith entered the race in the Penrose-McNichol camp, but quickly switched sides to align with the Vares. In attempting to control the results of the 1917 ward elections, Smith supported his own man, Isaac Deutsch. During the events of September 19, six gunmen presumably brought in by Deutsch attempted to kill the other Republican candidate, James Carey. During the tussle, Carey was severely beaten and policeman Epperley was shot and killed.

The next day, Smith was charged with conspiracy to murder, based primarily on the belief that he knew about the threats against Carey and the arrangements by Deutsch. Testimony to the grand jury ran the gamut, including accusations from the gunmen of drugging by Deutsch, and assertions that Smith was entirely unaware of the violent situation in the ward. Finally, Smith and his co-defendants were indicted by grand jury on December 20, 1917. Fourteen months later, Smith was acquitted by a jury while his co-defendants were found guilty and served anywhere from one to three years. During the investigation and trial, Smith continued to serve as mayor.

1924: As part of a larger initiative to end corruption and gambling in the city, ninety-two men are arrested for illegal gambling by the vice squad during a raid at the Union Republican Club of the Tenth Ward.

1987: The band Pink Floyd plays to 120,000 fans at JFK Stadium.

September 20

In 1777, the British under General Howe were threatening Philadelphia and engaging in military campaigns they hoped would defeat the colonials quickly. After a defeat at the Battle of Brandywine on September 11, General George Washington's forces retreated and regrouped as 6,000 British troops under Lord Cornwallis made their way toward the Schuylkill River and the city. Washington sent General Anthony Wayne and his 2,200 men in nine regiments to move behind the British, planning to cut off the British baggage wagons as they attempted to cross the river. Their efforts were doomed to failure.

Wayne arrived at Paoli Tavern on September 19, a distance of about two miles from the large British encampment. Wayne wrote to Washington that the British troops were concentrated together, but very quiet and that Wayne believed the British had no knowledge of the colonials' close presence. What Wayne did not know was that Washington's courier had been captured or deserted and that the British knew exactly where the Americans were located. Wayne moved his troops another mile and a half to farmland on top of South Valley Hill on the evening of the 19th. The next night the British, under Major General Charles Grey, led a surprise attack on the Americans and quickly routed them, losing only four soldiers killed and seven wounded. The attack was with bayonets, the British having removed the flintlocks of their guns to be able to march stealthily.

A total of 272 men in Wayne's division were killed, wounded, or missing after the battle. Wayne was tried by court-martial and declared to have acted with honor, but historians believe he made a serious tactical error. Rumors abounded that the British had "given no quarter" in the attack and executed surrendering American troops. Whether this was propaganda or reality, the battle became known as the Paoli Massacre. As a result of this loss, Howe then enjoyed complete access to the south side of the Schuylkill River, where he could choose to attack either Philadelphia or Reading. Washington chose to retreat toward Reading to protect his supplies and by September 23, 1777, the entire British force had crossed the river and occupied Philadelphia without opposition.

1783: The Pennsylvania Legislature confirms a deal with New Jersey, where six of thirteen islands in the Delaware River below Trenton (including Windmill Island) are granted to Pennsylvania.

1830: The first National Negro Convention convenes in Philadelphia with the intention of abolishing slavery.

1869: The Chestnut Street Theater under the management of actress Laura Keen opens.

1945: The Cleveland Buckeyes defeat the Homestead Grays, 5 to 0, to win game four and sweep the Negro World Series, four games to zero.

September 21

With the drone of nearly 150 airplane engines overhead, New Jersey governor Morgan Foster Larson and airport president Nicholas Luddington dedicated the new Camden Central Airport on this date in 1929, Larson proudly remarking that the airport was unquestionably "one of the greatest steps for progress ever taken for New Jersey." Located along the north side of the Cooper River, the new airport site was chosen for its nearly level ground and easy access to nearby roads and highways. Selected to serve as the airmail port for Philadelphia and provide a primary connection in the fledgling air travel industry, Camden Central Airport seemed destined to bring success and business to Camden County.

In addition to two paved take-off runways, the airport featured two unpaved runways, two large airplane hangars, and a plant for the Jacobs Engine Manufacturing Company. Over the next few years, additional sod runways were added, as well as a third asphalt runway. Air traffic in the area was still fairly limited to mail delivery, and Camden remained the center of all airmail traffic in the region. By 1936, Philadelphia's $4.5 million post office at 9th and Chestnut Street was receiving several deliveries each day. Once the mail arrived in Camden by airplane, it was transferred to an autogiro, an early form of helicopter. The autogiro then flew across the river to Philadelphia and landed on a special pad on the roof of the new post office.

Unfortunately, the use of airmail, an expensive postage option, declined during the late 1930s and early 1940s. The use of larger airplanes also put the Camden Central Airport at risk, since it was not large enough to accommodate them. With the opening of Philadelphia's airport in 1940, the four airlines working out of Camden moved across the Delaware River to the new facility. World War II brought temporary activity to Camden as the United States Navy used the airport as a landing field and training facility. Postwar commercial activity never reached the earlier level because of competition from both Philadelphia and New York City. By 1957, the airfield was all but abandoned.

1705: The first city burial ground "for strangers dying in this city" is established by Common Council.

1939: Mrs. Josephine Romualdo is sentenced to death for the arsenic murder of her husband, Antonio. Mrs. Romualdo is one of several "arsenic widows" implicated in a South Philadelphia poison ring.

September 22

Few neighborhoods in Philadelphia were as infamous for crime, corruption, and vice as the Fifth Ward of the late 1800s and early 1900s. Known as the "Bloody Fifth" among many of its residents and outsiders alike, the Fifth Ward was bounded to the north by Chestnut Street, to the east by the Delaware River, to the south by South Street, and to the west by Seventh Street. The heart of the city's history and home to significant icons of freedom and independence, the Fifth Ward served as the antithesis of all that was great about Philadelphia and represented the depths to which political corruption could drag even the best of histories.

In the nineteenth century, the Fifth Ward was home to a wide variety of folk, from Irish immigrants to long-established Jewish families to working-class blacks. Elections in particular brought out the most violence and corruption, as Philadelphia political warriors fought to maintain control over City Hall and local ward leadership, heavily expressed through racism and deep lines of political loyalty. In 1871, African-American activist Octavius Catto was shot and killed on Election Day, and in 1917, the mayor of Philadelphia was implicated in a murder enacted by his own followers. Both events received a great deal of attention in the press, and the trials that followed were carefully monitored.

On this date in 1886, another crime was committed on Election Day, but in this case no apparent trial followed. That evening, police lieutenant David B. Roche shot and killed a black man, William Powell, while Powell sat in a local bar. Extremely drunk, Roche and his pals panicked and kidnapped the mortally wounded Powell and abandoned him in Frankford. Roche and his colleagues returned to the ward and drank themselves into a stupor. Though a warrant was issued for Roche's arrest, he was back in uniform soon after and continued his career. Eventually, the Fifth Ward emerged from the 1950s as Society Hill, the most desirable and well-known neighborhood in the city. Today, the Bloody Fifth and its dark past are just a vague memory.

1777: John Bartram dies at the age of seventy-eight.

1960: Rocker Joan Jett is born in Philadelphia.

September 23

The Philadelphia Sesquicentennial celebrated the 150th anniversary of the founding of the nation in 1926. Built in South Philadelphia in the area now occupied by sports venues, the fair featured an eighty-foot-tall replica of the Liberty Bell covered with 26,000 lights. It rained on the day President Calvin Coolidge spoke at the opening ceremony in July, and it continued to rain throughout most of the rest of the fair. The weather and other factors led to financial difficulties, which some believe was the impetus for offering Sesquicentennial Stadium (later JFK Stadium) as the site of the Gene Tunney–Jack Dempsey heavyweight championship fight after plans to hold the fight at Madison Square Garden fell through.

Dempsey was world champion, a boxer much loved by the rabid boxing fans of the 1920s. Known as the "Manassa Mauler," he gained his early reputation following several round-one knock-outs. Out of the ring for most of the three years preceding the fight, he had appeared in movies and on the vaudeville circuit. Dempsey's challenger, Gene Tunney, was known as an "intellectual boxer," not only for his interest in defense, but also because he read Shakespeare and quoted poetry. A Marine veteran, he competed in a series of fights to earn the title fight.

Billed by promoters as "the fight of the century," the fight drew more than 120,000 spectators on this date in 1926, despite the pouring rain. Film stars such as Tom Mix and Charlie Chaplin, state governors, the mayors of Philadelphia and New York, financiers such as Andrew Mellon and Charles Schwab, and the publisher William Randolph Hearst contributed to the almost $2 million gate. It was a record attendance for a prize fight. Fans were largely disappointed in the fight itself. Dempsey seemed out of condition, slower, and less powerful than they remembered. The underdog Tunney made the most of his careful style, and he won the championship in a ten-round decision. Dempsey and his wife took the train back to the Midwest after the fight. At each train stop press conference, Mrs. Dempsey would ask, "Jack, what happened?" Jack would always reply, "Honey, I forgot to duck." The quip was famously echoed by President Ronald Reagan many years later, in his reply to First Lady Nancy Reagan after he was shot by a would-be assassin.

1784: Robert Bell, publisher, dies.

1926: John Coltrane, jazz saxophonist, is born.

In July 1862 Congress enacted legislation to permit the president to "employ as many persons of African descent as he may deem necessary and proper for the suppression of the rebellion." But no action was taken by the Federal government until June of 1863, when the Philadelphia mustering officer received orders to authorize the formation of one regiment of ten companies of black troops. Soon after, a camp was established north of the city limits in Cheltenham on land owned by financier Jay Cooke and named Camp William Penn. It was the first recruiting and training center for black troops operated by the United States government.

Lieutenant Colonel Louis Wagner, a German immigrant who had been wounded at the Second Battle of Bull Run, volunteered to command the camp. All of the officers were white and received special training provided by the "committee for the supervision of recruiting of colored troops" located at 1210 Chestnut Street. The first recruits arrived on July 4, 1863. The camp soon grew too large for its location and additional land west of Old York Road was leased to the Federal government by the son-in-law of abolitionist Lucretia Mott. Mrs. Mott, William Still, Frederick Douglass, and other famous abolitionists and preachers visited the camp and participated in activities for the troops. A total of 19,940 men in eleven regiments were trained at the camp and sent to battlefields, largely in the South.

The recruitment and arming of African-American troops was not without controversy. Although a "Grand Review" of the troops was held at the camp on September 24, 1863, the first regiment permitted to leave for active duty was not allowed to parade through Philadelphia. Commandant Wagner and others worked against this prejudice and on October 3, 1863, the Sixth Regiment and four companies paraded down Broad Street past a group of dignitaries and military leaders at the Union League. Two of the regiments, the Sixth and the Eighth, are included in a list of the best three hundred fighting regiments of the war and saw significant action at the Battle of Chaffin's Farm with heavy casualties. The Twenty-second escorted President Lincoln's casket through Washington. Following the war, the predominantly African-American community of LaMott was built on the land, and remains today a National Historic District.

1921: Jim McKay, ABC TV announcer covering the Munich Olympics Palestinian terrorist attack in which Jewish athletes were murdered, is born Jim McManus in Philadelphia.

September 25

As early as 1719, members of the religiously persecuted Brethren arrived in Philadelphia, drawn to the northwestern area of Germantown, established by German Mennonite settlers beginning in the early 1680s. Led by Peter Becker, the Brethren quickly founded a home base in Germantown, but also encountered internal conflicts held over from their initial refugee experiences in Krefeld, Germany. It was not until 1723 that the widespread Brethren returned to Germantown in hopes of solidifying their congregation and extending their mission. Following a series of baptisms in the Wissahickon Creek, the first Brethren congregation in America was born. A number of influential religious and community leaders emerged from this congregation, including Conrad Beissel, who later founded the Ephrata Cloister, and Christopher Sauer, a successful printer who found his life changed by Beissel but who himself forever changed the voice and role of German Pennsylvanians.

Arriving in Germantown in 1724, Sauer moved to Lancaster with his wife, Maria. At the same time, Beissel arrived intending to establish his own religious experiment. Sauer soon learned that his wife had joined Beissel and his followers in the Ephrata Cloister as Sister Maria, leaving Sauer and his young son behind. She continued there for the next twelve years, while Sauer returned to Germantown, bought land, and started over. His home served as the primary meeting place for the Brethren for nearly thirty years. Sauer never lost his connection to the Ephrata cloister or his wife, who returned to him in 1744, more than a decade after Sauer's establishment of a printing press in Germantown.

Inspired in part by the success of Benjamin Franklin, Sauer embarked on a new career as a printer in 1735. Franklin, the most prominent printer in Pennsylvania, served a large proportion of the German language audience but used roman type. Sauer's innovation was the use of the German text type, allowing for a more direct communication with his German immigrant customers through religious texts, calendars, almanacs, and readers. In 1743, he published the first German-language Bible in America, each page hand-set and hand-printed. Sauer also used his press to influence politics, specifically reaching out to the Germantown-based Quakers. The Sauer Bible remains a unique representation of the Bible in America; the first English-language version would not be printed in this country until just prior to the Revolutionary War. Sauer died on this date in 1758, leaving his business to his son and a legacy of strength in voice and opinion for the German-American community for decades to come.

1857: The Bank of Pennsylvania collapses at the beginning of the Panic of 1857.

1968: Musician and actor Will Smith is born.

1998: The largest recorded earthquake in Pennsylvania history, measured at 5.2 on the Richter Scale, occurs in northwestern Pennsylvania. It is felt over more than 75,000 square miles, including Philadelphia.

The history of Masonic lodges in Philadelphia goes back to the beginning of the eighteenth century, when members of the Masons, including Benjamin Franklin, met at Tun Tavern at Penn's Landing. On September 26, 1786, thirteen lodges combined to create one of the oldest grand lodges in the nation. Freemasonry continued to flourish and in 1867 the Masons purchased land near City Hall to build a temple. The Masons selected James Windrim, a member of the first graduating class of Girard College, as the architect. The Temple became the twenty-eight-year-old Windrim's second major commission. He later designed the Academy of Natural Sciences and the Agricultural hall for the Centennial Exposition.

On June 27, 1868, the cornerstone was laid in a ceremony featuring a gavel said to have been owned by another famous Mason, George Washington. The design of the building incorporated the architectural styles of the mystic ancestors of the Masons, with elements from Egypt, Greece, Italy, Germany, France, Scotland, and England. At a cost of more than $1.5 million for the exterior alone, the temple is a solid, imposing structure of granite and other stone. Following traditional Masonic practice, all stones were individually cut and finished at the quarry before being brought to the construction site. A 250-foot medieval-style tower crowns the building. The entrance to the building features four pairs of huge pillars with Norman-style arches. The ornate interior of the building, completed after fifteen years and designed by George Herzog, who also created the interiors for City Hall, is composed of seven major halls, each decorated in a different style. The grand Egyptian Hall features sphinxes and hieroglyphics, while the Oriental Hall is said to have been inspired by the Alhambra in Spain.

After five years of construction, a three-day series of parades and ceremonies culminated in the dedication of the building on this date in 1873, nearly a century after the first Lodge was organized. The dedication parade included 14,000 participants, and estimates of the crowd on Broad Street topped 200,000 people. The Temple, formally known as the Grand Lodge of Free and Accepted Masons of Pennsylvania, has been renovated and meticulously maintained over the years, and is on the National Register of Historic Places.

1777: Lord Cornwallis and the British enter and occupy Philadelphia. Congress is forced to move to York, Pennsylvania.

1881: King David Kalakana I of the Sandwich Islands (to become known as Hawaii) visits Philadelphia and lodges at the Continental Hotel.

1933: A rebellion of nearly 1,700 convicts flares at the Eastern Penitentiary and rages for six hours before 2 fire companies, 600 Philadelphia policemen, and several details of state police subdue the mob.

1979: The Bellevue-Stratford Hotel reopens following the Legionnaires' disease outbreak in 1976.

There are limited opportunities for golf in a densely populated urban setting like Philadelphia. The public course in Cobbs Creek Park serves as good recreation for its citizens, but the history of golf in Philadelphia has taken place at private golf clubs outside the city such as the Merion Golf Club. Begun in 1865, the Merion Cricket Club built a golf course in 1912 on the Main Line, a string of communities along a main railroad line west of the city. Designed by Hugh Wilson, a Scottish immigrant, the course featured steep-faced bunkers in the Scottish style. Instead of using pennants to mark the holes, the course featured woven red wicker baskets that did not reveal which way the wind was blowing. The course was a great success and hosted the 1914 United States Amateur championships. A fourteen-year-old golfer from Georgia, Bobby Jones, competed in the tournament that year. Returning to Merion eight years later, he won the first of his record five U.S. Amateur titles.

In 1930, Bobby Jones did what no other golfer has ever done: he won the Grand Slam. Starting with the U.S. Open, he went on to win the British Open and the British Amateur championships. This trifecta was considered such a triumph that New York City held a ticker tape parade in his honor when he returned from England. But Bobby Jones had one more tournament to win. On this date in 1930, Merion was the site of the U.S. Amateur championship, and a crowd of 18,000 filled the grounds to watch the final afternoon of play. State troopers and Marines escorted Jones off the tees and onto the greens in order to protect him from the large number of spectators. When the match ended, Jones had won the championship and what was called "the impregnable quadrilateral." Having won it all, Jones retired from golf at the age of twenty-eight, and golfers have been chasing his record ever since.

Merion Golf Club has had an impressive history, hosting more national United States Golf Association titles than any other club. Players such as Jack Nicklaus and Lee Trevino enjoyed their own notable victories at Merion, and have both been quoted praising the qualities of the courses. All told, Merion's East Course has hosted seventeen USGA championships. The club's glory may not be all in the past; Merion is scheduled to host the championship again in 2013.

1824: Arrival of the Marquis de Lafayette to Philadelphia by way of Frankford Arsenal. His visit was timed to kick off the 50th Anniversary observation of the Signing of the Declaration of Independence in 1776.

1976: Pope Paul VI names the city's Cathedral of Saints Peter and Paul a basilica.

September 28

The world influenza pandemic of 1918-19 was the worst recorded pandemic in world history, killing millions across the planet. Although it was dubbed "the Spanish flu," it is thought to have originated in the United States and to have been transmitted to Europe by American soldiers joining the war effort. Across the nation, more than 500,000 Americans lost their lives. Philadelphia, frequently victimized by epidemics since its founding, suffered more during the flu epidemic than any other leading Amcrican city. By the end of the epidemic, an estimated 15,000 Philadelphians had died out of a population estimated at about 2 million.

Although American public health officials knew of the emergence of a virulent strain of influenza spreading across Europe, attention was focused on the war effort in 1918, and governments around the world considered it necessary to suppress information about the pandemic that could prove valuable to the enemy. The first Philadelphia case was reported on September 12 at the Navy Yard, but the local papers did not report on the illnesses spread to nearly 600 sick sailors until September 19. The director of the department of health was quoted as saying, "There is little fear that the disease would spread to any great degree among citizens." On September 28, 1918, 200,000 people gathered for a parade to support Liberty Loan fund-raising for the war effort. Soon after, the rate of illness grew exponentially.

By October 9, more than four thousand cases were reported within in a 24-hour period. Hospitals were beyond capacity and doctors and nurses were in short supply because so many of them had been committed to service overseas. As the death rate increased, entire families were found dead and bodies began piling up in morgues. The city eventually resorted to mass graves. An estimated third of the patients hospitalized died as the disease proved most deadly for children and adults in their prime. In the third week of October alone, 9,500 Philadelphians succumbed to the flu or accompanying pneumonia. The flu disappeared almost as soon as it arrived, with cases dramatically decreasing in early November. Even today, it is not well understood why the flu appeared almost simultaneously across the world, and why specific cities like Philadelphia were so badly affected, though there is little doubt the severity of the epidemic affected the city for decades to follow.

1787: The newly completed United States Constitution is forwarded to state legislatures for ratification.

1876: "Pennsylvania Day" is held at the Centennial Exposition. Attendance reaches its peak on this day with 257,619 visitors.

September 29

The availability of a free education lay at the heart of Thomas E. Cahill's desire to form a Roman Catholic high school in Philadelphia. In 1890, twelve years after his death, Cahill's dream was finally realized when the Roman Catholic High School of Philadelphia opened its doors. The all-male school located at the corner of Broad and Vine streets and housed in a dramatic Gothic-styled building, honors Cahill through the school mascot known as the Cahillite. The state of Pennsylvania also honored Cahill with the placement of a historical marker on the site on this date in 2009.

Cahill, a successful dealer and businessman in the coal, ice, and wood industries, lived a frugal life but amassed great wealth. He and his wife dreamed of providing for the underprivileged population of Catholic boys in Philadelphia. Upon opening, the school served 500 students with a combination of a secular and nonsecular curriculum. The school continued with great success but found that, like many diocesan schools, a poor economy and dropping enrollment threatened its existence. A campaign launched by the alumni association saved the school and brought recognition to the importance of its history and the building's architecture. Initially a neighborhood school drawing from a select number of parishes, Roman now educates children from throughout the city, serving nearly 1,000 in 2010.

The school boasts of a number of successful graduates, many from among the sports, arts, and culture scene. The basketball team has produced a number of NBA players, among them Eddie Griffin and Michael Bantom, while the football program has seen the success of players like Marvin Harrison and Scott Paxson. John Facenda, whose voice is forever associated with the NFL films of the 1970s, was a graduate, as was the playwright Charles Fuller. A success from the beginning, Cahill's dream remains a symbol of educational excellence in Philadelphia more than a century after it began.

1902: A great baseball parade is held in honor of the American League Champions, the Philadelphia Athletics.

1915: The Philadelphia Phillies clinch their first national pennant. It was the last time they would win a World Series game until 1980.

1951: The first football game broadcast on television in color is played at Franklin Field.

September 30

Philadelphia is not known today as a particularly corrupt big city, but it has had its share of political scandals and criminal activity, especially at the height of the Gilded Age of the industrial era. One notorious affair involved one of the city's most successful businessmen of the 1870s. By the age of twenty, William H. Kemble went into business for himself, opening a general supply store and then starting a lace-importing business at 52 North Third Street in the city. Other business ventures followed until he was appointed as the stamp agent of Philadelphia by President Abraham Lincoln. During the Civil War, he and several business partners started the Union Passenger Railway Company of Philadelphia. His wealth in railroads and banking rapidly grew. From 1865 to 1868, he served as state treasurer while living at his town house on Green Street and his summer residence, "Marylawn" in Glenside.

Kemble was a businessman, but he was also the most powerful lobbyist in the state legislature, earning the nickname "King of the Lobby." It was said that any bill would pass if it was described as "Kemble's bill." In 1878, the "Riot Bill" went before the legislature, which proposed compensating railroad companies $3 million in damages incurred in 1877 when striking railroad workers in Pittsburgh fought with militia from Philadelphia and a subsequent fire destroyed private property belonging to the railroad. Taxpayer groups fought the legislation on the grounds that the legislature was not an insurance company, while railroad business interests in Pittsburgh and Philadelphia lobbied hard in favor of the bill.

Kemble and others were accused of offering bribes to those who would vote in favor of the bill. Kemble was convicted, but anticipating a pardon he and his fellow convicted defendants fled before the sentencing. Captured in Philadelphia, Kemble was returned to Harrisburg where he received a two-year sentence but was immediately pardoned. Kemble remained a powerful force in the city, promoting the interest of his railroad company over competitors through "ownership" of city council and other officials. At his funeral at Laurel Hill Cemetery on September 30, 1891, a throng of prominent persons including judges, United States senators and representatives, and railroad executives heard a eulogy by the Reverend Dr. Mutchmore of the Memorial Presbyterian Church, in which he stated that "there would be far fewer commercial failures if there were more men like Mr. Kemble to stand by their friends in the time of adversity."

1728: John Bartram purchases property formerly belonging to Frederick Schobbenhausen at a sheriff's sale in Kingsessing.

1963: Haile Selassie, the Emperor of Ethiopia, is greeted upon his arrival in Philadelphia.

1995: The Philadelphia Naval Shipyard closes.

In the pantheon of American patriots that includes names like Washington, Jefferson, Franklin, and Adams, the men and women of Philadelphia in the first half of the nineteenth century would most certainly add one more: Marie-Joseph Paul Yves Roch Gilbert du Motier, Marquis de La Fayette. Born in France in 1757, Lafayette's service in the War for Independence was known far and wide. He arrived in Philadelphia in 1777, and was soon afterward accepted as General George Washington's aide-de-camp. As such, he traveled with Washington everywhere, serving as an influential member of his staff. Lafayette's loyalty and bravery earned him a stellar reputation, and even after he returned to France in 1779, his influence was felt as he petitioned for French involvement in support of the American fight. He returned to service with Washington in time to help defeat British general Lord Cornwallis and end the war. The next four decades passed for Lafayette with many victories and losses, most notably surrounding the violence and upheaval of the French Revolution and the reign of Napoleon.

By the 1820s, America prepared to celebrate the fiftieth anniversary of the Declaration of Independence, which would come in 1826. In anticipation of this grand event, President James Monroe invited Lafayette to the United States to engage in a tour of locations associated with the American Revolution. Lafayette arrived in New York in August 1824, and began to make his way to Washington, D.C., and points south, including a visit with Thomas Jefferson at Monticello. Lafayette was greeted in Philadelphia on September 27, 1824, with a remarkable procession. The following description of his arrival was documented in *Memoirs of General Lafayette: with an Account of His Visit to America and His Reception by the People of the United States; From His Arrival, August 15th, to the Celebration at Yorktown, October 19th, 1824,* published by Samuel L. Knapp in 1824:

> His entrance into the fair city, founded by the wise and benevolent Penn, is described as most magnificent in all its accompaniments. The population poured forth to meet him at an early hour. Carriages, horsemen and pedestrians filled every avenue for a distance of five miles; and the windows and stagings were thronged with ladies eager to welcome him. Just at the entrance of the city, a division of militia, composed of cavalry, artillery and infantry was drawn up in a hollow square, on a piece of land of about forty acres, to receive the Patriot Hero, whose approach was announced by a salute of 100 rounds of artillery. Lafayette, uncovered and standing up in his barouche, was seen by the whole field. The car of Saladin could not have exceeded that of Lafayette. The troops were nearly six thousand. After the review, which the general made on foot, he received the saluting honors in his barouche.
>
> The line of march into the city was then taken up. It extended nearly three miles, and passed through numerous streets. More than six hours were consumed in proceeding from Frankfort to the State House, a distance of about four miles. A full description of the procession, and the decorated arches, &c. under which it passed, would occupy too great a portion of this volume—we can only give the outline of the procession.
>
> A cavalcade of 100 citizens preceded; followed by 100 general, field and staff officers.

Then came a square of cavalry; a band of music, mounted, and a corps of 160 cavalry. Next a brigade of infantry, with flank companies.

Committee of arrangements. General Lafayette and Judge Peters, in the splendid barouche.

Then followed four other barouches, drawn by four horses each, with Governors Shulze and Williamson, and suites, the general's family, and distinguished individuals

Then three cars, of large dimensions, containing 120 revolutionary heroes and worthies, each car characteristically decorated; bearing on their front "Washington," on the rear "LaFayette," and on the sides, "defenders of our country," "The survivors of 1776."

Then advanced 400 young men. After these the procession of trades, led by a car, containing a body of printers at work at case and press—the latter striking off, and distributing, copies of an ode on the occasion—followed by the typographical society, with a banner, with the inscription: "LaFayette—the friend of universal liberty, and the rights of the press."

Then followed 200 cordwainers (with banners, badges, emblems, &c. The other trades were also decorated;)—300 weavers;—150 ropemakers;—150 lads, uniformly dressed;—100 shipbuilders;—700 mechanics of different professions, not enumerated;—150 coopers, with a car containing a cooper's shop, the workmen fitting staves and driving hoops:—Then came 150 butchers, well mounted and neatly dressed in their frocks;—then 260 carmen, mounted, with aprons trimmed with blue; and a body of 150 riflemen, in frocks, dressed with plaids, leopard skins, &c. A company of artillery, with two pieces; a brigade of infantry and the New Jersey cavalry. A body of 300 farmers closed the procession.

Besides the above, there were the Red Men of the state, the Lafayette Association, the True Republican Society, the Washington and Lafayette Society; and the German American Society.

The appearance of the whole of this truly grand procession was august and imposing. As it passed, Lafayette! Lafayette! sprang from the voices of a multitude that rolled on, and on, and on, like wave after wave of the ocean, in numbers we shall not presume to name (but which were estimated at 200,000). Lafayette beat in every heart—Lafayette hung on every tongue—Lafayette glowed on every cheek—Lafayette glistened on every swimming eye—Lafayette swelled on every gale. The whole city and country appeared to have arrayed themselves in all their glory, and beauty, and strength, at once to witness and adorn the majesty of the spectacle; and the fashionable part of the community seemed determined to exhibit the perfection of taste in the beauty of the decoration of their persons, and the richness of their attire. In Chestnut-street wreathes were cast into the barouche, as it passed, and many of them were from the fairbands of Quakeresses.

After the procession had passed through the principal streets, the front halted at the old State-House, which contains the hall in which the Declaration of Independence was signed in 1776.

Here the general alighted, passed under a most magnificent triumphal arch, and was conducted to the hall, which is 40 feet square and was decorated in the most splendid manner. Among the decorations was a statue of Washington, and portraits of William Penn, Franklin,

Robert Morris, Francis Hopkinson, Greene, Wayne, Montgomery, Hamilton, Gates, Rochambeau, Charles Carroll, M'Kean, Jefferson, Hancock, Adams, Madison, Monroe, and Charles Thompson. The portrait of Washington, by Peale, occupied the first place, and was the most splendidly decorated. Here were assembled the city authorities, the Society of Cincinnati, the judges, officers of the army and navy, and the Committee of arrangements, all seated on superb sofas.

October

October 1

A theater in the grandest tradition, the Arch Street Theater opened to the public on this date in 1828, beginning a long tradition of excellence and drama on, and off, stage. Built on Arch Street near Sixth, the classically designed marble facade was based on the work of esteemed architect John Haviland. Owned by a New York company but managed by local W. B. Wood, the theater struggled during its first years. Envisioned as a rival to the much older and more established Walnut Street Theater and the Chestnut Street Theater, Arch Street benefited from the arrival in 1831 of William Forrest, brother to the acclaimed actor Edwin Forrest. Under his direction and with the additional presence of Edwin Booth through much of his most successful years, the Arch Street Theater remained a leading attraction in the city for more than a century.

Following its opening day, the first season lasted almost eleven weeks and featured a production of the play *The Honeymoon* and the more farcical *Three and the Deuce.* Offering a mixture of plays and short comedies, the theater hoped to attract a clientele made up of businessmen and professionals in the fast-growing city. As word of Forrest's skill grew, so too did the audience numbers, and the theater emerged as one of the best in the city. After thirty years, the theater changed hands as Mrs. John Drew, herself a famed actress, bought the property and managed it as a first-class playhouse. For another thirty years, the house thrived and offered a wide variety of productions until the last curtain fell on Mrs. Drew's ownership in 1892.

The next owner, Charles Blaney, proved less effective as a manager and the quality of productions declined. So, too, did the numbers of potential audience members as the well-to-do left the city for suburban enclaves. For a brief period starting in 1898, the theater featured the unique art of Yiddish comedy in hopes of appealing to the large immigrant community in Philadelphia, but quickly assumed the role of house of vaudeville. In 1909, Yiddish productions were revived along with vaudeville, but the theater closed for good and was demolished in 1936.

1940: The first section of the Pennsylvania Turnpike opens with a total of 160 miles of roadway.

1970: The last Phillies game is played at Shibe Park. Seats are ripped out and there is a melee on the field afterward.

October 2

In June 1775, the Continental Congress chose George Washington as commander-in-chief of the Continental Army, largely because he alone of the four men contending for that honor was a native Virginian and because his character was unquestioned. Charles Lee, a former British officer, was considered the most experienced military man serving in the Continental Army; he had served in the French and Indian War and as a general in the Polish army. Lee was also a controversial figure; ambitious, crude, and slovenly, he had earned the nickname "Boiling Water" from the Iroquois for his terrible temper. Lee always resented the selection of Washington as commander-in-chief.

Shortly after the start of the war, Lee participated in the siege of Boston and the defense of New York and South Carolina and Georgia, in effect serving as Washington's second in command. But he frequently and publicly derided Washington's abilities as a general and undermined Washington's authority or maneuvered to force a poor showing from Washington's command. In December 1776, Lee was captured by the British in Basking Ridge, New Jersey, and spent eighteen months as a prisoner. Released in a prisoner trade, Lee rejoined Washington at Valley Forge. Baron Von Steuben was then training the Continental troops, but Lee believed that they would never be able to fight against British regulars; he favored guerrilla campaigns using local patriots. In June 1778, Lee allegedly ignored orders by Washington to advance, turning a possible victory into a draw.

Lee was court-martialed for disobedience of orders, misbehavior before the enemy, and disrespect to the commander-in-chief. Such luminaries as the Marquis de Lafayette, Alexander Hamilton, and General Anthony Wayne testified, with Lee conducting his own defense. Lee contended that the orders from Washington were not clear and his movement of troops had been left to his discretion. After a long trial, punctuated by letters to newspapers by Lee arguing his overall case against Washington, he was convicted and suspended from the Army for a period of a year. Unable to turn public opinion in his favor even though he had been second in command of the revolutionary forces, Lee never returned to military service. He died of fever in poverty and obscurity on October 2, 1782, at an inn in Philadelphia.

1727: The first Amish settlers in America arrive in Philadelphia.

October 3

Ernest Evans was born on this date in 1939 in South Carolina, the son of tobacco workers. His family joined the African-American migration to the northern city of Philadelphia, where they settled in South Philadelphia. Interested in music as a small child, Ernest practiced his singing impressions of Elvis Presley, Fats Domino, and Jerry Lee Lewis on customers at the produce market on Ninth Street where he worked while attending high school. He and his singing group, the Quantrells, also performed at churches and other locations in the neighborhood. His boss at the market nicknamed him "Chubby" because of his plump physique and arranged for him to do a private recording for Dick Clark of *American Bandstand.* When Clark sent the recording as a Christmas present to business associates, Chubby Evans caught the attention of Cameo-Parkway Records.

Renamed Chubby Checker by Clark's wife as homage to Fats Domino, he had his first hit for Cameo-Parkway in 1959 with a recording of "The Class." Soon after, Checker recorded his signature hit, "The Twist," which had been a minor hit for singer and songwriter Hank Ballard. Checker's version sent the song to the top of the charts for eighteen weeks. In the early 1960s, Checker had additional hits with "Pony Time," "Let's Twist Again," and the "Limbo Rock." For the first and only time in recording history, his reissue of his original single "The Twist" reached the top of the charts again in 1962. Chubby Checker also starred in two movies that featured the Twist, *Twist Around the Clock* and *Don't Knock the Twist.*

The excitement over "The Twist" wasn't just about the music; the accompanying dance, in which Checker swung both arms in the opposite direction of his hips and one bent leg, swept the country like wildfire. On television and in film, Checker's style was seen and modeled by thousands of crazed teenagers. Perhaps the greatest cultural contribution Chubby Checker made was to make "dancing apart to the beat" the style for all rock and roll dancing since 1959.

1924: The first game of the first "Colored World Series," played between the Kansas City Monarchs and Philadelphia Hillsdale, is held at the Baker Bowl as 18,000 watch from the stands.

1979: Pope John Paul II visits Philadelphia.

October 4

After the departure of the British occupation force in 1778, Philadelphians fell on hard times. Inflation was rampant, with the Continental dollars paid to the troops worth less and less. Food shortages and poverty afflicted ordinary working people. During this period, Philadelphia almost fell into a civil war between radical patriots who supported price controls and held resentments toward merchants who had done business with the British, and the more conservative wing of the patriots, who were concerned that the destruction of business would lead to the economic failure of the revolution.

James Wilson, a signer of the Declaration of Independence, was a leading Constitutional lawyer and supporter of the Revolution. Along with Robert Morris and others, he was a member of the conservative contingent who opposed the 1776 Pennsylvania constitution with its single assembly and a governing committee instead of a governor. Opposed by the members of the Constitutional Party composed largely of farmers and the working poor, he lost his seat in the legislature over his views and left the Commonwealth in 1777. In 1779, he moved back to Philadelphia to a house on the corner of Walnut and Third streets and was heavily criticized for his legal defense of loyalists and his opposition to price controls.

On October 4, 1779, Wilson and about thirty-five others gathered at his house to defend themselves from radical patriots who they believed would be attacking them. A large contingent of citizens marched to the house armed with a cannon, possibly to tar and feather its inhabitants and drive them from the city. Reports of who may have fired first vary, but the march turned deadly and people in the house and on the street were killed and wounded. The riot was ended only by the arrival of the Continental Dragoons on horseback. The loss of life at "Fort Wilson" led to the decline of the radicals and ultimately Wilson and the conservatives prevailed, achieving changes to the Pennsylvania constitution. Wilson went on to serve on the Constitutional Convention and is often considered the Father of the United States Constitution.

1777: General George Washington attempts to defeat Howe's army in Germantown and is repelled. He retreats to Whitemarsh and later to Valley Forge to wait out the winter.

1832: During the first cholera epidemic to hit Philadelphia, the last case of the disease is reported on this date. Altogether, there are 985 deaths with more than 2,300 reported cases.

October 5

Among the many acts that led to the revolt of the American colonies from England, few were as protested or as detested as the Stamp Act. Intended to establish a mechanism to enforce the paying of taxes to the Crown as well as to assert the King's control over the American colonies, the Stamp Act applied to a wide variety of paper products and the legal documents printed on them. Land records, deeds, court pleadings, mortgages, and even playing cards were all taxed. Within days of the announcement that Parliament had passed the Act, the Massachusetts legislature drafted and sent a petition of protest demanding repeal. More violent and personal protests were also mounted, including in Philadelphia, where the first of the stamps intended to be affixed to paper and documents arrived in the city on this date in 1765.

A significant result of the Stamp Act, which was scheduled to be implemented on November 1, 1765, was the appointment of a Stamp Distributor who would oversee the placement of stamps on all appropriate materials and would also oversee receipt of the tax funds. In New Jersey, William Coxe was selected, while Pennsylvania and Delaware were to be represented by John Hughes. By mid August, both men were eagerly awaiting official notification of their new, presumably prestigious positions. Within two weeks, however, word of planned mass protests and threats against Coxe and Hughes led Coxe to resign his position on September 2. Hughes continued as Distributor but by October 2 was refusing to take possession of the stamps scheduled to arrive shortly.

Fueling the local protests were a number of groups, most significantly the Sons of Liberty, who were strongest in New York, Boston, and Philadelphia. On the day the stamps arrived, bells in the State House and Christ Church were rung in protest, while muffled drums beat to call Philadelphians to the State House yard. Hundreds of people responded to the call, many demanding an end to the act and others going further to threaten the life and property of John Hughes. Afraid for his life, Hughes resigned on October 8, and no one was ever selected to replace him. The Stamp Act was repealed by Parliament on March 18, 1766, but the battle lines were drawn and the result would be war.

1777: The Battle of Germantown takes place; Howe's British troops defeat the colonials under George Washington's command. The battle is reenacted annually on the grounds of Cliveden, in Germantown.

1902: Larry Fine, to become famous as Larry (with Moe and Curly) of the Three Stooges, is born in Philadelphia.

October 6

A city of many neighborhoods and ethnic backgrounds, Philadelphia has benefited over the last three centuries from the contributions of its manifold citizenry. Today, the extended neighborhood of Germantown, in the northwest region of Philadelphia, is one of a few city communities that have born witness to a long line of history-making people and events with both regional and national impact. From the beginning, Germantown has stood for much of what Philadelphia and Pennsylvania seemed to offer new arrivals: tolerance, acceptance, and an opportunity to succeed in business as well as in life.

Founded on this date in 1683 by thirteen Quaker and Mennonite families from Krefeld in Germany, Germantown was the first municipality created in Philadelphia County, chartered by William Penn in 1689. German Township, encompassing the whole of the northwest wing of the city, consisted of a borough and outlying township, the borough under the supervision of a bailiff, burgesses, and committeemen. Most early leaders were Quakers, some of whom initiated the first white protest against slavery in 1688. Early businesses thrived, among them farming, brick making, and printing. Later, textile weaving, furniture, and toy manufacture and larger industries such as the railroads made their mark on the borough. In 1777, during the American Revolution, Germantown Avenue, the main route in and out of the city toward the northwest, was the scene of the Battle of Germantown as the British began their occupation of Philadelphia.

By the early 1800s, Germantown was a thriving economic and cultural center. In 1854, the consolidation of all townships and boroughs into the City of Philadelphia ended Germantown's autonomy, but new interest in its resources and as a retreat from the densely populated city center encouraged the area's development as a residential community. In part due to its industry as well as its history of tolerance, Germantown attracted a variety of new arrivals, including Irish, Italian, Jewish, and African-American families. Throughout its history, names as notable as Rittenhouse, Pastorius, Chew, Logan, Alcott, Washington, and Wister all called Germantown home. In the twentieth century, Germantown faced racial and economic tensions much as did the rest of Philadelphia. Today, Germantown represents a unique blending of past, present, and future, standing as one of Philadelphia's most historic and storied neighborhoods.

1723: Benjamin Franklin is said to have arrived in Philadelphia from Boston at the age of sixteen years.

1952: *American Bandstand* makes its television debut on WFIL with host Bob Horn.

October 7

Inspired by the 1825 opening of the Erie Canal, which enabled inexpensive shipping between New York and the Midwest, businessmen in Philadelphia began demanding their own transportation system to better connect Philadelphia and Pittsburgh. In 1828, the Commonwealth's legislature approved a plan of canals linked by railroads. The Philadelphia and Columbia Railroad was part of this plan, starting at Broad and Vine streets in Philadelphia and winding across eighty-two miles to the Columbia, a town on the Susquehanna River in central Pennsylvania.

Construction began in 1829 with iron rails laid on top of stone blocks. This approach replaced the wooden tracks of earlier train systems. Laborers building the railroad were largely immigrants from Ireland; fifty-seven of these men, whose names were not recorded, died in a cholera epidemic in 1832 on route at Duffy's Cut. To solve the problem of how to get the engines out of the Schuylkill Valley at Philadelphia and to lower the cars when they reached the canal at Columbia, an ingenious system of inclined planes was developed. Although the project was widely supported by Pennsylvanians concerned about business and economic development, railroads were a relatively new technology and the success of the effort was not guaranteed.

The first twenty miles of track were opened in 1832, and the line was completed on this date in 1834. In celebration, special steam trains carrying Governor George Wolfe and other dignitaries left Columbia at 8:00 A.M. and arrived in Philadelphia at 6:00 P.M. Despite the use of steam trains at the inauguration of the line, horses were the primary source of power employed until 1844. The railroad was a success, and the twenty-two days it took to cross the state by wagon was reduced to just three and one half. Over time, the canal system was abandoned in favor of a complete steam railroad system to link east and west. In the 1870s, the railroad tracks became the backbone of the development of suburban Philadelphia communities known today as the Main Line, a direct reference to the significance of the first Philadelphia and Columbia Railroad as the primary route westward from Philadelphia.

1849: Edgar Allan Poe dies in obscurity in Baltimore, Maryland.

1954: Marian Anderson is hired by the New York Metropolitan Opera as their first African-American performer.

October 8

Like many big American cities, Philadelphia suffered from a plague of graffiti in the early 1980s. The Philadelphia Anti-Graffiti Network was organized and funded to work directly with graffiti artists to give them alternatives, help businesses and homeowners clean up graffiti, and promote art in the city through the creation of urban murals. In the early years of the Mural Arts Program, reformed graffitists served community service "sentences" by cleaning marred properties and working with professional artists. In 1991, the program won the Innovations in American Government award for the city. The Mural Arts Program became an independent entity in 1996, raising private funds for its work in a public-private partnership.

As a result of the Mural Arts program, Philadelphia is known internationally as the "city of murals" for having created more than 3,000 public works of mural art spread across the city. Art education programs also sponsored by the Mural Arts program have served more than 20,000 youth in the city, and its programs for youth and adult offenders work to combat crime and violence "through the power of art." The murals appear in all parts of the city, including its poorest neighborhoods. The Mural Arts Program executive director, Jane Golden, has been honored as an expert in urban transformation and was named in 2007 as one of the 75 Greatest Living Philadelphians by the *Philadelphia Daily News.*

The 3,000 murals encompass a variety of artistic styles, themes, and sizes, with *The History of Immigration* the largest at 600 feet in length. Colorful references to nature in such works as *Honey's Garden* and *Butterflies of the Caribbean* brighten the street while other murals promote reading, anti-smoking, peace, and hope such as *If You Dream It You Can Achieve It.* Many of the murals honor individuals such as Wilt Chamberlain, Paul Robeson, Mayor Frank Rizzo, Martin Luther King, Jr., and Patti LaBelle. Less than successful in curtailing illegal graffiti over the last decade, the program is better at promoting neighborhood involvement and outreach, with many murals designed by way of collaboration between artist and residents. In South Philadelphia on October 8, 2005, the South Philadelphia Musicians mural was dedicated. Smiling, over-life-sized paintings of rock and roll stars of the 1960s including Fabian, Chubby Checker, Eddie Fisher, and Frankie Avalon watch over the neighborhood of their youth, one of thousands of unique and compelling murals around the city.

1883: Franklin Square is first lit with electricity.

October 9

Did you know that the Schuylkill River has its own navy? Formed in 1858, the Schuylkill Navy is the oldest amateur governing body in American sports. Long before the Navy's organization, Philadelphia residents fished, swam, ice skated, hunted, and sleighed on the river and along its banks. Construction of the Fairmount Water Works early in the nineteenth century created a relatively calm and smooth surface that provided ideal conditions for rowing and sometimes froze in the winter. A competitive rowing regatta took place in 1835, leading to the formation of a number of rowing clubs, which constructed sheds along the river in the early 1850s. The city condemned the poorly constructed shacks in 1859, and in 1860 an ordinance was passed permitting the construction of three houses for the Pacific Boat Club, the Schuylkill Navy, and the Philadelphia Skating Club.

By the early 1870s, clubs had built stone boathouses, primarily in a Victorian Gothic style, along the east side of the river starting at the Fairmount Water Works. Other architectural styles soon followed including Mediterranean, Picturesque, Shingle, and Colonial Revival, in brick, shingle, and stucco as well as stone. The first National Regatta was held on this date in 1873, and in 1876 the first international regatta was held as part of the Centennial celebration.

One of the features of the Schuylkill Navy was its strict requirement that rowers be amateurs. Rowing was a professional sport in many areas, subject to gambling and other unsavory activities. The Navy's refusal to permit the participation of paid rowers helped define the difference between amateur and professional sports in America. In the 1920s, rowers from Philadelphia, like Jack Kelly, Sr., won medals in international regattas and at the Olympics, giving the Schuylkill Navy even more recognition. The beautiful boathouses built by the clubs are actively used today by amateur and collegiate rowing clubs, and important regattas take place on the river every year. T0he houses in the historic boathouse row continue to draw people to the riverside, especially at night when their rooflines and corners are brightly lit, making them an attractive and romantic sight for Philadelphians and visitors alike.

1823: Scientist Joseph Leidy is born.

Many black Philadelphians were active in supporting the Union cause in the Civil War and pursuing civil rights for African-Americans after the victory. Octavius V. Catto, one of the most accomplished African-Americans of the city, became a martyr to that struggle. The son of a Presbyterian minister, Catto was educated in city schools, tutored in classical languages in Washington, D.C., and was a student at the Institute for Colored Youth in Philadelphia, which later became Cheyney University. Soon after his graduation as valedictorian, Catto taught English literature, classical languages, and higher mathematics at the school. Catto founded the Banneker Literary Institute, and was a member of the Franklin Institute and the Library Company of Philadelphia. He was also an accomplished athlete and was the founder and captain of the Pythias Baseball Club.

Catto was also heavily involved in politics, joining with Frederick Douglass to raise companies of black soldiers for the Union Army and founding the Equal Rights League in 1864. In 1867, he led the successful effort to integrate public transportation in the city. An ardent supporter of the Republican Party, Catto was a forceful voice in favor of civil rights and was honored by the Union League when the city celebrated Pennsylvania's adoption of the Fifteenth Amendment to the Constitution guaranteeing blacks the right to vote.

The Democratic Party machine, dominated by Americans of Irish ethnicity, controlled politics in the city after the Civil War. Fearing a Republican reform victory, the machine sought to intimidate black voters using gangs who violently attacked black voters in the streets. Knowing the risk, Catto was nevertheless instrumental in urging African-American voter participation during the elections in 1871. On his way home from the polls on October 10 that year, Catto was shot to death at South and Eighth streets by Frank Kelly, a Democratic Party operative. Word of his death at the age of thirty-two spurred even more voter participation that day and beyond, and the Democratic machine control of the city ended. Frank Kelly was hidden in Moymensing taverns and then fled to Chicago. He was returned for trial in 1877, but despite his identification as the killer by black and white witnesses alike, he was acquitted.

Voter intimidation and fraud in Philadelphia politics is not necessarily limited to the remote historical past. On Election Day 2008, African-Americans King Samir Shabazz and Jerry Jackson, of the New Black Panther Party, stood outside a Philadelphia polling station on Fairmount Avenue, one of the men brandishing a nightstick. When the case against the men was dismissed by U.S. Attorney General Eric Holder after it had been won, accusations of Justice Department misconduct arose, igniting a controversy that remains unresolved.

1717: George Boone and his wife, the future parents of Daniel Boone, arrive in Philadelphia after emigrating from England.

October 11

Since the first election in 1789, Philadelphia has born witness to the power and posturing of presidential campaigns. George Washington, reluctant candidate but seen by most as the only choice, showed through his extraordinary leadership during war and peace that he was the man for the job. John Adams, self-doubting and driven to receive recognition for his many years of work toward establishing American independence, launched his own, insider's campaign while serving as Vice President. In the last century and more, candidates as varied as Abraham Lincoln, Harry S. Truman, and Richard Nixon have all stumped for votes in Philadelphia, seeking to gain favor with voters as a pivotal moment in each campaign. In 2008, the man who would become the first African-American president of the United States also looked to Philadelphia for support.

In the early spring of 2008, Illinois senator Barack Obama was positioned as a front-runner in many states as primary season began. Obama faced uncertainty about his previous work as activist and brief stint as senator, and challenges to his positions on issues as broad as unemployment, the economy, and civil rights. In particular, Obama faced questions about a religious mentor whose recorded remarks led to accusations that he was preaching racism from the pulpit. On March 18, Obama came to the National Constitution Center in Philadelphia to address those concerns. His speech, in which he discussed issues of race and religion, relating them to his own family history, was seen by some as a healing answer to the divisiveness of the campaign. For others, it did not answer the questions.

The campaign continued, and by late spring 2008, Obama was clearly the Democratic front runner. On this date later that year, Obama returned to Philadelphia for a last swing through what would prove to be a pivotal voting area in the final election. Obama visited four separate Philadelphia neighborhoods: West Philadelphia, Germantown, Mayfair, and North Philadelphia. He was received by tens of thousands of supporters, and many protesters. In West Philadelphia, Obama was supported by Mayor Michael Nutter and Governor Ed Rendell. In Germantown's Vernon Park, a predominantly African-American community, Obama spoke to more than 20,000 people. On Election Day, Obama received 3 million Pennsylvania votes, over 55 percent of the state's total, while Republican opponent John McCain received 45 percent with approximately 2.4 million votes. As was the case so many times before, Pennsylvania and Philadelphia provided the keystone to the success of a presidential journey.

1793: The highest number of deaths from yellow fever is recorded in one day, totaling 119 people.

1912: Renowned conductor Leopold Stokowski debuts with the Philadelphia Orchestra. He remained until 1940, but returned for another nine years in 1960.

1949: Daryl Hall of Hall & Oates is born.

October 12

Philadelphia has always been a city of neighborhoods, each with its own character, mix of ethnicities, and commercial specialties. The "Italian Market" in the Belle Vista neighborhood is one of America's oldest continuously operating open-air markets. Begun early in the twentieth century, the market first featured pushcarts where Italian fruit and vegetable stands stood next to Jewish merchants selling eggs and poultry from New Jersey, fabrics, and other household goods. Pushcarts gave way to buildings on the narrow streets as buildings took their place and the market flourished.

Located at 9th Street between Washington and Christian avenues, the market looks very much as it did a hundred years ago. Row houses line the streets with businesses on the ground floor and residences on the upper floors. Open early and late, the market traditionally catered to working families from the industrial neighborhoods ringing the market. Awnings shade the outdoor displays in the summer, and merchants light fires in barrels in the street to warm customers during the winter months. Vendors still call out to customers about their wares. In addition to traditional Italian goods, the influence of recent immigrants from other nations diversify the many offerings. Visitors today can find live ducks, in-season fruit, a wide array of vegetables, spices, Italian cheeses and delicacies, flower stalls, and meat and seafood of any kind.

Although many Americans of Italian descent have moved to the suburbs, coming to the Italian market to shop is still a tradition. At Christmas, long lines queue at Italian bakeries and people carry home Christmas trees along the narrow streets. Two establishments, Cannuli's Meats and Isgro Pasticceria, have been in operation at the market since early in the twentieth century and have been joined recently by outdoor cafes. An icon known throughout the country, the market was featured in the film *Rocky* as Sylvester Stallone began his long run to the Art Museum steps, miles away in distance and in culture. On October 12, 2007, the Market was recognized with a Pennsylvania State Historical Marker at the corner of 9th and Christian streets, formally acknowledging the importance of the market and the people it serves.

1832: British actress Fanny Kemble first appears on a Philadelphia stage.

1906: A run of one hundred miles is made by an electric car from Jersey City to Philadelphia on a single charge and using only its regular stock batteries.

October 13

Before 1800, the only way for wagons to cross the Schuylkill River was to use floating pontoon bridges or to cross by ferry, dramatically reducing the speed and efficiency of travel to points west of the city. Unfortunately, these structures were frequently destroyed by floods, most notably in 1789 when all were lost. On March 16, 1798, the legislature passed an act creating a company to build a stone bridge spanning the Schuylkill at High Street (now Market Street) with initial capital of $150,000. The plan was to have the members of the company collect tolls until the bridge was paid for and to eventually make it a free bridge. Work began on this date in 1800 with the laying of the cornerstone and the construction of stone abutments.

The eastern pier in the river was built in a cofferdam in twenty-four feet of water. The western pier, which proved more difficult to construct, was built at a depth of forty-one feet. No pier of masonry at that depth was known to exist in the world at the time. After the cost of the stone work escalated, the decision was made to abandon the idea of a stone bridge and complete the project as a wooden structure. Timothy Palmer, an experienced bridge builder from Philadelphia, was brought in to finish the job. By the time the single-arch, 552-foot-long bridge was completed, the cost had risen to double the original investment of $150,000.

In order to lengthen the life of the bridge, a wooden covering was built soon after the bridge opened on January 1, 1805. The "Permanent Bridge" was the longest covered bridge in the world and either the first or the second to be built in America. The bridge was an immediate success and when it was threatened with fire in 1806, more than 5,000 Philadelphians braved snow and ice to protect it. Beautiful as well as functional, the bridge sported wood statues of "Commerce" and "Agriculture" sculptured by William Rush and a marble obelisk and sun dial at the western entrance. In 1840, the city purchased the bridge and eliminated tolls. The bridge continued to serve the citizens of the city well until its destruction by fire on November 20, 1875.

1775: The Continental Congress orders the construction of a naval fleet, to be built in the fledgling Philadelphia shipyard.

Philadelphia's reputation as the workshop of the world is well known. There is little question that the city was a powerhouse of production and progress through the end of the nineteenth century into the twentieth century. However, it was the life and struggles of its hundreds of thousands of factory workers that was the primary agenda on this date in 1889 when a special conference was held by the American Federation of Labor and the Knights of Labor, two of the most powerful and influential unions in the country. Of particular interest was a discussion of the eight-hour workday. The Knights, under the leadership of William Powderly, had for several years refused to take a formal position on this long-fought debate. In contrast, the members of the Federation, led by Samuel Gompers, took a stand the previous December by declaring May 1, 1890, as the target date for the establishment of an eight-hour workday. The purpose of the conference was reached with an agreement from the Knights of Labor to add their voices to the increasing demand for better working hours.

As early as the 1790s, Philadelphians took a stand to demand the regulation of the workday. In 1791, city carpenters staged a strike demanding a ten-hour day. In 1835, Irish coal workers staged a similar protest, while the following year the first calls for eight hours were heard throughout the country. The federal government eventually weighed in on June 25, 1868, with the creation of a standard eight-hour day for all government employees. Limited in its impact, the action nevertheless served as encouragement for the growing number of unionized workers. Some individual industries soon capitulated, among them the building trades, but others resisted. In 1886, the Haymarket Riot in Chicago resulted in the deaths of four strikers and further galvanized the labor movement.

In Philadelphia, just two months after the conference attended by Powderly and Gompers, the city government announced it would enforce a law on the books a remarkable twenty-one years, applying the eight-hour day to city workers. In a major shift, the Ford Motor Company under Henry Ford announced in 1914 their doubling of salaries and the adoption of a shorter day, while the federal government enforced similar protections for railroad workers in 1916, the first federal intervention in private companies. Finally, the eight-hour day was formally established by the Fair Labor Standards Act of 1938, completing the legacy of decades of protest and negotiation.

1644: William Penn is born.

1952: The House Un-American Activities Committee makes slow progress in its investigation of alleged Communist subversion in Philadelphia when five witnesses refuse to answer questions on the grounds of self-incrimination.

October 15

An unusual accusation came to light on this date in 1911, over a decade after the presumed crime was enacted. The destructive and mysterious explosion which sank the USS *Maine* in the Havana, Cuba, harbor on February 15, 1898, could not have occurred farther from the streets of Philadelphia, nor from the Spanish operatives initially blamed for the explosion. However, as home to the Dittmar Powder Company, the city held the potential to be the point of origin for an event that would ultimately lead the country to war.

The USS *Maine* was ordered to Cuba to protect American interests in an increasingly hostile political and military environment resulting from local unrest and the potential for civil war. Later investigations of the incident that followed indicate that on the night of February 15, five long tons of powder charges on board the vessel exploded. Over 260 men lost their lives. Many Americans, and the United States government, looked to the influence of Spanish spies and operatives as the cause of the explosion, providing a primary impetus for the start of the Spanish-American War. Those who supported the war began to use the battle cry "Remember the *Maine!*" in hopes of rallying American citizens.

In 1911, a second Naval Board of Inquiry was opened to revisit the question of what happened to the USS *Maine.* The Dittmar Powder Company of Philadelphia was accused by an unidentified source of selling 8,000 pounds of dynamite, 225 miles of copper wiring, and an electric motor to a representative of the Spanish forces in Cuba. The proof, it was said, was the discovery of a section of wire from the wreck of the USS *Maine* that was similar to that manufactured by Dittmar. The sale, purported to have taken place in 1896, was denied by the owner of the company, who believed it unlikely an employee would knowingly engage in such a betrayal. In an odd twist to the story, a former consul soon after accused President McKinley of knowing the USS *Maine* would be attacked. Though the accusations were deemed quite serious at the time, no further investigation into the company was initiated, and the matter was dropped. The true cause of the explosion on the USS *Maine* has remained a mystery ever since, some linking it to the Spanish, some blaming Americans, and some believing it to have been accidental.

1947: The pioneering Better Philadelphia Exhibition exploring the city's urban planning possibilities ends after a month, attracting 385,000 visitors.

1954: Hurricane Hazel disrupts the unveiling of the Northeast Extension of the Pennsylvania Turnpike in King of Prussia.

October 16

On this date in 1839, an employee of the United States Mint in Philadelphia crafted the first known photograph ever taken in America. Joseph Saxton, an inventor and machinist, was born in Huntington, Pennsylvania, on March 22, 1799. The son of a nail manufacturer, Saxton quickly grew uninterested in factory work during a two-year apprenticeship. Instead, he pursued clock-making and engraving as a career, and established his own shop in Philadelphia by 1820. His scientific interests led him to join the Franklin Institute, as well as traveling to England to explore various innovative approaches to electrical engineering. Many of his inventions proved to be ingenious improvements over existing technology, including a rotating coil current generator, a device for measuring the velocity of electricity, and an ever-pointed pencil.

It was his scientific curiosity that led Saxton, for two years previous the constructor and curator of weighing instruments at the Mint, to try out a new and exciting photographic process. In France, many advances in the processing of light into photographic images were made over the years. Louis Daguerre and Joseph Nicéphore Niépce, in particular, struck upon a particular method almost at the same time, though Daguerre retained claim to the name. By way of a fine, polished ribbon of silver, mercury, and iodine, a reverse image was produced. In September of 1839, the process was first described in American newspapers, including details about individual ingredients and the many steps necessary to create the daguerreotype, or heliograph.

Saxton was certainly one of many who read the September article, but unlike most others, he elected to try the process himself. Using a cigar box and a variety of improvised ingredients, Saxton constructed the ground-breaking new camera obscura. On the afternoon of October 16, he placed the device on the windowsill of his second-floor office and allowed the proper time for exposure. The result, permanently impressed on a silver plate, was a perfect view of the cupola of Central High School and the State Arsenal. The photograph, preserved today in the collections of the Historical Society of Pennsylvania, initiated a new era in modern America and remains one of the great treasures of Philadelphia.

1773: Philadelphia citizens hold a mass meeting in protest of the tea tax and the East India Company monopoly. The protests were later endorsed by Boston and are seen as a precursor to the Boston Tea Party.

October 17

Philadelphia is a city that loves its sports heroes. One of the most beloved is basketball's Julius "Dr. J" Erving. Erving was born in Roosevelt, New York, and spent his college career at the University of Massachusetts. At the time he was drafted in 1972 as a professional by the Milwaukee Bucks of the American Basketball Association, that fledgling league was in serious competition with the National Basketball Association for the attention of fans. With its free style of play and innovations such as the three-point shot, the ABA was a perfect home for the above-the-rim, spectacular-dunking Dr. J.

During his years on the New York Nets, Dr. J led the team to the 1974 and 1976 ABA championship and won the 1976 All-Star Game Dunk Championship. In the five years he spent in the ABA, Erving won two championships, three MVP awards, and three scoring titles. In 1976, the ABA and the NBA merged and the Nets sold his contract to the Philadelphia 76ers for $3 million just one day before the start of the 1977 season. Philadelphia fans embraced Erving immediately, and he delivered amazing basketball athleticism and grace, seeming to float in midair as he scored. He also became one of the first professional basketball players to endorse and sell basketball shoes.

On October 17, 1980, Philadelphia fans rejoiced when Erving signed an extension contract that would keep him on the team until the end of his career. Dr. J had made the 76ers a highly competitive team, but they frequently lost to the Los Angeles Lakers in the championships because they lacked a dominating center. In 1983, the 76ers added Moses Malone as the center and the team went on to win the NBA championship, the first of Erving's career with the team. In eleven seasons with Philadelphia, he averaged 22 points a game and scored more than 30,000 points. Following his retirement from basketball in 1987 at the age of thirty-seven, Dr. J. was inducted into the Basketball Hall of Fame in 1993. A successful businessman today, Philadelphia honors him with a mural at 1234 Ridge Avenue and with their memories of the dominant and most exciting player of his time.

1858: The Quaker City Barge Club is founded.

1953: The Reverend Dr. Benjamin Glasco is named the first African-American Moderator of the Philadelphia Presbytery, the largest in the Presbyterian Church in the United States.

1954: An eight-man Philadelphia syndicate purchases control of the Philadelphia Athletics, ending the 54-year-old dynasty of the Connie Mack baseball family.

1999: The Martin Luther King Plaza Homes at 13th and Fitzwater streets are imploded at 8:50 A.M. by Controlled Demolition and Bianchi-Trison corporations.

October 18

When Connie Mack announced his retirement at age eighty-eight on October 18, 1950, he had been in professional baseball for longer than anyone in history. Born in 1862 in Podunk, New York, Cornelius Alexander McGillicuddy played thirteen seasons as a catcher, but his notable contributions to baseball and Philadelphia were as the longtime manager and owner of the Philadelphia Athletics. Shortening his name to Connie Mack so that it would fit on scoreboards, he was offered the manager's job and partial ownership of the new American League franchise in 1901. He continued to manage the A's for the next fifty years, a record in Major League baseball.

Mr. Mack, as his players always called him, dressed in a business suit, hat, and tie for the games, reflecting his philosophy that baseball was a game, but also a business. He once said, "It is more profitable for me to have a team that is in contention for most of the season, but finishes about fourth. A team like that will draw well enough during the first part of the season to show a profit for the year, but you don't have to give the players big raises when they don't win."

His business sense led him to one of the most significant "fire sales" in baseball history during the Great Depression, when he traded most of his winning team rather than agree to the salaries they demanded. The "Tall Tactician" was elected to the Baseball Hall of Fame in 1937, some thirteen years before he retired as an active manager. In his career overall, he holds the record for the most games managed (7,887), most games won (3,776), and most losses (4,025). His teams won nine American League pennants, and five World Series titles: in 1910, 1911, 1913, 1929, and 1930. The Athletics played at Shibe Park for most of their history, and in 1953 it was renamed Connie Mack Stadium in his honor. A year later, the team was sold and moved to Kansas City. At his death in 1956, there was no other figure in baseball who commanded more respect and affection.

1850: Jenny Lind, "the Swedish Nightingale," managed by P. T. Barnum, sings on the first of two evenings at Musical Fund Hall, on Locust Street. The two concerts netted $19,000, a sum unprecedented for such entertainment.

1918: The week ending on this date records a death toll of 4,596 persons as the Spanish influenza pandemic continues.

1968: The Spectrum is officially dedicated. The stadium would be demolished in fall 2009.

October 19

A cornerstone of the fine arts institutions of the city, the Philadelphia Art Alliance was born out of a belief in the beauty of American theatrical and visual arts, and of the value of ensuring a place to explore and experience all that the city has to offer. Founded by heiress and actress Christine Wetherill Stevenson in 1915, the Art Alliance is among the oldest multidisciplinary arts centers in the United States and is committed to "presenting emerging and established artists from the visual, literary and performing arts." In addition to Stevenson, founding members include the finest regional artists, among them Leopold Stokowski, Violet Oakley, and Eva Stotesbury. Inspired by the New York Armory Show of 1913 and the impending threats against America from Europe, Stevenson hoped to reinforce the depth and strength of American artistry by providing a venue for its expression. On this date in 1917, the first official home of the Alliance opened to the public on Walnut Street.

Stevenson, daughter of millionaire paint manufacturer Samuel Wetherill, was no stranger to the arts. An actress and playwright in her own right, Stevenson helped found the Plays and Players Theater in 1911, as well as co-founding the Hollywood Bowl in Los Angeles. Following her visit to the Armory Show in 1913, Stevenson began to sponsor "salons" in her father's house on Rittenhouse Square. These continued for two years until two adjacent homes in the 1800 block of Walnut Street were purchased by the Art Alliance in 1917 and converted to artist studios and apartments. Stevenson died in 1922 at the age of forty-seven, and following the death of her father in 1926 his mansion on Rittenhouse Square was sold to the Art Alliance, where the Alliance remains today.

Among the many artists who have shown or performed at the Alliance, names like Wyeth, Klee, Cage, and Venturi suggest the diversity of opportunity. For many years, membership to the Alliance granted special dining opportunities as well, where guests sat among the exhibits and enjoyed fine food and good company. Today, the Wetherill Mansion hosts three to four exhibitions annually, as well as dozens of performances, lectures, workshops, and special events. Listed on the National Register of Historic Places, the Art Alliance stands as a jewel on Philadelphia's most cultured Square.

1836: The first interment is held at Laurel Hill Cemetery.

1968: First-year Philadelphia Flyers play their first home game in the newly dedicated Spectrum, where they shut out the Pittsburgh Penguins, 1–0.

Early in the twentieth century, public mural art was generally the domain of male artists. The large canvases or wall paintings, picturing historical events, were projects in their scope and content generally believed to be better executed by men. Violet Oakley's work in the Commonwealth's capitol changed that perception and in her long life she painted forty-three murals, including fourteen in the reception room of the capitol depicting the life of William Penn and his founding of the Pennsylvania colony.

Born in New Jersey, Oakley studied art in Philadelphia at the Drexel Institute. In 1902, she was chosen to paint the murals of William Penn at the capitol and was also given the commission to paint the evolution of the law in world history for the Supreme Court chambers. Her work was in the style of the day, depicting idealized heroes such as Washington and Lincoln, but her approach communicated her pacifist views. In her depiction of Lincoln at Gettysburg, for example, she focuses his gaze on a wounded soldier and a grieving family instead of on military or political figures.

In 1906, Oakley moved to the Mt. Airy neighborhood of Philadelphia, establishing a household called "Cogslea" for the three other women artists who lived with her in an artistic and economic collective. Later, she and her companion, Edith Emerson, the director of the Woodmere Art Museum, renovated the building complex's barn as a home and studio. Violet Oakley continued her work at this location until 1961, including a series of ten murals on the role of women in the Bible that she painted for the First Presbyterian Church of Germantown. Her work is part of the permanent collection of the Woodmere Art Museum, and she is viewed today as one of America's great muralists. In 1977, the Violet Oakley Studio was listed in the National Register of Historic Places, and on October 20, 1998, Pennsylvania dedicated a historical marker about Oakley at St. Georges Road and McCallum Street in Mt. Airy.

1840: Today is the first day of the first-ever electorate-selected Mayoral Administration. The previous year marked the city's first mayoral election, but the victor lacked the majority and was ultimately selected by City Council. Swift served a one-year term.

October 21

American jazz made a dramatic shift in the 1940s from "swing" to "bebop." John Birks "Dizzy" Gillespie was not only a principal architect of the bebop movement, he was also one of the greatest trumpeters of the twentieth century. Born in Cheraw, South Carolina, on October 21, 1917, Gillespie made Philadelphia his home at the age of 18. His father, James, was a bricklayer, pianist, and bandleader. When Dizzy was a child, his father kept all of the band instruments in the Gillespie home. By the age of thirteen, in 1930, Dizzy started playing the trumpet and was inspired by a recording of Roy Eldridge to become a jazz musician.

After the family moved to Philadelphia in 1935, Gillespie played with bands all over Philadelphia and picked up the nickname "Dizzy" because of his fun-loving antics. In 1937, he had the honor of replacing his idol Eldridge in Teddy Hill's Orchestra, and only two years later joined Cab Calloway's band. During the 1940s, Gillespie played with a number of bands, partnering with Charlie Parker in 1945. They developed the bebop style with Gillespie as composer and arranger of such classic songs as "Groovin' High," "A Night in Tunisia," and "Manteco."

In 1953, someone fell on his trumpet onstage and bent his instrument. Dizzy liked the sound, and after that lucky accident, he had his trumpets constructed that way. A great showman, Dizzy was the first jazz artist to tour abroad as a representative of the United States government. Later in his career, he incorporated Afro-Cuban, Caribbean, and Brazilian rhythms into his music. In 1989, Gillespie received a lifetime achievement award at the Grammy Award ceremonies and was presented with the National Medal of Arts by President George H. W. Bush. The next year, Dizzy received the American Society of Composers, Authors, and Publishers Duke Award for fifty years of music achievement. A member of the Philadelphia Music Alliance Hall of Fame, Dizzy Gillespie died at the age of seventy-five in 1993.

1838: Central High School opens.

1980: The Philadelphia Phillies win their first World Series against the Kansas City Royals.

October 22

In 1787, influenced by Quaker beliefs and principles, a group of Philadelphians set about to reform the prison system in the city. The idea was to build a penitentiary, an environment that would end corporal punishment and ill treatment and encourage contemplation and penitence among convicted criminals. On October 22, 1829, Eastern State Penitentiary, with a new prison design and operating principles, admitted its first prisoner. It was an experiment in prison reform that spread across much of the world and ultimately failed, but thousands of prisoners were incarcerated there over a period of 142 years.

Designed by John Haviland, the facility consisted of seven cell blocks radiating out from a central surveillance core. The interior of the prison was lit by skylights and featured private cells for each prisoner with running water and central heat. Gothic in design on the outside, the building resembled a church, with vaulted hallways and tall arched windows. Prisoners were not allowed outside contacts, with the Bible as their only reading material. Conversation was prohibited and each prisoner was engaged in some form of work. International visitors disagreed about the prison's approach. Alexis de Tocqueville in 1831 wrote, "Can there be a combination more powerful for reformation than that of a prison which hands over the prisoner to all trials of solitude," but Charles Dickens was appalled on his 1842 visit, writing that "I hold this slow and daily tampering with the mysteries of the brain to be immeasurably worse than any torture of the body." The total isolation of prisoners was relaxed over time and the prison continued to expand, finally adding a death row in 1956.

Infamous prisoners such as Al Capone and bank robber Willie Sutton, who successfully engineered an escape in 1945, were incarcerated at Eastern State Penitentiary. By the 1960s the facility needed significant modern repair but instead was closed, in 1971. After remaining vacant for many years, the Pennsylvania Prison Society opened the facility for tours in 1994, and it has been preserved and has grown as a popular tourist destination. The prison is said to be haunted, and the frightening Halloween tours attract many visitors and raise funds for the continued maintenance of this architectural treasure and part of Philadelphia history.

1829: Eastern State Penitentiary is opened for prisoners.

1917: Leopold Stokowski leads the Philadelphia Orchestra in their first recording for the Victor Talking Machine Company.

1980: After winning the Pennant on October 21, the Philadelphia Phillies host a victory parade down Broad Street to JFK Stadium.

October 23

As the fiftieth anniversary of the Declaration of Independence approached, more Philadelphians than ever enjoyed the benefits of a strong economy and a diversity of booming industry and national identity. However, a continuing mark of social status and wealth was the consumption of certain European goods that reflected a sense of taste and quality unmatched outside France and England. On this date in 1827, a Philadelphia manufacturer broke through the taste barrier, creating the nation's first commercial porcelain and china and succeeding at providing products of the highest quality, enough to firmly establish American porcelain in the hearts and homes of its citizens.

William Ellis Tucker, the son of a merchant of fine china, grew up fully aware of the attraction and popularity of European porcelain. In the early 1820s, many Americans were interested in finding ways to assert their superiority over England and other European nations. When he opened his factory at 23rd and Chestnut streets, he believed he could refine the porcelain process using raw materials, feldspar and kaolin, from local mines in Delaware. In a desire to appeal to his customers used to foreign taste, initially he drew from European designs in the creation of pitchers, urns, and coffee and tea sets. Within a few years, however, he looked to distinctly American and Philadelphia motifs to decorate his pieces. His younger brother, Thomas, began as an apprentice to the business but quickly assumed the position of primary design manager. Under his guidance, the company produced beautifully hand-painted items with scenes of local landscapes and flowers, all of which sold well.

In 1827, Tucker won recognition from the Franklin Institute for the quality of his porcelain. Unfortunately, his success did not translate well to the economic side, where the company suffered from unstable finances. In 1832, Tucker recruited several partners to the business, but had not yet seen the fruits of his labor when he died unexpectedly that same year. Younger brother Thomas attempted to continue with the business, but larger economic and political forces in the form of tariff-free imported goods and a sagging economy forced the company to close in 1838. Today, Tucker porcelain is highly prized by collectors, a single piece selling for nearly $300,000 in a recent auction. Largely forgotten by all but the most interested collectors, Tucker nevertheless stands as a symbol of American quality and success at a time when being the best meant everything.

1696: Philadelphia Quakers rule that Friends should "be Careful not to Encourage the bringing in of any more Negroes, & that such that have Negroes be Careful of them, bring them to Meetings, or have Meetings with them in their Families, & Restrain them from Loose, & Lewd Living." This is probably the first institutional attempt to limit slave trading in America.

1920: Police Commissioner and Mayor Frank Rizzo is born.

October 24

The first food and goods markets in Philadelphia were located on High (later Market) Street, but as the city grew citizens wanted more convenient access to markets in the Cedar (later South) Street area. Early in the eighteenth century, stalls and markets were established around Second and South streets in an area known as New Market. As early as 1745, wooden sheds or "shambles" to offer produce, meat, salted fish, and other goods were built. Wooden open-air structures with roofs, the shambles enabled farmers to enter with their wagons and sell their goods directly to customers. Dolley Madison, Martha Washington, Stephen Girard, and other notable Philadelphians frequented the market, which offered tobacco, wines, and imported goods of all kinds in addition to food products. Philadelphia was dependent on the ships that brought imported products like molasses, limes, oranges, coffee, and brandy.

In 1804, a Head House for the market, designed by architect John Haviland, was completed at Second and Pine streets. Immediately adjoining the shambles, it was built to house a very necessary fire company. Most of the shambles and the New Market were demolished in the 1950s, but due to the efforts of a group of citizens, the Head House was spared as a prime example of late colonial architecture. On October 24, 1959, the restoration of the deteriorated Head House was announced. Mayor Richardson Dilworth inaugurated the renovation, which included a new roof, a new cupola, and the relocation of several doors and windows.

The renovation served as a keystone to the larger 1960s redevelopment of the area, which became known as Society Hill and is today one of the more exclusive yet lively neighborhoods in the city. If Dolley Madison were to visit Head House Square today, she would find that it is again being used as a market. Sponsored by the Food Trust, the market hosts local farmers, who offer fresh vegetables, fruits, and other products from stalls in the shambles and Head House to Philadelphians seeking a source of locally grown food.

1682: William Penn lands at New Castle, Delaware.

1799: Zeigler's Plains in Spring Garden is inaugurated by scene of "a grand Jubilee" in honor of the election of Judge McKean as Governor of Pennsylvania.

1896: August Schrader, known to many as the "Divine Healer," arrives in Philadelphia charged with the special mission of curing the bodily afflicted.

1931: Leopold Stokowski, conducting the Philadelphia Orchestra in a program of ultra-modern music, walks out on his audience in the Academy of Music when he is disturbed by a sudden sneeze.

October 25

In the wake of the Stamp Act, the impact of British trade policies on the colonies was felt by more Americans than ever. Indeed, the eventual repeal of the Stamp Act in 1766 did not occur soon enough for independence-minded businessmen and dealers in British goods in Philadelphia. On this date in 1765, a number of significant traders and importers in Philadelphia signed a non-importation agreement declaring their intention to boycott British goods and support an American economy and manufacture. Their efforts, however, proved less than successful as the pressure of reduced income and the prospect of an extended boycott threatened the financial security of the city's most powerful businessmen.

Indeed, Philadelphia was not the only city to utilize an organized protest against British taxes. In New York and Boston, similar agreementswere drafted. In Boston, the cry among the Sons of Liberty to "save your money and country" attempted to appeal to a newly aroused sense of unity among the colonies against a common enemy: the British Parliament. Merchants increasingly challenged British Chancellor of the Exchequer Charles Townshend and his post–Stamp Act taxes known as the Townshend Acts. New, expanded taxes on glass, paper, lead, paint, and tea imported from Britain struck more directly than those of the Stamp Act, which primarily affected items on paper. In response, patriots in Philadelphia and Boston urged colonists to block English trade. Homespun goods and the handful of American-manufactured goods were proffered as alternatives, with limited success.

The reality, however, was much more difficult to reconcile. American merchants dependent on British trade felt the boycott deeply as the colonies suffered an economic depression. Slowly, the number of boycott supporters dwindled and British goods reappeared in Philadelphia shops. Most non-importation agreements were set to expire on January 1, 1770, and as a result both sides increased pressure on citizens to choose. With the repeal of the Townshend Acts in 1770, the non-importation movement appeared to die. However, within a few years the remaining tax on tea and the application of the so-called Intolerable Acts inspired resistance once again. Practiced by way of the 1765 agreement, Philadelphia and its colonial neighbors were prepared for the fight ahead.

1701: William Penn grants a Charter of Privileges to Philadelphia.

1829: The first prisoner is admitted to Eastern State Penitentiary.

October 26

Gunsmithing was a skilled trade in Pennsylvania from very early in its history. A number of innovations in the design and construction of guns were accomplished in the Commonwealth, but perhaps none more famous than the deringer. Henry Deringer, Sr., emigrated from Germany just before the Revolution, establishing himself in the gunsmith business in Easton and producing versions of Kentucky rifles and pistols with flintlock action. His son, Henry Deringer, Jr., was born on October 26, 1786, and apprenticed to his father in the trade.

In 1806, the family moved to Philadelphia where they established a factory that manufactured flintlock pistols and muskets, later adding percussion rifles for the U.S. Army. The business and the family's home were located on what is now Fairmount Avenue in the Liberties neighborhood. The Deringer "pocket" pistol had a capacity of just one shot, leading many owners to carry two matching guns. The gun was popular as a carrying weapon for civilians because it was lightweight and could be concealed. One of its drawbacks was that each pair of guns came with a unique mold to produce ammunition only for those particular pistols. The large-caliber ammunition was never standard for the models of the gun. For this reason, the gun was generally not purchased for military use. A typical Deringer pistol had a black walnut stock with mountings engraved with German silver and some had gold-plated mountings.

In 1865, John Wilkes Booth used his one-shot Deringer to assassinate President Abraham Lincoln at Ford's Theatre. Booth dropped the gun during his leap to the stage, and today it is on display in the museum of the theater. Deringer was the victim of numerous instances of trademark infringement and spent a great deal of time taking legal action against those who used the Deringer name. Some of the forgeries were stamped "Derringer," especially those made by Slotter and Company, a firm established by former workmen at the Deringer plant. Production of the Deringer ceased in 1870, but the term "Derringer" was used as a generic description for small hand guns, most famously the Remington derringer, and remains in use today. Henry Deringer died in 1868 and is buried at Laurel Hill Cemetery.

1774: The First Continental Congress convenes in Philadelphia.

1879: Angelina Grimke, abolitionist, dies.

1990: William Samuel Paley, the Philadelphia-based businessman who created the Colombia Broadcasting System (CBS) from a group of sixteen struggling local radio stations, dies.

October 27

On February 15, 1898, the American battleship USS *Maine* exploded and sank in waters near Cuba, signaling the start of the Spanish-American War. Patriotic fervor, signified by the call to "Remember the Maine," inspired this brief war, which earned Teddy Roosevelt fame with the Rough Riders and ended with America being awarded control of Spanish colonies in the Philippines, Guam, and Puerto Rico. To celebrate the victory and the return of the troops, a grand "Peace Jubilee" in Philadelphia took place over four days in October 1898.

Decorative elements, including a huge illuminated arch built to span Broad Street, and lamps on City Hall spelling out "the Star-Spangled Banner in Triumph Doth Wave," added to the festive and patriotic tone of the event. On October 27, President William McKinley and Vice President Garret Hobart and their wives, cabinet members, a host of generals, and other dignitaries reviewed a long parade of troops. More than 25,000 troops marched, including four Pennsylvania regiments and a contingent of Rough Riders. The Navy was not ignored, with a naval parade of ships on the Delaware overseen by the Secretary of the Navy, John Long. Warships, some built in the city, were led by the USS *Columbia.* The ships sailed up and down the river accompanied by firing salutes and the "Stars and Stripes Forever" played by the Marine band on the USS *New Orleans.*

Thousands of people visited the city for the jubilee, many taking advantage of the Pennsylvania Railroad offer of a round trip for the price of a single fare. Over the four days of the jubilee, speeches, more parades, and church services culminated in a rededication of Independence Hall, which had been historically renovated through the efforts of the Daughters of the American Revolution and others. Although most Philadelphians praised and enjoyed the jubilee, some anti-war groups opposed its focus on military power. While the formal peace treaty with Spain was not signed until December 1898, President McKinley also attended jubilees in Atlanta and Chicago in November and December of that year, none so glorious as the Philadelphia celebration.

1919: Albert I, King of the Belgians, together with Queen Elizabeth and Prince Leopold, visits Philadelphia.

1929: Black Friday—the day the Great Depression begins. In Philadelphia, a record number of shares—423,019—are sold on the Philadelphia Stock Exchange.

October 28

From the moment William Penn set foot on the land granted to him by King Charles II, he was prepared to put into place a frame of government. Penn arrived in 1682 with the knowledge that indigenous peoples, Swedes, and Englishmen were already living on the land, each under their own laws. Before he even left England, Penn drafted what was the first of his plans for organizing the laws and provisions of his new colony. It would take three additional efforts and almost a decade before the fourth and final plan, known as the Charter of Privileges, was formally signed and enacted by William Penn on this date in 1701.

As a Quaker, Penn knew well the discrimination and intolerance faced by thousands of people from various religions in Anglican England. As a result, central to all four of the Frames of Government was the guarantee of freedom of religion. However, Penn was also aware of the need to balance the rights of individuals with the control and management of a government leadership. In addition to protection of personal civil rights, Penn recommended the establishment of a 72-member Council, a 500-member General Assembly, and a governor with veto power. His plan was rejected by the legislature because it allowed too much power for the governor. A second plan proposed by Penn reduced the governor's role and was accepted in 1683. Just three years later, Deputy Governor William Markham proposed a plan that further strengthened legislative powers to include crafting legislation, which was quickly accepted without debate, as Penn himself was back in England and could not dispute the changes.

In 1699, Penn returned to Pennsylvania with the hope of reestablishing the plan of 1683. However, he once again met with resistance, due primarily to the tremendous population growth and subsequent shift in diversity of opinion of desire for leadership among fractious groups. As in the earlier versions, fundamental rights and privileges were protected under the new plan, in particular religious liberty and freedom of conscience. The Council was stripped of its lawmaking abilities, which were returned to the Assembly, firmly establishing a unicameral legislature. Finally, the three lower counties were established as the colony of Delaware. Remarkably, the Charter of Privileges remained the defining plan of government for Pennsylvania until the American Revolution, serving as one of the most liberal, longest running, and strongest of colonial constitutions in American history.

1776: The first state constitution is adopted, establishing a Supreme Executive Council instead of a governor and one assembly.

One of the most controversial Union generals of the Civil War, George Brinton McClellan was born in Philadelphia in 1826. The son of Dr. George McClellan, a surgical ophthalmologist and founder of Jefferson Medical College, he enrolled in the University of Pennsylvania at age thirteen and was admitted to West Point two years later. Following a successful career at West Point, McClellan served with distinction in Mexico and spent several years studying military operations in Europe. After a few years working for the railroads, he returned to army service, eventually rising to commander of the Army of the Potomac, where he made significant contributions to the Union cause while also drawing criticisms.

After the defeat at Bull Run, McClellan actively sought the appointment from President Lincoln as commander. His organizational and preparation skills were seen as key to Union success. But his strength was also his weakness. Time and time again, he engaged the enemy but did not pursue them when he could have achieved a victory. McClellan consistently overestimated the size of the Rebel armies opposing him, and cautiously withheld reserves rather than advancing toward victory. In this way, McClellan let Joseph Johnston's army withdraw at the Second Battle of Manassas and failed to defeat Robert E. Lee at Antietam. Known as "Little Mac" to the Union troops, his caution was believed by some to be owing to concern about casualties in a war that claimed thousands of deaths in every major battle. McClellan's relationship with Lincoln deteriorated, with McClellan's demands for more men, equipment, and horses substituting for action on the field. Lincoln relieved McClellan of his command in November 1862, and McClellan returned to his home in New Jersey to wait for new orders that never arrived.

In 1864, McClellan opposed Lincoln as the Democratic Party presidential nominee. The Democratic platform called for negotiation with the Confederacy, but McClellan rejected that approach, calling instead for a military victory. He won only three states as support for Lincoln remained strong. Later in life McClellan served as governor of New Jersey and published a book defending his actions during the war. McClellan died on this date in 1885. He is honored in the city of his birth by McClellan Street in South Philadelphia and by a prominent statue of himself on horseback, which stands at the northern entrance to City Hall.

1682: William Penn arrives at Chester on the *Welcome*.

At the start of the twentieth century, northeast Philadelphia along Route 1 was the location of one of the world's largest reinforced concrete commercial buildings, the Sears, Roebuck & Company warehouse and catalog shipping facility. Sears had built its business on mail orders since 1888, and the new building, designed by George C. Nimmons & Company of Chicago and completed in 1920, was to serve not only as a retail outlet but for shipping Sears goods from Mainc to Virginia. The five-million-square-foot complex on 120 acres at Adams Street and Route 1 included a retail store, numerous warehouses, a power station, and regional offices for the company. Goods were transported by trains running past the warehouses. Constructed in a Gothic style with a red-brick exterior, the building featured a 14-story clock tower. In the 1960s, the company built a subway station beneath the complex, but the city never completed the line.

At its peak, the complex employed 4,500 people, many of whom lived in the post–World War II housing developments in northeast Philadelphia. As the mail order business declined, operations were slowly curtailed, and with the end of the general distribution of catalogs in 1993, the complex closed. The Rubin Organization purchased the main building and 48 acres in that year and planned to demolish the structure to build a new 455,000-square-foot shopping center with 2,300 parking spaces.

Despite last-minute attempts to save the tower, the building was demolished on October 30, 1994. Over a period of three months, more than 300 employees of the Mercer Wrecking Recycling Corporation of Trenton, New Jersey, drilled 15,000 holes, laid 25 miles of wire and planted 12,000 pounds of dynamite for the implosion. Tens of thousands of spectators gathered to witness the event, which was the largest implosion in city, and perhaps, world history. In only 7.5 seconds, the building was reduced to a pile of rubble estimated at 25 million cubic yards, and a significant part of life in northeast Philadelphia came to a definitive end.

1872: The cornerstone is laid for the new Academy of Natural Sciences museum at 19th and Race streets.

October 31

The founding of a new colony required men of a variety of talents, including administration. When William Penn sailed to the new world in 1699, he brought James Logan with him as his assistant. Logan was a Quaker schoolmaster in Bristol, England, who had also been involved in the shipping trade. When Penn returned to England in 1701, Logan remained in Pennsylvania, where he held many offices during his lifetime and amassed a fortune investing in land and trading with Native Americans in the fur business.

By 1704, Logan became a member of the Council of the proprietorship and stayed in that post for forty-three years. A leader of the proprietary party, he favored aristocratic interests and served as an agent for the Penn family. In 1722, he was elected Mayor of Philadelphia, notably allowing Catholic immigrants to hold the city's first public mass. From 1731 to 1739, he served as the Chief Justice of the colony and was selected to serve as Acting Governor from 1736 to 1738, during which he oversaw the Walking Purchase Treaty, which tricked the Lenape into turning over 1,200 square miles of Pennsylvania land. In addition to his political activities, he was a natural scientist who published a work on the propagation of seed corn and tutored the plant scientist John Bartram in Latin. A scholarly man, he also translated Cato's poetry, which was published and printed by Benjamin Franklin. Franklin declared it "a happy omen that Philadelphia shall become the seat of the American muse."

Logan's home, Stenton, was built in 1730 on five hundred acres in northwest Philadelphia. One of the best examples of Georgian architecture in the city, the house features Flemish bond work and the symmetrical design typical of expensive homes of the period. The house has paneling throughout and was furnished by Logan with pieces imported from England and made by skilled Philadelphia craftsmen. The library of the house held Logan's huge 3,000-volume library of literature and scientific books. At his death on October 31, 1751, he left his library to the city, where it is now part of the collection of the Library Company of Philadelphia. Stenton remained in the Logan family until the twentieth century and is now a historic museum open to the public.

1791: The *National Gazette* newspaper is established.

1929: The Philadelphia Electric Company is incorporated.

1989: Mob boss "Little Nicky" Scarfo is shot eight times in a Philadelphia restaurant and survives.

October

In late 1835, Philadelphia librarian and businessman John Jay Smith noted in his diary the state of Philadelphia's burying grounds, in particular the graveyard at the Cherry Street Friends Meetinghouse, where his daughter was interred a number of years before. The overcrowding of the city, paired with unstable ground, resulted in his inability to locate his daughter's grave. From that point, Smith determined to establish a neat, orderly, and suitably rural location for the citizens of Philadelphia to place their loved ones. He ultimately established Laurel Hill Cemetery, the second-oldest rural cemetery in the country, along the banks of the Schuylkill River in 1836. On October 19, 1836, Laurel Hill held the first interment, for Mercy Carlisle, a local Quaker woman.

Smith, an amateur horticulturalist, was interested in creating a serene, beautiful landscape in which both the living and the deceased could enjoy a pastoral place unlike the burgeoning city to the east. By the mid-1800s, Laurel Hill welcomed tens of thousands of visitors each year, many coming to remember lost loved ones in addition to partaking of the beautiful vistas and tranquil parkland. In hopes of attracting only the finest of clientele, Laurel Hill Cemetery published a number of guidebooks, specifically highlighting famous people or particularly notable views. In the 1844 *Guide to Laurel Hill Cemetery,* the purpose and value of the cemetery is outlined in the following way, seemingly predicting the growth of the city and the current meaning of Laurel Hill as an oasis in the midst of everyday life:

> Would it not be desirable, when interments in populated districts shall be prohibited by law, which most assuredly will be the case in the course of a few years, to convert the burial-grounds within these limits into open squares, similar to those already possessed by the public? We need more of these enchanting places of resort; they are demanded like by a due consideration for the health as well as the pleasure of all classes of our citizens. Why then lose what space we have? Besides, this plan would not only embellish the city, but would prevent the horrid and barbarous practice of disturbing the remains of those already interred for the sake of a few dollars. Who ever read of the Grecians, the Romans, the Egyptians, the Persians, the Assyrians, or the Hebrews, those civilized people of by-gone ages, desecrating the graves of their ancestors to make room for city improvements? Even the people of the so-called barbarous nations have ever cherished the tombs of their forefathers with the deepest veneration, and a violation of the grave among them deemed a most sacrilegious act, punishable alike by the gods and men. Alas! this abominable practice is only characteristic of enlightened Christians of the nineteenth century.
>
> If it is a curious inquiry for the antiquarian to trace the migration of nations by their graves, it is equally interesting to note the progress and growth of cities by their graveyards. When the cemeteries just mentioned were first established, they were "far out of town;" now, with few exceptions, they are, for the most part, in the midst of densely populated districts. Perhaps the chronicler of 1952, as he scans these pages, will note "the cities of the dead," which we place at present at a distance from the city, as being in the midst of the "living tide," and the solitude of Laurel Hill and the Woodlands be no more.

November

Descended from a family of accomplished freedmen, educator and scholar Sadie Tanner Mossell Alexander was born into a distinguished African-American family in Philadelphia in 1898. Her father, Aaron Albert Mossell II, was the first African-American graduate of the University of Pennsylvania law school. Educated in Washington, D.C., as a child, Alexander followed in her father's footsteps and returned to Philadelphia, where she graduated from the University of Pennsylvania's school of education and began her graduate education at the university in economics in 1918. In 1921, she became the first African-American woman in the country to earn a doctorate, completing her dissertation on standards of living among African-American immigrants in Philadelphia. Throughout her life, she continued to lead the way, pioneering in both education and civil rights.

Unable to find work in her field, she joined an African-American insurance company in North Carolina. After marrying Raymond Alexander, a Philadelphia lawyer, she returned once again to the city to enroll in the University of Pennsylvania School of Law. After becoming the first woman to pass the bar exam, she specialized in family and estate law and soon after became the first woman to practice law in the Commonwealth. By 1930, she was an active leader in the National Urban League. Her law firm worked diligently to desegregate movie theaters, hotels, and other public services in the city. In 1948, President Harry S. Truman appointed her to his Committee on Civil Rights, whose charge was to prepare a report on the state of civil rights and suggest solutions. She believed that the gap between American ideals and the reality of the treatment of African-Americans was threatening American democracy.

After her husband became a judge in 1959, she opened her own firm and practiced law in Philadelphia until 1974. She focused on family law and continued her commitment to equality, working for many years with the national committee of the American Civil Liberties Union (the ACLU) and the Philadelphia Bar Association. For five years she served as the chair of the Commission for Human Relations in the city. In 1978, President Jimmy Carter appointed her as chair of the White House Conference on Aging. Sadie Alexander died on November 1, 1989, at her home in Philadelphia, leaving a legacy of achievement to her community and her two daughters.

1701: William Penn is believed to have left Philadelphia for the last time.

November 2

The Centennial Exposition of 1876 was designed to be a celebration of the country and proof of the progress of the nation since the Civil War. A group of African-Americans from Arkansas, led by Bishop John Miflin Brown, decided in 1873 to organize something that would testify to the presence of African-Americans at the Centennial and their role in the history of the nation. The product of their efforts has a story as remarkable as the man it commemorated.

Brown and his associates commissioned a monument to be placed in Fairmount Park in memory of Bishop Richard Allen, who was the founder and first bishop of the African Methodist Episcopal Church and a leading figure in Philadelphia history. Designed by Cincinnati monument maker Alfred White, the monument was 22 feet tall and consisted of 4 Roman-style pillars topped by a roof. It was crowned by a 3-foot bust of Richard Allen sculptured from Italian marble. As the monument was being transported by train from Cincinnati to Philadelphia, a train wreck destroyed the base of the monument, but the bust of Richard Allen was in another car and was undamaged. After regrouping to procure another base, the group dedicated the monument in Fairmount Park on November 2, 1876, just eight days before the end of the Centennial Exposition.

Not approved to become a permanent fixture of the park, the bust was taken for safekeeping to Wilberforce University, founded by the A.M.E. in Ohio. The bust survived a tornado in the 1970s and was placed on the reference desk in the college library. Largely forgotten, the bust's significance was recently discovered and it was brought back to Philadelphia. Fully restored in 2010, the bust will remain on display at Mother Bethel A.M.E. Church for a least a year in celebration of the 250th anniversary of Richard Allen's birth. It will then return to Wilberforce University where it will undoubtedly stand as a new legacy of the life and work of Richard Allen.

1895: Infamous serial killer Herman W. Mudgett, also known as H. H. Holmes, is convicted of murder in the first degree for killing Benjamin F. Pietzel in Philadelphia on September 2, 1894.

1915: Pennsylvania defeats a suffrage amendment by 62,000 votes, of which the majority is from Philadelphia.

1965: In an upset victory over the Democratic machine, Arlen Specter, the Republican nominee, defeats the Democratic incumbent, James C. Crumlish, Jr., for District Attorney.

November 3

When one thinks of Washington, D.C., and the monumental structures that welcome government representatives, foreign dignitaries, and hundreds of thousands of tourists each year, it is not likely that one will think of John McShain, the Philadelphia-born son of an Irish immigrant. McShain's father owned a local construction company, and upon his death, John was left with little choice but to assume control of the family business. Over the next forty years, McShain carved out a unique niche for his particular talents, earning the nickname "the Man Who Built Washington."

McShain was just twenty-one years of age when his father died in 1919. For the decade leading up to the Great Depression, McShain struggled to establish the company, focusing primarily on business and religious projects. A devout Catholic, McShain married Mary Horstmann in 1927, herself the daughter of a well-established Catholic family of merchants. When economic disaster struck the nation, McShain was prepared and sought out the area of construction most likely to show growth: government contracts. Beginning with an annex to the Library of Congress in 1934, McShain's company went on to become one of the largest construction contractors in the nation.

In 1939, McShain was invited by President Franklin D. Roosevelt to build the Roosevelt Presidential Library in Hyde Park, New York. Despite McShain's Republican loyalties, he continued to win government projects, including an extension to the Pentagon, the Jefferson Memorial, National Airport, Philadelphia International Airport, and the Bethesda Naval Hospital. On this date in 1949, it was announced that McShain would oversee one of the most significant renovation projects in American history, that of upgrading and reconstructing the White House. The $4.25 million contract took four years to complete, during which time President Harry S. Truman and his family lived at the nearby Blair House. Interests in horse racing and returning to his father's birthplace led to McShain's eventually retiring in County Kerry, Ireland, where he died in 1989 at the age of ninety.

1929: In an attempt to curtail rampant voter fraud, Philadelphia voters support a $2 million bond issue to install voting machines in the city for the first time.

1973: Former heavyweight boxing champion Joe Frazier announces the establishment of a new clinic to treat sickle cell anemia and other blood diseases affecting African-Americans.

 November 4 

After independence was declared, itself a treasonous act as defined by the king of England, Pennsylvania and the other states passed laws to deal with traitors to the new government. In Pennsylvania, legislation was passed in February 1777 defining treason and adopting as punishment the death penalty and forfeiture to the Commonwealth of all property owned by a convicted traitor. Treasonable acts included accepting a commission from the enemy, joining the enemy army or encouraging others to join, and providing the enemy aid and comfort. The occupation of Philadelphia by the British from September 1777 to mid-June 1778 and their departure provided an opportunity to test the law and led to the conviction and hanging of John Roberts, a prominent Quaker.

John Roberts was a very successful Quaker businessman in Merion, outside the city. He fled Merion during the British occupation and lived in Philadelphia, where he sold provisions to the British, guided raids for food in the countryside, and attempted to raise a cavalry troop of other loyalists. After the British left in 1778, Roberts and at least twenty others were ordered to surrender to the authorities. At his trial, he was defended by James Wilson, a signer of the Declaration and a highly respected lawyer. Roberts' defense was based largely on his assertion that he had been "under the influence of fear when he took the impudent step of leaving his family and joining the enemy." Though his attempts to recruit troops had largely been unsuccessful, Roberts was convicted, with some evidence to suggest that the jury believed that the sentence would be lenient.

The chief justice of Pennsylvania, Thomas McKean, pursued treason cases partly because he wanted to establish the rule of law. By sentencing Roberts to death, he made an example of a prominent man. Some historians believe McKean thought the sentence would be overturned or commuted. Appeals to the State Executive Council failed, despite the submission of petitions for leniency from Quakers and others, and on November 4, 1778, John Roberts and Abraham Carlisle, another prosperous defendant, were hanged.

When signing the Declaration of Independence, Benjamin Franklin famously advised, "We must, indeed, all hang together, or most assuredly we shall all hang separately." The other fifty-six men who united to sign the declaration understood the risk. Although none of them were hanged, not one escaped unscathed, many of them losing their fortunes, their property, and their families during the Revolution, and all of them targets of the British military.

1776: The 56th and final member of the Continental Congress, Matthew Thornton of New Hampshire, signs the Declaration of Independence while in Philadelphia.

1953: The management of the Frank Seder Department Store, a twelve-story establishment in the center of the Philadelphia shopping district, announces it is going out of business.

November 5

At a time when the automobile was growing in significance across the country, Philadelphia and its manufacturers stepped in to meet the demand for parts and components of the industry. In 1912, Edward Gowen Budd resigned his position with Hale & Kilburn, a local manufacturer of rail-car parts, to begin his own company. At heart a steel and metal parts fabricator, the Budd Company proved to be innovative enough to regularly meet the changing demands of transportation technology. What would later become the Budd Manufacturing Company established a diversified and highly successful manufacturing business in Northeast Philadelphia, with two plants and at its height more than 20,000 employees.

The first Budd plant opened at Tioga and Aramingo avenues in 1912, but moved to I and Ontario streets within a year. Budd specialized in the first all-steel touring automobile bodies, producing them in the plant and shipping them by rail to Michigan. In 1921, the company produced its one millionth automobile body and in 1924 expanded to Europe. During the Great Depression, Budd pursued alternative products and manufacturing processes, including improvements in welding technology that led to a shift toward the production of rail cars. During World War II, Budd contributed to the region's war effort by producing ammunition. After the war, the company returned to rail car production and continued to expand and diversify, adding defense and testing technologies to its roster.

In 1963, Budd received a number of large contracts, most notably for 660 subway cars. Within a few years, Budd was also selected to provide new rail cars for the Pennsylvania Railroad, precursors to the Metroliners on Amtrak. Other innovations were unveiled in the 1960s, including automobile disc brakes, a storm radar detector processor for the Air Force, and a mobile airplane disembarking lounge known as the "plane-mate" unveiled on this date in 1969. In 1972, the company headquarters left Philadelphia after sixty years for Troy, Michigan, where it continues to provide innovative rail and transportation products.

1935: Two years after authorizing Sunday baseball and football games, Philadelphia makes another successful attack upon the Pennsylvania "Blue Law" of 1794 by voting to permit the exhibition of movies after 2:00 P.M. every Sunday.

2004: A historical marker honoring tennis and basketball great Ora Washington is dedicated in Germantown.

November 6

William Penn and the Religious Society of Friends (Quakers) brought a tradition of nonviolence to Philadelphia. Their beliefs were tested during the Revolution and in the Civil War era in particular, because of their strong support of abolitionism. In 1917, the American Friends Service Committee was founded in Philadelphia with a mission to provide conscientious objectors with alternatives to military service that could be conducted in war zones and to assist civilian war victims. Operating from its offices at 15th and Cherry streets, the AFSC has expanded its work through the decades and has sent volunteers around the world. On November 6, 1999, a historical marker was dedicated noting the work of this significant but sometimes controversial group.

During the First World War, Quakers collected relief supplies to be shipped to France by the AFSC, and following the war AFSC worked with orphans and helped with reconstruction efforts. Preceding World War II, the AFSC worked to rescue refugees from Nazi Germany, and after the war ended, AFSC sent relief workers to Europe, Japan, India, and China. As during the Civil War, many Quakers chose to serve in the armed forces, while others sought alternative service. In 1947, the AFSC was awarded the Nobel Peace Prize along with the British Friends Service Council, in recognition of the work of Quakers around the world. As the cold war and the threat from nuclear arms escalated, AFSC members worked to stop the production of nuclear weapons and promote disarmament.

In 1966 during the Vietnam War, AFSC programs assisted children in South and North Vietnam. Medical supplies and artificial limbs for injured civilians were also provided. The materials for North Vietnam were sent through Canada, because the AFSC was unable to get State Department approval to send medical supplies to Communist-run North Vietnam, where they would likely be redirected to Communist troops. The work on behalf of North Vietnamese citizens was very controversial in Philadelphia, a city that had 80,000 Vietnam vets and 646 deaths in the conflict. Thomas Edison School lost 54 alumni, the single largest number of casualties of any American school. Although no longer dominated by Quakers, the AFSC continues its work today, reaching out across the globe to aid those in need.

1892: The statue of William Penn is placed in the courtyard at City Hall in preparation for placing it atop the tower.

1893: The Liberty Bell is welcomed home from the World's Columbian Exposition in Chicago.

November 7 

In the midst of the rapid growth of industry in Philadelphia during the 1880s and 1890s, an equally compelling demand for labor provided new opportunities for both advancement and exploitation. Immigrants, children, and women were particularly at risk for the devastating effects of poor labor management, poor working conditions, and bias. A further desire to attain suffrage for women led to the establishment of women's guilds, leagues, and organizations devoted to serving the female residents of most leading cities. In Philadelphia, in 1877, a particular niche was filled with the organization of the New Century Guild, which was established on the central agenda of providing an "organized center of thought and action among women, for the protection of their interests."

Led by Eliza Sproat Turner and Charlotte L. Pierce, the Guild intended to provide women with a place to learn the new skills necessary to be successful modern women. Additionally, the guild hoped to support women seeking to enter the new workforce by providing vocational training in evening classes. Programs included night classes in literature, French, music, and history to enlighten the minds of members. More practical vocational training was offered through courses in bookkeeping, dressmaking, millinery, and home nursing, among others. The demand for classes soon outstretched the guild's capacity to the point where a new home was purchased on Girard Avenue in the early 1890s. As word of the high quality of skills and general abilities of New Century Guild graduates spread throughout many local businesses, the young women were in high demand. Facing the economic depression of 1893, the guild began to provide more services, including meals, temporary lodging, and emergency financial support.

At heart an organization committed to the advancement of women, it was not uncommon for the suffrage movement to be reflected in guild activities. On this date in 1903, the guild sponsored a special banquet in honor of Susan B. Anthony, pioneering activist and suffragist. Civic engagement was further reinforced through a current events group and the publication of a newspaper and works about the role of women in society. In the years following the successful passage of the Nineteenth Amendment granting women the right to vote, the guild turned its attention once again to working women, providing support and opportunity for women of all ages. In the twenty-first century, at a time when more women than men are graduating from college, the guild continues to foster self-sufficiency and community among women at their headquarters, located at 1307 Locust Street.

1932: The USS *Indianapolis* is launched from New York Shipbuilding in Camden, New Jersey.

1933: Philadelphians vote overwhelmingly to permit the playing of sports games on Sunday, countering a 1794 "Blue Law" designed to protect the Sabbath.

Local elections in Philadelphia are rarely enacted without a great deal of passion and just a taste of notoriety, especially when they involve issues of race. The mayoral primary election of 1982 was no different, as incumbent Democratic mayor William Green chose not to run again and opened the field to the polarized camps of former mayor Frank Rizzo and City Managing Director W. Wilson Goode. A highly controversial but popular figure with a long history in the city, Rizzo was nevertheless defeated by Goode, who benefited significantly from the black voters in Philadelphia. After a hard-fought campaign, Goode defeated Philadelphia Stock Exchange chairman John Egan to become the first African-American mayor of Philadelphia on this date in 1983.

Born in North Carolina into a family of tenant farmers, Goode seemed an unlikely candidate for mayor of a leading mid-Atlantic city. However, after attending high school in Philadelphia and graduating from Morgan State University, Goode returned to Philadelphia to begin work as a neighborhood activist and served as campaign manager for Hardy Williams' 1971 campaign for mayor. A number of state senators, concerned about the lack of African-American representation within state government, persuaded Governor Milton Shapp to appoint Goode as commissioner of the Public Utilities Commission, where he worked toward improving consumer protections. Appointed City Managing Director by Green to fulfill a campaign promise, Goode was well positioned to meet Rizzo in the 1982 primary. In the first few years of his administration, Goode focused on managing environmental, education, and budgetary crises. Unfortunately, he found it very difficult to convince City Council to agree with his plans.

The Goode administration was forever altered by the events of May 13, 1985, when city police bombed the West Philadelphia compound of the MOVE organization. Though Goode was not held criminally responsible for the deaths of eleven people, including five children, his reputation was badly damaged. Support among the African-American community was enough, however, to ensure his re-election in 1987. His second administration was fraught with poor fiscal management and the enactment of a particularly high increase in a very unpopular city wage tax. Since his retirement from government service in 1992, Goode has continued to serve Philadelphia as a social activist and founder of Amachi, a mentoring program for the children of incarcerated parents.

1731: The Library Company of Philadelphia opens.

1809: The first telegraph is received, probably of a semaphore design, courtesy of the Reedy Island Telegraph Company.

November 9

The tradition of serializing novels which was popular in England includes Charles Dickens and Arthur Conan Doyle, among many others. In America, the most famous serialized novel was Harriet Beecher Stowe's *Uncle Tom's Cabin,* which appeared in 1852 in the abolitionist newspaper *National Era*. In the 1930s and 1940s this tradition was continued in Philadelphia by the *Philadelphia Inquirer.* Between 1934 and 1949, 356 "Gold Seal" illustrated novels were published in their entirety in Sunday newspaper supplements.

At the time, the two major Philadelphia newspapers were the *Inquirer* and the *Bulletin*. The *Bulletin* had the largest circulation, bringing truth to the slogan "Almost everybody reads the *Bulletin.*" The serialized novels were designed to attract readership to the *Inquirer* and to appeal to a wide spectrum of readers. The novels, with their two-color illustrations, presented the works of well-known writers. The mystery genre was represented by such famous authors as Philip MacDonald, Ellery Queen, Agatha Christie, and Erle Stanley Gardner. F. Scott Fitzgerald's *The Great Gatsby* was an example of popular, but classic, literature appearing in the supplements. Westerns, family drama, romance, and historical tales were also published.

On November 9, 1941, *Strange Victory* by Franken Meloney and illustrated by Ben Dale was the featured novel, and had been previously serialized in *Good Housekeeping* magazine in 1938. Franken Meloney was the pen name of Rose Franken and her second husband, William Meloney. Rose Franken was a Broadway playwright who specialized in stories about family and relationships. After she was widowed, she and her second husband published a number of novels, with Meloney taking care of the plot and Franken writing the dialogue. Franken's most famous work was a dramatization of one of her novels, *Claudia,* which starred the newly discovered Dorothy McGuire and Jennifer Jones for more than 700 performances on Broadway and in a 1941 film. Serialization of novels in the *Inquirer* meant that thousands of Philadelphians were reading the same book at the same time. Today, the Free Library of Philadelphia's "One book, One Philadelphia" program brings Philadelphia readers together in a similar way, offering a common experience in an uncommon way.

1954: The Philadelphia Athletics baseball team is given permission to move to Kansas City.

November 10

Within just a few months of the start of the American Revolution in April 1775, American forces were already on the march to Canada in hopes of gaining military control over British Quebec and convincing French-speaking Canadians to join the Americans in defeating the British. In Congress, however, many believed the two expeditions led by Richard Montgomery and Benedict Arnold would not be sufficient to manage the complex military demands of land and sea, a fear that proved warranted when Montgomery and Arnold were handed the first true defeat against the British at the Battle of Quebec. Congress hoped a different approach would help and wanted to launch a similar attack against a British fort in Nova Scotia. The special skills and mission of a marine battalion seemed appropriate, and on this date in 1775, what would later become the United States Marine Corps was born in Tun Tavern in Philadelphia.

Key to the military strategy in the first stages of the war was the ability to meet the British on land as well as at sea. One month earlier, Congress had authorized the formation of the Continental Navy, which would consolidate the various ships already in service to the individual colonies. Drawing from the protocols of the British Royal Navy, Congress drafted rules and regulations specific to the marines, who would protect and support the naval mission as well as serve as a landing force for initial engagements. By order of Congress, two battalions were called up and the first commission was issued to Captain Samuel Nicholas on November 28, who established a recruiting station to raise the sufficient number of marines. Initially, Congress hoped to recruit primarily from the Continental Army, but General Washington suggested to Congress that unemployed merchant seamen be used instead.

Under the authority of the newly created Congressional Marine Committee, ships were prepared and men trained. Ten additional Marine officers were appointed by Captain Nicholas, many of whom were Philadelphia merchants, laborers, and tradesmen. Five companies of 300 men were raised. By March 1776, the first Marine landing occurred when, under Nicholas' command, New Providence Island in the Bahamas was captured from the British. The Marines went on to serve with great distinction during the American Revolution, but at the end of the hostilities the organization was disbanded. When the United States Navy was created under the constitutional government in 1798, the Marines were revived, and have since served in all American wars, honoring their Latin motto, *Semper Fidelis*, "Always Faithful."

1876: The Centennial Exposition closes today after opening on May 10. The nation's first world's fair has drawn, all tallied, 10 million visitors.

November 11

Like those in other large cities, Philadelphia's Chinatown has its own long and storied history. Growing out of the influx of Chinese immigrants seeking wealth and opportunity in the 1870s and 1880s, Chinatown was initially populated by mostly single men. Faced with exclusionary immigration laws, limited work opportunities, and with a desire to re-create the social connections they knew at home, the new arrivals settled in the area around 10th Street and Arch Street, which remains today the heart of Philadelphia's Chinese-American community.

Following the start of World War II, restrictive immigration laws were lifted as attention turned away from China and toward the threat from Germany, Japan, and Italy. Chinese-Americans stood side by side with other Americans to serve their country. When they returned from overseas, many arrived as newlyweds, quickly establishing their own families. Other young families followed, and Chinatown grew. Churches, businesses, and social and cultural organizations were formed to support the community.

In the 1960s, Urban renewal and other development projects began to threaten Chinatown, even as residents sought to improve their community. The proposed construction of the Vine Street Expressway served as a motivator for a growing number of community activists who worked to unify their voice and preserve their neighborhood. Unable to fully stop the development, the residents of Chinatown successfully negotiated a modified plan. Today, community activism remains an important part of life in Chinatown.

On this date in 1982, a Port Agreement in Tianjin, China, was signed that authorized the creation of a Friendship Gate for Philadelphia. Located at 10th Street near Arch Street at the heart of Chinatown, the gate was a joint project between Philadelphia and Tianjin. Handcrafted by artisans using traditional methods, the colorful gate is the only one of its kind in the United States. It was officially dedicated on January 31, 1984, and following a complete restoration in 2008, was rededicated on November 19, 2008.

1797: John Adams gives his first State of the Union address in Congress Hall.

1807: Rickett's Circus burns down.

1872: General George Meade's horse Baldy marches in the funeral procession for Meade in Laurel Hill Cemetery.

1918: The end of World War I is celebrated, becoming known as Armistice Day.

1932: Girl Scouts begin the commercial sale of cookies by making and selling them in the windows of the Philadelphia Gas and Electric Company.

November 12

Competition among department stores demands quick action, clever marketing, and an exaggerated sense of the unique or surprising. In addition to rivalries within cities (Strawbridge & Clothier and Wanamaker's in Philadelphia, for example), across the country some of the largest retail businesses in the world historically fought to be the first or the best at something that would make a difference in the bottom line. In June 1945, Chicago-based Marshall Field & Company attempted to lay claim to being the first department store to sell an airplane from within its walls and advertised the event in national newspapers.

At Wanamaker's, innovation and ingenuity were nothing new to the company, often credited with inventing modern concepts of marketing and personalized retail service. In response to the Marshall Field announcement in 1945, a longtime employee of Wanamaker's rebutted their competitor's claim. He stated that a full-sized duplicate of the Bleriot plane that flew the English Channel was available for purchase on this date in 1909 at the Philadelphia store, a full thirty-six years earlier than the Marshall Field airplane. The sale of the $5,000 airplane, yet another clever Wanamaker advertising ploy, was likely arranged by Rodman Wanamaker, son of the store founder and avid supporter of aviation.

Indeed, Rodman Wanamaker, born in 1863 in Philadelphia, continues to hold a special place in aviation history. In partnership with pioneer businessman and aviation engineer Glenn Curtiss, Wanamaker developed a flying boat design that is still in use today and fostered a new industry, that of seaplane travel to and from New York City and Florida. His financial sponsorship of long-distance improvements in airplane design contributed to Admiral Richard Byrd's successful transatlantic flight completed just days after Lindbergh's history-making flight in 1927. From the retail halls of Wanamaker's store to the Atlantic Ocean, Rodman Wanamaker's interest in airplanes and his influence in their advancement are clear to see.

1929: Actress and Princess of Monaco Grace Kelly is born.

November 13

One of the first specialty hospitals to be established, Wills Eye Hospital was founded in 1832 through the specific bequest of $116,000 by Quaker merchant James Wills. Within two years, it moved to 18th and Race Street, where the hospital's ward of seventy beds served as an asylum for indigent blind and lame Philadelphians. As early as 1839, Wills Hospital began training new doctors in a residency program. Thousands of doctors were trained at Wills, and today its alumni association supports research, scholarships, and an annual scientific clinical conference. At the first clinical conference in 1949, live eye surgery was performed on television with cameras beaming the scene from the operating room to an audience in the lobby. Still the oldest continuing specialty hospital in the nation, it helped to make ophthalmology recognized as a distinct branch of medicine.

On November 13, 1932, a new facility at 16th and Spring Garden streets was dedicated. Bed capacity increased to 120 with expanded outpatient services, teaching facilities, and conference space. By the 1960s, sub-specialty services in contact lens, cornea, glaucoma, neuro-ophthalmology, euplastic, oncology, pathology, pediatric, pediatric ophthalmology, and retina were established. Wills Eye Hospital research and development led to a number of advances in instruments and techniques in ophthalmology. Wills Eye Hospital doctors were the first to replace a clouded cataract lens with an artificial intraocular lens in 1952, and a machine for eye microsurgery was developed at Wills in 1972.

In 1972, Wills became affiliated with Thomas Jefferson University, and all Jefferson medical students now receive training at Wills. In 1980, continued growth in the number of services and patients led to the move to a new facility at 9th and Walnut streets twice as big as the Spring Garden facility, where it operates today. Serving 20,000 patients in the cataract and primary care division, today the hospital also performs more than 400 corneal transplants every year and operates the nation's largest service for the treatment of glaucoma. Internationally recognized for its innovative work, Wills Eye Hospital continues to serve the citizens of Philadelphia and beyond by ensuring the finest eye care and pioneering medicine, much as it has done for over 175 years.

1930: Jules Junker, a leading banker and importer of the first motorcar from France in 1899, dies.

1939: Judge John E. Walsh, who served on the municipal court bench for eighteen years and was known popularly as "the judge who sent Al Capone to jail," dies.

November 14

In the late evening hours of November 14, 1939, buildings in Philadelphia were seen to be rocking and dishes in cupboards rattled as the city felt the tremors of an earthquake. A rare but not entirely unknown phenomenon in the mid-Atlantic region, the earthquake was most strongly felt to the south and west of the city, particularly along the Main Line and points south. Throughout the history of the city, similar events have reminded residents of the passage of time and the fragility of the land.

Pennsylvania's unique geology and location contribute to the extent to which tremors and geologic shifts are felt through the southeastern corner of the state. Currently situated far from the active intersection of tectonic plates 2,000 miles into the Atlantic Ocean, the region is home to the older plate boundaries visible in the ridges and folds of the Pocono Mountains and Appalachian Mountains to the west of the city. In addition to natural shifts in the land plates that cover the earth, some think that earthquakes can also be caused by man-made events such as mining and drilling, essential to Pennsylvania's coal, steel, and natural gas industries. These quakes are highly localized, affecting only a small area. The earthquake of 1939 was strong enough in Philadelphia to knock bricks from buildings and drive people from their homes and businesses in fear of worse damage. The quake was also felt in southwest New Jersey and as far as Baltimore.

Among the earliest recorded earthquakes felt in Philadelphia, one that occurred in 1737 was an event strong enough to topple chimneys in New York City. In March and November of 1800, two quakes described as "severe" were felt, and a similar event in 1840 was accompanied by high swells on the Delaware River. In more recent decades, the ground has again trembled occasionally, with an earthquake of magnitude 2.8 felt throughout the region that once again rattled dishes.

1749: The Constitution of the Publick Academy is signed and Benjamin Franklin is named president.

1970: A twenty-mile-long oil slick drifts toward the Delaware Bay despite efforts to contain it before it reaches the mouth of the Schuylkill and enters the Delaware River.

November 15

In 1632, the English king Charles I awarded a grant of what is now Maryland to George Calvert. William Penn received his grant of what is now Pennsylvania from King Charles II in 1682 and an additional piece of land in 1683 on the Delmarva Peninsula. These generous awards led to the successful development of both colonies, but the imprecise boundaries of the two grants as described in the charters led to conflict for eighty years. The Calverts contended that the border was at the 40th parallel, encompassing the city of Philadelphia; the Penns argued that the border was some fifteen miles south of the city.

In 1730, this debate escalated to violence when a Marylander, Thomas Cresap, moved to disputed territory in Pennsylvania and began attacking Quaker settlements. Cresap was eventually arrested by Pennsylvania authorities and marched in chains through the Philadelphia streets. In 1734 and 1737, tensions escalated even further to the point where Pennsylvania and Maryland militias engaged in military skirmishes. King George II ordered a truce and in 1750 the English courts ruled that the border should be fifteen miles south of Philadelphia. Finally, in November 1763, Charles Mason and Jeremiah Dixon arrived in Philadelphia to conduct a definitive survey.

Mason was an astronomer from the Royal Observatory and Dixon was a respected surveyor. They began on November 15, 1763, by precisely locating Philadelphia and establishing the "Post mark'd west" fifteen miles south of the city at latitude 39 degrees 43 minutes 18.2 seconds north. Over the next five years, they worked to complete the various surveys that permanently established the borders among Maryland, Delaware, and Pennsylvania. At one-mile intervals, they laid huge stone blocks with a P on one side (for Pennsylvania and Delaware) and an M (for Maryland) on the other. Recent GPS tracking of more than 300 miles of the line indicates that it was never more than 800 feet off, and more frequently was accurate within a few feet. In 1820, the Missouri Compromise prohibited slavery north of the Mason-Dixon Line, and it is by this association that their achievement is most remembered today.

1777: The Articles of Confederation are adopted in York, Pennsylvania, when Congress is there during the occupation of Philadelphia.

1777: American troops evacuate Fort Mifflin following a six-week bombardment by the British, during which 400-450 Americans held firm, allowing for the repositioning of the Continental Army and their subsequent withdrawal to winter in Valley Forge.

1932: The USS *Indianapolis,* the first 10,000-ton cruiser to be completed after the ratification of the London naval limitation treaty, is commissioned at the Philadelphia Navy Yard.

November 16

Philadelphia gained a singular artist when Hermann Herzog was born on this date in 1831. Not a native Pennsylvanian, Herzog was born in Bremen, Germany, and trained as an artist in the Dusseldorf Academy from a young age. An accomplished landscape artist known for his realistic depiction of the beauty of the natural world, Herzog soon gained in popularity throughout Europe. The recipient of numerous awards, he immigrated to Philadelphia from Germany in the late 1860s, where he lived in a house at 4101 Pine Street. He maintained his home and studio in Philadelphia for the next sixty years until his death in 1932 at the remarkable age of 100 years.

While still in Europe, Herzog benefited from the purchase of his works by royalty and nobility, among them Queen Victoria of England, the Grand Duke Alexander of Russia, and the Countess of Flanders. Committed to careful study and preparation for each piece, Herzog traveled far and wide seeking a diversity of views. Water is apparent as a repeated motif in his work, however, as he attempted to portray the working of light through water and in the broader landscape. In the United States, Herzog visited many states, once again seeking natural treasures, among them the Yosemite Valley, the Florida Everglades, and the coast of Maine. He also traveled more locally, to Bucks County, and farther north, up the Hudson River in New York.

A prolific and financially savvy professional, Herzog was able to live off the proceeds of his sale of artwork and the subsequent investments of his savings. In 1876, he received an award for his painting of Sentinel Rock in Yosemite at the Centennial Exposition, and befriended Pennsylvania native and fellow artist George Cope, known for his still-lifes. Herzog continued to exhibit his work throughout his life, enjoying a shared gallery showing with his son, also an artist, in New York City in November of 1931. Herzog died three months later on February 6, 1932, leaving a legacy of work seen today in museum collections across the country.

1937: The 10,000-ton cruiser *Wichita,* the last of eighteen vessels of its class to be built under terms of the London treaty, slides gracefully into the Delaware River at the Philadelphia Navy Yard.

November 17

Efforts toward social change were a hallmark of the late 1960s. Young leaders emerged in the black community in particular, and David P. Richardson, Jr., of Germantown was among the most notable. When he was eighteen years old, he organized high school students in a citywide protest over the suspension of sixteen students and a call for education reform. On November 17, 1967, several thousand black students, joined by adult activists, staged a walk-out and marched to the Board of Education building on the Benjamin Franklin Parkway. Their demands included more black teachers, principals, and members of the school board, black history courses, and exempting black students from saluting the flag "because justice and liberty did not exist at all."

By all reports, the demonstration began peacefully, but clashes broke out between police and demonstrators. Commanded by police chief Frank Rizzo, more than a hundred police charged the demonstrators with nightsticks. The police stated later that the charge was a response to rock-throwing and the need to maintain public order. School board president Richardson Dilworth was attempting to negotiate with thirty representatives of the demonstrators when the violence broke out. Dilworth concluded that "a serious effort . . . to speak creatively to the major tension in our city was tragically destroyed by inept and precipitous police action." As fighting escalated, seventeen people were injured and fifty-seven were arrested. Subsequently, attempts were made to remove Rizzo from his post, but he was supported strongly by the mayor, local media, and many white parents and citizens. Conflict in the schools and occasional violence among black and white students continued throughout the 1960s.

Only six years after the demonstrations, David Richardson was elected to the State House of Representatives for the 201st district and was reelected twelve times. In his legislative career he served as Democratic Chair of the Health and Human Services Committee, and the Pennsylvania and national black legislative caucuses. A champion of social justice, welfare reform, and prison reform, he sponsored more than 400 bills. He died in office at the age of forty-six in 1995. Today, he is remembered in his home neighborhood of Germantown for his passionate commitment to his district. A post office and Chelten Avenue at the intersection of Germantown Avenue have been named in his honor.

1863: Streetcars with small steam engines, known as "dummies" by Philadelphians, are put into use for the first time, running on the Frankford extension of the Frankford and Southwark Passenger Railway. They remained in use until 1893, when electric trolley cars supplanted them.

In the mid eighteenth century, much of North America was held either by the British or the French. Conflict over settlements in the Ohio Valley led to the French and Indian War, known as the Seven Years War in Europe, which ensured British sovereignty over what is now Canada. Approximately 80,000 French-speaking Catholic Acadians lived in the maritime provinces of Canada, and they had refused to sign loyalty oaths to the British Crown, intending to remain neutral in the conflict. In 1755, Governor Laurence ordered the deportation of all Acadians to American colonies, to the Caribbean, and to France.

On November 18, 1755, an earthquake struck Philadelphia and other locations on the East coast, causing panic among the populace. That same day, ships carrying an estimated 450 Acadian refugees arrived in the Delaware River. Discovery of smallpox on board led to the refusal to allow the ships to dock, and they remained in the river until mid December. Two months earlier, Canadian governor Laurence had written a letter widely published in Philadelphia describing the Acadians as "secret enemies" who assisted the Indians and poisoned local wells. Governor Morris of Pennsylvania wrote to the governors of Massachusetts and New Jersey, fearing that the Acadians would join with Irish and German Catholics in a conspiracy against the colony's government and worrying that he did not have enough troops to maintain order.

Quaker and Catholic good Samaritans reported deplorable conditions on the ships and attempted to assist the Acadians with food and clothing once they were allowed to embark and live in rough "neutral huts." Many Acadians who died were buried in what is now Washington Square. Because the Acadians were so distrusted, the colony passed an act dispersing them to Bucks, Lancaster, and Chester counties. Eventually, some Acadians returned to Canada, while many others went south and settled in Louisiana. When Henry Wadsworth Longfellow wrote his epic poem *Evangeline* in 1847about the deportations, he set much of the story in Philadelphia. Known for its tolerance of different races, religions, and creeds, the city's reaction to the Acadians serves as a reminder that political turmoil can easily undermine the best of intentions.

1769: The Friendship Carpenters' Company is formed; it is merged with the first Carpenters' Company on March 1, 1786.

Organized crime has at times flourished in Philadelphia, as in many large American cities. Although it was smaller and less profitable than the New York mafia, the Philly mob made its mark in crime circles and in Philadelphia history. Like other family businesses, family connections and loyalties were a way to get in and move up. Early in the 1940s, Nicodemo "Little Nicky" Scarfo used his family connections to get his first mob jobs, ultimately rising to head of the Philadelphia mob. More than a dozen mob murders were attributed to Scarfo in his rise to the top.

Angelo Bruno, Philly's mob boss, exiled Scarfo to Atlantic City in the early 1960s to resolve a dispute among mobsters. In Atlantic City, Scarfo ran bookmaking and loan sharking operations and invested in an adult bookstore, but he struggled to make his operations profitable. That changed when legalized gambling came to Atlantic City in the late 1970s. Establishing ties with shady unions and bribing local officials, Scarfo soon began making a lot of money for himself and the mob. The opportunities in Atlantic City caught the attention of the New York mob, and the murder of Bruno in 1980 led to the selection of Phil Testa as boss. Testa promoted Scarfo to Consigliere and was then himself murdered in 1981, allegedly by Scarfo associates. Scarfo made a deal with New York families to share the bounty of Atlantic City and became the undisputed boss of the Philadelphia mob, partially through disposing of those who opposed him.

In 1982, a war broke out among members of the Philadelphia mob, with many killings and some notable misses, which led the media to refer to Scarfo's outfit as "the Gang that Couldn't Shoot Straight." Scarfo was convicted on November 19, 1988, of conspiracy to commit extortion of the waterfront developer Willard Rouse III, as well as for drug trafficking, loan sharking, and murder. Members of his own mob had turned informant and testified against him. Scarfo was sentenced to forty-five years in prison and remains incarcerated in the federal penitentiary in Atlanta. Though Scarfo's son and others have attempted to revive the family business, the mob has never been as strong a presence in the city since.

1686: King's Highway from Philadelphia to the falls of the Delaware at Trenton is ordered by Council to be built; it is later called the Frankford Turnpike.

1921: Roy Campanella, baseball Hall of Fame catcher, is born.

November 20

During World War II, the Philadelphia shipyards built fleets of ships for the war effort. Engineers worked there as well, perfecting parts and designs to improve the quality and speed of shipbuilding. In 1943, engineer Richard James was experimenting with springs to help stabilize ships during storms. He knocked several large springs off a workbench, and recognized that the "walking" springs would probably make a good toy. Over the next two years he refined the idea, and the Slinky, named by his wife Betty, was born.

Richard and Betty James convinced Gimbels Department Store in downtown Philadelphia to let them demonstrate the toy on an inclined plane in November 1943. Children were delighted and the toy sold out immediately. James Industries was founded in the city with a $500 loan to manufacture the toy, using equipment that Richard had created and built. In the 1950s, related toys such as the slinky dog and the slinky train made their debut, with the song lyric "everyone knows it's Slinky" featured in extensive advertising. In 1960, Richard James left his family to become a missionary in Bolivia, and Betty took over the company. Betty soon shifted company manufacturing to Hollidaysburg, Pennsylvania, where the Slinky is still made.

Committed to keeping the toys affordable, Betty James once told a reporter that she felt an obligation to children who couldn't have expensive toys. In 1959, John Cage composed music scored for many instruments, including an amplified Slinky. In 1985, Space Shuttle *Discovery* astronauts made a video illustrating how the Slinky, when free of Earth's gravity, could not walk as usual. In reflection of its place as a Pennsylvania first, the Slinky was made the official toy of the Commonwealth of Pennsylvania in 2001, and in that same year, Betty James was inducted into the Toy Industry Association Hall of Fame. Since 1945, more than 300 million Slinky toys have been sold. Betty James continued to manage the company until she sold it in 1998. She died on November 20, 2008, having provided decades of simple fun for kids all over the world by way of her husband's marvelous invention.

1864: The newly completed Cathedral of Saints Peter and Paul is dedicated by Archbishop James Frederick Wood.

November 21

Patriotism would not be enough to ensure the success of the Revolution; the cause also needed supplies and ammunition. One of the most important providers in the Philadelphia area was the Durham Furnace in Bucks County. Founded in 1727 by a group of Philadelphia investors who formed a stock company to build it, the furnace produced iron and steel for nearly 150 years. In 1728, the furnace exported three tons of pig iron to England, but the American product could not compete with cheaper Russian iron. Among the products produced by the furnace were the popular "Adam and Eve" stoves, a competitor to Benjamin Franklin's more famous stove.

In 1773, ownership of the furnace was transferred to Joseph Galloway and his wife and leased to George Taylor. The two men could not have had more different political views. Galloway was a Tory who joined the British in New York in 1776 and managed the city of Philadelphia for the British during their occupation in 1777. Taylor was a patriot active in political affairs who was a radical member of the Pennsylvania Assembly, organized militia companies, and signed the Declaration of Independence as a Pennsylvania representative. Taylor turned the furnace into a munitions factory for the revolutionary forces. The Durham furnace produced cannon, cannonballs, shot, and other military equipment for the Continental Army, most likely at a financial loss to Taylor.

When the colonials reoccupied Philadelphia in 1777, Galloway was declared a traitor and forfeited his property, including the furnace, but the courts later ruled that the furnace belonged to his wife and could not be confiscated. After Galloway's death, George Taylor married his widow and became the sole owner of the furnace. After the Revolution, successors to the original furnace continued to operate, employing as many as 350 men in 1849. Rail networks brought iron ore to the furnace, and first the canals, and then the railroads, carried coal to fire the furnaces, until production ceased in the late nineteenth century. On November 21, 1947, a historical marker was dedicated to memorialize the value of the furnace to the American cause and its role in the economy of the region.

1747: The Association Battery is erected at Society Hill on the banks of the Delaware at approximately Lombard Street (its construction is described as "the final break-up of the Quaker nonresistance policy" in Philadelphia).

1859: Demolition begins on Market sheds on High Street between Front and Eighth streets.

November 22

Newspapers and their publishers have long been a part of the fabric of Philadelphia, and from here spread to the rest of the country. At various points in the last three hundred years, the city has been home to the first American daily, the first political cartoon, the first newspaper "help wanted," and the first foreign language daily. Today, just a handful of the city's newspaper legacies remain in publication. One of them, the *Philadelphia Tribune*, holds the distinction as the oldest continually running African-American newspaper in the country, founded on this date in 1884 by Christopher J. Perry.

Born in Baltimore in 1854, Perry moved to Philadelphia as a young man in hopes of acquiring a better education than that available in a southern city. He attended night classes and as a teenager began to write for local newspapers, generally in the "colored" departments writing for the African-American community exclusively. By the early 1880s, he was writing for the *Northern Daily* and soon after became editor of the Colored Department of the weekly *Sunday Mercury,* which went bankrupt in 1884. Jobless, Perry understood the need for a newspaper committed to the needs of the black community, and seized the opportunity to establish the *Tribune.* A strong writer and manager, Perry guided the *Tribune* to the height of its field, gaining recognition as one of the leading African-American newspapers in the country.

One of the key goals of the *Tribune* under Perry's leadership was its support of Republicanism, and the larger place of blacks in American politics, arts, education, culture, and community. The newspaper served as a voice for the voiceless, often bringing to light events and concerns reflecting a defense of civil rights causes, community connections, and the diversity of life in black Philadelphia. Today, publisher Robert W. Bogle maintains the newspaper's role in Philadelphia. The son of a former *Tribune* employee, Bogle embraces the original intent of the paper and expands it to include items that represent the full diversity of Philadelphia, frequently covering stories not seen in other media. As it approaches the 130th anniversary of its founding, the *Philadelphia Tribune* reminds us daily of the strength and richness of the city's publishing history.

1829: The first riot of a racial character against black residents occurs in Philadelphia, a precursor of many to come in the 1820s and 1830s in opposition to the abolition of slavery.

November 23

The name Septimus Winner may be unfamiliar, but chances are one is very familiar with his most famous songs. Published under the pseudonyms Alice Hawthorne, Percy Guyer, Mark Mason, Apsley Street, and Paul Stenton, Winner was one of the most popular songwriters and successful music publishers of the nineteenth century. Born in Philadelphia in 1827, Winner was the son of a musical instrument maker who specialized in violins. A graduate of Philadelphia Central High School, Winner was largely self-taught when it came to music. Between 1845 and 1854, he and his brother Joseph partnered in the music publishing business, releasing their first successful song with lyrics by Septimus, "What Is Home Without A Mother?"

In addition to teaching music and performing with local groups, Winner continued his songwriting, publishing "Listen to the Mocking Bird" in 1854, which was one of the most popular tunes of the time. Other hit songs include "Oh, Where, Oh Where Has My Little Dog Gone," "Ten Little Injuns," "Abraham's Daughter," and "Carry Me Back to Tennessee." During the Civil War, Winner was arrested and jailed for a brief time for treason on the basis of his popular tune "Give Us Back Our Old Commander: Little Mac, the People's Pride," a plea to Lincoln to reinstate General George B. McClellan. He was released only when he agreed to destroy all remaining copies, but more than 80,000 copies had already been distributed. The song was also used during McClellan's unsuccessful candidacy for the presidency in 1864.

During his lifetime, Winner wrote more than 200 popular songs. He also excelled as an arranger of more serious music, writing over 1,500 musical arrangements for a variety of instruments and 2,000 arrangements specifically for the violin and piano. As part of his teaching activities, he published musical instruction books for twenty-three different instruments. A founder of the Philadelphia Musical Fund Society and a contributor to Edgar Allan Poe's *Graham's Magazine,* Winner would be inducted into the national Songwriters Hall of Fame. He died in Philadelphia on November 23, 1903. In 2005, Winner was identified as the composer of the Three Stooges song "Swinging the Alphabet."

1832: Matthias Baldwin's new steam locomotive, *Old Ironsides,* makes its first trial run from Germantown to 9th and Green streets.

November 24

As the twentieth century began, soft drinks became hugely popular. Until the Coca-Cola Company built a national following, most sodas were produced locally without brand names. New trends in advertising led to the success of Coca-Cola, and other manufacturers sought to establish a name for their product to stay competitive. There were many competitors to Coca-Cola in the early years, one of the most successful being Koca Nola. Produced by a rival Atlanta company, Koca Nola began in 1904 to sell franchises to bottling works and drugstores. One of the earliest franchises went to the James Esposito Soda Bottling Works of Philadelphia.

James Esposito, an Italian immigrant, founded his company in 1900 and began bottling ginger ale, birch beer, sarsaparilla, and other soft drinks at 812-814 Washington Avenue. After he acquired the Koca Nola franchise in 1905, his business grew. Copying Coca-Cola's business model as well as its product, Koca Nola made much of the assertion that it was "Delicious, Dopeless Koca Nola," a reference to the early use of cocaine as an ingredient in Coca-Cola. But in 1909, Koca Nola was accused of having cocaine in one bottle of its syrup. Although the owner vigorously denied the charge, it was a fatal blow and Koca Nola filed for bankruptcy on November 24, 1910. Esposito continued bottling Koca Nola until he lost a suit filed by Coca-Cola to stop using the name. Ultimately a judge allowed him to call his beverage Primo Cola, and he continued to sell the product at good profit for many years.

Esposito also went on to develop his own lemon-lime beverage, Primo Gassosa (Italian for "first carbonated water") in 1916. For a time it became the largest selling soft drink in America and was compared favorably in taste to the national 7-Up brand. Esposito's soft drinks were always bottled in glass, and the trend to plastic that began in the 1960s led to the decline of the company. In 1974, the plant closed and James Esposito and his Primo Gassosa disappeared into soft drink history.

1703: Justus Falckner is ordained at Gloria Dei, as the first Lutheran pastor in the United States. He served New York and East Jersey.

November 25

A tradition beloved by Philadelphians and Americans alike began on this date in 1920 when the Gimbels Department Store sponsored the first Thanksgiving Day Parade in front of their store on Market Street. Envisioned by Gimbels founder Ellis Gimbel as an enjoyable attraction to draw shoppers to its holiday-themed Toyland, the parade was staged by more than fifty volunteers, employees of the store who dressed in costumes and engaged onlookers with their celebratory antics. The main attraction was the arrival of Santa Claus (usually portrayed by a Philadelphia firefighter) on a truck and ladder. Climbing up to a ninth-floor window, Santa Claus kicked off the shopping season with dramatic flourish.

Gimbel Brothers, known locally as simply Gimbels, began as a small general store in Indiana before moving to Milwaukee. Adam Gimbel expanded the store franchise when he purchased the Granville Haines store in Philadelphia in 1894. By 1910, the New York branch was facing off with its primary rival, Macy's. Their carefully cultivated and publicized competition drove both businesses to the heights of the retail industry. With the success of Gimbels' parade in Philadelphia, Macy's established its own, now-world-famous event in New York four years later. In Philadelphia, Gimbels expanded its parade to include balloons, floats, and marching bands, which was first televised in 1953.

Like many large department stores, Gimbels faced economic challenges through the 1970s and 1980s. In 1973, the Gimbels family sold the business to Brown & Williamson, the American subsidiary of British-American Tobacco, which owned a number of large department stores. In 1980, the store left its home at Ninth and Market streets for the newly completed Gallery Mall. The new building did not have windows, and so the Santa Claus tradition died. Gimbels continued to decline through the 1980s and closed for good in 1987. In order to preserve the great Philadelphia tradition, local television channel WPVI-6 assumed responsibility for the parade, which has since been sponsored by Stern's Department Store, Boscov's Department Store, and IKEA. Today, the parade continues with as many as 7,000 volunteers and tens of thousands of onlookers completing their annual pilgrimage to mark the start of the holiday season.

1790: Trenton becomes the capital of New Jersey.

November 26

Philadelphia's only native-born saint, Katharine Drexel, was born in Philadelphia on November 26, 1858, the second child of wealthy banker Francis A. Drexel and his wife. Katharine's mother died soon after her birth and she was reared by her stepmother, a pious woman who welcomed the poor into her home. Katharine's early life was spent in luxury, with trips to Europe and other trappings of wealth. In 1887 after the death of her stepmother, Katharine and her sisters had a private audience with Pope Leo XIII in Rome. Katharine asked the pope to send missionaries to the American Indians, but he suggested she might be a missionary herself.

Katharine's father died in 1885 and his will left the earnings of his estate to his three daughters during their lifetime, reserving the principal for their children and charity. Her share of the earnings alone was enough for her to establish the order of the Sisters of the Blessed Sacrament in 1891, becoming the first sister in the order. She and the Sisters established boarding schools for African-American children, founded numerous Indian schools for various tribes, especially among the Navaho and the Sioux and the Chippewa, and chartered Xavier University in Louisiana to prepare teachers for the many schools across the nation where Sisters of the Blessed Sacrament taught.

In 1935, Sister Katharine had a heart attack and retired from active participation in the activities of the order, entering the contemplative life she had planned in her youth. She died in 1955 as the last survivor of the three siblings, and her father's large estate was distributed to charity. John Cardinal Krol introduced her name in Rome in 1964 as a potential candidate for sainthood, and in 1987 she was declared Venable, a step toward sainthood. Two miraculous cures of deafness were attributed to her, and on October 1, 2000, Pope John Paul II proclaimed her Saint Katharine Drexel, patron saint of racial justice and philanthropists. The Sisters of the Blessed Sacrament maintain a shrine to Saint Katharine Drexel in Bucks County north of Philadelphia and continue the charitable work that defined her life.

1792: Abolitionist Sarah Grimke is born in South Carolina.

November 27

Valley Forge is revered as the location of General George Washington's long encampment in the winter of 1777-78, where American troops trained to fight under Baron Von Steuben. Many died of the cold and disease, and solidified their commitment to the Revolution. But despite its sacred connection to the history of the nation, it wasn't protected from development for many years until Pennsylvania made it the Commonwealth's first state park. The Centennial and Memorial Association of Valley Forge was formed by private citizens in 1878 and was able to preserve Washington's Headquarters. Unable to secure federal funds, Governor Robert E. Pattison signed an act in 1893 for the acquisition of land at Valley Forge for a public park.

A great supporter of the park, Governor Samuel Pennypacker, in his farewell address in 1907, said that "every Pennsylvanian ought to go to Valley Forge as the saints of Mohammed went to Mecca." Governor Martin Brumbaugh subsequently used a grant from Congress to build the Great Arch of Victory at the park in 1910. Engraved on the arch is Washington's statement that "naked and starving as they are we cannot enough admire the incomparable patience and fidelity of the soldiery." On this date in 1936, Governor George Earle met with members of the Valley Forge Park Commission and announced plans to appropriate funds to expand the park from 1,500 to 5,000 acres. Reconstruction of the huts and streets as they appeared in 1777 would be accomplished with the assistance of laborers enrolled in the Civilian Conservation Corps. In 1976, President Gerald R. Ford visited Valley Forge to sign legislation authorizing the federal government to create Valley Forge National Historical Park.

In recent years, the park has continued to be threatened by development. In 2002, a housing development on private land within the park's boundaries was stopped when the federal government paid $4 million to developers, and in 2009 a controversial plan for a visitor's center, hotel, museum, restaurant, and campground on private land surrounded on all sides by the park led to a compromise. The nonprofit American Revolution Center and the National Park Service agreed to a land exchange that will establish a national museum of the American Revolution at Independence National Historical Park, in Philadelphia, preserving twenty acres at Valley Forge.

1820: Edwin Forrest makes his first stage appearance at age fourteen at the Walnut Street Theatre, in *Douglas* by John Home.

November 28

Music and the people who make it have long been a part of Philadelphia history. Birthplace to countless vocalists, musicians, composers, and performers of all kinds, the city can lay claim to being one of the most musically talented and appreciative in the country, if not the world. For a period of time, when the streets rang not with the sounds of music but with the pinging of hammers and the grinding of saws and drills, Philadelphia was also birthplace to the instruments that brought variety and beauty to all four corners of the world.

As early as the 1750s, musicians could purchase published sheet music from a local music store. Though at times in conflict with the Quaker concepts of appropriate forms of public entertainment, artists of all kinds played pianofortes, violins, and flutes in performances on stage and in homes. By the time of the American Revolution, Philadelphia had acquired its first piano manufacturer: Johann Behrent. Within two decades, John Isaac Hawkins followed suit, inventing an upright form of piano that he believed could easily challenge the use of larger, more unwieldy grand pianos. Even with the endorsement of luminaries like Thomas Jefferson and Charles Willson Peale, Hawkins' business foundered. However, within a few years another patent for an upright piano was claimed, this time by Thomas Loud, who was successful in establishing a piano manufactory by the early 1820s.

Improvements in manufacturing techniques and the growth of Philadelphia as an industrial center in the 1830s and 1840s led to a number of new instrument manufacturers setting up shop, most notably in the making of violins, accordions, nickelodeons, and pianos. The Centennial Exposition of 1876 permitted the display and marketing of a whole new range of makers and instruments, many based in Philadelphia. At the turn of the century, the rise of retail marketing innovations, many of them led by Wanamaker's department store, allowed for greater purchasing access to musical instruments including pianos. Unfortunately, the economic dips of the twentieth century led to the closing of many businesses, and musical instrument manufacture was one of many industries badly affected. Some, such as the Lester Piano Company of Delaware County, held on for a time and benefited from commercial and educational business. On this date in 1961, however, the Lester company succumbed, and one of the last great piano manufacturers of the city closed, ending a unique chapter in city history.

1894: Installation of the William Penn statue is completed atop the tower at City Hall.

November 29

Reuben Haines retired from business at age twenty-three and devoted himself to "the pursuit of knowledge and the society of genuine friends." In addition to helping found the Franklin Institute, the Academy of Natural Sciences, and the Pennsylvania Horticultural Society, he had an interest in school reform and education. That interest led him to invite Amos Bronson Alcott to come to Germantown from Boston in 1830 to open a school. Alcott's philosophy included opposition to corporal punishment, critical thinking as compared with lectures and drills, and teaching writing by having students write about things they knew instead of endless memorization and rote learning of grammar, spelling, and vocabulary.

Alcott and his family lived in a boardinghouse at 5425 Germantown Avenue, and there on November 29, 1832, his second daughter, Louisa May, was born. Writing to a friend, her father described her as having "a fine foundation for health and energy of character." After the death of Reuben Haines, the school closed and the family returned to Massachusetts, settling in Concord. Alcott became a member of the Transcendental Club, whose most prominent member was Ralph Waldo Emerson. Over the years, Alcott founded or taught in a number of schools, but he was never a financial success and the family lived in extreme poverty. Louisa's passion was for writing, and she was determined to help support the family, writing in her journal that "I'll be rich and famous and happy before I die, see if I won't."

Louisa's prediction came true when she published a number of books, most notably *Little Women* in 1868. The beloved American novel about girls coming to age in difficult economic circumstances in Civil War New England brought her both wealth and fame. The characters and stories in *Little Women* were taken from the Alcott family's experiences. Louisa based the character of "Jo" on herself; she was a tomboy and loved the theatrical presentations the children wrote to entertain themselves. Louisa never married and cared for her father until his death in 1886; she survived him by only two days and is buried in Sleepy Hollow Cemetery in Concord.

1828: The House of Refuge opens at 15th and Fairmount Avenue.

November 30

In the midst of the First World War, anger, hatred, and prejudice against African-Americans, Catholics, and Jews resulted in the revival of the Ku Klux Klan. Initially arising from the post–Civil War conflicts of the nineteenth century, in particular the North's flawed approach to Reconstruction, the KKK at its outset was centered primarily in the former slave-holding states of the American South. Following the failure of the original KKK to sustain its actions through the turn of the century, the influx of immigrants and increasing competition for jobs and economic success led to a rise in anti-immigrant sentiments. Several years after its revival, the KKK still wielded little influence on American society.

In the unstable economic atmosphere of post–World War I industrial America, however, it seemed to offer an answer to many Americans competing for jobs. In 1920, the Invisible Empire, as it was called, staged an attempt to advance the movement in the mid-Atlantic states of Pennsylvania, New Jersey, and New York. Focusing its attacks on what it deemed to be foreign outsiders, the KKK burned crosses, used violent intimidation, and conducted public marches to threaten its intended victims. However, as its activities increased, so too did attention to its crimes among city police and within the local media. Journalistic investigations into KKK crimes led to a congressional inquiry, which threatened the Klan's future. On this date in 1921, internal conflicts within the KKK leadership resulted in nearly 3,000 Philadelphia members of the Klan renouncing their membership and further threatening the organization's hold on Pennsylvania.

Though local media coverage suggested that the Klan was losing steam, in reality it would only continue to grow throughout the region. Essentially abandoning Philadelphia and Pittsburgh, the Klan instead focused on the interior regions of the state, appealing to long-established farming communities by way of outlining the risk from outsiders. Indeed, KKK membership is estimated to have reached its peak throughout the nation in 1924, with as many as 3 million members. In 1925, however, with the conviction of a grand dragon on charges of second-degree murder, the Klan's membership began to decline precipitously and its power waned. Today, the KKK survives in Pennsylvania, much reduced but a reminder of the region's painful past.

1782: A preliminary peace treaty is signed in Paris, entailing recognition of the independent United States of America by the British.

1929: Dick Clark is born in Philadelphia.

As one of the nation's single most significant symbols of freedom and independence, Philadelphia's Liberty Bell continues to honor its original purpose to call people together in times of peace as well as in times of crisis. Installed in the newly completed tower of the Pennsylvania State House in 1753, the Bell we know and love today began with a request to cast a bell suitable for the colony's most significant building, but also capable of working daily for many years to come. On November 1, 1751, Isaac Norris sent a letter to the Whitechapel Foundry in London requesting a bell, which arrived in good shape the following September. Unfortunately, the quality of this initial bell was deemed unsuitable, whereupon local craftsmen John Pass and John Stow were asked to recast it, using the original metal. They did so, and finally, in 1753, the future Liberty Bell was hoisted to the tower, where it remained until the American Revolution, when it was temporarily removed during the British occupation of Philadelphia.

In his letter, Isaac Norris carefully outlined the basic need for the bell, as well as what the Assembly of Pennsylvania wished to have inscribed on its surface, which was intended in part to honor the fiftieth, or jubilee, anniversary of the Charter of Privileges of Pennsylvania. The letter, reproduced below, established the words that ring today as inspiration for all who read them:

Philadelphia
November 1, 1751

Respected Friend Robert Charles:

The Assembly having ordered us (The Superintendents of our State House) to procure a Bell from England to be purchased for their use we take the liberty to apply ourselves to thee to get us a good Bell of about two thousand pounds weight the cost of which we presume may amount to about one hundred pounds Sterling or perhaps with the Charges something more and accordingly we have now enclosed a first Bill of Exchange viz. John Perrin and Son on Messrs. Thomas Flowerdew and Company for £100 Sterling. We would have chosen to remit a larger Bill at this time, but will take care to furnish more as soon as we can be informed how much may be wanted.

We hope and rely on thy care and assistance in this affair and that thee will procure and forward it by the first good opportunity as our workmen inform us it will be much less trouble to hang the Bell before their Scaffolds are struck from the Building where we intend to place it which will not be done till the end of next Summer or beginning of the Fall. Let the Bell be cast by the best workmen and examined carefully before it is Shipped with the following words well-shaped in large letters round it Viz.

By order of the Assembly of the Province of Pennsylvania for the Statehouse in the City of Philadelphia 1752

And Underneath

Proclaim Liberty through all the Land to all the Inhabitants thereof. Levit. XXV.10

As we have experienced thy readiness to Serve this province on all occasions we desire it may be our excuse for this additional trouble from

Thy Assured Friends,
Isaac Norris
Thomas Leech
Edward Warner

Let the package for the transportation be examined with particular care and the full value insured there.

December

December 1

The sport of basketball was invented by James Naismith, in Massachusetts in 1891, but Philadelphia claims the first professional organization in basketball. In the beginning, players shot a soccer ball into peach baskets, which were replaced with closed nets on iron hoops in 1893. The game became very popular very quickly, and Philadelphia was chosen as home to the first professional basketball league in 1898. The National Basket Ball League consisted of six teams ranging from Trenton, New Jersey, to Delaware. The first game was played on this date in 1898 between the Trenton Nationals and the Hancock Athletic Association at Textile Hall in the Kensington section of the city. More than nine hundred fans attended the first game, which was won by the Nationals 21–19.

The score was very low by today's standards, partially because the ball needed to be retrieved from the closed hoops every time a player scored. Two other Philadelphia teams, the Clover Wheelmen and the Germantown Nationals, competed in that first season. Over the next few years, the league expanded and contracted, playing on average about forty games a season. Team names were colorful and sometimes quite obscure, and included the Bristol Pile Drivers, the Burlington Shoe Pegs, and the New York Wanderers. The Camden team was nicknamed the "skeeters," an acknowledgment of that insect's abundance in the Garden State. In the short history of the league, however, none of the Philadelphia teams won the championship, which was instead dominated by the Trenton team and the Camden Electrics.

After only a few years the league fell into decline. Teams dropped out before seasons ended and the final season of 1903 featured only five teams: the Camden Electrics, Trenton Potters, Conshohocken, Millville Glass Blowers, and St. Bridget's Biddies. The Burlington team, which did not compete that year, had fired all its players. The Philadelphia Phillies had been disbanded by its manager and future member of the Basketball Hall of Fame, Frank Morgenweck. On January 4, 1904, the league ended, but litigation followed when Frank's brother, William Morgenweck, was sued by disgruntled investors in the Camden Electrics. Professional leagues came and went in subsequent decades, with professional basketball permanently becoming part of Philadelphia sports history with the formation of the National Basketball League and the Philadelphia Warriors in 1946.

1800: The federal seat of government officially changes from Philadelphia to Washington, D.C. John Adams is the first president to reside in the White House.

1837: John Amble is awarded a patent for improvements in the mode of constructing saw mills for sawing timber.

2009: The city bans cell phone talking and texting while driving.

December 2

Most families have an oral history passed down from generation to generation. Some of the tales of our ancestors are true, although details may change over time; some stories are embellished; and some may be fanciful creations that we wish were true. The tale of Lydia Barrington Darragh, whose story of heroism during the Revolution was first told by her daughter Anne many years after the event, is one such example of oral history.

During the British occupation of Philadelphia in 1777, General William Howe had his headquarters at a neighbor's home on Second Street. Major John Andre (who later recruited the traitor Benedict Arnold to change sides in the conflict) ordered Lydia Darragh to vacate her house so that it could be used by British officers. Owing to the intervention of a cousin who was a British officer, she was permitted to stay in the house with two of her children as long as it could be used for meetings of British officers. That December, Howe was intending to attack the American forces under George Washington at their winter camp in Whitemarsh outside the city.

On December 2, 1777, as the story goes, Howe and his officers made final preparations for the attack in a meeting at Lydia's house. She hid in a linen closet and learned of their plans. Her son, Charles, was serving with Washington's troops as part of the Second Pennsylvania and she sought to alert the Americans. Getting permission to go to the countryside in search of flour, she trudged through the snow until she was able to get a message to Thomas Craig, a member of the militia and a friend of her son, who then took the news to Washington. Washington was warned that 5,000 British troops, 13 cannon, and other equipment were to be sent after him the next morning. Because of Lydia Darragh's information, the Americans were prepared. We will never know if the story of Lydia Darragh's heroism is accurate, but we do know that the Americans were aware of the impending attack. Lydia Darragh continued to reside in Philadelphia until her death on December 28, 1789, and is buried at the Quaker cemetery on Fourth Street.

1816: The Philadelphia Savings Fund Society, the first savings bank in the country, opens.

1822: The second Chestnut Street Theater opens. Designed by William Strickland, it remained an active theater until 1855.

December 3 

John Brown was viewed as either an inspirational martyr to the cause of freedom, or a dangerous madman by the citizens of Philadelphia. An unyielding abolitionist who believed violence was necessary to cleanse the nation of slavery, he devised a plan to attack the federal armory at Harper's Ferry, Virginia, and move down the Shenandoah Valley, freeing slaves. He consulted prominent African-Americans from Philadelphia, including the artist David Bustill Bowser, caterer Thomas J. Dorsey, and Underground Railroad organizer William Still, who declined to participate in what he considered an ill-advised plan. With the help of twenty-one followers, Brown captured the armory on October 16, 1859, and held it for three days, killing several Harper's Ferry citizens. Faced by a contingent of troops under the command of Robert E. Lee, most of Brown's followers were themselves killed. Brown and several others were captured, tried, and found guilty of treason, murder, and inciting an insurrection among slaves. All were sentenced to hang.

Brown's wife, Mary, stayed with Lucretia Mott and other abolitionists in Philadelphia between the trial and the execution. She traveled to Harper's Ferry accompanied by Philadelphia abolitionists James McKim and his wife, as well as Hector Tyndale. She intended to see her husband for the last time and accompany his body back north for burial. On the day of Brown's execution, December 2, 1859, many African-Americans and abolitionists in Philadelphia draped their homes and businesses with black to honor "Martyr Day." A racially integrated crowd of 4,000 gathered for a prayer vigil and speeches in National Hall on Market Street. Robert Purvis, a nationally significant abolitionist leader, gave an impassioned speech describing Brown as "the Jesus of the nineteenth century," as the police closed down the meeting. At the same time, 20,000 citizens of Philadelphia held their own rally in support of Brown's execution.

A Philadelphia-Wilmington-Baltimore railroad train brought the body to Philadelphia on December 3, 1859, and was greeted by thousands of supporters and opponents of Brown at the station. Fearing violence, Mary Brown and Mayor Alexander Henry secretly arranged to have an empty coffin displayed at the station, while they spirited the body of John Brown to the Philadelphia waterfront to be taken by ship to New York. Within a few years, the bloodshed that John Brown predicted as he went to his death had indeed consumed the nation.

1864: George W. Childs purchases the *Public Ledger* with partners Anthony J. Drexel and Francis A. Drexel. He continues as publisher until his death in 1894.

1881: The Brush Electric Light Company lights up Chestnut Street from river to river for the first time, using forty-seven arc lamps.

1976: *Rocky* is released nationally. Written by and starring actor Sylvester Stallone, the iconic movie was filmed in just 28 days for $1.1 million. Nominated for ten Academy Awards, the film won three Oscars, including Best Director and Best Picture.

December 4

When Condy Raguet, a businessman and former Ambassador to Brazil in the James Monroe administration, learned of the development of savings banks in Britain, he and his partners established the first savings bank in the United States. Intentionally avoiding the term "bank," which carried a negative connotation at the time, the Articles of Association of the Philadelphia Savings Fund Society were eventually adopted on December 4, 1816.

The company grew and prospered, and by 1917 PSFS was first in the number of depositors and second in the funds deposited in the nation. The bank emphasized the value of savings to children, with a special counter for student accounts and a program of plays and pageants on the value of savings that were produced for audiences at settlement houses and playgrounds. Located at a number of different addresses in the city since its founding, the bank constructed a new central headquarters in 1932 on Market Street at 12th Street. The 36-story building was the first modern skyscraper of the international style constructed in America. It was also the second office building in America to be air-conditioned. A huge, twenty-seven-foot red neon sign spelling out PSFS crowned the building and became (and remains) a Philadelphia icon.

As the banking business changed in the 1970s, PSFS began to decline. In the 1980s, PSFS was doing business as Meritor Financial Group, and in 1990 Mellon Bank purchased all fifty-four of its branches and the PSFS name. For a time, the PSFS sign was turned off, until public protest led to its relighting. In 1992, the FDIC seized Meritor and sold off the rest of its banking business to Mellon. The FDIC kept possession of the PSFS building, and in 1994 the building was purchased by developers who renovated it into a hotel and added an addition. Today, the Loews Hotel proudly displays the neon PSFS sign on the building, which was awarded "Building of the Century" by the American Institute of Architects Philadelphia chapter in 1969.

1682: William Penn convenes the first General Assembly in Chester, which subsequently unites the three lower Delaware counties with Pennsylvania.

1833: The American Anti Slavery Society is formed by Arthur Tappan.

1973: The Who perform live at the Spectrum. The concert is recorded and the resulting album becomes arguably one of the greatest live albums in music history.

December 5

Philadelphia was a center for many early technological breakthroughs that led to the development of motion pictures, as well as home to many of the most talented and successful performers and producers of films. As early as 1870, Henry R. Heyl projected photographs on a screen at the Academy of Music, while Coleman Sellers of Philadelphia invented the kinematoscope, a precursor to Edison's film projector. In 1888, John Carbutt invented a form of celluloid film. Philadelphia was also home to an early mogul of silent pictures—Siegmund "Pop" Lubin. Lubin came to Philadelphia late in the nineteenth century and established an optical shop. He had spent some time as a vaudevillian, and his interest in movies led him to develop his own motion picture projector. The optical shop manufactured movies with the slogan "Clear as a Bell." Soon, Lubin (and Philadelphia) was in the business of making movies.

In 1897, Lubin hired two railway men to reenact the Corbett-Fitzsimmons prize fight on film, and the company began to prosper. In 1910, Lubin built the most modern film studio in the world in North Philadelphia. Called "Lubinville," its indoor lighting system and huge size allowed up to five pictures to be filmed at once. Lubin also opened several movie theaters in the city. In 1913, Lubin purchased 500 acres in Valley Forge to create the Betzwood studio and followed this purchase with the development of studios in Florida, California, and Germany.

At their peak, Lubin's enterprises employed more than 2,000 actors, directors, and technicians, including Pearl White and Oliver Hardy. Philadelphians flocked to the new "nickelodeons" and independent movie theaters to enjoy the glowing attractions. Philadelphia was also the birthplace of a number of silent-film stars, including Alice Gale (born on this date in 1858), Lionel Barrymore, W. C. Fields, and Charles Douglas MacLean, each of whom appeared in locally produced films. In pursuit of commercial success, Lubin often plagiarized the work of others, most notably Edwin Porter's 1903 film *The Great Train Robbery,* but he also filmed original comedies, dramas, and westerns. In 1914, a fire destroyed all the negatives at Lubinville and soon after Lubin went bankrupt. By 1917, he had returned to the optical shop and died in 1923, leaving many of his pioneering films lost forever.

1792: President George Washington and Vice President John Adams are elected to a second term.

1882: Broad Street Station opens for general train service.

1933: The Eighteenth Amendment is repealed and National Prohibition ends.

December 6

The soul music scene in Philadelphia in the 1970s was lively, with local record labels such as Philadelphia International Records recording the hits of the day by such groups as the Stylistics and the Spinners. One of the elements of the success of both these groups was the work of the songwriter Linda Creed. Creed was born on December 6, 1949, and grew up in the Mt. Airy neighborhood. She first got interested in music as a student at Germantown High School. After a brief sojourn in New York, she returned to Philadelphia and had her first hit "Free Girl," recorded by British artist Dusty Springfield.

Creed soon joined songwriters Kenny Gamble, Leon Huff, and Thom Bell at Philadelphia International Records in the Shubert Building. With Thom Bell, Creed wrote hit after hit for the Stylistics, including "You Are Everything," "I'm Stone in Love with You," "Betcha, By Golly Wow," "Break Up to Make Up," and "Rock 'n' Roll Baby." Creed's happy marriage to Stephen Epstein led to writing "You Make Me Feel Brand New." Subsequently she also wrote hits with Thom Bell and others for the Spinners, including "Rubber Band Man."

Creed was diagnosed with breast cancer at the very young age of twenty-six, but continued to work in the music business and care for her daughters and family. A warm person, she spent much time with Teddy Pendergrass after his devastating car accident. In 1986, "The Greatest Love of All," a ballad that she wrote with composer Michael Masser, became a huge hit for Whitney Houston. Tragically, Creed lost her battle with breast cancer at the young age of thirty-seven on April 10, 1986. Following her death, her family and friends founded the Linda Creed Breast Cancer Foundation, which seeks to provide education, screenings, and care in the fight against the disease. Creed was posthumously inducted into the Songwriters Hall of Fame in 1992.

1790: Congress moves from New York City to Philadelphia, where George Washington serves two terms as president.

1882: A transit of Venus across the Sun is observed from the roof of the Central High School buildings.

December 7

Avram Noam Chomsky, noted American linguist, political activist, and self-described libertarian socialist, was born in Philadelphia on December 7, 1928. His father was a Russian immigrant and renowned Hebrew scholar. Although the family's first language was Yiddish, Hebrew was spoken in the home and Chomsky was immersed in Hebrew language and culture. He received his early education at Oak Lane Country Day School and then later graduated in the 184th class of Central High School.

In 1945, Chomsky entered the University of Pennsylvania, where he met and studied with Zelig Harris, who founded the first department of linguistics in the country while at the university. Chomsky ultimately earned a doctorate from the University of Pennsylvania and went on to become one of the founders of the modern study of linguistics. He pioneered significant theories about the universality of grammar of human communication. His argument that children are born with certain innate grammatical principles, known as the concept of transformational-generative grammar, was contrary to the thinking of the time and led the study of linguistics in a new direction.

Chomsky's opposition to the Vietnam War and his influential book *American Power and the New Mandarins* led him to become one of the most widely quoted political intellectuals in America, and one of the most controversial. Teaching at the Massachusetts Institute of Technology for more than fifty years, Chomsky continues his criticism of U.S. foreign policy today.

1682: The First Pennsylvania General Assembly adopts the Great Law, a humanitarian code that guaranteed liberty of conscience and became the fundamental basis of Pennsylvania law.

1736: The Union Fire Company is founded by Benjamin Franklin, becoming the city's first organized voluntary fire-fighting service.

1833: James Boxall begins operating the first omnibus in Philadelphia, running between the Merchant's Coffee House at 2nd Street to the corner of 16th and Chestnut Street. Boxall went out of business within the year, but his initial success laid the foundation for Philadelphia's pioneering transportation initiatives.

1872: The cornerstone is laid to the new Frank Furness–designed Pennsylvania Academy of Fine Arts building at Broad and Cherry streets.

1952: A 500-bed Veterans Administration hospital, dedicated to the service of some 250,000 veterans of all wars living in this area, is dedicated on the anniversary of the attack on Pearl Harbor.

December 8

First established in 1824, the Franklin Institute is a museum dedicated to science, engineering, and invention in honor of Benjamin Franklin. For more than a hundred years, the institute was located at the current site of the Atwater Kent Museum on South 7th Street, but at the start of the Great Depression private funds were raised for the construction of a new building on the Benjamin Franklin Parkway near 20th Street. Opening in 1934, the massive building features the national Franklin Memorial in a domed hall decorated in marble. A favorite destination for Philadelphians and visitors to the city, the Institute offers permanent displays, hands-on science experiments, interactive learning experiences, the second-oldest planetarium in the nation, and traveling exhibitions of all kinds. On December 8, 2006, the Institute proudly announced its one millionth visitor for that year, a significant annual event and a reflection of the thousands of people who visit each month.

Among its permanent exhibits, the giant heart has been a favorite since 1954. Visitors can walk through the two-story-tall heart or view its interior in 3-D. Now visitors can take their own electrocardiogram, or crawl through an eight-foot-long artery. Other longstanding visitor favorites have included a full-sized jet liner, which was removed in the 1980s, a Wright Brothers Model B Flyer, the planetarium, and a domed IMAX theater. The electricity exhibit illustrates Franklin's work and offers a simulation of lightning from a giant Tesla coil mounted on the ceiling. Popular traveling exhibitions have featured topics as broad as King Tutankhamen, Charles Darwin, the human body, and the Titanic.

In addition to exhibitions, the Institute sponsors programs to improve science teaching and has been host to many demonstrations of new inventions and technology. The world's first demonstration of an electronic television system was presented at the Institute in 1934. In 1940, a publicist for the Institute issued a news release that Institute astronomers had discovered that the world would be ending the next day at 3:00 P.M. Because the Institute and its scientists were so well respected, this announcement caused panic in the city. Of course, the publicist was dismissed, and the Institute retained its reputation as one of the city's most visited and beloved attractions.

1776: Washington's retreating army crosses the Delaware River from New Jersey to Pennsylvania.

December 9

With the horrors of the Civil War fading from view, Americans at the end of the nineteenth century were hoping to establish American dominance in world affairs. That opportunity came when conflict with Spain over Cuba and the sinking of the battleship USS *Maine* led to the Spanish-American War. The war was fought largely in two disparate locations and in two different ways: on land in Cuba and on the sea in the Philippines. The USS *Olympia,* an iron armored cruiser captained by Charles V. Gridley, served as Commodore George Dewey's flagship at the Battle of Manila Bay in May of 1898.

Built in California, the *Olympia* was a typical steel warship at 5,886 tons and 344 feet in length. It carried 30 guns, including four 6-pounders and 6 torpedo tubes. After slipping into Manila Bay at night, the *Olympia* led a group of American ships in attacking the inferior Spanish navy. Commodore Dewey began the fight at 5:41 A.M. on May 7 with the famous words, "You may fire when you are ready, Gridley." Dewey's complete victory led to his promotion to the special rank of Admiral of the Navy, which has never been awarded since. His popularity also led to a presidential run in 1900, but Dewey eventually withdrew in favor of President William McKinley.

After leading the victory at Manila Bay, the USS *Olympia* served in the Caribbean, Atlantic, and Mediterranean, and when World War I broke out the ship patroled off Nova Scotia and transported sailors to Murmansk in Russia. In October 1921, the USS *Olympia* had the honor of bringing the remains of the World War I Unknown Soldier from France to Washington for interment. The end of active service came on this date in 1922, when the USS *Olympia* was decommissioned at the Philadelphia Navy Yard. In 1995, the ship was docked at the Independence Seaport Museum on the Delaware River, where it can be toured by the public. As the world's oldest steel warship still afloat and the only surviving naval ship of the Spanish-American War, the ship is a one-of-a-kind treasure but is in need of significant repair. The museum is currently seeking $10 million for hull repairs to prevent the ship from sinking, which is considered imminent.

1833: The Philadelphia Female Anti-Slavery Society is formed.

1869: The Noble Order of the Knights of Labor, a secret society and a precursor to labor unions, is organized in Philadelphia.

1958: The first commercial jet flight from Philadelphia International Airport is scheduled, nine days before the formal dedication of the 10,000-foot runway from which the huge Boeing 707 took off.

December 10

In entertainment history, music stars have transformed themselves into movie stars, but perhaps none so successfully as Philadelphia's Will Smith. Born and raised in the West Philadelphia Wynnewood neighborhood, Willard C. Smith, Jr. (Will Smith), got the nickname "Prince" at Overbrook High School because of his ability to get out of trouble by using his humor, wit, and charm. He started rapping at age twelve, and at age sixteen he met Jeff Townes at a party and they partnered as DJ Jazzy Jeff and the Fresh Prince in Philadelphia's emerging rap music scene. In contrast to "gangsta" rap, their music was positive, wholesome, and mainstream, leading to immediate commercial success.

The duo was among the first to "scratch" records in rap music, which became an important element of hip hop music. Their debut album in 1988 built on the success of the single "Girls Ain't Nothing But Trouble" and they won the first Grammy for Best Rap Performance for their single "Parents Just Don't Understand." Their album, "He's the DJ, I'm the Rapper" was the first hip hop album to reach double platinum sales. Smith was a millionaire by the time he was eighteen, but broke by twenty. Partly to address his financial problems, he turned to acting. He was cast in the lead role in a television sit-com series, "The Fresh Prince of Bel-Air," which ran for six seasons and brought him to the attention of an even wider audience. In that series, he essentially played himself, but his charm and charisma soon brought movie offers and more.

Known in the media as "Mr. July" for his summer blockbusters, Smith has starred in a record eight $100 million–grossing movies, including *Independence Day* and *Men in Black.* While he has appeared most frequently in big special effects action films, he was also nominated for an Academy Award for his dramatic performances in *Ali* and *The Pursuit of Happyness.* On December 10, 2007, he placed his prints at the legendary Grauman's Chinese Theatre in Los Angeles. Smith remains close to family and friends in Philadelphia and has used the city in films and music videos.

1787: Thomas Gallaudet is born in Philadelphia. He later founded the first free school for the deaf in America in Connecticut. One of his eight children founded Gallaudet University in Washington, D.C.

December 11

Philadelphia has always held a unique place in the history of publishing. The city has been home to many American firsts, including the first Bible in English, first volume of Shakespeare, first novel, first popular magazine, and first foreign-language newspaper. Much of the publishing industry was centered in the area around Independence Hall and Washington Square. Successful firms headquartered in Philadelphia include W. B. Saunders, which was founded in 1888 and specialized in medical books; *The Farm Journal,* begun in 1877 and ultimately reaching a circulation of over 600,000; the Curtis Publishing Company, home of *Ladies Home Journal, Saturday Evening Post, Jack and Jill, Holiday,* and other magazines; and the Lippincott Company, once the largest book distributor in the world.

One of the oldest and most prolific firms was founded in 1785 by Matthew Carey, who served as an apprentice printer to Benjamin Franklin in France. The Marquis de Lafayette funded Carey's first publishing enterprise, which later evolved through mergers and dissolutions into several key publishing houses. As a businessman, Carey was known for his pioneering and focused efforts to promote his company. He organized the first book fair, the first American booksellers association, utilized outside proofreaders for the first time, and adopted innovations in marketing and book distribution.

James Fenimore Cooper, one of the century's greatest authors, had a long relationship with the firm, which published his first book in 1826 and ultimately published a total of twenty-four of Cooper's works. The relationship was not always smooth. By December 11, 1830, when *The Water Witch* was published by the firm, Carey was offering less and less money for each new novel, an indication of Cooper's waning popularity and Carey's success-driven agenda. After Carey's death in 1839, the company operated under many names and partnerships, including Carey and Lea, Lea and Blanchard, and Lea Brothers and Company. Under the leadership of Carey's son Henry C. Carey, the business flourished, with publications as diverse as the *Encyclopedia Americana,* maps of all kinds, the first Catholic Bible printed in America, and the works of Sir Walter Scott, Edgar Allan Poe, Washington Irving, and others.

1783: George Duffield preaches a sermon of thanksgiving at the Third Presbyterian Church, on the day appointed by Congress as a day of thanksgiving for the restoration of peace and the establishment of our independence.

December 12

A passionate patriot and staunch supporter of the need for a strong centralized government, New York politician and statesman John Jay was born on this date in 1754 to a successful family of Huguenot merchants in New York City. A graduate of Kings College (later Columbia University), Jay pursued a career as lawyer and political representative of the conservative Whig factions in New York circles. Jay soon embraced the revolutionary ideology but retained a reputation for fairness and careful consideration of the law. It was because of this reputation that Jay was selected to represent New York in the First and Second Continental Congresses, beginning his close association with Philadelphia and the events that birthed a nation.

Balancing his political obligations in New York with his participation in Philadelphia, Jay helped draft the New York Constitution of 1777 and served as president of the Continental Congress from 1778 to 1779. As Minister to Spain, Jay successfully lobbied for a $170,000 loan from Spain to support the war. As the Revolutionary War drew to a close, Jay's diplomatic skills were called in to assist Benjamin Franklin in negotiating with the British to end the war in 1783. Returning to Philadelphia, Jay worked to support the Articles of Confederation but also believed in their inherent weakness and pushed for a new centralized government. In partnership with Alexander Hamilton and James Madison, the three men authored eighty-five Federalist Papers, successfully arguing for the creation of the United States Constitution.

In 1789, President George Washington offered Jay the position of first chief justice of the Supreme Court. At a time when the true powers of the three branches of government were still untried, Jay and his fellow judges enacted a number of significant judgments establishing procedure and ensuring a separation of powers.. Jay continued to serve his country and his state, however, negotiating with the British to resolve shipping and trade conflicts and sitting as governor of New York from 1795 to 1801, for which he resigned as chief justice. As governor, Jay successfully pushed for the abolition of slavery in New York, a cause of great importance to him. Jay retired in 1801 and remained on his family farm until his death in 1829, having proudly and passionately honored both state and country, ensuring the foundations of law in the United States.

1776: The Second Continental Congress leaves Philadelphia for Baltimore, fearing an impending British attack on Philadelphia.

1787: The Pennsylvania Assembly ratifies the United States Constitution, the second state in the country to do so.

1872: Edwin Forrest is found dead in his bed, evidently from apoplexy.

1922: John Wanamaker dies.

December 13

Fox hunting in America can be traced as far back as 1650, and George Washington's diaries from the 1750s frequently mention his enthusiastic participation in the hunts. Although individual men of wealth bred their own dogs and hunted before 1766, the first organized fox hunting club was formed in Philadelphia in that year. The first meeting of the Gloucester Fox Hunting Club took place on December 13, 1766, at the Philadelphia Coffee House at Front and Market streets. The twenty-seven original members were primarily from Philadelphia and adopted a code of rules for the club at the first meeting. The original members included prominent Philadelphians such as Benjamin Chew (former chief justice of the Pennsylvania Supreme Court), Robert Morris (the Financier of the American Revolution), Thomas Mifflin (member of the First Continental Congress), and Samuel Nicholas (first officer commissioned in the U.S. Marine Corps). Samuel Morris was the club's first president.

The hunts were scheduled twice a week, taking place primarily in Gloucester County, New Jersey. The Inn of the Dead Fox in that county is where the hunt frequently rested, and it is still standing today. Samuel Morris' African-American slave, Natty, served as Master of the Hounds from 1769 and received as compensation $50 a year, a house, and a horse—enough to eventually enable him to purchase his freedom. By 1773, the club ran thirty-one hounds, the riders wearing their signature uniform of a dark-brown cloth coat, white buttons, and frock sleeves, buff waistcoat and breeches, and a black velvet cap.

When the American Revolution began, the club ceased operations for a time and the members of the club signed up together as the First Troop Philadelphia City Cavalry. Joining Washington's army in 1776, they played an important role in the Battle of Trenton, swimming their horses across the ice-filled river to the New Jersey bank and serving as escort to Washington during the battle. The troop also participated in the Battle of Princeton, counterattacking with Washington and routing the British. After returning to the Philadelphia area, the troop also fought in the battles of Brandywine and Germantown. After the American victory in the Revolution, the club began meeting again and continued fox hunting until 1818. The First City Troop continues today as a private military unit in service to the country.

1759: The first music store in America opens in Philadelphia.

December 14

Over dinner and drinks in the dining room of Camden County gentleman John E. Hopkins, fossil hobbyist William Parker Foulke first heard the tales of a strange find: bones discovered twenty years before in a steep ravine just yards away. It was the summer of 1858, and Foulke was so drawn to the stories he asked to be shown the site immediately. Hopkins obliged and within a few weeks Foulke arranged for a new excavation of the rich marl deposits along the stream bed at the bottom of the ravine. What he found there would ultimately change the way humans saw their place in history, and their understanding of the history of the earth.

One by one, Foulke and his workers uncovered the remains of animals long gone. Seashells by the hundreds were discovered, a reflection of New Jersey's history as the ocean floor 100 million years before. Foulke also uncovered the almost-complete remains of an animal larger than an elephant but with unique features that were reminiscent of birds and reptiles. Fossils were not new to the scientific community; indeed, in Philadelphia fifty years earlier, Thomas Jefferson and Charles Willson Peale both exhibited the remains of large mammoths and other specimens. In 1841, British scientist Richard Owen proposed the existence of giant, prehistoric reptiles and coined the name "dinosaurs," Latin for terrible lizard.

What was different about the Haddonfield, New Jersey, discovery was the sheer size and quality of the fossils, which allowed a complete picture of the living animal to be created. Unlike earlier discoveries, Foulke's discovery was virtually complete, allowing for a highly accurate reconstruction of the anatomy of the animal. Foulke called on his friend and anatomist Joseph Leidy, who examined the specimens and made the first sketches of the dinosaur he called *Hadrosaurus foulkii,* in honor of its origin and discoverer. On this date in 1858, Foulke and Leidy announced their discovery to the members of the Academy of Natural Sciences of Philadelphia, forever influencing the new science of dinosaur paleontology.

1799: George Washington dies at Mount Vernon in Virginia.

December 15

As almost any politician will tell you, crafting the law is a time-consuming and often contentious process. Compromise and diplomacy are always required, as opposing sides seek opportunities to represent their individual agenda while also recognizing that without a certain willingness to give up closely held beliefs, no larger goal will be met. The earliest days of the creation of the laws which established the United States and its government were undoubtedly fraught with the strong positions and firm beliefs which challenge lawmakers today. In particular, many who attended the Constitutional Convention in Philadelphia in 1787 recognized that certain significant rights and protections were not being included in the Constitution, which was mostly concerned with establishing a working frame of government. Amendments would be necessary, and in light of this need to adjust and build on the strengths of the Constitution, a process was put into place.

On this date in 1791, just over four years after the Constitution was ratified, the first ten amendments were ratified while Congress was seated in Philadelphia and the Bill of Rights was born. The result of a deal to convince anti-Federalists to support ratification of the United States Constitution, the Bill of Rights was intended to specifically ensure individual rights of American citizens. In 1789, James Madison assumed the role of shepherding the initial seventeen proposed amendments through Congress. His participation was seen as key, because as the primary architect of the Constitution, his support of the effort to alter or amend it was perceived as necessary. Madison was at first reluctant, believing the Constitution adequately protected citizens, but he came to understand the need for compromise and willingly supported the effort. The United States Senate approved just twelve, and through the process of ratification in the states, the final number agreed upon became ten.

At heart a declaration of rights and deeply inspired by the complaints that led to the war with England, the Bill of Rights guarantees freedom of speech, freedom of the press, freedom of religion, and freedom of assembly. Further protections include those against unreasonable searches and seizures, the right to a speedy trial, the right to bear arms, and freedom from cruel and unusual punishments. Since 1791, an additional seventeen amendments have been ratified, many providing significant impacts on American lives. Always debated but firm in their place within our government and daily lives, the Bill of Rights remains a defining icon of our national history.

1854: The first street-cleaning machine in the United States, with revolving brooms attached to a cylinder on a cart, is put into operation in Philadelphia.

1968: Philadelphia Eagles fans boo and attack Santa Claus with snowballs, establishing their reputation as the worst behaving fans in professional sports.

In the mid twentieth century, Dr. Margaret Mead was unquestionably one of the most famous women in the country. Born in Philadelphia on December 16, 1901, Mead was the daughter of a Quaker academic family; her father was a professor of economics at the University of Pennsylvania, and her mother was a sociologist. Able to attend college at a time when few women did, she studied anthropology at Barnard College under Professor Franz Boas and worked closely with his assistant, Ruth Benedict, with whom she developed a lifelong friendship. In 1925, Mead began her first field expedition to the island of Tau in Samoa. It would define her professional career and personal life for the next fifty years.

Studying the development of adolescent girls in Samoan society, she published *Coming of Age in Samoa,* which reported that Samoan girls entered womanhood without the emotional crisis and drama attendant to that transition for many American girls. This book, with its somewhat racy investigation of adolescent sex, was widely read by the general public, becoming both highly influential for its anthropological insights and widely criticized of faulty research methods and for promoting free love. Mead continued her work, publishing many more studies conducted in the Admiralty Islands, New Guinea, and Bali. Her books included *Coming Up in New Guinea, Sex and Temperament in Three Primitive Societies,* and a memoir, *Blackberry Winter.* Mead also served as Dr. Ruth Benedict's literary executor and published an anthology of Benedict's diaries, letters, and other works.

Much of Mead's work was done under the auspices of the American Museum of Natural History in New York, where she served as a member of the staff. She also taught at a number of universities, including Fordham and Columbia. Always a dynamic and exciting personality, she created a stir wherever she appeared. One of the hallmarks of her work was her belief that the ultimate value of studying others was what we could learn to improve our own society. Her publications and lectures on women's rights, child-rearing, and education influenced American women in particular. Married three times, Mead died in 1978 leaving a daughter who also became an anthropologist and academician.

1841: The Pennsylvania Hospital for the Insane is opened in West Philadelphia, far from its parent, Pennsylvania Hospital.

December 17

Born and raised in Buffalo, New York, Grover Washington, Jr., first learned to play the saxophone on an instrument given to him by his mother. As a young man serving in the military, he played with an Army band. Following his discharge from the service in 1967, he settled in Philadelphia, the hometown of his wife, and began his career in jazz. Honing his skills in jazz clubs in Philadelphia and New York, he worked during the day at a Philadelphia record wholesaler. After his second album, *Inner City Blues,* was released in 1971, Grover commented that "I was unloading boxes of records with my own name on them."

During the 1970s he further developed a soulful sound, playing in concert halls and recording more albums. In 1981, his album *Winelight* earned two Grammys for "Best Jazz Fusion Recording" and "Best R&B Song" for the single "Just the Two of Us," recorded with Bill Withers. Over the next decade, Washington recorded and produced increasingly sophisticated music, earning four gold records for sales over one million. A beloved adopted son, Washington was the headliner at one of Philadelphia's July Fourth celebrations at Penn's Landing, drawing an audience of one million people. In the early 1980s, Washington played an important role in establishing and producing the Philadelphia singing group, Pieces of a Dream.

A devoted Philadelphia 76ers fan always occupying a seat in Section F Row 12, Washington played the national anthem ten times for ten 76er victories, most notably in game three of the Eastern Conference Finals against Milwaukee in 1983. He expressed his admiration for Julius Erving by writing a song for the *Winelight* album titled "Let It Flow (For Dr. J.)." Washington was quoted as believing that every athlete is a frustrated musician and every musician is a frustrated athlete. His height of 5 feet 8 inches ended a debate about basketball versus music as a career. Grover Washington, Jr., died on December 17, 1999, of a heart attack at age 56. The Grover Washington Jr. Middle School in the Olney neighborhood was named for him in 2001.

1777: George Washington sets up the Continental troops at Valley Forge.

The Fugitive Slave Act, enacted in 1850 by the federal government in support of slave holders in the South, inspired a number of brave, as well as cowardly, acts on the part of Pennsylvania and Philadelphia citizens. A strong Quaker presence in the southeastern region of the state resulted in an active and highly successful branch of the Underground Railroad. However, business interests and a general suspicion among many of the dangers of an increased role in politics and culture for freed slaves inspired a highly tense and often conflicted population. In September 1851, an incident occurred in Christiana, Pennsylvania, near Lancaster, that would ultimately influence the national debate on slavery for years to come.

In August of that year, Maryland slave owner Edward Gorsuch arrived in Philadelphia in hopes of filing a claim on four runaway slaves he believed were being aided by an African-American activist in Christiana. With a sheriff and members of his own family in tow, Gorsuch set out by train. Word of his intent was sent ahead, however, by sympathetic anti-slavery activists, and upon his arrival at the home of William Parker, he met with armed resistance. The stand-off continued for several hours until the arrival of three local, white Quaker neighbors boosted the resisters' confidence and shots rang out. Gorsuch was killed while Parker and most of his family and the runaways fled for Canada; Parker was eventually aided by Frederick Douglass in New York.

In response to the murder of a white slaveholder by his black slaves, the federal prosecutors filed treason charges against thirty-eight men from Christiana. The first man tried, local miller Castner Hanway, was soon acquitted and the remaining charges dropped. One week after his acquittal, on December 18, 1851, Hanway and fellow defendant Elijah Lewis appeared at an anti-slavery meeting in Philadelphia. Flanked by noted abolitionists Lucretia Mott and Joshua R. Giddings, the men were received with great enthusiasm by the audience. The long-term impact of the trial, including the inability of prosecutors to convict on treason charges, was felt for many decades afterward. In a more chilling effect, John Wilkes Booth was said to have viewed the riot as a prime example of northern aggression against the South, influencing his decision to commit the greatest act of violence by assassinating President Abraham Lincoln nearly fifteen years later.

1865: The Thirteenth Amendment abolishing slavery is declared in effect.

1949: The Philadelphia Eagles crush the Los Angeles Rams, 14–0, to win the National Football League Championship for the second straight year.

December 19

Defeated and demoralized by a string of difficult losses, General George Washington and the Continental Army sought a strategic site to overwinter in late 1777. British general William Howe had successfully pursued Washington and his men through the towns and townships to the west of Philadelphia. In September, the British assumed control of Valley Forge in the wake of his decisive victory over the Americans at the Battle of Brandywine. Howe chose not to pursue the weakened American forces, however, due primarily to a severe lack of provisions. Washington struggled to protect the city, positioning his army between Howe and the main roads in from the west. Following defeats at Paoli and Germantown, Washington's army retreated and Howe gained control of Philadelphia.

As winter set in and the possibility of engaging Howe diminished, Washington looked for a secure location to regroup and wait until spring. He chose Valley Forge, named for the iron forge nestled along Valley Creek. Flanked by high ground and positioned for better defending areas west of the city, Valley Forge seemed perfect. On December 19, 1777, Washington and nearly 12,000 men marched into the camp. Defense lines, training grounds, and encampments were laid out, with priority given to the construction of shelter and the procurement of provisions. Within six weeks, huts and tents for the men were completed. Food, fuel, and clothing proved much more difficult to locate, however. Despite pleas to the Congress, Washington and his men suffered frigid cold and lack of food. Disease spread rapidly, resulting in the deaths of more than 2,000 men. Sick, tired, and undersupplied, the army struggled for survival through the worst of the winter.

In addition to food, clothing, and shelter, Washington recognized that his men also lacked proper military training. Baron Friedrich Wilhelm von Steuben, a Prussian of great training skill, was selected to improve soldiering among the men. Steuben designed a training curriculum that included a standard text (written by him in French and translated for the men) as well as regular drills and a personal approach virtually unheard of at the time. As the men departed Valley Forge on June 19, 1778, the Continental Army proved stronger and more prepared for battle. Out of the depths of the cold winter, a true army was born.

1732: Benjamin Franklin begins publishing *Poor Richard's Almanac.*

1790: The First-Day or Sunday-School Society is founded (the full title was the Society for the Institution and Support of First-Day or Sunday-Schools in the City of Philadelphia and the Districts of Southwark and the Northern Liberties).

December 20

Philadelphia has many "firsts" of political or economic interest, but it also has a social history of note. The city was the location of the origin of a series of balls and social events, called the Philadelphia Assemblies, which began in the winter of 1748-49, the first in the colonies. Philadelphia was the biggest city in America at the time, with a substantial population of wealthy upper-class businessmen and entrepreneurs. Assemblies were quite exclusive and a number of rules were established to govern the dances and card playing. For the first Assemblies, the cost was forty shillings, and fifty-nine men signed on as the first subscribers. According to the rules, Assemblies were to be held every Thursday from six to twelve from January 1 to May 1, ladies and visitors were admitted only by ticket, and each dancing set was to be composed of ten couples.

During the American Revolution, attempts were made to continue the Assemblies, with the specific prohibition of Tories. A notice appeared in a 1780 newspaper stating, "It is expected that no man who has not taken a decisive part in favor of American independence will in future intrude on the Dancing Assembly of the city; such characters are either too detestable or too insignificant for Whig Society." During the 1780s and 1790s, the assemblies flourished in the city, with the president, cabinet members, and foreign dignitaries frequently in attendance. At a special assembly in honor of his birthday in 1793, Washington gave a toast: "The Dancing Assembly of Philadelphia—May the members thereof, and the Fair who honor it with their presence, long continue in the enjoyment of an amusement so innocent and agreeable."

Unlike assemblies in other parts of America that died out (with the notable exceptions of New Orleans and Savannah), the Philadelphia assemblies were sustained. During the Gilded Age at the end of the nineteenth century, they were a place to enjoy dancing, exhibit wealth, and introduce young women to proper society. On December 20, 1957, the Philadelphia Assembly marked the two hundredth anniversary of the tradition with a glittering event at the Bellevue-Stratford Hotel, continuing a social tradition born of the city's elegant past.

1870: Rothermel's painting *The Battle of Gettysburg* is unveiled at the Academy of Music. The 16-inch x 32-inch painting is now a focal point of the Pennsylvania State Museum in Harrisburg.

December 21

On this date in 1849, a group of avid ice skaters gathered at Sigman's Hotel on George Street (now Sansom Street) near Sixth with the intent of establishing a social and sporting club. Located at the conjunction of two rivers, Philadelphia is perfectly suited for the art and sport of ice skating. With the organization of the Skater's Club of the City and County of Philadelphia that day, the nation saw the creation of the first skating club in North America. Beyond the opportunity to teach and improve the art of ice skating in a friendly and social atmosphere, the club also addressed an unusual sport-related risk: the possibility of falling through the natural ice that formed on the rivers.

As ice skating grew in popularity, so too did the frequency of ice breaks and drowning. The Humane Society of Philadelphia was formed as early as 1770 to perform rescue work, but the club addressed the specific need on the ice. All members were required to wear a special identifying pin in the shape of an ice skate. Further, each carried a ball of twine for use in the immediate assistance of an unlucky skater. According to the club minutes, rescues were enacted frequently, illustrating the significance of their role along the river banks. By 1861, the Humane Society was absorbed by the Skater's Club and for the next quarter century, skating on the rivers thrived. A clubhouse on the Schuylkill River served as a popular gathering site.

In the early 1900s, competition for quality ice between the sportsmen and ice dealers and conflicts with boat captains who wanted a clear path through the ice resulted in a dramatic reduction in the activities of the Skaters Club. With the development of indoor, artificial rinks in the 1910s, skating experienced a revival. Headquartered at the Philadelphia Ice Palace at 45th and Market streets, the club offered skating lessons, carnivals, and competitions. Finally, in 1937, the club purchased land near Haverford College in Ardmore and built a new rink. Over the years several national championships have been held at the rink, and well-known members include skating superstars Dick Button and Scott Hamilton. Today, the club continues to serve as a training ground for aspiring professional as well as amateur figure skaters, even as the risk of ice breaks is no more.

1933: Dried human blood serum is first prepared at the University of Pennsylvania and later used to great effect during World War II.

December 22

In 2010, the Denver Art Museum presented the first museum retrospective of the work of Charles Deas, an artist who helped form Americans' ideas of the West in the 1840s. Born in Philadelphia on December 22, 1818, to a family that was prominent in colonial Philadelphia, Deas studied art at the National Academy of Design in New York. Settling there, he built a decent reputation in the 1830s painting portraits and scenes of literary subjects. During an economic downturn his commissions declined and like many young men of his time, he went West, settling in the Missouri Territory near St. Louis.

In 1840 he joined his brother, a soldier, at Fort Crawford and began visiting Sioux, Winnebago, and other Indian communities in the area. Inspired by what he saw and experienced, he began painting Western themes. His paintings of ordinary life of Indian tribes, dramatic pieces on hunting, and wilderness travel, and his rather formal portraits of individual members of the tribes, became very popular. His *Council of the Shawnees at North Bend* portrays General George Rogers Clark in a historical event. His most famous painting, *Long Jakes, the Rocky Mountain Man,* romanticized the hunter and made him nationally known. He also painted vivid scenes from his imagination. Before the age of photography, paintings were the primary means for Easterners to learn something about the culture and look of the West. Deas had a strong impact on what people thought they knew about the expanding Western territories of America.

Immensely popular, Deas influenced the work of other major artists such as William Tylee Ranney and Arthur Fitzwilliam Tait, but his fame soon faded. When he was institutionalized in a mental asylum in New York at the young age of twenty-nine, Deas' career was tragically cut short. His illness had an impact on his work at the time, and one of his paintings featuring a sea monster was described as "so horrible, that a sensitive artist fainted at the sight." Deas remained institutionalized until his death in 1867.

1719: The first issue of the *American Weekly Mercury,* the city's first newspaper, is published.

1775: John Paul Jones receives his naval commission from John Hancock in Philadelphia.

December 23

The deep, rich tones of a bell ring through the air every hour on the hour. Often presumed to be the clock in the tower at City Hall, it is in actuality the eighth-largest bell in the world, hanging inconspicuously at the top of One South Broad Street, formerly known as the Liberty-Lincoln Building and the PNB Building. Weighing in at over seventeen tons, the Founder's Bell, as it is known today, stands as a commemoration of one of the city's greatest retailers and philanthropists, John Wanamaker. Though it resides today in a seemingly perfect home, it began its journey thousands of miles away, much as the city's other famous bell did in the 1700s.

Upon the death of John Wanamaker in 1922, his son, Rodman Wanamaker, sought a compelling and appropriate way to commemorate his father's lifelong work. He determined to commission the creation of a bell, and ordered the construction of a tower atop the Wanamaker Department Store building at Juniper and Market streets. The bell was cast in England, and was said at the time to be the largest ever completed in that country. The bell features a facsimile of John Wanamaker's signature and the words, "Let those who follow me continue to build with the plumb of honor, the level of truth and the square of integrity, education, courtesy and mutuality." Measuring over nine and a half feet in diameter and almost eight feet tall, the massive bell is tuned to a low D bass clef, said to be a half-tone lower than the bell in St. Paul's Cathedral. The bell was so large that the first ocean liner engaged to ship it to Philadelphia had to decline because of the weight. Finally, in mid-December 1926, the bell arrived in New York on the Cunard liner *Ascania,* and traveled by train to Philadelphia.

On this date, hundreds of people gathered to watch the bell as it was hoisted to the top of Wanamaker's store 325 feet above street level. It was first rung on New Year's Eve that year, and was designed to swing freely in ringing. Unfortunately, the swinging bell caused the building to shake, so it was remounted. After the Liberty-Lincoln Building was completed in 1932 to house the Men's Store for Wanamaker's, the bell was moved to its new location. Today, it continues to ring out hourly and on a good day can be heard for twenty-five miles, reaching all corners of the city it presides over.

1909: The battleship *Utah* is launched from New York Shipbuilding in Camden, New Jersey. It is the most powerful United States naval vessel to date, with ten 12-inch guns.

December 24

Charles Willson Peale was a man of many talents and interests. As one of the best and most well-known artists of his day, he painted a number of Revolutionary War heroes and leading Philadelphians. Peale also had a keen interest in the natural world, especially that of the new nation. He founded a museum, which was housed partially at the Pennsylvania State House (now Independence Hall) and at the American Philosophical Society on Fifth Street. One of the first of its kind in the nation, his museum contained many natural specimens including plants and minerals, as well as preserved and live mammals, birds, and insects, often displayed in naturalized dioramas. Peale himself experimented with taxidermy and some of his work survives today. On this date in 1801, he introduced one of his most significant specimens to an awe-struck public.

In 1801, news of the discovery of three new mastodon skeletons came to Peale's attention and he traveled to Newburgh, New York, with his son Rembrandt to obtain the fossils for his museum. Working with Caspar Wistar, a noted expert on anatomy, he and Rembrandt mounted a full skeleton that measured eleven feet tall and seventeen feet long. Peale initially displayed the skeleton to members of the American Philosophical Society, and the general public was admitted soon after. The mastodon quickly became the most famous part of his museum. In his acclaimed 1822 self-portrait *The Artist in His Museum,* the mastodon's tooth is at his feet. After Peale's death, the specimen disappeared, but it was found in Germany a hundred years later, and can be viewed there today.

Jefferson, in particular, was interested in the mastodon and believed that live animals could still be found in the West. In 1803, he sent Meriwether Lewis to Peale's museum in preparation for his expedition to the Pacific. The mastodon was significant because European scientists had argued that North America could only support weak or small animals and plants. Jefferson disagreed, arguing that the mastodon was proof of the vigor of the American climate and environment. Although Lewis and Clark did not find a living mastodon or the Northwest Passage, the mastodon continued to hold a special place in the pantheon of American natural history.

1680: Edward Drinker is born, said to be the first child of English descent born in Philadelphia. He died on November 17, 1782.

1728: Samuel Keimer founds the *Pennsylvania Gazette* newspaper.

1994: A late-night fire at the primate house at the Philadelphia Zoo results in the deaths of twenty-three primates, including a family of six lowland gorillas, a family of three orangutans, and ten lemurs, among others. The scarcity of fire detection equipment in the animal habitats at the zoo was blamed for the deaths, and the zoo responded by improving all animal buildings.

December 25

A visitor to Philadelphia in 1749 noted that the Quakers who founded the city did not celebrate Christmas as a special day. But as Anglicans, Catholics, Lutherans, and Moravians settled in the city, they brought their religious traditions and services as well as their secular traditions like the Christmas tree, the Yule Log, and the parties surrounding Twelfth Night. Throughout the 1800s, Philadelphians enjoyed the addition of traditions such as Santa Claus, holiday parties, and street and window decorations. By the mid-1900s, many of these traditions had moved outside of the privacy of the home into the shops, streets, and public square of Philadelphia.

In hopes of bringing in more shoppers, many of the city's department stores initiated special holiday attractions. The Wanamaker holiday light show, accompanied by concerts on the world's largest pipe organ, has been an attraction for more than five decades. A huge curtain almost five stories tall holds lighted shapes and figures from children's Christmas stories that switch on and off in time to the music. At Strawbridge and Clothier, the attraction was a life-sized walk-through display of the story and characters of Charles Dickens' *A Christmas Carol.* Spectacular trees and garlands decorated all floors of the store. The Lit Brothers store on Market Street featured a Christmas Village display, a life-sized presentation of a colonial village at Christmas, with moving figures. The display is now a part of the holiday celebrations at the Please Touch Museum. A long tradition that has ended was the annual arrival of Santa Claus at Gimbels. Transported in a fire engine and portrayed always by a Philadelphia firefighter, Santa scampered up the tall ladder of the truck into the upper floors of the store. Thousands came to witness this annual event.

City neighborhoods also found ways to expand community participation in Christmas celebrations. In South Philadelphia, entire blocks are lighted with garlands of Christmas lights, often strung completely across the narrow streets. More modern and less family-oriented traditions have also evolved, among them the Running of the Santas, a bar-hopping event that raises money for charity, which was started in the city. Through these public gatherings and highly anticipated traditions, people continue to celebrate the holiday season in a uniquely Philadelphia way.

1685: The *Kalendarium Pennsylvaniese* is published as the first almanac printed in America.

1776: General George Washington and his troops cross the Delaware River to surprise Hessian troops camped at Trenton.

1946: W. C. Fields dies.

December 26

Two years after leaving the presidency, George Washington was retired at Mount Vernon in Virginia when he became ill and died suddenly on December 14, 1799. News traveled slowly in the eighteenth century, and news of his death reached the national capital of Philadelphia days later. Congress immediately proclaimed December 26, 1799, as a national day of mourning and contemplation. Ceremonies and funeral events took place across the nation, but the formal national funeral for the beloved hero of the Revolution and the nation's first president was planned for Philadelphia.

The City Council, directed by Mayor Robert Wharton, requested that the bells of Christ Church be muffled for three days "as a mark of deep regret with which the citizens of this place view the melancholy news." Washington had attended services at the church for three years during his residence in Philadelphia. On the morning of the 26th, sixteen cannon were fired early and one cannon was fired every half hour until the start of a funeral procession at 11:30. The procession started at Sixth and Chestnut streets with members of Congress, a military guard, and local leaders accompanying a bier to Zion Lutheran Church at 4th and Cherry streets. According to witnesses, the streets and windows along the route were crowded with Philadelphia citizens offering their respects. Zion Lutheran was chosen because it was the largest church in the city. Bishop William White, rector of Christ Church, conducted the service while General Richard Henry Lee (later the father of Robert E. Lee) gave an undistinguished eulogy to a crowd of about 4,000, including President John Adams. The speech's only highlight was the phrase "first in war, first in peace, first in the hearts of his countrymen."

Two days later, Congress approved another resolution calling for the erection of a monument honoring Washington in the new capitol under construction along the Potomac. Plans were made with the Washington family to inter his body in the city to be named for him. But Congress did not appropriate funds for the monument until the 1880s and Washington's remains still rest at Mount Vernon.

1683: A meeting of the Provincial Council, at which the Proprietor presided, asks Enoch Flower to become the first schoolmaster in Philadelphia. His school operated until 1689, when it was superseded by the Public Grammar School established by the Monthly Meeting of Friends.

1831: Financier of the War of 1812 Stephen Girard, with an estate valued at $7,500,000, dies.

1878: Electric lights are first used commercially in a store in Philadelphia.

1940: The *Philadelphia Story* is released, starring Katharine Hepburn and Cary Grant.

December 27

The tragic fire at One Meridian Plaza in 1991 was an example of what can happen when almost everything goes wrong, and it led to significant changes in building requirements for Philadelphia's hi-rise structures. Built in 1972, the thirty-eight-story office building was located in the center of the business district at 15th and South Penn Square, across the street from City Hall. The tallest building constructed in the city since the early 1930s, the building code that governed its construction dated from 1949 and made no distinction between ordinary buildings and massive hi-rises. Sprinklers were installed at first only in the underground portions of the building; by 1991, retro-conversion of the fire protection system had been completed only on the four upper floors.

On Saturday night, February 23, 1991, a fire started in a pile of linseed-soaked rags on the floor on the 22nd story. By the time firefighters were called, heavy smoke and flames were coming out of the windows and the fire was rapidly spreading. The pressure valves on the water standpipes had not been adjusted properly and there were problems getting enough water to the fire. Back-up generators did not work, making it impossible for the firefighters to use the elevators. Three firefighters became disoriented in the black smoke on the 28th floor and perished in the fire; another twenty-four firefighters were injured. At seven o'clock the next morning, the fire commissioner ordered the building evacuated because of imminent danger of collapse. The fire was finally stopped when it reached the 30th floor where sprinklers were activated.

In the aftermath of the tragedy, efforts toward improved safety resulted in a law requiring every nonresidential building in the city taller than seventy-five feet to have sprinklers installed by 1997, affecting about 300 structures in the city. The blackened and burned building was the subject of lawsuits and wrangling over its future for many years. Because of its proximity to other buildings, in particular the historically and municipally significant City Hall, it could not be imploded, requiring a slow manual process of demolition. On December 27, 1998, demolition began on the last of the damaged floors. One Meridian Plaza was replaced in January 2009 by a forty-eight-story condominium complex. On October 21, 2009, a plaque was unveiled at the site honoring the three firefighters who lost their lives in a fire that affected more than just a single skyscraper.

1773: The tea ship *Polly* is turned away by American colonials and forced to return to England with its contents.

1862: The Union Club unanimously adopts a plan to form the Union League of Philadelphia.

December 28

Grand homes and even grander lifestyles seemed destined for the design style of architect Horace Trumbauer. Known for his work on the homes of the nation's wealthiest financiers and industrialists of the Gilded Age in the late nineteenth century, Trumbauer built his reputation by creating extravagant and elegant homes for the likes of sugar magnate William W. Harrison, partners George W. Elkins and Peter A. B. Widener, and coal millionaire Edward J. Berwind. After nearly twenty years of success in residential design, Trumbauer turned his attention to commercial and industrial structures, forever changing the look and grandeur of Philadelphia's built landscape.

Born the son of a salesman in Philadelphia on this date in 1868, Trumbauer trained with the local architectural firm owned by G. W. and W. D. Hewitt before opening his own office by age twenty-one. After several years of smaller commissions notably with Wendell and Smith, developers of Overbrook Farms, Trumbauer received his first solo job. He designed an affordable suburban home at a cost of just $178. Within a few more years, however, Trumbauer was designing massive homes for the elite of the city, some with as many as 110 rooms and hundreds of thousands of dollars worth of fine marble and plaster work. Generally considered a classicist, Trumbauer's work reflected a detailed view of many revival styles, among them Italian Renaissance, Gothic, and Colonial. Just prior to World War I, however, Trumbauer and his firm turned their attention to the demand for large municipal and commercial designs.

Among his commissions can be found a variety of railroad stations, hospitals, hotels, office buildings, and factories. Most notable in Philadelphia are the main branch of the Free Library on Logan Circle (1925-27), the Philadelphia Museum of Art (1916-28), the Irvine Auditorium (1926-32), and the Public Ledger Building (1923). In most cases, his commercial works have survived to be used as they were designed, though some have been adapted to new demands. For example, in 1980 the Ben Franklin Hotel at 834 Chestnut Street, built by Trumbauer in 1925, was closed and renovated into apartments. At the cusp of a new housing trend in Philadelphia, the hotel represents the beginning of a revival of many grand old structures, ensuring their presence in the city and contributing to the elegant, historical atmosphere for which Philadelphia is known, much of it the result Trumbauer's work.

1732: The first advertisement for Benjamin Franklin's *Poor Richard's Almanac* appears in his *Pennsylvania Gazette* newspaper.

December 29

E. C. Brown and Andrew Stevens, Jr., owned one of the most successful African-American banks in the northern states at the beginning of the twentieth century. On December 29, 1919, they opened the Dunbar Theatre at South and Broad streets to provide a venue for African-American theater and music revues. The theater hosted the Lafayette Theatre group from Harlem, hosted benefits for the NAACP, and offered quality entertainment, including "Shuffle Along," which made its debut in Philadelphia before opening as the first all-black musical revue on Broadway. But they could not make a business success with the venture and sold the theater in 1921 to another African-American entertainment entrepreneur, John T. Gibson.

John T. Gibson was already a successful entertainment entrepreneur, and ran Gibson's Auditorium on South Street, booking black vaudeville acts. In 1914 he bought the Standard Theatre on the 1100 block of South Street. The Standard offered vaudeville, music, and stage shows to the increasing number of blacks who moved to the city after World War I. Bessie Smith and Ethel Waters, the "Black Rockettes," and jazz bands led by Duke Ellington and Louis Armstrong all played the Standard. When he purchased the Dunbar in 1921, he installed the larger acts at that location. As the owner of two successful black theaters, Gibson became the wealthiest African-American citizen of Philadelphia at the time. As time went on, racially mixed audiences flocked to the theaters to enjoy jazz until the Standard closed in 1931.

More than thirty years later in the 1960s, the city experienced a revival of black performing arts venues with the founding of Freedom Theatre, a black community-based theater and locale for arts education by John Allen and Robert Leslie. Located at the home of Edwin Forrest, a leading white tragic actor of the nineteenth century, Freedom Theatre started a black professional theater company in the 1990s. Works by African-American playwrights such as Leroy Jones, Ossie Davis, and James Baldwin were offered. Today, more than 800 students annually participate in its performing arts training program, helping to develop African-American talent for the future, ensuring Philadelphia's place in the history of African-American theater history.

1719: The first non-publisher advertisement in an American newspaper appears in Andrew Bradford's *Weekly Mercury*. The ad regarded a runaway slave from Virginia.

1769: The first announcement is published advertising the opening of a fine china factory in Southwark, likely the first in the state. Refused a loan by the Pennsylvania General Assembly, the factory closed in 1772.

1870: An ordinance is passed providing for a paid fire department.

December 30

The Philadelphia Zoo is America's oldest zoo, opening on July 1, 1874. It prides itself today on its collection of 1,300 animals, and it attracts over a million visitors a year. Although the emphasis of the modern zoo is on conservation and providing the most appropriate living conditions for the animals, its most famous resident lived a confined life that would not be permitted under today's standards.

Born in West Africa, the western lowland gorilla named Massa came to America as the pet of Gertrude Lintz, an eccentric woman from Brooklyn. Massa lived in her home, where she taught him to do household chores. When he was four years old, Lintz accidentally dumped a pail of water on him that he was using to scrub the floor, surprising the gorilla. She required more than seventy stitches after the attack that followed, and decided she could not keep him any longer. Massa arrived at the Philadelphia Zoo on December 30, 1935. For the next half a century, his home at the zoo was a concrete-floored cage about ten paces long and five paces wide. Beloved by zoo visitors, Massa stayed in the cage alone, sometimes turning his back on visitors, but also exhibiting gentle characteristics toward his human handlers.

Gorillas are considered by many to be humanity's closest relatives and are known to live as long as thirty-five years in the wild. Fed on a high-protein, low-cholesterol diet with plenty of fruit and vegetables, the aging gorilla lived far longer. Weighing 400 pounds at his prime, by 1984 he was bald, suffered from arthritis, and weighed about 250 pounds. On December 30, 1984, a fiftieth birthday celebration was held at the zoo, with hundreds of visitors and a birthday sundae made with fruit, whipped cream, and ice cream. That night, Massa suffered a stroke and died; autopsy results showed advanced hardening of the arteries. In July 1999, the zoo opened a new primate center on the site where the old monkey house and Massa's cage were located. Featuring wide open spaces and trees to climb, the primate center provides the current zoo gorillas with a totally different life experience. Massa is memorialized at the zoo with a bronze sculpture of him in his prime by artist Eric Berg.

1851: Barnum's Museum, located at Seventh and Chestnut streets, burns down.

1895: The Bourse building on Seventh Street formally opens, organized around the idea that all businessmen could meet and exchange their views. Founded in 1890, the exchange was initially conceived by George E. Bartol.

1911: The new Wanamaker Department Store building is dedicated at Juniper and Market streets with President William H. Taft attending.

1918: Three homes are bombed by anarchists, those of Justice Robert von Moschzisker of the State Supreme Court, Judge Frank L. Gorman of the municipal court, and acting Superintendent of Police William Mills. All homes are destroyed but no one is injured. The case is never solved.

December 31

New Year's Eve, celebrated by millions all over the world with fireworks, horns, funny hats, parties, and public countdowns from ten to one has become much more to African-Americans across the country as "Watch Night." On this date in 1862, thousands anxiously awaited the moment at 12:01 A.M. on January 1, 1863, when the Emancipation Proclamation became law, forever changing the history of America and starting a tradition continued today in churches and homes in every state. Though primarily associated with African-American traditions in the minds of many, the practice of commemorating the end of the calendar year with church services and community events began much earlier, grounded in the religious observations of the Moravians and from there spreading to other denominations.

The earliest Moravian observation of Watch Night is believed to have occurred in 1733 in Germany. One of the several religious groups to seek a new life in Pennsylvania, Moravians brought their tradition with them. Inspired by the Moravians, John Wesley and the Methodist Church incorporated a similar practice into their rituals, with the first known service in the United States held in Philadelphia in 1770 at Old St. George's Church, where it continues today as "Covenant Renewal Services." Viewed as an opportunity to give thanks for the blessings of the previous year and to express wishes for a happy and healthy new year, services generally involve friends and extended family in a spiritual alternative to nonsecular celebrations.

In September 1862, President Abraham Lincoln released a preliminary version of the Emancipation Proclamation, which would free a large percentage of enslaved blacks. The official release of the document was planned for January 1, 1863. As the hours passed, those who would be most affected by the Proclamation must have waited with tense anticipation. Combining their political freedom with the spiritual freedom of the coming of Jesus Christ, many African-American communities today honor Watch Night in deeply personal and yet largely community-oriented ways. Dinners, prayer services, and celebrations remind many of the moment when life changed completely and a new era dawned.

1800: William Birch's *Views of Philadelphia* is published, featuring twenty-four hand-colored prints depicting scenes of Philadelphia.

The cold winter of 1776 seemed far from the hot days of July, when independence was declared and all of Philadelphia seemed poised for the push toward war with England. General George Washington, appointed commander of the American Continental Army in May 1775, on the first day the Continental Congress met in Philadelphia, was now facing a demoralized and poorly outfitted military. Following defeats in New York, Washington and his troops were forced to retreat to New Jersey, leaving Congress to worry about the impending threat to their own safety. Crossing into Pennsylvania in early December, the Americans watched and waited while the majority of the British troops returned to New York to regroup over the winter. The remaining Hessian troops occupied Trenton. Washington, aware of the thin thread of strength left within his own ranks, determined to attack Trenton, and silently crossed the Delaware River on Christmas Day. His three-pronged attack was ultimately reduced to just one, as two of his officers, Lieutenant Colonel John Cadwalader and General Ewing, were unable to cross owing to severe weather and ice in the river. Ultimately, the Americans achieved victory, defeating the Hessians and reviving morale and purpose throughout the Army and within Congress.

One participant of the winter maneuvers was Charles Willson Peale, already a noted artist, but destined to become one of Philadelphia's most famous citizens. In a daily diary, Peale recorded his experience as a member of Cadwalader's Associators, a Philadelphia militia group called up specifically to lend aid to Washington but who were unable to cross the river because they could not manage with their heavy artillery. The following excerpt from Peale's diary suggests both the hardships and the mundane challenges of that cold winter along the Delaware River:

December 1776

(7th) Go with Mr. Barker on Shore and Buy some milk. Settle our Expenses; I pay 1/5. we arrive at Trent-Town about 1 O'clock. Have just Rested and eat when Major Bradford says we must Cross the River, each man delivered the Complements of Cartridges, we are ordered to prepare to march and send our heavy luggage across the River, <I expected> we were to advance to toward the Enemy, but it was to retreat across the River, which we accomplished in the Evening. We put up a few Tents for this Night on the Shore.

(25th) we were ordered to join Brigade, many of the men was unwilling to turn out, as it was a Day that [they] would wish to enjoy themselves, however with small Battalions we went through: several Maneuvers . . . we were marched over [Neshaminy] ferry and down to Dunkins Ferry Rather a round about way nearly in all 6 miles when the first and 3rd <with artillery> was nearly landed on the other side. The Wind began to Blow and the Ice gathering so thick at a considerable distance from the Shore there was no possibility of Landing and they were ordered back with the Troops that had landed, the 2nd. Ordered to March back to Bristol, at which place I arrived just before the day of the 26th. When the wind had increased with Rain & hail, [I was] very much fatigued having walked since 4 O'clock of yesterday 18 miles at least, 11 of them with heavy luggage. The Storm continues with hail & Rain.

Sources

A Note About Sources

To date, there is no single publication, Web site, or database that documents every moment of Philadelphia history. Indeed, while there are a number of truly remarkable published sources available to the interested reader or researcher, it is not uncommon for the particulars (such as exact dates) to be a side note to the larger narrative. As a result, research for this volume could not have been conducted without the manifold sources listed below in tandem with the World Wide Web.

The Internet has proven invaluable for projects such as this one, and for the conscientious and cautious user it can offer information literally not available anywhere else. Unfortunately, as an organic, democratic community, the Web also poses pitfalls and challenges. Personal blogs, memoirs, hobby sites, neighborhood and community historical pages, and uploaded sources were all used for this volume, many cross-checked when possible against a second source.

A further complication for historians is the unique moment on September 2, 1752, when the British Colonies adopted the Gregorian calendar. In a moment, what would have been September 3, 1752, under the older Julian calendar shifted by more than ten days to become September 14, 1752. The resulting confusion in a world in which accurate timekeeping was already somewhat challenging led to inconsistencies in the assignment of particular dates for several years.

In choosing to assign particular events to singular dates, the author has elected to use those most commonly accepted within the community of historians and lovers of history. In instances where events are documented in newspapers or in personal documents such as diaries or letters, accuracy is generally easier to affirm. History is more an art than a science, and as such all responsibility for selection of date assignments is assumed by the author.

Bibliography

Finkel, Kenneth. *Philadelphia Almanac and Citizens' Manual for 1994.* Philadelphia: Library Co. of Philadelphia, 1993.

Fisher, Sidney George, and Nicholas B. Wainwright. *A Philadelphia Perspective; The Diary of Sidney George Fisher Covering the Years 1834-1871.* Philadelphia: Historical Society of Pennsylvania, 1967.

Jackson, Joseph. *Encyclopedia of Philadelphia.* Harrisburg: National Historical Association, 1931.

Sources

Klein, Philip Shriver, and Ari Arthur Hoogenboom. *A History of Pennsylvania.* University Park: Pennsylvania State University Press, 1980.

Miller, Randall M., and William Pencak. *Pennsylvania: A History of the Commonwealth.* University Park: Pennsylvania State University Press, 2002.

Mires, Charlene. *Independence Hall in American Memory.* Philadelphia: University of Pennsylvania Press, 2002.

Nash, Gary B. *First City: Philadelphia and the Forging of Historical Memory.* Philadelphia: University of Pennsylvania Press, 2001.

———. *Forging Freedom: The Formation of Philadelphia's Black Community, 1720-1840.* Cambridge: Harvard University Press, 1988.

Robson, Charles. *The Manufactories and Manufacturers of Pennsylvania of the Nineteenth Century.* Philadelphia: Galaxy Pub. Co., 1875.

Rosenfeld, Richard N., and William Duane. *American Aurora: A Democratic-Republican Returns: the Suppressed History of Our Nation's Beginnings and the Heroic Newspaper That Tried to Report It.* New York: St. Martin's Press, 1997.

Taylor, Frank H. *Philadelphia in the Civil War 1861-1865.* [Philadelphia]: The City, 1913.

Weigley, Russell Frank, Nicholas B. Wainwright, and Edwin Wolf. *Philadelphia: a 300 Year History.* New York: W. W. Norton, 1982.

Wolf, Edwin, and Walton H. Rawls. *Philadelphia, Portrait of an American City.* Philadelphia: Camino Books, 1990.

Web Sites

HTTP://WWW.BOOKS.GOOGLE.COM
HTTP://WWW.EXPLOREPAHISTORY.COM
HTTP://WWW.GOOGLE.COM (TIMELINE)
HTTP://WWW.HISTORY.COM
HTTP://WWW.MASSHIST.ORG/DIGITALADAMS
HTTP://WWW.MEMORY.LOC.GOV
HTTP://WWW.NYTIMES.COM/REF/MEMBERCENTER/NYTARCHIVE.HTML
HTTP://WWW.USHISTORY.ORG

Index

Aaron, Hank, 187
Abbey, Edwin Austin, 110
Abolition Society, 123
abolitionism: American Anti-Slavery Society, 385; Germantown Petition in Opposition to Slavery, 61, 72-73, 76; importing slaves banned, 184; Liberty Bell, 148; opposition to, 86, 145; Pennsylvania Anti-Slavery Society, 10, 148; Female Anti-Slavery Society, 390; Quakers, 72-73, 76, 86, 123, 336; Underground Railroad, 104, 131, 229
Abu-Jamal, Mumia (Wesley Cook), 133
Academy of Music, 31, 48, 51, 70, 179, 337, 386
Academy of Natural Sciences: architect, 305; Audubon and, 135; cornerstone laid, 343; Darwin elected member, 102; dinosaur discovery announced, 395; founders, 376; location, 235; members of, 204; organized, 32
Acadians, 80, 365
Act Concerning Aliens, 202
"Action News" format, 292
Adams, Abigail, 213, 271
Adams, John: Act Concerning Aliens, 202; Alien and Sedition Acts, 205, 225; on Declaration of Indepen dence, 213, 243-44; first State of the Union address, 358; Great Seal of the United States, 197; letter to Abigail, 213, 243-44; theater attendance, 77
Adams, Lynn G., 271
Adams, Robert, Jr., 119
aerial flight, 16, 55, 202
Aero Post, 55
affirmative action, 132, 195
Africa, John, 133
African Americans: Banneker School, 165; Centennial Exposition, 349; Civil War period, 303, 323; "great migration," 273; post-World War I period, 377; race riots, 273, 276, 369; theater for, 410; voting rights for free blacks, 145; yellow fever epidemic (1793), 277-78
African Church, 121
African Episcopal Church of St. Thomas, 228
African Methodist Episcopal Church, 118
air service, 217
airmail, 55
airplane racing, 251
airports, 300
Akihito, Crown Prince, 293
Albert Einstein Healthcare Network, 217
Albert I, King of Belgium, 340
Alcott, Amos Bronson, 376
Alexander, Grover Cleveland, 207
Alexander, Raymond, 348
Alexander, Sadie Tanner Mossell, 348
Alfonsi, Ferdinando, 138
Alfonsi, Stella, 138
Ali, Muhammad, 83
Alien and Sedition Acts (1798), 205, 225
Allen, Alfred Reginald, 147
Allen, Carl, 257
Allen, Harrison, 49
Allen, John, 410
Allen, Richard: African Methodist Episcopal Church, 118, 240; birth, 57; death, 101; National Negro Convention, 294; Philadelphia Free African Society, 121, 123; St. George's Methodist Church, 228; yellow fever epidemic (1793), 277-78
Allen, Richie, 265
Allende, Carlos, 257
almanacs, 406
Amble, John, 382
American Anti-Slavery Society, 385
American Anti-Vivisection Society, 66
American Bandstand, 64, 172, 292, 297, 319
American Baptist Historical Society, 148
American Catholic Historical Society, 233
American Colonization Society, 294
American Federation of Labor, 327
American Friends Service Committee, 353
American Institute of Architects, 145
American League, 35
American Legion convention (1976), 232
American Magazine, The, 56
American Museum, 282
American Philosophical Society, 9, 129, 179, 180, 405
American Society for Promoting Useful Knowledge, 9
American Society of Free People of Colour, 294
American spelling reform, 262
American Sunday School Union, 168
American Swedish Historical Museum, 120, 235
American Weekly Mercury, 403, 410
Amish settlers, 315
An Essay Toward the Present and Future Peace of Europe, 93
anarchists, 411
Anderson, Marian, 70, 320
Andre, John, 117, 161, 383
Annenberg, Walter, 29
Anthony, Susan B., 271, 354
anti-abolitionism, 160
Apprentice's Library Company of Philadelphia, 111
Aramingo Canal, 90
Arch Street Theater, 314
arctic expeditions, 79
Argo, 79
Armstrong, Lance, 200
Armstrong, Louis, 172
Arnold, Benedict, 117, 161, 196, 357
arsenals, 117, 162, 329
"arsenic widows," 300
Artcraft Silk Hosiery Mills, 130
Articles of Confederation, 64, 362
Artists' Fund Society, 128
Ashbridge, Samuel H., 178
Ashburn, Richie, 122, 288
Asian immigrants, 3
assemblies, 401
Association Battery, 368
Associators, 269, 413
Athenaeum, 52, 114
Atwater Kent Museum, 389
Audubon, John James, 135
aurora borealis, 105
Autenrieth, Charles, 139
automobile parts, 352
Avalon, Frankie, 297

Bache, Benjamin Franklin, 205, 257, 289
Bacon, Edmund, 163, 170
Bacon, Kevin, 219
Bailey, Lydia, 67
Bailey, Pearl, 104, 172
Baird, Alexander, 67
Baker, William F., 207
Baker Bowl, 207, 251
Balachine, George, 125
Baldwin, Matthias, 134, 183, 370
Baldwin family, 3
Baldwin Locomotive works, 3
ballet, 125
ballooning, 16, 202, 228, 269, 287
Baltimore and Ohio Railroad, 219
bananas, 182
bank clearinghouse, 32
Bank of North America, 14, 151, 169
Bank of Pennsylvania, 281, 304
Bank of the United States, 68, 79
banking, 385
Banneker Literary Institute, 323
Banneker School, 165
Bantom, Michael, 308
Barber, Bill, 18
Barkley, Charles, 105
Barnes, Albert C., 236
Barnes Foundation, 236
Barnum, Phineas Taylor, 62
Barnum's Museum, 62, 411
Barry, John, 126, 221, 222, 292
Barrymore, John, 58, 386
Bartol, George E., 411
Bartram, John, 179, 204, 235, 301, 309, 344
Bartram, William, 32, 233, 268
baseball, 263, 283, 285, 299
basketball, 44, 110, 158, 308, 330, 352, 382
Bassett, Lewis, 226
Battle of Brandywine, 191
Battle of Germantown, 317-18
Battle of Gettysburg, 214
Battle of Gettysburg, The (Rothermel), 401

Index

"Battle of the Kegs," 39-42
Battle of Trenton, 413-14
Beam-Fletcher Transportation Company, 197
Beatles, 124, 154, 261, 281
Becker, Peter, 304
Beggar's Opera, 269
Behrent, Johann, 375
Beissel, Conrad, 304
Bell, Bert, 220
Bell, Robert, 302
Bell, Thom, 387
Belle Vista, 325
Bellevue Stratford Hotel, 156, 232, 305, 401
Belmont, 123
Belsterling, John Jacob, 275
Ben Franklin, 269
Ben Franklin Hotel, 21, 409
Ben Franklin Parkway, 200
"Benecia Boy" (John E. Heenan), 260
Benezet, Anthony, 76, 123
Benjamin Franklin Bridge, 13, 106, 212
Benjamin Franklin Parkway, 3
Bentley, Robert J., 86
Berg, Eric, 411
Berliner, Emile, 159
Berman, Reuben, 207
Berwanger, Jay, 51
Bethel African Methodist Church, 118
Bethel African Methodist Episcopal Church, 228, 240, 294
Bethey, Lincoln, 251
Betsy Ross House, 37
Better Philadelphia Exhibition, 287, 328
Betzwood studio, 386
Bianchi-Trison Corporation, 330
"Bible Riots," 149
Biddle, Anthony J., 113
Biddle, Nicholas, 70
Bielek, Al, 257
Big Five, 110
bike racing, 200
Bill of Rights, 396
Bingham, William, 83
Birch, Thomas, 20
Birch, William Russell, 20, 118, 412
birds, 19
Birds of America, 135
Birdsong, Cindy, 167
Black Panther Party, 276
black troops, 303
blackouts, 182
Blanchard, Jean-Pierre, 16
Blaney, Charles, 314
Blavat, Jerry, 154, 214
Blibber-Bubble, 15
blizzards, 86
Blob, The, 291
Blockley, 239
blood serum, 402
Blue Devil barge club, 123
blue laws, 195, 352, 354
Bluebelles, 167
Bluford, Guion Stewart "Guy," 275
Bogle, Robert W., 369
Bolber, Morris, 138
bombings, 411
Bond, James, 11
Bond, Thomas, 54
Boone, George, 323
Booth, Edwin, 314
Booth, John Wilkes, 339, 399
bootleggers, 136
Bourse building, 411
Bowser, David Bustill, 384
Boxall, James, 388
boxing, 83, 302
Boyle, George L., 55
Bradford, Andrew, 56, 239, 410
Bradford, Odessa, 273
Braman, Norman, 149
Brandenburg Industrial Services Company, 97
Brandywine, Battle of, 191
Brethren, 304
Bridesburg, 112
bridges: Benjamin Franklin Bridge, 13, 106, 212; Delaware River Bridge, 13, 212; floating bridge, 90; "Permanent Bridge," 326; Tacony-Palmyra Bridge, 259; Walt Whitman Bridge, 158; "Wire Bridge," 9
Bridges, Robert, 81
Brill family, 3
"Bring Back Our Darling," 212
Britannia Fire Company, 168
"Broad Street Bullies," 162
Broad Street Station, 187, 386
Broadway Limited, 188
Brown, Barzilai S., 164
Brown, Charles Brockden, 24
Brown, Denise Scott, 202
Brown, E. C., 410
Brown, Henry "Box," 104, 105
Brown, John, 384
Brown, John Miflin, 349
Brown, Larry, 158
Brown, Mary, 384
Brown, Nathan, 87
Brownrigg, William, 165
Brown's Department Store, 117, 136
Brumbaugh, Martin, 374
Bruno, Angelo "the Gentle Don," 96, 366
Brush Electric Light Company, 384
Budd, Edward Gowen, 352
Budd Company, 230, 352
builders' associations, 237
Bunker, Chang and Eng, 49
Burham, Carrie, 271
buses, 178, 388
Bushnell, David, 18
busing, 290
Bustleton Airport, 55
butchers, 90
Butler, Pierce, 22
Button, Dick, 402

Cadwalader's Associators, 413
Cafone, Pete, 10
Cahill, Thomas E., 308
Calder, Alexander Milne, 215, 233
Calvert, George, 362
Camden, New Jersey, 88
Camden Central Airport, 300
Cameo-Parkway Records, 316
Camp William Penn, 303
Campanella, Roy, 366
Campbell, Bebe Moore, 62
Campbell, Bill, 288
Cannuli's Meats, 325
Capitol Communications, 292
Capone, Al, 23, 335, 360
Caponigro, Anthony "Tony Bananas," 96
Carbutt, John, 386
Carey, James, 298
Carey and Lea, 392
Carlin, John, 192
Carlisle, Abraham, 351
Carlisle, Mercy, 345
Carman, Caleb, 39
Carnes, Peter, 228
Carpenters' Company, 28, 237, 365
Carpenters' Hall, 28, 66, 237, 281, 284
Carson, Ann Baker, 27
Carson, John, 27
Carter, William, 130
Carter Hawley Hale Stores, 136
Caruso, Enrico, 120
Casale, Gerard F., 200
Cathedral of Saints Peter and Paul, 129, 285, 306, 367
cattle, 78
Catto, Octavius, 283, 301, 323
Cedar Hill Cemetery, 100
cell phones, 382
Centennial and Memorial Association of Valley Forge, 374
Centennial Exhibition (1876): agricultural hall, 305; American spelling reform, 262; bananas sold, 182; closing, 357; Eakins' Gross Clinic rejected, 236; featured exhibits, 3; logo, 148; phonograph, 159; *Public Ledger,* 175; site, 153, 235; soda fountain craze, 203; John Philip Sousa and, 157; visitors, total, 357
Center City, 216, 256
Center Square, 34, 128
Center Square Waterworks, 34
Central High School, 104, 236, 334, 370, 387, 388
Central Library, 61
Chamberlain, Wilt, 22, 45, 77, 114, 266
Chambers, Charlotte, 86
Chancellor Records, 297
Chaney, John, 110
Chang and Eng, 49
Chapman, Maria Weston, 160
Charter of Pennsylvania, 79
Charter of Privileges (1701), 19, 69, 148, 181, 338, 341, 378-79
Chauner, David M., 200
Checker, Chubby (Ernest Evans), 316
Cheeks, Mo, 158
Chestnut Street Theater, 60, 112, 181, 299, 314, 383
Chevalier, Jack, 10
Chew, Benjamin, 394
Chew family, 114
Cheyney University, 323
Childs, George W., 46, 100, 384

Index

Chinatown, 38, 252, 358
cholera, 317, 320
Chomsky, Avram Noam, 388
Christ Church, 205, 237, 249, 407
Church of Christ, 113
Church of the Advocate, 240
Cianfrani, Buddy, 91
Citizens Alliance for Better Neighborhoods, 91
Citizens Bank Park, 122, 288
City Council, 45
City Hall: clock, 8; Free Library moves to Concert Hall, 54; interiors, 305; as tallest building in U.S., 215; William Penn statue, 4, 233, 353, 375; work begins, 257
City of Philadelphia, 20
Civil War: mustering for defense, 206; pro-Southern support, 17, 86, 275; Refreshment Saloons, 164; supplies for the Union, 112; textile industry, 250; volunteers for the Union, 275; war weariness, 214
Clark, Dick, 127, 292, 297, 377
Clark, Joseph, 290
Clarke, Bobby, 18, 162
Clarke, Mae (Violet Mary Klotz), 261
Clarkson, Matthew, 277
Claver, St. Peter, 240
Clinton, Henry, 151, 195
Cloister, Ephrata, 304
Clover Wheelmen, 382
Clymer, George, 253
Coatesville, Pennsylvania, 258
Coca Cola, 165
College of Apothecary, 66
College of Physicians, 9, 49
colleges and universities: Cheyney U., 323; C. of Apothecary, 66; C. of Physicians, 9, 49; Girard C., 59, 215, 248, 290; La Salle U., 110; Philadelphia C. of Pharmacy and Science, 66; Philadelphia U., 44; Pierce C., 251; St. Joseph's U., 110; Temple U., 29, 157; Thomas Jefferson U., 360; U. of Pennsylvania, 57, 131, 147, 402; U. of the Arts, 153; U. of the Sciences of Philadelphia, 66; Villanova U., 110
Collins, Arthur Francis, 50
Collinson, Peter, 138, 179
Colonel Woods Museum, 282
Coltrane, John, 230, 302
Columbia (the elephant), 85
Comcast Center, 170
Common Council, 19
Common Sense (Paine), 16
Communist Party, 241
Concert Hall, 54
Congress Flag, 191
Congress of the Confederation (1781-1789): Constitution adopted, 215; Constitution forwarded for ratification, 307; Constitution in effect, 213; Constitution signed, 296; return from Princeton, 198; withdrawal to Princeton, 198, 201
Connie Mack Stadium, 252, 331
Consolidation Act (1854), 45, 123, 149
Constitutional Convention, 64, 168, 196, 251, 396
Constitutional Party, 317
Consultation of Older Adults, 248
Continental Congress, First (1774), 2, 284, 339; Second (1775-1781): Baltimore, flight to, 393; Baltimore, return from, 87; Canadians urged to join rebellion, 172; chaplain appointed, 113; colonies placed in state of defense, 158; flag design selected, 191; Great Seal of United States adopted, 197; House of Representatives proposed, 227; Lancaster, flight to, 290; Lancaster, return from, 213; naval fleet ordered, 326; opening day, 153; peace commission appointed, 188; "United States" made official, 288; Washington appointed commander, 192, 315; York, flight to, 305; *see also* Congress of the Confederation
Controlled Demolition, 30, 186, 330
Convention Center, 164
Convention Hall, 60, 253
Conwell, Russell, 203
Cooke, Jay, 297
Cooke, Sam, 154
Coolidge, Calvin, 302
Cooper, William, 133
Cooper and Bailey's Great London Shows, 85
Cooper Shop Volunteer Refreshment Saloon, 164, 169
Cornwallis, Lord, 305
corruption in city offices, 130
Cosby, Bill, 223
Cosby, William, 249
Coxe family, 114
Craig, Thomas, 383
Cramp, William, 295
Cramp family, 3
Cramp Shipbuilding Company, 181, 286, 295
Cramp Yard, 125
Creed, Linda, 387
Cresap, Thomas, 362
crime, 3, 89, 119, 138, 366, 377
"crime of the century," 169
Croce, Jim, 17
Cruiser Olympia Association, 293
Crumlish, James C., Jr., 349
"Curse of Billy Penn," 170, 215
Curtis Building, 251
Curtis Publishing Company, 392
Curtiss, Glenn, 359
Custer, George, 259
Custis, George Washington, 23

Daily News, 292
dairy industry, 78
Dale, Ben, 356
d'Amboise, Christopher, 125
Darkow, Martin, 293
Darragh, Lydia Barrington, 383
Darrow, Charles, 82
Darwin, Charles, 102
Dash, Sara, 167
Davis, Jefferson, 214
Davis, Sammy, Jr., 172
daylight savings time, 94
deaf, the, 192
DeAngelis, Peter, 297
Deas, Charles, 403
Decatur, Stephen, 59
Declaration of Independence: adoption of, 213; broadside distribution, 25; date commemorating, 243-44; first printing, 216; first public reading, 219; first publishing, 217; signing of, 247, 351
Declaration of Rights and Sentiments, 271
Delaware and Schuylkill Navigation Company, 119
Delaware and Schuylkill Railroad, 183
Delaware River, 152, 389, 406
Delaware River Bridge, 13, 212
Delaware River Railroad Company, 28
Delaware tribe, 50
Delon, Mademoiselle, 202
Democratic National Convention (1936), 200, 204; (1948), 171, 223
Democratic Party, 86, 323
Demolition Dynamics, 97
Dempsey, Jack, 302
Department of City Transit, 152
department stores: Brown's, 117, 136; Carter Hawley Hale, 136; Frank Seder, 351; Gimbels, 92, 139, 367, 372; "Grand Depot," 87; Lit Brothers, 139, 292, 406; Oak Hall, 117; Triangle Clothing, 146; Wanamaker's, 117, 136, 198, 273, 404, 406, 411
Deringer, Henry, Jr., 339
Deringer, Henry, Sr., 339
Design of Cities, The, 163
Deutsch, Isaac, 298
Dewey, Thomas E., 223
Dickens, Charles, 20, 81, 206, 335
Dickinson, John, 33
Diemer, Walter E., 15
Dies, Martin, 221
DiGildo's Saloon, 89
Dilworth, Richardson, 124, 337, 364
"dime museum," 282
dinosaurs, 395
Diocese of Philadelphia, 117
District of Belmont, 123
Dittmar Powder Company, 328
"Divine Healer" (August Schrader), 337
Divine Lorraine hotel, 289
Dixon, Jeremiah, 362
DJ Jazzy Jeff, 29, 391
Dock Creek, 34

Index

docks, 68
Dorsey, Thomas J., 384
Dougherty, Dennis Joseph, 184
Douglas, David, 8
Douglas, Joe, 212
Douglas, Mike, 172
Douglass, Frederick, 303, 323, 349
Downingtown, 291
Drew, Mrs. John, 314
Drexel, Anthony, 100, 231, 384
Drexel, Francis A., 373, 384
Drexel, Katharine, 196, 373
Dreyfuss, Barney, 71
Drinker, Edward, 405
Dubble Bubble, 15
duels, last, 119
Duffield, George, 392
Duggleby, Bill, 130
Dumont, Frank, 282
Dunbar Theatre, 410
Dunlap, John, 216, 219
Dunlop, John, 21, 25
Dunsmore, John Ward, 111
Durham Furnace, 368

"Eagles Court," 97
Eakins, Thomas, 56, 236
Earle Theatre, 99
earthquakes, 25, 304, 361, 365
East Falls, 127
Eastern European immigrants, 3
Eastern State Penitentiary, 23, 119, 165, 305, 335, 338
Eckertt, J. Presper, 57
Eckfeld, Adam, 192
Eddy, Nelson, 147
Egan, John, 355
Egan, Michael, 117
eight-hour workday, 327
Eighty-eighth Regiment, 275
electric cars, 325
electric trains, 35, 53
electrification, 384, 407
electron microscopy, 129
elephants, 85
Elisabeth, Queen of Belgium, 340
Elverson family, 206
Emerson, Edith, 333
English orthography, 262
ENIAC, 57
epidemics: cholera, 317, 320; influenza pandemic, 296, 307, 331; typhoid, 127; yellow fever, 60, 228, 277-78, 324
Episcopal Academy, 8
Epperley, George A., 298
Equal Rights League, 323
equestrian shows, 260
Erving, Julius "Dr. J," 158, 330, 398
Esposito, James, 371
Evangeline, 365
Evans, Oliver, 227
Evans, Wilbur, 147
executions, 152

Fabian, 49, 297
Facenda, John, 308
Fagan, John, 67
Fahnestock, George, 214
Fahnstock, Violet, 15
Faire Mount, 128
Fairmount Park, 101, 128, 153, 158, 235, 266, 349
Fairmount Park Transportation Company, 129
Fairmount Water Works, 128, 322
fairs, 163, 218
Falckner, Justus, 371
Farm Journal, The, 392
Farnsworth, Philo T., 264
Father Divine, 289
Faulkner, Daniel, 133
Favato, Maria, 138
Fellowship Fire Company, 168
Fernandez, Chico, 146
ferries, 91, 106, 152
Ferris, J. L. G., 263
Fields, W. C., 36, 195, 386, 406
Fifth Ward, 298, 301
filmmaking, 251, 291
Fine, Larry, 318
fire insurance, 154
firefighting, 37, 168, 388, 410
fires: 1735, 168; Assembly buildings, 93; Barnum's Museum, 411; Broad Street Station, 187; Chestnut Street Theater, 112; cigar factory, 139; Friends Home for Colored Orphans, 160; Gulf Refinery, 271; Metropolitan Opera House, 120; One Meridian Plaza, 408; "Permanent Bridge," 326; Philadelphia Coke Company, 231; Philadelphia Zoo, 405; Phillies' wooden stadium, 207; Port Richmond tire dump, 88; railroad property, 309; Rickett's Circus, 358; schoolhouse, 51; Shibe Park, 265; sprinklers required, 408; Triangle Clothing store, 145; warehouses, 115
First-Day or Sunday-School Society, 400
First District, 91
First Penn Bank, 91
First Presbyterian Church of Germantown, 333
First Troop Philadelphia City Cavalry, 394
First Unitarian Church, 131
First World War. *See* World War I
Fisher, Eddie, 255
Fisher, Sydney George, 140-41
Fitch, John, 267
Fitzgerald, Thomas, 283
Flag Day, 191
Flew Chewing Company, 15
floods, 26, 90
Flora, or Hob in the Well, 150
Flower, Enoch, 407
Foglietta, Tom, 154
Food Trust, 337
football, 261, 308
Ford, Gerald, 253
Forrest, Edwin, 51, 84, 111, 374, 393, 410
Forrest, Thomas, 95
Forrest, William, 314
Forrest Home for Retired Actors, 84
Fort Mifflin, 362
Forten, James, 81
fossils, 395
Foulke, William Parker, 395
Fountain, Pete, 172
Fox, Gilbert, 134
Fox, Josiah, 222
Fox, Margaret, 46
Fox, William C., 221
fox hunting, 394
Frank Seder Department Store, 351
Franken, Rose, 356
Frankford and Southwark Passenger Railway, 364
Frankford Arsenal, 112, 306
Frankford Elevated line, 152
Frankford Turnpike, 366
Frankford Yellow Jackets, 220
Franklin, Benjamin: American Philosophical Society, 9; arrival in Philadelphia, 319; daylight savings time, 94; death, 126; Dock Creek swamp, 34; electrical experiments, 138, 153, 192, 208-9; epitaph, 264; Great Seal of the United States, 197; historical marker for, 207; lending libraries, 61; local militia, 50; Masons, 305; paid police, 89; Penn family, 181; Pennsylvania Abolition Society, 123; *Philadelphische Zeitung*, 149, 219; Plain Truth, 269; *Poor Richard's Almanac*, 24, 400, 409; as postmaster general, 237, 255; Public Academy, 361; public hospitals, 54; retirement, age at, 67; Union Fire Company, 388
Franklin, John, 46
Franklin Field, 97, 136, 159, 187, 308
Franklin Institute, 48, 159, 264, 269, 323, 376, 389
Franklin Square, 321
Franklinia alatamaha, 179
Fraser, John, 131
Frazier, Marvis, 106
Frazier, "Smokin" Joe, 83, 350
Free African Society, 123, 228
free blacks, 145, 294
Free Library of Philadelphia: Barbara Gittings collection, 252; Central Library groundbreaking, 155; charter adopted, 61; Logan Circle branch, 409; main building opens, 179; move from City Hall to Concert Hall, 54; "One book, One Philadelphia" program, 356; "The Raven" manuscript, 26; unit for blind, 182
Free Society of Traders, 99
Freedom Theatre, 410
Freedom Train, 296
Freemasons. *See* Masons
French, Daniel Chester, 235
French Revolution, 11
Friends Home for Colored Orphans, 160
Friendship Carpenters' Company, 365

 Index 

Friendship Gate, 38, 358
Fry, William H., 181
Fryer, John E., 252
Fuller, Charles, 308
Fulton, Robert, 267
Fumo, Vincent J., 91
Furness, Frank, 131, 388

Gabor, Zsa Zsa, 172
Gale, Alice, 386
Gallatin, Albert, 79
Gallaudet, Thomas, 391
Galloway, Joseph, 274, 368
Galludet, Edwin, 192
Gamble, Kenny, 101, 256, 387
Gamble & Huff, 101
gambling, 120, 298
gangs, 3
garages, 254
garbage removal, 231
Garrison, William Lloyd, 160
Gaye, Marvin, 124
Geator Gold radio, 154
Geiger, Emily, 130
George, Henry, 82
Geppert Brothers, 186
Gere, Richard, 276
German Americans, 56, 72, 86, 147, 155, 201, 293, 304
Germantown: Brethren, 304; founding and history, 319; Italian immigrants, 144; Mennonites, 235, 319; Petition in Opposition to Slavery, 61, 72-73, 76; Quakers, 72, 319
Germantown, Battle of, 317-18
Germantown Nationals, 382
Gettysburg, Battle of, 214
Gibson, John T., 410
Gibson, Litzka R., 291
Gibson, Walter Brown, 291
Gibson's Auditorium, 410
Gillespie, Elizabeth Duane, 191
Gillespie, John Birks "Dizzy," 334
Gimbels Department Store, 92, 139, 367, 372
Girard, Stephen, 59, 290, 337, 407
Girard Bank, 268
Girard College, 59, 215, 248, 290
Girard Life Insurance Annuity and Trust Company, 92
Girl Scouts, 358
Girls' High and Normal School, 44
Gittings, Barbara, 252
Glasco, Benjamin, 330
Gloria Dei Church, 120, 161, 171, 268, 371
Gloucester Fox Hunting Club, 394
"God Bless America," 144, 162
Goddard, Mary Katherine, 25
Goddard, William, 33
Godfrey, Thomas, Jr., 133
Gola, Tom, 20
Golden, Jane, 321
Golden Boys of Bandstand, 297
golf, 306
Gompers, Samuel, 327
Goode, Wilson, 124, 156, 355
Gorgas, Josiah, 112
gorillas, 411
Gorman, Frank L., 411
Gorsuch, Edward, 399
Gradual Abolition Act, 76
Graeff, Abram op de, 73
Graeff, Derick op de, 73
Graff, Frederick, 122
graffiti, 321
gramophone, 159
"Grand Depot" store, 87
Grand Lodge of Free and Accepted Masons, 305
Grant, Maxwell, 291
Grant, Ulysses S., 153, 259
Granville, Haines & Co., 372
Grateful Dead, 99, 218
Gratz, Rebecca, 31, 272
Gray, William, 278
"Great Builder," 184
Great Central Fair, 218
Great Depression, 340
Great Law, 388
"Great Law," 195
Great Seal of the United States, 197
Great Wigwam, 259
Greaton, Joseph, 69
Green, William J., III, 287, 355
Greene, Robert, 226
Grey, Charles, 299
Grey Panthers, 248
Grice, Hezekiel, 294
Gridley, Charles V., 390
Griffin, Eddie, 308
Grimke, Angelina, 63, 160, 339
Grimke, Sarah, 373
Grinnell Expeditions, 46
Griswold, Roger, 37, 58
Griswold, Rufus Wilmot, 35
Gross Clinic, The, 236
Grover Washington Jr. Middle School, 398
Guardians of the Poor, 239
Gulf Refinery, 271
Gunner's Run Improvement Company, 90
Gustav Vasa Bible, 120

Haddonfield, New Jersey, 395
Hagler, Marvin, 20
"Hail Columbia," 134
Haile Selassie, 309
Haines, Reuben, 376
Haines & Kibblehouse, 30
Hale, Robert, 24
Hale & Kilburn, 352
Haley, Bill, 52
Hall, Daryl, 324
Hallam company of actors, 150
Hamilton, Alexander, 79, 115, 242
Hamilton, Andrew, 249
Hamilton, James, 249
Hamilton, Scott, 402
Hancock, John, 403
Hancock Athletic Association, 382
hangings, 150, 152, 169, 351
Hanway, Castner, 399
Hardart, Frank, 188
Harper's Ferry raid, 384
Harris, Zelig, 388
Harrison, Marvin, 308
Harshaw, Margaret, 147
Haviland, John, 314, 335
Hawkins, John Isaac, 375
Hayden, Ferdinand, 32
Head House, 337
Heart in Hand Fire Company, 168
Heberton, Mahlon Hutchinson, 53
Heenan, John E. ("Benecia Boy"), 260
Heiden, Eric, 200
Heimer, Steve, 89
Heinz, John, 113
Hemsley, Sherman, 44
Henderich, Garret, 73
Hendryx, Nona, 167
Henning, C. J., 293
Henry, Alexander, 17, 193
Hermits of Wissahickon, 201
Herzog, George, 305
Herzog, Hermann, 363
Hess, James J., 89
Hesselius, Gustavus, 168
Hewitt, George, 131
Hextall, Ron, 120
Heyl, Henry R., 48, 386
Hibernian Society for the Relief of Emigrants, 78
Hickel, Walter J., 125
Hicks, Charles, 290
Hicks, Marie, 290
Hilldale Daisies, 207
Hires, Charles Elmer, 203
historical societies, 120, 148, 233, 235, 284, 329
Historical Society of Pennsylvania, 284, 329
History of Immigration, The, 321
Hoban, Russell, 47
Hobart, Garret, 340
Hockley, Thomas, 131
Hoff, Max "Boo-Boo," 136
Hog Island Shipyard, 55, 173, 179, 180, 250
Holiday Records, 52
Holme, Thomas, 45, 216
Holmes, Henry Howard (Herman Webster Mudgett), 150, 349
Holte, Patricia (Patti Labelle), 167
Honey's Garden, 321
Hopkins, Charles, 89
Hopkins, John E., 395
Hopkins, Samuel, 242
Hopkinson, Francis, 18, 39-42, 197
Horn, Bob, 319
Horn, Joseph, 189
Horn and Hardart automat, 189
Horowitz, Vladimir, 48
horse-drawn carriages, 183
horse racing, 97, 155
horseback, travel by, 112
Horstmann, Mary, 350
hospitals, 54, 121, 217, 388
House of Refuge, 376
House Un-American Activities Committee investigation, 327
Howe, William, 151, 161, 274, 290, 299, 317, 318, 383
Hudson, George Vernon, 94
Huff, Leon, 101, 256, 387

Index

Hughes, Charles, 260
Hughes, John, 318
Hull, Isaac, 46
human blood serum, 402
Humane Society, 402
Humphrey, Hubert, 223
Humphreys, Joshua, 222
Humphreys and Wharton Shipyard, 222
Hunter, William, 255
Hunting Park Racecourse, 155
Hurricane Hazel, 328
hydrofoil demonstration, 190

I-95, 4, 88, 125
ice, 33
ice cream, 226
ice skating, 195, 402
If You Dream It You Can Achieve It, 321
immigrants, 3, 86, 138, 144
implosions, 30, 97, 186, 330, 343
Imps barge club, 123
Independence Day, 213
Independence Hall: Carpenters' Company, 237; Liberty Bell moved from, 8; Lincoln and, 65, 132, 140-41; Masaryk marker installed, 234; as a nickname, 148; Peale's Museum at, 85; rear tower, 34; tower restoration, 71
Independence National Historical Park, 205, 374
Independence Seaport Museum, 390
Independence Square, 91, 287
influenza pandemic, 296, 307, 331
Inn of the Dead Fox, 394
Inspecting the First Coins, 111
Institute for Colored Youth, 283, 323
instrument manufacturers, 375
International Commercial Conference, 179
International Electrical Exhibition, 280
International Eucharistic Congress, 253
International Exhibition of Arts, Manufactures, and Products of the Soil and Mine. *See* Centennial Exhibition

Irish Americans, 86, 149, 301
Irvine, William, 120, 240
Irvine Auditorium, 409
Isgro Pasticceria, 325
Italian immigrants, 138, 144
"Italian Market," 325
Iverson, Allen, 158
Ivory, Henry, 169

Jackson, Augustus, 226
Jackson, Michael, 124
Jacobs Engine Manufacturing Company, 300
Jacquett, Peter, 94
Jagger, Thomas Augustus, Jr., 31
Jahn, Helmut, 170
James, Betty, 367
James, Richard, 367
James Esposito Soda Bottling Works, 371
James Industries, 367
James Reesides & Company, 178
Jay, John, 115, 393
Jefferson, Thomas, 197
Jessup, Morris K., 257
Jett, Joan, 301
Jewish Hospital, 217
JFK Stadium, 97, 124, 218, 253, 261, 298, 302
"Jim Crow," 178
John, Elton, 68
John Paul II, 316
Johnson, Andrew, 259
Johnson, Francis "Frank," 193
Johnson, Jane, 229
Johnson, Nancy, 288
Johnstown flood, 174
Joint Committee on Railroads, 185
Jones, Absalom, 121, 123, 228, 277-78
Jones, Bobby, 158, 306
Jones, John Paul, 403
Jones, Mary Harris ("Mother Jones"), 262
Junker, Jules, 360
Junto, The, 9

Kahn, Louis I., 63
Kahn, Stan, 172
Kalakana I, 305
Kalas, Harry, 122
Kalendarium Pennsylvaniese, 406
Kane, Elisha Kent, 46, 93
Kane, John Kintzing, 229

Katzenstein, Carolyn, 271
Keeping, Edwin, 130
Keimer, Samuel, 405
Keiser, Roy, 125
Kelly, Frank, 323
Kelly, Grace, 127, 359
Kelly, Jack, Sr., 322
Kelpius, Johannes, 201
Kemble, Frances (Fanny) Anne, 22, 51, 325
Kemble, William H., 309
Kennedy, John, 146
Kennedy, John F., 156
Kensington, 45, 80, 125, 149, 382
Kethians, 90
kidnappings, 212
King, Martin Luther, Jr., 114, 154, 248, 273, 290
King, Robert P., 67
King's Highway, 366
Klotz, Violet Mary (May Clarke), 261
Knapp, Samuel L., 310-12
Knights of Labor, 327, 390
Knight's Wharf, 161
Know-Nothing Party, 182
Knox, Henry, 107-8
Koca Nola, 371
Kosciuszko, Thaddeus, 263
Kosloff, Irv, 158
Krimmel, John, 90
Krol, John, 253
Ku Klux Klan, 377
Kuhn, Margaret "Maggie," 248
Kurland, John, 199
KYW TV, 172

La Salle University, 110
Labelle, Patti (Patricia Holte), 167
Lafayette, Marquis de, 193, 238, 242, 306, 310-12
LaMott, 303
Lancaster, Pennsylvania, 249
Landlord's Game, 82
Lanza, Mario, 38
Larson, Morgan Foster, 300
Lasorda, Tommy, 134
Latrobe, Benjamin Henry, 34, 128
Laurel Hill Cemetery, 122, 130, 235, 309, 332, 339, 345, 358
Layman, Dan, 82
Le Sacre du Printemps, 120
Lea and Blanchard, 392

League Island, 152, 194
League Island Navy Yard, 253
Lee, Charles, 315
Lee, Richard Henry, 213, 407
Lee, Robert E., 206, 214
Lee Brothers and Company, 392
Leech, Thomas, 379
legionnaire's disease, 232, 305
Leidy, Joseph, 288, 322, 395
Lemke, Herman, 293
Lenape tribe, 50, 80, 200, 270
Lennon, John, 172
Lenora, 181
Leopold, Prince of Belgium, 340
Leslie, Robert, 410
Lester Piano Company, 375
"Letters from an American Farmer," 33
Lewis, Elijah, 399
Lexington, 126
Liberty Bell: arrival in Phila delphia, 280; crack, 85, 220; move from Independence Hall to Liberty Bell Pavilion, 8; need and requirements for, 378-79; Panama-California Exposition in San Francisco, 216; prior name, 219; sound broadcast over radio, 183; as a symbol, 148; usage, 148; George White and, 246; Whitecha pel Foundry, 148; World's Columbian Exposition, 353
Liberty Bell Pavilion, 8
Liberty-Lincoln Building, 404
Liberty Place, 170
libraries: Apprentice's Library Company of Philadelphia, 111; Central Library, 61; first lending library, 61; Franklin and, 61; Philadel phia Public Library, 61; U. of Pennsylvania, 131; *see also* Free Library of Philadelphia
Library Company of Philadelphia, 32, 323, 344, 355
Lilly, Eli, 66
Lilly, Josiah, 66
Lincoln, Abraham: arrival in Philadelphia, 64; first visit, 184; funeral cortege, 131; Independence Hall, 65, 132, 140-41; opposition to, 86,

214; visits Sanitary Fair, 193
Lind, Jenny, 51, 62, 331
Lindbergh, Charles, 190
Lindsay, John, 138
Lintz, Gertrude, 411
Lipman, Hyman, 105
Lippard, George, 53
Lippincott mansion, 264
liquor sales, 182, 195
Liquori, Mary, 159
Lit, Jacob, 139
Lit, Samuel, 139
Lit Brothers Department Store, 139, 292, 406
Live Aid, 124, 224
Lloyd, Thomas, 99
Loews Hotel, 385
Logan, James, 344
Longfellow, Henry Wadsworth, 365
Loud, Thomas, 375
Loyalist Convention, 259
Lubin, Siegmund "Pop," 386
Lubinville, 386
Luddington, Nicholas, 300
Lurie, Jeffrey, 149
Luzerne, Chevalier, 226
Lye, Henry, 85
lynchings, 258
Lyon, Matthew, 37, 58
Lyon, Patrick, 281

Machen, John Gresham, 188
Mack, Connie, 285, 330, 331
MacLean, Charles Douglas, 386
Maclure, William, 204
MacMillan expedition to North Pole, 187
Madison, Dolley, 294, 337
Madison, James, 294
Magdalene Society, 113
Magee, Herb, 44
"magic lantern," 48
Magie, Elizabeth, 82
Makover, Henry B., 217
Malone, Moses, 158, 330
Manayunk, 200
Mann Music Center, 235
Marconi Plaza, 25
Market Street East shopping district, 139, 256
markets, 139, 149, 226, 256, 325, 337, 368
Markham, William, 168, 341
Marshall, John, 217, 220
Marshall Field & Company, 359
Martin, Edward, 199
Martin Luther King Plaza Homes, 330
Martins, Peter, 125
Marucci, Robert, 297
Masaryk, Tomas Garrigue, 234
Mason, Charles, 362
Mason, William, 264
Mason-Dixon Line, 362
Masonic Club of Manyunk, 283
Masonic lodges, 201, 305
Masonic Temple, 131
Masons, 201, 305
Massa (a gorilla), 411
Massimino, Rollie, 110
Matlack, Timothy, 247
Mauchly, John, 57
mayors, 19
McArthur, John, 215
McCaffery, Seamus, 97
McClellan, George B., 86, 342
McKay, Jim, 303
McKean, Thomas, 201, 351
McKim, James, 384
McKinley, William, 179, 340
McLean, George P., 275
McLean, Joseph A., 275
McNeil, Robert, 66, 91
McNeil Laboratories, 91
McNichol, James, 298
McParlan, James, 82
McQueen, Steve, 291
McShain, John, 350
McVay, Charles, III, 218
Mead, Margaret, 397
Meade, George, 358
meat industry, 78, 90
medical schools, 217
Mellon Bank, 385
Meloney, Franken, 356
Melvin and the Blue Notes, 101
Memorial Hall, 153, 235
Mennonites, 235, 319
Mercer, Singleton, 53
Mercer Wrecking Recycling Corporation, 343
Merchant's Coffee House, 388
Merchants' Exchange Building, 65
Merion Cricket Club, 306
Merion Golf Club, 306
Meritor Financial Group, 385
Metroliner, 230
Metropolitan Opera House, 120
Mifflin, Thomas, 394
Mike Douglas Show, 172
Mills, William B., 135, 411
Mischianza, 161
Mrs. Drew's Arch Street Theater, 157
Mister Softee, 92
Model School, 44
Monks of Monk Hall, The, 53
Monopoly board game, 82
Montgomery, Richard, 357
Moore, Cecil B., 56, 290
Moore, George, 199
Moore, J. Hampton, 11
Moravians, 412
Morgenweck, Frank, 382
Morgenweck, William, 382
Morris, Robert, 13, 14, 151, 235, 317
Morris, Samuel, 394
Mosher, Bill, 212
Moss, Roger, 114
Mossell, Aaron Albert, II, 348
Mott, James, 10
Mott, Lucretia (née Lucretia Coffin), 10, 229, 271, 303, 384
Mt. Airy, 333
Mount Airy School for Deaf, 192
Mount Sinai Hospital, 217
MOVE, 133, 147, 156, 253, 355
movie industry, 386
Moy, Lawrence M., 252
Moyamensing Prison, 150, 229
Moylan's Horse, 12
Mozart, Amadeus, 51
Mudgett, Herman Webster (Henry Howard Holmes), 150, 349
Mummers Parade, 8
Municipal Auditorium, 185
Mural Arts Program, 321
murders, 150, 169, 300, 301, 349
Murphy, Charles W., 71
museums: American M., 282; American Swedish Histori cal M., 120, 235; Atwater Kent M., 389; Barnum's M., 62, 411; Colonel Woods M., 282; "dime museum," 282; Independence Seaport M., 390; Peale's M., 85, 134, 229, 282, 405; Pennsylvania M. and School of Industrial Art, 153; Philadelphia M. of Art, 3, 34, 101, 115, 153, 235, 409; Please Touch Children's M., 139, 153, 406; Woodmere Art M., 333
Music Fund Hall, 331
music halls, 51
music performance and pub lishing, 193, 224, 375, 387
music stores, 394
Musical Fund Society of Philadelphia, 51
musicals, 77
Musiq Soulchild, 295
mutiny, 198, 253
Mutual Fund Society, 133
Mutumbo, Dikembe, 158

Naismith, James, 382
Nanny Goat Market, 149
National Basket Ball League, 382
National Basketball Association, 158
National Constitution Center, 324
National Football League, 132
National Gazette, 344
National Historic District, 303
National Hockey League All-Star game, 25
National Negro Convention, 294, 299
National Register of Historic Places, 305, 333
National Shrine of Saint John Neumann, 196
National Union Convention, 259
Natty, 394
Negro League games, 207
Negro League World Series, 207, 299, 316
Neumann, John, 12, 196, 203
New Century Guild, 354
New Jersey, 91, 106
New Market, 337
New Sweden, 120
New Years Associations, 8
New Year's Eve, 412
New York Shipbuilding, 354, 404
Newspaper Guild, 185
newspapers, 185, 206, 239, 252, 369
Nicholas, Samuel, 357, 394
Nixon, John, 219
Nixon, Richard, 31, 132, 290
non-importation movement, 338

Index

Normal Schools, 44
Norris, Isaac, 378-79
North Penn Railroad, 28
North Philadelphia, 273, 276
Northern Liberties Hospital, 217
novels, serialized, 356
nuclear power, 103
Nutter, Michael, 324

Oak Hall Department Store, 117
Oak Lane Country Day School, 388
Oakley, Violet, 332, 333
O'Brien, "Philadelphia" Jack, 83, 113
Odom, Vernon, 295
O'Donnell, Francis, 352
oil spills, 361
"Old Drury," 60
Old Ironsides (locomotive), 370
Old St. George's Church, 412
Old Swedes Church, 120, 161, 171, 268, 371
Olympics (baseball team), 283
One Liberty Place, 4, 215
One Meridian Plaza, 66, 408
Ono, Yoko, 172
opera, 269
Opportunities Industrialization Center, 286
Ord, George, 268
organized crime, 366
Ormandy, Eugene, 31
Orphan Asylum, 31
Orthodox Presbyterian Church, 188
Orukter Amphibolos, 227
Overbrook High School, 266, 391
Owen, Robert, 204
Oxford Provident Building Association of Philadelphia County, 10

Pacific Boat Club, 322
Paine, Thomas, 76, 123
Palestra, the, 60, 110
Paley, William Samuel, 339
Palmer, Timothy, 326
Pancoast, William H., 49
Panic of 1873, 297
Paoli Massacre, 299
parades, 8, 90, 292, 372
Parent, Bernie, 18, 162
Parker, William, 399
parking, 254
Parking Wars, 254
Pass, John, 148, 378-79
Pastorius, Francis Daniel, 72-73
Paul VI, Pope, 306
Paxson, Scott, 308
Peace Mission, 289
Peale, Charles Willson: army service, 413-14; collects swordfish beak, 267; death, 65; museum founded by, 85, 134, 229, 282, 405; Benjamin West and, 280
Peale, James, 120
Peale's Museum, 85, 134, 229, 282, 405
Pearson, Leonard, 78
Pellegiano, Louise, 159
Pemberton, John Styth, 165
pencil manufacturing, 105
Pendergrass, Teddy, 101, 387
Penn, John, 270
Penn, Thomas, 270
Penn, William: as absentee landlord, 93; arrives at Chester, 341; assistant to, 344; birth, 327; blue laws, 195; calls for schools, 237; Charter of Privileges, 69, 181, 338, 341; convenes first General Assembly, 385; "Curse of Billy Penn," 170, 215; death, 241; first mention of a town, 222; "Great Law," 195; grid plan, 168; horse racing, 155; lands at New Castle, 337; leaves Philadelphia for last time, 348; Lenape tribe, treaty with, 50, 200, 270; liberty of conscience, 181; Quaker ideals, 181; religious tolerance, 69, 76; sails to new world, 344; statue in City Hall, 4, 233, 353, 375
Penn Central, 230
Penn Relays, 136
Penn Square, 217
Penn's Landing, 88, 305
Penn's Treaty with the Indians, 80
Pennsylvania Abolition Society, 76, 123
Pennsylvania Academy of Fine Arts, 56, 131, 135, 145, 388
Pennsylvania Anti-Slavery Society, 10, 148
Pennsylvania Association of Amateur Base Ball Players, 283
Pennsylvania Ballet, 125
Pennsylvania Bank, 218
Pennsylvania Canal, 120
Pennsylvania Chronicle and Universal Advertiser, 33
Pennsylvania Evening Post, 173
Pennsylvania Gazette, 152, 405
Pennsylvania Hall, 160
Pennsylvania Horticultural Society, 376
Pennsylvania Hospital, 54, 121, 154
Pennsylvania Hospital for the Insane, 54, 397
Pennsylvania Human Relations Commission, 195
Pennsylvania Journal, 254
Pennsylvania Liquor Control Board, 23, 195
Pennsylvania Museum and School of Industrial Art, 153
Pennsylvania National Guard, 269
Pennsylvania Navy Yard, 221
Pennsylvania Packett, 260
Pennsylvania Prison Society, 335
Pennsylvania Railroad, 53, 105, 187, 188, 230
Pennsylvania School for the Deaf, 113, 192
Pennsylvania Special, 188
Pennsylvania State House, 34, 85, 148, 249
"Pennsylvania System," 119
Pennsylvania, 33
Pennsylvania Turnpike, 314
Pennypacker, Samuel, 374
Penrose, Boies, 215, 298
People's Wigwam, 270
Pepper, George S., 61
Pepper, William, 61
Perigord, Charles-Maurice Tallyrand, 124
"Permanent Bridge," 326
Perry, Charles, 169
Perry, Christopher J., 369
Petrillo, Herman, 138
Petrillo, Paul, 138
pharmacists, 66, 91
"Phasmatrope," 48
Philadelphia: biggest snowstorm, 13; city flag, 102; consolidation, 28, 45, 123, 149; corruption in city offices, 130; expansion, 45; first burial ground for visitors, 300; first mayoral election, 333; first street-cleaning machines, 396; first telegraph received, 355; grid plan, 168; highest temperature, 252; hottest June, 212; last duel, 119; last gas-lit street lamp, 119; longest-serving mayor, 19; lowest temperature, 52; most marriage licenses in a day, 122; motto, 102; nickname, 2, 56; population, 3, 45; as a port city, 33, 123; seal and arms, 57, 102; year established, 2
Philadelphia, Germantown and Norristown Railroad, 183
Philadelphia 76ers, 60, 105, 158, 330
Philadelphia Alcoholics Anonymous, 71
Philadelphia Almshouse, 239
Philadelphia and Columbia Railroad, 320
Philadelphia and Trenton Railroad, 183
Philadelphia Anti-Graffiti Network, 321
Philadelphia Arcade, 146
Philadelphia Art Alliance, 332
Philadelphia Assemblies, 401
Philadelphia Athletics, 35, 71, 121, 203, 285, 308, 330-31, 356
Philadelphia Aurora, 205
Philadelphia Bank, 253
Philadelphia Bar Association, 241
Philadelphia Baseball Club, 139
Philadelphia Bettering House, 239
Philadelphia Bulletin, 10, 14, 36, 206, 356
Philadelphia Children's Aid Society, 174
Philadelphia City Planning Commission, 163
Philadelphia Coffee House, 394

Philadelphia Coke Company, 231
Philadelphia College of Pharmacy and Science, 66
Philadelphia Committee of Safety, 219
Philadelphia Contributionship, 154
Philadelphia Convention Center, 281
Philadelphia Country Club, 155
Philadelphia Daily News, 321
Philadelphia Dispensary, 121
Philadelphia Eagles, 26, 49, 51, 97, 113, 149, 207, 220, 396, 399
Philadelphia Electric Company, 162, 344
Philadelphia Evening Bulletin, 194
Philadelphia Evening Post, 219
Philadelphia Experiment, 257
Philadelphia Federation of Teachers, 287
Philadelphia Fellowship Commission, 45
Philadelphia Female Anti-Slavery Society, 390
Philadelphia Fire Department, 37, 168, 410
Philadelphia Flyers, 10, 18, 60, 80, 120, 144, 162, 332
Philadelphia Free African Society, 121
"Philadelphia Freedom," 68
Philadelphia Freedoms, 68
Philadelphia, 59
Philadelphia Gas and Electric Company, 358
Philadelphia Gas Works, 51, 96, 106
Philadelphia General Hospital, 239
Philadelphia Herald, 139
Philadelphia High School for Girls, 44
Philadelphia Home Show, 118
Philadelphia Hospital, 121
Philadelphia Ice Palace, 402
Philadelphia Inquirer, 118, 185, 206, 292, 356
Philadelphia International Airport, 127, 173, 390
Philadelphia International Championship, 200
Philadelphia International Records, 101, 387
Philadelphia Jockey Club, 155
Philadelphia Medical Society, 47
Philadelphia Mint, 111, 215, 242, 329
Philadelphia Morning Gazette, 147
Philadelphia Municipal Airport, 173, 197
Philadelphia Museum of Art, 3, 34, 101, 115, 153, 235, 409
Philadelphia Musical Fund Society, 370
Philadelphia National Shrines Park Commission, 254
Philadelphia Naval Hospital, 186
Philadelphia Navy Yard: closes, 309; *Eldridge* made invisible (Philadelphia Experiment), 257; *Indianapolis* commissioned, 218, 362; *Kitty Hawk* commissioned, 138; MacMillan expedition to North Pole, 187; *Olympia* decommissioned, 390; origin, 68; *Pennsylvania* launched, 229; sabotage alleged, 221; *Wichita* launched, 363
Philadelphia Newspapers, LLC, 206
Philadelphia Orchestra, 51, 324, 335
Philadelphia Orphan Society, 31
Philadelphia Park, 155
Philadelphia Parking Authority, 254
Philadelphia Perspective, A, 140-41
Philadelphia Phillies, 12, 71, 113, 122, 134, 139, 146, 151, 167, 170, 187, 215, 226, 261, 265, 283, 297, 308, 314, 334, 335
Philadelphia Plan, 132
Philadelphia Police Department, 85, 89, 156, 183, 252, 258, 276
Philadelphia Presbytery, 330
Philadelphia Preservation Alliance, 238
Philadelphia Public Library, 61
Philadelphia Rapid Transit system, 152
Philadelphia Record, 185
Philadelphia Red Cross, 174
Philadelphia Saturday Courier, 21
Philadelphia Savings Fund Society, 246, 383, 385
Philadelphia Skating Club, 322
Philadelphia Society for Alleviating the Miseries of Public Persons, 151
Philadelphia Society for Assist ing Distressed Prisoners, 50
Philadelphia Society for Promoting Agriculture, 26
Philadelphia Spelling Book, 186
Philadelphia Sports Hall of Fame, 288
Philadelphia Stock Exchange, 340
Philadelphia Story, The, 251, 407
Philadelphia Transit Company, 246
Philadelphia Transportation Company, 64
Philadelphia Tribune, 369
Philadelphia University, 44
Philadelphia Walk of Fame, 255
Philadelphia Warriors, 158, 382
Philadelphia Zoo, 85, 212, 235, 405, 411
Philadelphische Zeitung, 149, 219
Phillie Phanatic, 134, 261
Philly Sour (Sound of Philadelphia), 101, 256
Phoenixville, 291
Physick, Philip Syng, 165
Pierce, Charlotte L., 354
Pierce, Franklin, 194
Pierce College, 251
Pietzel, Benjamin, 150
Pinchot, Gifford, 23
Pink Floyd, 97, 298
Pinkerton National Detective Agency, 212
Pius XII, Pope, 144
Plain Truth, 269
plays, prohibition of, 8
Plays and Players Theater, 332
Please Touch Children's Museum, 139, 153, 406
Plumstead warehouse, 150
PNB Building, 404
Poe, Edgar Allan, 21, 26, 27, 35, 81, 206, 320
Poe, Virginia Clemm, 27, 35
"poison widows," 138
police brutality, 258
police deaths, 89
police dogs, 148
Polly, 408
Pool, Thomas, 260
poor and indigent, the, 239
Poor Richard's Almanac, 24, 400, 409
porcelain, 336
Port of Philadelphia, 123
Port Richmond, 88
Portues, James, 237
Potter, James, 71
Potts, Albert, 84
Powderly, William, 327
Powell, William, 301
Powelton Village, 156, 169
Pratt, Henry, 235
Pratt, Matthew, 16
premieres, 120, 133, 134, 181
Presbyterian Church of America, 188
Presbyterian Hospital, 100
Priestley, Joseph, 165, 209
Primo Cola, 371
Primo Gassosa, 371
Prince of Parthia, The, 133
printing industry, 67, 100
Printz, Johan, 120
Prison Society, 113
prisons: Eastern State Penitentiary, 23, 119, 165, 305, 335, 338; Moyamensing P., 150, 229; Quaker reformers, 119; riots, 19, 305; Walnut Street P., 16, 19, 119
Procession of the Victualers, 90
Procter, William, 66
Progressive Party, 234
Prohibition, 23
"Project PX," 57
Provincial Council, 156, 163
Public Academy, 361
Public Grammar School, 407
Public Ledger Building, 409
Public Ledger, 46, 118, 136, 175, 384
public performances, 77
public transportation, 28
publishing industry, 392
Purvis, William, 14, 384

Pythians (baseball team), 283, 323

Quaker City Barge Club, 330
Quakers: abolitionism, 72-73, 76, 86, 123, 336; anti-Quaker attitudes, 181; Banneker School, 165; Christmas and, 406; Germantown, 72, 319; Holy Experiment, 181; ideals, 181; monitoring of, 56; music and stage performances, restrictions on, 51, 77, 195; prison reforms, 119
Quantrells, 316
Queen Village, 88

racing, 195
radio, 154, 292
Radnitzky, Emmanuel (Man Ray), 272
Rafill, Stewart, 257
railroads, 183, 219, 309, 320
Ramsay, Jack, 110
Randolph, A. Philip, 171
Rawle, William, 26
Reach, Alfred, 71
Reading Terminal Market, 226
Reedy Island Telegraph Company, 355
Reid, Andy, 26
religious tolerance, 69, 76, 388
Remington, Frederic, 235
Remington, Joseph, 66
Rendell, Ed, 227, 324
Republican National Convention (1856), 51, 194; (1940), 184, 201; (1948), 198; (2000), 242
Republican Party, 17, 86
reservoirs, 34
restaurant tippers, 158
retailing, 87
Rice, Edgar, 258
Richardson, David P., Jr., 364
Richie Ashburn Foundation, 288
Ricketts, John Bill, 260
Rickett's Circus, 79, 121, 131, 358
"Riot Bill," 309
riots: anti-Catholic, 69, 216; anti-immigrant, 69; "Bible Riots," 149; "flash mob" incident, 99; Friends Home for Colored Orphans, 160; King assassination, 114; prison inmates, 19, 305; race, 273, 276, 369; Walnut Street Prison, 19
Rittenhouse, David, 111, 180, 204, 242
Rittenhouse Square, 51
Rizzo, Frank: 1967 student protests, 364; 1982 mayoral primary, 355; birth, 227, 336; career, 227; civil rights lawsuit against, 258; commuter tunnel groundbreaking, 199; declares state of emergency, 114, 276; recall movement, 106
robberies, 235
Roberts, John, 351
Robeson, Paul, 30
Rochambeau, Comte de, 274, 280
Roche, David B., 301
rock concerts, 224
Rocky, 325, 384
Rodham, Robert, 125
Rogers, John, 71
Rolling Stones, 97
Roman Catholic High School of Philadelphia, 308
Romualdo, Antonio, 300
Romualdo, Mrs. Josephine, 300
Roosevelt, Eleanor, 45, 70
Roosevelt, Franklin Delano, 23, 124, 171, 204, 350
Roosevelt, Theodore, 262
Roosevelt Boulevard, 178
root beer, 203
Rose, Pete, 12, 230
Ross, Betsy, 37, 169, 191
Ross, Charles Brewster, 212
Ross, Christian K., 212
Ross, John, 37
Rothermel, Peter, 401
Rouse, Willard, III, 366
Rouse and Associates, 170
rowing, 123, 322
Royden, William, 106
Rundgren, Todd, 199
Rush, Benjamin, 103, 121, 123, 128, 151
Rush, William, 34, 326
Ruska, Ernst, 129
Rydell, Bobby, 297

Saam, Byrum, 122, 288
Sabo, Albert F., 133
St. Augustine's Roman Catholic Church, 149, 251
Saint-Gaudens, August, 235
St. George's Methodist Church, 118, 228
St. James Hall, 147
St. Joseph's Church, 54, 69
St. Joseph's University, 110
St. Mary's Catholic Churchyard, 126
St. Michael's Evangelical Lutheran Church, 48
St. Michael's Roman Catholic Church, 149
St. Peter the Apostle Church, 196
St. Peter's Church, 113
St. Peter's Protestant Episcopal Church, 264
St. Thomas' African Episcopal Church, 81
Samuel, Bernard, 254
Sanitary Fair, 193
sanitation services, 231
Saturday Evening Post, 249
Sauer, Christopher, 304
Sauer, Maria, 304
Sauer Bible, 304
Saunders, W. B., 392
savings banks, 385
Savoy Opera Company, 147
Saxe, Susan, 102
Saxton, Joseph, 329
Say, Thomas, 204
Scarfo, Nicodemo "Little Nicky," 344, 366
Scheib, Carl, 285
Schienfield, Lou, 162
Schmidt, Mike, 288
Schobbenhausen, Frederick, 309
school masters, 407
schools: Banneker S., 165; busing begins, 290; fires, 51; Normal Schools, 44; racial imbalances ordered eliminated, 195; Roman Catholic High S., 308; Rush and, Benjamin, 103; strike by high school students, 364; strike by teachers, 287; William Penn Charter S., 237
Schrader, August ("Divine Healer"), 337
Schultz, Dave "the Hammer," 162
Schuylkill Arsenal, 162
Schuylkill Falls Bridge Company, 111
Schuylkill Water Works, 145
Schweppe, Jacob, 165
seal of the United States, 198
Sears, Roebuck warehouse, 343
Second Bank of the United States, 119
Second World War. *See* World War II
Segal, Mark, 252
"Selective Patronage" boycott, 286
Sellers, Coleman, 386
serialized novels, 356
Sesquicentennial Exposition (1926), 63, 174, 217, 302
Sesquicentennial Stadium, 124, 302
Shadow (character Lamont Cranston), 291
Shapp, Milton, 355
Sharpless, Barry, 137
Sharps Rifle, 291
Sherman, Roger, 227
Shibe Park, 97, 121, 124, 215, 224, 265, 314
Shifler, George, 149
shipbuilding, 68, 125, 173, 221, 295, 367
Shippen, Edward, 220
Shippen, Margaret "Peggy," 117
Shippingport Atomic Power Station, 103
Shirelles, The, 64
Shuman, Frank, 292
Shyamalan, M. Night, 251
"Siamese Twins," 49
Sidebotham, Thomas, 10
Sigman's Hotel, 402
Simitiere, Pierre Eugene du, 197
Singerly, William, 185
Sisters of the Blessed Sacrament, 373
Sixth Sense, The, 251
Skater's Club of the City and County of Philadelphia, 402
Slate Roof House, 237
Slinky, 367
Slotter and Company, 339
Smith, John Jay, 345
Smith, Kate, 144, 162
Smith, Thomas B., 298
Smith, Will, 304, 391
Smith, William, 280

Index

Smith, William Burns, 219
Smith family, 114
Smith Island, 152
Smyth, Richard, 27
snowstorms, 13, 26
Snyder, Simon, 27
soccer, 174
Socialists, 56
Society Hill, 88, 163, 301, 368
Society Hill Towers, 226
Society of Cincinnati, 150
Society of Colonial Dames, 191
Society of Friends, 16
Society of the Sons of Saint George, 132
Society of the Woman in the Wilderness, 201
soft drinks, 165, 203, 371
Solomon, Haym, 13
Some Fruits of Solitude, 93
Sons of Liberty, 318
Sons of St. Patrick, 91
soul music, 387
Sound of Philadelphia (Philly Soul), 101, 256
Sousa, John Philip, 157
South Philadelphia, 144, 321
South Philadelphia High School for Girls, 70
South Philadelphia Sports Complex, 97, 124
Southeastern Pennsylvania Transportation Authority, 136
Southern European immigrants, 3, 144
Southwark, 216, 410
Southwark Theater, 269
Southwark Towers, 30
"Spanish flu," 307, 331
Speakman, Townsend, 165
Specter, Arlen, 60, 137, 349
Spectrum, the, 18, 20, 60, 99, 162, 332, 385
Spinelli, Eileen, 261
Spinners, 387
Spring Garden, 45, 337
Springsteen, Bruce, 97
Spirit of Transportation, The, 187
Stamp Act, 163, 318, 338
standard time, 94
Stanton, Elizabeth Cady, 271
State Arsenal, 329
state-controlled liquor stores, 9
State Farm Insurance Company, 178
States Rights Party, 234
steamboats, 267
Steuben, Friedrich Wilhelm Augustus von, 66, 315, 400
Stevens, Andrew, Jr., 410
Stevenson, Christine Wetherill, 332
Still, William, 229, 303, 384
Stirling, Amos ("William Field"), 169
Stokowski, Leopold, 292, 324, 332, 335, 337
stores. *See* department stores; music stores; state-controlled liquor stores
Stotesbury, Eva, 332
Stow, John, 148, 378-79
Stravinsky, Igor, 120
Strawberry Mansion, 238
Strawbridge and Clothier, 139, 292, 406
Street, John F., 287
street-cleaning machines, 396
street lamps, last gas-lit, 124
streetcars, 28, 64, 364
Strickland, William, 71, 383
strikes: 1900, 144; 1927 longshoremen, 89; Artcraft Silk Hosiery Mills, 130; carpenters, 327; high school students, 364; Newspaper Guild, 185; railroad workers, 309; "Selective Patronage" boycott, 286; teachers', 287; transit, 151, 246; truckers, 249
subways, 64, 246, 247
suffrage, women's, 271, 354
suffrage amendment, 349
Sullivan, Leon, 286
Sun Power Company, 292
Sutton, Willie, 335
Swaine, Charles, 79
Swann Fountain, 233
Swedish settlers, 102, 120, 216, 341
Swift, John, 160
swimming, 195
swimming pools, public, 198
Syracuse Nationals, 158

Tacony, 144
Tacony-Palmyra Bridge, 259
Tageblatt, 293
Tamanend, 80
Tappan, Arthur, 385
Tate, James H. J., 60, 114, 127, 273, 276
Taupin, Bernie, 68
Taylor, Frederick W., 95
Taylor, George, 368
tea tax protest, 329
Team America, 174
Teddy Pendergrass Alliance, 101
telegraphs, 355
television, 292, 308, 389
Television Laboratories, 241, 264
Temple of the Independent Order of Odd Fellows, 164
Temple University, 29, 157
tennis, 68, 352
Testa, Phil, 366
Textile Hall, 382
textile industry, 250, 262
Thanksgiving Day Parade, 372
Thayer, John B., 130
theaters, 51, 77, 150
Thespian Club, 84
Third Presbyterian Church, 67, 392
30th Street Station, 187
Thomas Edison High School, 101, 353
Thomas Jefferson University, 360
Thomson, Charles, 190, 197, 247
Thomson, Elihu, 104
Thornton, Matthew, 351
Three Mile Island, 103
Throneberry, "Marvelous" Marv, 288
Tierney, Brian, 206
Tinicum Island, 120
Tinicum National Wildlife Refuge, 125
Titanic, 130
Tocqueville, Alexis de, 335
Toney, Andrew, 158
tornados, 25, 248
Torresdale, 178
Tower, Zealous Bates, 275
track and field, 136, 159; *see also* Penn Relays
trains, 35, 106, 230
transatlantic cables, 36
transit of Venus, 387
Treaty Elm, 80
Treaty of Friendship (1682), 270
Treaty of Paris, 21, 282
Trenton, Battle of, 413-14
Trenton Nationals, 382
Triangle Clothing store, 146
Triangle Publications, 292
Trocadero Burlesque Theater, 110
trolleys, 129, 246, 364
trucking, 197
Truman, Harry, 171, 191, 205, 223
Trumbauer, Horace, 21, 409
tuberculosis, 78
Tucker, Robert, 336
Tucker, Sandy, 167
Tucker, William Ellis, 336
Tun Tavern, 305, 357
tunnels, 199
Tunney, Gene, 302
Turner, Eliza Sproat, 354
Tyndale, Hector, 384

Uncle Tom's Cabin, 356
Underground Railroad, 104, 131, 229
Union Baptist Church, 70
Union Club, 408
Union Fire Company, 168, 388
Union League, 157, 408
Union League Building, 131
Union Passenger Railway Company, 309
Union Republican Club, 298
Union Volunteer Refreshment Saloon, 164
U.S. Constitution, 157, 213, 215, 296, 307, 393, 396
U.S. Marine Corps, 269, 357
U.S. Mint, 111, 215, 242, 329
UNIVAC I, 191
universities. *See* colleges and universities
University of Pennsylvania, 57, 131, 147, 402
University of the Arts, 153
University of the Sciences of Philadelphia, 66
Uptown Theater, 154
USS *Columbia,* 295, 340
USS *Eldridge,* 257
USS *Indiana,* 295
USS *Indianapolis,* 218, 354, 362
USS *Jacob Jones,* 71
USS *Kitty Hawk,* 138
USS *Maine,* 328, 340, 390
USS *Massachusetts,* 295
USS *Monitor,* 199
USS *New York,* 295
USS *Olympia,* 293, 390
USS *Pennsylvania,* 229

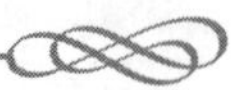

Index

USS *Philadelphia,* 285
USS *Quistconck,* 250
USS *United States,* 221, 222
USS *Utah,* 404
USS *Wichita,* 363

Valley Forge, 66, 196, 362, 374, 398, 400
Valley Forge National Historical Park, 374
Van Kannel, Theophilus, 255
Vare, Edwin H., 298
Vare, Mrs. Flora Morris, 170
Vare, William S., 298
Vaux family, 114
Vauxhall Garden, 287
Venturi, Robert, 202
Vertol helicopter, 154
Veterans Administration hospital, 388
Veterans Stadium, 97, 113, 122, 134, 224, 261
Victor Talking Machine Company, 159, 335
Views of Philadelphia, 118, 412
Vigilance Society, 229
Villanova University, 110
Vine Street Expressway, 38
Violet Oakley Studio, 333
Voight, Henry, 267
von Moschzisker, Robert, 411
voting machines, 350
voting rights, 145

Wachovia Center, 60, 162
Wagner, Louis, 303
Walcott, Jersey Joe, 232
Walker, Zachariah, 258
Walking Purchase, 270
Walnut Street Prison, 16, 19, 119
Walnut Street Theater, 23, 45
Walsh, John E., 360
Walt Whitman Bridge, 158
Walter, Thomas Ustick, 215
Wanamaker, John, 87, 189, 222, 293, 393
Wanamaker, Rodman, 185, 359, 404
Wanamaker family, 3
Wanamaker's Department Store, 117, 136, 198, 273, 404, 406, 411
Warner, Edward, 379
Warner, William, 66
Washington, George: 1789 election, 115; appointed commander, 153, 192, 315; ballooning, 16; Jean-Pierre Blanchard and, 16; Congress Flag, 191; Constitutional Convention, 168; crosses the Delaware, 389, 406; death, 395; Fairmount Park statue, 158; fox hunting, 394; Germantown battle, 317, 318; Lafayette and, 242; letter to Henry Knox, 107-8; Masons and, 305; metals for coins, 111; Rickett's Circus, 79, 131, 260; Rochambeau and, 280; Society of Cincinnati, 150; theater attendance, 77; Valley Forge, 196; whiskey tax, opposition to, 294
Washington, Grover, Jr., 398
Washington, Martha, 337
Washington, Ora, 352
Washington Hall, 133
Watch Night, 412
water supply, 34, 128
waterways, 33
Watts, Bobby "Boogaloo," 20
Wayne, Anthony, 299
WDAS-AM, 154
Weaver, John, 120
Wedell, Rachel, 139
"weeping time," 22
Weiner, Charles R., 132
Weisberger, Barbara, 125
Weld, Theodore, 160
Wesley, John, 412
West, Benjamin, 80, 280
West Oak Lane, 231
West Philadelphia, 144, 324
Westervelt, William, 212
WFIL-FM, 29
WFIL-TV, 292, 319
WGL, 51
Wharton, Joseph, 161
Wharton, Robert, 19, 23, 407
Wharton, Thomas Isaac, 114, 222
Wharton & Humphreys shipyard, 173
Wharton family, 114
WHAT-AM, 154
Wheeler, John, 229
Whig Party National Convention (1848), 184
White, Alfred, 349
White, Caroline Earle, 66
White, George, 246
White, Roy Wilson, 169
White, William, 113, 119, 228, 407
Whitechapel Bell, 280
Whitechapel Foundry, 148
Whitman, Walt, 101
Who, 124
Who, The, 385
Widener, Eleanor, 130
Widener, George Dunton, 130
Widener, Harry Elkins, 130
Widener, P. A. B., 115, 130
Widener family, 3
Widener Memorial School, 130
Wilkinson, Thomas, 152
William Birch & Son, 20
William Cramp & Sons, 125
William Horstmann and Sons, 250
William Penn Charter School, 237
Williams, Hardy, 355
Williams, John Foster, 222
Williamson, Passamore, 229
Willing, Charles, 151
Willing, Morris & Company, 151
Willing, Thomas, 151
Willit, William, 94
Willow Grove Park, 157
Wills Eye Hospital, 360
Wilson, Alexander, 120, 268
Wilson, C. Colket, III, 125
Wilson, Hugh, 306
Wilson, James, 317, 351
Wilson, Woodrow, 82, 106
Windmill Island, 152, 299
Windrim, James, 305
Wine, Bobby, 265
Winner, Septimus, 370
WIP, 92
"Wire Bridge," 9
Wissahickon Creek, 201
Wistar, Caspar, 405
Wister, Owen, 225
Witching Wave Company, 255
Wolfe, George, 320
Woman Suffrage Association, 271
women's suffrage, 271, 354
women's wages, 66
Wood, James Frederick, 367
Wood, W. B., 314
Woodmere Art Museum, 333
Woods, Georgie, 154
Woodside, John Archibald, 69
workday, 327
World Team Tennis, 68
World War I, 3, 56, 173, 250, 293, 377
World War II, 4, 221, 250, 285, 367
Worrell, Richard, 72-73
Wortman, Jacob L., 31
WPGR, 154
WPVI-TV, 292
Wray, Lud, 220
WRTI-AM, 29
WWRL-AM, 154
Wyeth, John, 66

yellow fever, 60, 228, 277-78, 289, 324
Young, William J., 24
Young Ladies Baseball Club, 263
Young Men's Hebrew Association, 155

Zagat survey, 158
Ziegler's Plains, 337
Zion Baptist Church, 286
Zion Lutheran Church, 407
Zoological Society of Philadelphia, 96
zoos, 85
Zworykin, Vladimir, 129